Korean-American
Relations

Korean-American Relations

DOCUMENTS PERTAINING TO THE FAR EASTERN DIPLOMACY OF THE UNITED STATES

VOLUME III

The Period of Diminishing Influence,

1896–1905

Edited and with an Introduction by

Scott S. Burnett

UNIVERSITY OF HAWAII PRESS

HONOLULU, HAWAII

94 93 92 91 90 89   5 4 3 2 1

Library of Congress Cataloging-in-Publication Data
(Revised for vol. 3)

McCune, George McAfee, 1908–1948, ed.
  Korean-American relations.

  Vol. 2–   edited, with an introd., by Spencer
J. Palmer and others.
  Vol. 3–   published by University of Hawaii Press,
Honolulu.
  Includes bibliographical references and index.
  Contents: v. 1. The initial period, 1883–1886.—
v. 2. The period of growing influence, 1887–1895.—
v. 3. The period of diminishing influence, 1896–1905.
    1. United States—Foreign relations—Korea.
2. Korea—Foreign relations—United States.   3. Korea—
Foreign relations—1864-1910.   I. Harrison, John A.
(John Arnold), joint ed.   II. Title.
E184.K6M33   1951   327'.730519   51-1111
ISBN 0-8248-1202-6 (v. 3)

To M. E. B.

CONTENTS

PREFACE

In 1937 George M. McCune returned to Korea to finish his research on the Yijo Sillok, which culminated in his Ph.D. dissertation.[1] While in Korea he and the Honorable U. Alexis Johnson, who was then serving as Vice-Consul in Seoul, decided to make copies of the extensive Legation documents in the U.S. Consul in Seoul. Dr. McCune used his Leica camera and the film was developed in the Yonsei University laboratory by Arthur L. Becker, the father of McCune's wife, Evelyn.[2] These microfilms contained all of the official correspondence between the U.S. diplomatic representative in Korea and the State Department from 1883 until 1905, when the diplomatic representative was removed from Korea and Japan officially took control of Korean foreign relations. This microfilm collection was one of the great pioneering efforts in the study of U.S.- Korean relations and for a number of years comprised the single most important Western record of modern Korean history. The collection, however, was largely inaccessible until 1951, when George McCune and John A. Harrison published the first of "a projected three-volume series on Korean-American relations from 1883-1905."[3] *Korean-American Relations, Documents Pertaining to the Far Eastern Diplomacy of the United States, Volume One, The Initial Period, 1883-1886*, was published to "help to make more clear the processes of American diplomacy and the record of American representatives in East Asia."[4]

Dr. McCune was unfortunately unable to finish work on the final two volumes before his early death in 1948, and the project lay dormant until 1960, when two professors at the University of California at Berkeley, Dr. Woodbridge Bingham, professor of History, and Dr. Robert A. Scalapino, professor of Political Science, encouraged Dr. Spencer J. Palmer, a former student, to begin work on volume II, covering Korean-American relations from 1887 to 1895. Under the sponsorship of the University of California, Palmer began the arduous task of reading and analyzing the original McCune

---

[1] It was also during this visit that McCune and Dr. Edwin O. Reischauer developed the McCune-Reischauer system for the romanization of the Korean language.

[2] Evelyn McCune indicates that the film was developed at Yonsei "to avoid Japanese confiscation of the film." Letter, February 1985.

[3] Volume I, p. vii.

[4] Ibid.

ix

microfilms provided by Evelyn McCune. Professor Palmer was able to greatly enhance the value of the series by using additional materials and by adding useful appendixes. Volume II was published in 1963 and entitled *The Period of Growing Influence*.[5]

During the thirty-five years since the publication of volume I, the *Korean-American Relations* series has continued to provide an "accurate and convenient source-book."[6] The significance and relevance of the series is given further credence in light of the widespread use that both volume I and volume II have enjoyed and continue to enjoy in the efforts of other scholars. There are few histories of the early period of Korean relations with the Western world that do not cite some portion of these two volumes. It is in view of this continued value that I have worked toward the completion of volume III.

There are three sources of primary materials that have been used as references in compiling this volume: the original McCune microfilm, the National Archives microfilm,[7] and *Foreign Relations of the United States*. Each has particular strengths and weaknesses that should be indicated for those who might wish to refer directly to the microfilm, or who need to work with documents not found in the *Korean-American Relations* series.

The McCune microfilm consists of the original dispatches as they were recorded by hand in the Legation ledgers. They do not contain the often extensive enclosures that accompanied the dispatches, but do show the occasional changes in spelling, syntax, and word choice that occurred before the documents were duplicated and sent on to the State Department. These films were produced in 1937 under less than satisfactory conditions and, consequently, about 20% are unreadable. The McCune microfilms comprise only a small part of the George McCune collection at the University of Hawaii's Center for Korean Studies and have recently been refilmed, which makes their handling much easier.

The National Archives microfilms covering this period are in excellent condition, are much more varied and useful than any of the other sources, and were used almost exclusively for the transcription of the documents in this volume. The major collection consists of copies of the original dispatches received by the State Department, including almost all of the sometimes lengthy enclosures. Although not as immediately important for the needs of the collection in this volume, other documents that have been consulted and that are available in the National Archives material include various instructions from the State Department to the U.S. Representative in Korea and correspondence to and from the

---

[5] Spencer J. Palmer, ed., *Korean-American Relations: Documents Pertaining to the Far Eastern Diplomacy of the United States, Volume Two, The Period of Growing Influence, 1887-1895* (Berkeley and Los Angeles: University of California Press, 1963).

[6] Volume II, p. xi.

[7] A complete listing of the pertinent National Archives microfilm is listed in Appendix D along with the appropriate catalog reference numbers.

Korean Legation in the United States. These films are all bright and clear, and for the final nine years most of the correspondence was typed (rather than written out longhand), which greatly facilitated reading and transcribing. For those individuals who need to make a more extensive consultation of the documents than this volume provides, the National Archives microfilm should be preferred over the McCune microfilm, unless the particular needs of the research project dictate differently.

The *Foreign Relations* series published by the State Department contains only a small portion of the documents found in this volume.[8] It is instructive, not only because of what it contains, but because of what it does not contain. A close comparison of the materials in the *Foreign Relations* series with the materials contained in the two microfilm collections reveals that not only were the documents presented in *Foreign Relations* chosen selectively, but the materials were heavily edited as well. On the whole the quality of this series is quite uneven. But despite the obvious drawbacks and limitations, this source is usually available in most university libraries. Because of this accessibility and the obvious space constraints of the present volume, I have chosen to omit those documents that are only marginally important and appear in a reasonably true form in *Foreign Relations.*[9]

This volume, of course, owes its very existence to the previous efforts of George McCune, John Harrison, and Spencer Palmer. To ensure continuity, the organization and layout of the book are patterned on those of volumes I and II. As was the case in the two previous volumes, all documents are cited verbatim, without regard for spelling or grammatical inconsistencies, and the Victorian salutations and conclusions have been routinely omitted.

In volume I, McCune and Harrison stated that "The selection of documents for this volume was based upon the principle that nothing essential to an understanding of the American role in Korea should be omitted, within the limits of the space available for publication."[10] Although dealing with a longer period of time and considerably more available documents, I have attempted to keep to that original standard. It was initially easy to eliminate the routine messages that traveled between Seoul and Washington. It was also quite simple to do without those documents that could easily be found in other publications

---

[8]From 1896 to 1905 there were 58 separate pieces of correspondence included in the *Foreign Relations* series under the heading of Korea. Virtually nothing was included in that series that dealt with internal Korean matters, nor did any of the dispatches marked "confidential" find their way into the collection. All spelling and punctuation was standardized and the texts were freely edited to remove anything that was either superfluous, or that might have been potentially embarrassing to the United States.

[9]Nine pieces of correspondence were included that are duplicates of highly edited documents found in the *Foreign Relations* series.

[10] Volume I, p. vii.

such as *Foreign Relations of the United States*. From that point on, however, my own interests and biases played a considerable role in the selection process. It must be admited from the outset that the documents contained in this volume do not represent every historically significant communication found in the original collections. I have chosen to eliminate most of the enclosures, as they are quite often sufficiently detailed in the main piece of correspondence. I have also chosen to leave out dispatches that repeat material found in previous dispatches. Some attempt has been made to include a certain number of documents that reveal the day-to-day official duties of the Korean diplomatic corps, but they are by no means commensurate with the actual amount, which is overwhelmingly large. It has been one of my greatest regrets that I could not include some of the more "chatty" correspondence which breathes some life into diplomatic materials that can often be imposing. In short, this volume reflects a sincere effort to represent fairly the historically significant details as seen from my perspective. That I have chosen documents that seem unimportant to some and rejected what seems significant to others must be readily acknowledged.

To further aid those who I hope will be able to use this volume in their research as a companion to volumes I and II, I have included four appendixes. Appendix A is a list of the pertinent U.S. diplomatic personnel from 1895 to 1905, and Appendix B is a somewhat more complete list of Korean diplomatic personnel, including the Chinese characters for Korean names. Appendix C is a short chronology of the last ten years of Korean - American diplomatic relations, and Appendix D is a list of the National Archives microfilm holdings on Korea from this early period and their corresponding reference numbers.

Each of the documents included in this series were copied directly from the originals. Those copied pages were then read aloud while an assistant simultaneously checked them once more against the originals to ensure the authenticity of spelling and punctuation. All spelling errors and inconsistencies in punctuation have been deliberately retained as they appeared in the original legation documents.

I am considerably indebted to a number of people for their assistance in the completion of this volume. Evelyn B. McCune, John A. Harrison, and Spencer J. Palmer, all of whom were involved in the first two volumes, have freely offered much appreciated advice and support. Dr. Palmer has been a particularly effective and rigorous teacher for years and has continued to teach and give of his experience throughout the period of this project. John I. Benson, librarian at the Center for Korean Studies at the University of Hawaii, made an extraordinary effort to make the McCune microfilm available to me. His efforts, and those of the Center for Korean Studies and the University of Hawaii Press have been invaluable. My wife Marie E. Burnett, and brother, Stanton P. Burnett, have endured my reading aloud some 2,000 typewritten pages and proved to be most enthusiastic companions for what otherwise would have been a rather lonely endeavor.

Brigham Young University, Provo, Utah S.S.B.

INTRODUCTION

An American Financed Street Car on the Streets of Seoul

Reprinted from Peter A. Underwood, Samuel H. Moffett, and Normen R. Sibley, eds., *First Encounters: Korea 1880–1910* (Seoul: Dragon's Eye Graphics, 1982).

INTRODUCTION1

Korea, 1896-1905

By the end of the nineteenth century most of the world had been sliced up into selfish spheres of influence by just a handful of nations. Russia, France, Great Britain, Germany, and the United States had, through diplomatic and military means, literally gained control of the world. Japan would soon join this elite group of imperialists. Africa, South America, and Asia were fought for, bartered over, and in the end subdued for a time.

Scores of nations have endured this process of control. All of them present valid case studies in the workings of imperialism. The case of Korea is particulary interesting and useful because all of the major world powers of that time were present and actively involved in its ultimate demise.

Korea was and still is important primarily because of its geographical relationship to powerful nations. The defeat of China in the Sino-Japanese War reduced by one the number of neighboring nations that would use Korea as both weapon and shield. This left Russia and Japan to glare at each other across the peninsula while making preparations for the battle that was to come.

Japan fought China to ensure the "full and complete independence and autonomy of Korea" and then proceeded to keep King Kojong under virtual imprisonment, install a sympathetic Korean Cabinet, and initiate a series of restrictive "reforms." It is worth noting that Korea enjoyed considerably greater independence as the "Hermit Kingdom" before its freedoms became an international issue than it ever did afterwards.

Though Japan's influence in Korea was considerable, its position of power was to be short- lived. The intervention by a Russian-German-French diplomatic alliance on April 23, 1895 dramatically reduced the concessions granted to Japan after the Sino-Japanese War and severely challenged Japan's "privileged" position in Korea. The Japanese still held the King under virtual house arrest until February of 1896, when the King and the Crown Prince disguised themselves as court women and escaped from the Palace to the Russian

---

[1] The references contained in this introduction are all taken from documents in this volume. Although documents are certainly available from sources other than U.S. Legation files, I have chosen to work exclusively within this context so as to highlight material that might prove useful.

Legation, where they remained under the protection of Russia for nearly one year. At that point Japan's position in Korea collapsed, leaving the mobs free to vent their anger on the Japanese and pro-Japanese Korean officials.[2] The first reports of Russian influence to reach Washington from Seoul were positive. "I think I see plain indications," reported U.S. Minister John Sill, "that the present policy of Russia is to suggest the appointment of intelligent and reputable foreign advisers to the new government from nationals other than her own. No indications of material interference by Russia. Russian Minister earnestly disclaims such interference."[3] At least in the eyes of the American Minister, the Russian Minister Plenipotentiary A. N. Waeber made an effort to "make the least possible show either of force or of prevailing influence" and because of these new circumstances "His Majesty feels a sense of personal security unknown to him since the seizure of the palace on July 23. [sic] 1894."[4]

Minister Waeber's policies were too mild for many of the Russian expansionists and indeed his policies were responsible for the independent action of Korean conservatives.[5] On February 20, 1897, at the urgent request of his Cabinet, the King left the Russian Legation, further undercutting the Russian position. Waeber was replaced in September of 1897 by the strident Alexis de Speyer, who fancied himself "a true Russian."[6] This appointment marked a distinctly different Russian attitude toward Korean matters. Minister Allen made this comparison,

> It was the carefully pursued policy of the late Russian Representative, Mr. Waeber, to abstain from all appearance of meddling in Korean affairs, often going to the extreme of allowing certain abuses to continue rather than speak, when a word of rebuke from him would have had much, if not a conclusive effect. In this way he was able to control Korean affairs so far as he desired without seeming to work against, or weaken, the pet idea of independence, so dear to the better Koreans. His successor has taken a directly opposite course, and his first two months of service here have been very stormy, but successful in a way.[7]

De Speyer worked energetically and often ruthlessly to reassert Russian control. He made demands for the exclusive use of Deer Island in Pusan Harbor,[8] replaced

---

[2] No. 195, Sill to Olney, February 11, 1896.

[3] No. 201, Sill to Olney, March 2, 1896.

[4] No. 226, Sill to Olney, July 17, 1896.

[5] See No. 245, Allen to Olney, November 13, 1896.

[6] No. 22, Allen to Olney, October 16, 1897.

[7] No. 29, Allen to Sherman, November 7, 1897.

[8] See No. 8, Allen to Sherman, October 1, 1897.

uncooperative Korean ministers with ones inclined to be more supportive,[9] and tried to replace the Director of Korean Customs, James McLeavy Brown, a British subject, with Kiril A. Alexeev, a Russian subject.[10] De Speyer also struck out at the Americans, particularly the American missionaries, who he claimed were supporting the activities of the Independence Club. At a gathering of diplomatic personnel, de Speyer announced that ". . . no Korean entertaining friendly sentiments toward America should have a place in the Government."[11] Upon assuming his duties as U.S. Minister to Korea, Horace N. Allen reported that "Russian interference in Korea now extends to the most intimate matters connected with military and political affairs." He continued, "I am privately informed from the Palace, that Mr. de Speyer, the new Russian Chargé d'Affaires, has informed the King very plainly and forcibly, that he must take Russian advice upon all matters and advise only with Russia; that Russia will see that he is not troubled, and that he will have ample funds for his enjoyment."[12]

Throughout this period France made no attempt to disguise its close and careful collusion with Russia. Minister Allen reported that "the French Representative seems to be almost as influential here as is the Russian. They seem to work together very harmoniously."[13] The Franco-Russian "Dual Alliance" formed primarily to deal with European policy was applied with some success long before the Anglo-Japanese Alliance caused them to specifically and formally include Asia within its scope.[14]

Russian policy throughout this period of time was clumsy and inconsistent. The caution of Waeber allowed opposition forces to grow and gain power. The policies of de Speyer further alienated the Koreans and offended the other foreign powers. Russia was unwilling to give Korea the aid that was sorely needed, yet would not allow Korea to look for loans from any other source.[15] De Speyer attempted to provide strong leadership that would reestablish Russian dominance, but instead his efforts left the Russian position in Korea weaker than ever.

Other than limiting the growth of Japanese influence, Russian interest in Korea centered primarily around securing an ice-free port. When the Russians occupied ice-free Port Arthur, on the Liaotung Peninsula, the aggressive policy in Korea gave way to a

---

[9] See No. 10, Allen to Sherman, October 2, 1897.
[10] See No. 17, Allen to Sherman, October 9, 1897.
[11] No. 9, Allen to Sherman, October 1, 1897 (not included).
[12] No. 3, Allen to Sherman, September 17, 1897.
[13] No. 48, Allen to Sherman, December 20, 1897.
[14] Ibid.
[15] Ibid.

surprising retreat. On March 7, 1898 de Speyer presented Emperor Kojong[16] with an ultimatum from the Tsar, threatening to withdraw Russian financial and military advisors if the Emperor did not make a clear statement of his desire to retain them. In an unusual show of fortitude, the Emperor forced the Russian's hand and accepted the offer of withdrawal.[17] Accordingly, on March 23, 1898 all Russian military and civilian advisors were withdrawn from Korea.

This sudden withdrawal gave the Russian-Japanese struggle in Korea a sense of equilibrium that allowed the Emperor and a pro-American political movement called the Independence Club (Tongnip Hyop'hue) to assert themselves with relative freedom from interference from either faction.[18] The Independence Club was led primarily by Koreans who had been educated in the United States, or who had been given diplomatic assignments in the United States. The most notable of the Independence Club leaders was its founder, Philip Jaisohn (So Chae-p'il). A member of a group responsible for an unsuccessful coup in 1884, Jaisohn fled to Japan and from there to America, where he was educated. He returned to Korea as an advisor to the Korean Government in January of 1896 with an American passport and began to organize the Independence Club and publish a newspaper.

The fledgling political party and its newspaper began to have an impact on the Korean Emperor and on the Koreans in Seoul. They were successful in driving out of office several "obnoxious" officials and in influencing the Emperor to appoint a Cabinet that met with their approval. Although the influence of the Independence Club was, for the most part, limited to a small minority of the people of Seoul, it was responsible for encouraging the beginning of what can certainly be called mass consciousness in Korea. So impressed was Minister Allen with the public expressions of support for the Independence Club by numbers of men and women that he reported, albeit incorrectly, that the movement had "grown till it now represents the mass of the Korean people" and declared that "a peaceful revolution has taken place."[19]

The Independence Club found the Emperor responsive during most of 1898, until conservative officials finally convinced him that the organization's real purpose was to establish a republic in Korea. He promptly dismissed the Cabinet supported by the Independence Club, replaced them with men that Minister Allen thought to be "corrupt and unscrupulous," and ordered the arrest of nineteen Independence Club leaders. Thousands

---

[16] King Kojong took the title of Emperor on October 12, 1897.

[17] See No. 89, Allen to Day, March 19, 1898.

[18] See No. 116, Allen to Day, June 24, 1898.

[19] No. 152, Allen to Hay, October 13, 1898.

of Koreans gathered outside the gates of the prison demanding that they be arrested along with their leaders.[20] The Korean police force was reportedly "in more or less open sympathy with the people" and could not be counted on to control the crowds. The question of control was soon answered when an ancient guild of peddlers (Pobusang) descended on Seoul in support of the conservative Korean leadership and in opposition to the massed supporters of the Independence Club. Violence broke out and several people were killed or injured.[21] The government finally restored order by calling in troops to disperse the people and by banning further gatherings. With this the efforts of the Independence Club came to an end.

This period was indeed one of the most remarkable in the history of Korea. The Independence Club, though limited in scope and effectiveness, was an impressive attempt to make Korea truly free of foreign domination and improve the quality of life in Korea. During this short period of "independence" the Independence Club was able to effectively move the Emperor in several instances, but he was so easily swayed from one opinion to another that real progress was difficult to achieve. Even though Minister Allen doubted the ability of Korea to govern itself, stating that the "Koreans must lean upon and advise with some foreign power" and that conditions in Korea "had gone from bad to worse since the complete withdrawal of Russian influence,"[22] this period of progressive social and political activity is clear evidence of an unfulfilled potential for political independence and mass participation in Korea.

From 1898 until the Russo-Japanese War in 1904, neither Russia nor Japan were completely successful in gaining control of Korean matters to the exclusion of the other. Despite Russia's general withdrawal, de Speyer and subsequent Russian representatives made consistent efforts to gain concessions from the Korean government and hinder Japanese progress as much as possible. Japan, on the other hand, had already established extensive commercial interests from which it began to take a much more active roll in Korea. The whole period is replete with the diplomatic, and quite often undiplomatic, banterings of these two powerful neighbors. Korean independence suffered the most.

On April 25, 1898 Russia and Japan concluded what is known as the Nishi-Rosen Agreement. This agreement mutually limited the two parties from interfering in Korean affairs, but more important, it recognized Japan's superior commercial interests in Korea. Though Japan lost control of the Korean monarch in 1896 it had continued to dominate Korean trade. Although Korea was retaining relative autonomy in matters of government,

---

[20] No. 161, Allen to Hay, November 14, 1898.
[21] Ibid.
[22] No. 167, Allen to Hay, December 23, 1898.

the Seoul *Independent* protested as early as 1896 "against the gradual absorption of Korea by the Japanese, who are complained of as living all about through the Interior, contrary to treaty stipulations, and engaging in trade."[23] According to Minister Allen it was widely held that "the steady influx of Japanese into Korea, and their rapid scattering about through the whole interior, is due to a well devised plan for a kind of peaceful absorption of the country."[24] Regardless of whether or not such a plan existed, the presence and activities of Japan throughout the interior gave it a strategic advantage that none of the other powers could match.

Russia's attention was diverted from Korea by its occupation of Manchuria in August of 1900. This occupation, ostensibly to protect Russian interests from the rampaging Chinese "Boxers," shifted Russia's attention and strategic interests to the north and allowed Japan to operate with relatively greater freedom in Korea. Minister Allen reported that "the impression is gaining ground in Seoul that Korea must come under Japanese influence as a result of the present crisis in China" and that "the Russians feel that they must acquiesce in letting Japan control Korea for the present." To which he added, "it seems equally true that they have intentions regarding the peninsula for the future when Russian communications with these parts are perfected."[25]

The Russian encroachment in northern China caused great concern in Great Britain, the United States, and Japan, all of whom had interests in Manchuria. The United States moved to limit Russia diplomatically in the form of Secretary of State John Hay's corollary to his own "Open Door" policy. Britain and Japan formed the Anglo-Japanese Alliance in 1902, pledging assistance in the event a third party became involved in any conflict and recognizing Japan's predominant position in Korea.

By 1903 Korea was clearly in Japan's "sphere of influence." When Russians began harvesting a timber concession on the Yalu River that they in fact had legal title to, the Japanese became "considerably exercised."[26] What Minister Allen assured his superiors was "more or less local friction between the Japanese and Russians over the timber operations of both on the Yalu River"[27] became the *cause bellé* for the Russo-Japanese War.

Japan attacked Russian positions at Port Arthur on February 8, 1904, and the next day sank two Russian ships in Korea's Chemulp'o harbor. Though hostilities continued

---

[23] No. 153, Allen to Hay, October 20, 1898.
[24] Ibid.
[25] No. 272, Allen to Hay, August 23, 1900.
[26] No. 604, Allen to Hay, April 24, 1903.
[27] No. 612, Allen to Hay, May 26, 1903.

well into 1905, Japan moved quickly in Seoul to establish order on its own terms. Minister Allen, in a cable report of the Korean-Japanese Protocol of February 23, 1904, gave a clear example of how seriously Korean independence was actually considered.

> Last night articles of agreement has (have) [sic] been signed establishing the Japanese protectorate of Korea. It is very strong. The *Japanese agree to maintain the independence and integrity of Korea* in consequence of which *Korea is to follow the advice of Japan implicitly* in all matters of reform and other political measures. The Japanese also obtain use of territory for military purposes.[28]

One by one the Japanese assumed control of Korean agencies; the police on January 5;[29] the Bureau of Communications on March 30;[30] Korean Customs on October 5;[31] and finally, Korea's Foreign Office on November 17.[32] On November 24 the foreign legations began to withdraw and on December 21, before the last legation left Seoul, Ito Hirobumi was officially appointed Resident General of Korea.[33]

The United States in Korea, 1896-1905

The period from 1896 to 1905 saw the United States break from its traditional isolationism and appear as a world power and also as a new expansionist power. The old paradigms of Manifest Destiny and the Monroe Doctrine combined with new ones such as Social Darwinism and what might be called "White Man's Burdenism" to give the United States a purposeful attitude of expansionism. U.S. involvement in areas that were traditionally not within its sphere of influence increased dramatically. In Asia and the Pacific, where it was a late-comer among Western powers, the United States annexed the Hawaiian Islands in July of 1898, acquired the Philippine Islands and Guam as a result of war with Spain in December of 1898, and split the Samoan Islands with Germany in November of 1899.

Although this change of attitude was evident throughout the world, U.S. policy in Korea remained essentially the same as it had been from the beginning. This policy might best be described as "disinterested neutrality." In a letter of instruction to Minister Allen

---

[28] No. 676, Allen to Hay, February 22, 1904. Emphasis added.
[29] No. 856, Allen to Hay, January 6, 1905.
[30] No. 902, Allen to Hay, May 30, 1905.
[31] No. 14, Morgan to Root, August 28, 1905.
[32] No. 34, Morgan to Root, November 20, 1905.
[33] No. 50, Paddock to Root, February 26, 1906.

marked "Confidential" because of "the frankness with which it deals with the question, and the earnestness with which it expresses the hope of this Department," Secretary of State John Sherman clearly outlined three points of U.S. policy with regard to Korea:

> 1. The U.S. representative in Korea is not to "take sides with or against any of the interested powers."
> 2. The U.S. is not "bound to Korea by any protective alliance" despite the "good offices" clause in Article 1 of the Treaty of 1882.
> 3. The U.S. does not wish to take on the role of "counsellor (sic) of Korea as to its internal destinies."[34]

The result of this policy was that, at least officially, the United States showed little support for Korean sovereignty and independence and acknowledged whatever power happened to be controlling the Emperor and his court. Although this policy had little moral basis, it reflected the reality of the U.S. position in Korea. The clear and overwhelming national interests of Japan and Russia, the inpracticality of the United States establishing a military presence in Korea, the delicate and potentially disastrous nature of dealing with two volatile powers, the limited nature of U.S. interests, and the acceptance in principle of many of Russia's and Japan's rationalizations for infringing on Korean sovereignty all led to a weak, but consistent, U.S. policy.

Americans in Korea from 1896 to 1905 were generally there as diplomats, missionaries, advisors, or entrepreneurs.

There were three U.S. Ministers in Korea during this period: John M. B. Sill, Horace N. Allen, and Edwin V. Morgan. Sill ended his tenure as Minister in 1897 under severe reprimand from Washington for activities that compromised the U.S. policy of neutrality. Morgan was a caretaker Minister who served only five months during 1905. Allen was the most influential U.S Minister of this period and was responsible for representing the United States in Korea for eight of the twenty-three years that diplomatic relations existed with the Yi dynasty. Allen was one of the first American missionaries to take up residence in Korea and because of his many years of exposure to Korean court life he was able to describe himself as "particularly well posted as to Korean customs and politics"[35] and asserted to his superiors that his "long years of friendly acquaintance with His Majesty" very often gave him "opportunities which others might wish to enjoy."[36]

The American missionaries in Korea had been situated mainly in Seoul, but from 1895 to 1905, they spread throughout Korea to P'yôngyang, Taegu, Suwôn, Pusan and

---

[34] No. 23, Sherman to Allen, November 19, 1897.
[35] No. 168, Allen to Sherman, Dec. 23, 1898.
[36] No. 52, Allen to Sherman, December 30, 1897.

other areas. Minister Allen, in his report on "Missionaries and the Far Eastern Question," estimated that out of 250 Americans in Korea,150 of them were missionaries.[37] These he described elsewhere as being "an unusually select and high class of missionaries."[38] These American missionaries attained a status in Korean society and in the court of King Kojong that was unparalleled in its day, and they often became involved in international political issues, usually on the side of the Koreans and usually out of genuinely sincere regard for Korean independence. They were highly successful, and Korea became renowned as a productive mission field. American missionaries in Korea also became well known for their strongly stated criticisms of Russia and Japan and became the subject of protests from Moscow and Tokyo and numerous admonitions from Washington.[39]

From 1896 to 1905 the number of Americans employed by the Korean government as advisors declined from seven to one. Although the United States was asked several times to provide additional advisors, it continued in its longstanding reluctance to take on a responsibility that might in some way make the United States liable to the Korean government or responsible for the actions of the Korean government. It was the opinion of Minister Allen that "American interests have never been enhanced by any of the American advisors Korea has employed in the past" and that "no advisor has been able to accomplish much however for the reason that the Koreans have not acted upon any such advice unless it conformed with their own desires and intentions."[40] Although Japan, Russia, Britain, and (before 1895) China pressed Korea for additional positions of influence for their nationals, and in fact furthered their own self-serving policies through those advisors, the United States actively avoided such situations.

U.S. commercial interests in Korea had been almost nonexistent before 1895. Beginning with a concession given to American entrepreneurs Hunt and Fasset for mining gold at Unsan in Pyongan Province in 1895, U. S. firms began to generate real economic influence in Korea. In 1896 a financial syndicate represented by American James R. Morse was given rights to construct the first railway in Korea between Seoul and Chemulp'o,[41] and in 1898 a large contract was awarded to the firm of Collbran and Bostwick to build an electric railway and lighting plant.[42] Despite the disapproval of the Korean Government, Morse sold the railway rights to the Japanese after the Independence Club riots of 1898

---

[37] No. 281, Allen to Hay. September 15, 1900.
[38] No. 3, Allen to Sherman, September 17, 1898.
[39] See No. 179, Sherman to Sill, March 30, 1897; No. 9, Allen to Sherman, October 1, 1897; No. 57, Allen to Sherman, January 7, 1898.
[40] No. 466, Allen to Hay, May, 26, 1902.
[41] See No. 266, Sill to Sherman, April 12, 1897
[42] See No. 73, Allen to Sherman, February 15, 1898; No. 746, Allen to Hay, May 27, 1904.

frightened investors. The Unsan mines and the electric works were by far the most successful of all the American business ventures and were profitable well into the twentieth century.

By 1902 the friendly atmosphere that had typified U.S. - Korean personal relations had slowly diminished, until Minister Allen was forced to report that "with a Foreign Office without power, and without access to the ruler, I am unable to even secure considerations for matters however important they may be. Formerly, by my personal influence with His Majesty I was able to accomplish more than the others."[43] Allen blamed this reduction of influence on many things, including the lack of substantial U.S. policy, the unfair machinations of other powers, the poor state of repair of the U.S. Legation, and on the interference of a powerful Korean government official named Yi Yong Ik, who he described as a "man who cannot read or write, is corrupt and stupidly brutal beyond description."[44] Yi Yong Ik made difficulties for every segment of the American community in Korea and, in conjunction with other things such as the increasing influence of Japan and the tacit U.S. acceptance of Japanese suzerainty over Korea, contributed to the diminishing influence of the United States in Korea.

On November 24, 1905, U.S. Secretary of State Elihu Root telegraphed instructions to U.S. Minister to Korea Edwin V. Morgan to "withdraw from Korea and return to the United States, leaving the premises, legation property and archives in custody of the Consul General."[45] In obedience to these instructions, the United States became the first nation to recognize the Japanese Protectorate over Korea just twenty-three years after it had been the first Western nation to enter into a diplomatic agreement acknowledging the independence of Korea.

In retrospect, the most significant generalization that can be made about the relationship between the United States and Korea is that throughout the period the United States saw that relationship as subordinate to its other commitments and interests in the Far East. Virtually from the very beginning the United States distanced itself from a close association with Korea and continually stressed to the U.S. delegation in Korea the need to limit relations to strictly diplomatic formalities. The close and important ties and relationships that existed between the Korean Government and American businessmen, numerous missionaries, and key members of the American delegation in Korea were looked on with suspicion and were often the object of censure. Nowhere in any of the

---

[43] No. 534, Allen to Hay, November 21, 1902.
[44] Ibid.
[45] Telegram, Root to Morgan, November 24, 1905.

documents that I have examined is there any indication that the United States was interested in any special position in Korea or was willing to support Korean independence, if that meant opposing one of the other interested parties.

On the other hand, it is clear that the Korean Monarch and many individuals in Korean society looked, perhaps wishfully, on that relationship as one that was qualitatively different than that which existed between Korea and any other nation. Kojong spoke more than once about Article One of the *Treaty of Peace, Amity, and Commerce,* signed between the two nations in May of 1882, hopefully suggesting that this Article indicated a commitment on the part of the United States to Korean sovereignty. Although continually rebuffed through official channels, Kojong got a very different message from his person-to-person relations with Americans, which were in sharp contrast to the U.S. policy of "disinterested neutrality." That difference may have been a source of confusion for the Koreans. The work that was done by Americans in education, health and medical care, and building and construction was unparalleled in Korea. It would have been very easy for the Emperor to mistake the personal commitments of American citizens in Korea as evidence of a strong national commitment to Korea. In almost every way the Americans in Korea were closer to and more kindly regarded by the Koreans than their counterparts from China, France, Russia, or Japan.

Whatever the desires of American nationals or the wishful thinking of Kojong may have been, the reality of the situation was simply that those individuals in charge of the diplomacy of the United States cared very little if Korea was a free and independent nation, or a colony of some other power. Our "neutrality" with regard to the many international conflicts in Korea during that period was based purely on self-interest and not on any moral compunction to steer clear of Korean sovereign rights.

PERIOD OF RUSSIAN PREDOMINANCE

The Russian Legation in Seoul, Korea

Reprinted from Peter A. Underwood, Samuel H. Moffett, and Normen R. Sibley, eds., *First Encounters: Korea 1880–1910* (Seoul: Dragon's Eye Graphics, 1982).

No. 195   Legation of the United States
                                           Seoul, Korea, Feb. 11, 1896

Secretary of State

Sir:-

I have the honor to inform you that this day has witnessed another wholesale change in the Korean Cabinet. For some time the Kingdom has been disturbed by more or less serious insurrections. Within the last few days the situation has rapidly grown more dangerous.

The enforcement of decrees by the late Government requiring the Koreans to cut off their top knots of hair has been the cause of many alarming uprisings, some of them within 20 or 30 miles of this city. The Government has almost exhaused its military force in futile attempts to put down the insurgents. These have now cut all the telegraph lines leading to the outside world and we are now, so far as telegraphic communication is concerned quite isolated. I have an opportunity to send a telegram by ship to Chefoo and hence on by wire.

I am sending it to night for reading see enclosure No. 1.

This morning at about 8-30 there came a letter from Mr. Speyer the Russian Chargé D'Affaires here, a copy of which I enclose 2, informing me that the King had taken refuge at his Legation. Rumors to the same effect had reached me a half hour earlier. At 11 oclock a letter came from Mr. Ye Wan Yong the newly appointed Minister for Foreign affairs. It had the seal of His Majesty and requested me to inform my colleagues as Dean of the corps that His Majesty would receive us in Audience. See Enclosure 3.

I circulated this letter at once. It was nearly 1 oclock P. M. when all the Foreign Representatives except Mr. Komura and Mr. De Speyer had a very brief audience with His Majesty and the Crown Prince. He merely informed us that fearing great danger at the Palace, he had this morning sought and obtained refuge at the Russian Legation and had immediately invited us all to see him at that palace. See enclosure 4

I also enclose translation of a proclamation pasted up upon the gates of the Russian Legation.

I learn now 6 p.M. that the late Cabinet have been dismissed and many of its members arrested. That Kim Hong Gip late Prime Minister and Chung Pyong Ho, late Minister of Public Works Agriculture and Commerce while under arrest by the police and on his way to prison were seized by a mob and killed in the broad street not far from the entrance to the Palace; that You Kill Chun late Minister of the Home (Interior) Dept. was seized and roughly handled by a mob but was rescued from death by Japanese soldiers stationed in barracks in front of the Palace Gates; that Kim Yun Sik , late Minister of Foreign Affairs and Cho Hui Yun late Minister of War are under arrest.

So far as I am yet able to learn, the new Cabinet is made up of the following friends of the King:
Prime Minister and Acting Minister of the Home Department- Pak Chung Yang formerly Korean Minister at Washington.
Minister of Foreign Affairs and Acting Minister of Education - Ye Wan Yong, also at one time Korean Representative at Washington.
Minister of War - Ye Yin Yong, brother of Ye Wan Yong.
Inspector of Police, An Kyung Soo, lately imprisoned by the ruling party.
Minister of Justice, Cho Pyeng Chick who was Foreign Minister in 1894.

The excitement here is intense and the killin by a mob as noted above may easily be the beginning of very serious trouble.

I sent my telegram asking for a guard this morning as soon as I knew of the action of His Majesty in seeking asylum in the Russian Legation for I knew the city would be terribly and dangerously excited. I have very secretly informed Commander Houston of the U. S. S. "Mathias" of the situation and had asked him to be in readiness to send a guard on short notice, naming 20 as a suitable number.

I have just heard from him that eleven men will start up tomorrow.

Mob violence is more to be feared than anything else, though the large number of Japanese Soshi in the city whom Mr. Komura, the Japanese Minister has but recently said he cannot control are an element of danger. The death of one Japanese from mob vilence is already reported in this city, while seven Japanese were killed in the county a few days ago by the insurrectionists.

It is idle to ask for Korean assistance. They cannot take care of themselves and their soldiers have nearly all been sent out to fight insurgents and have not been heard from since their departure.

If the present condition of affairs lasts many days we have to remember that a very large number of insurrectionists are within a good days march of Seoul and are professedly headed this way.

I suppose there are several hundred Japanese soldiers in the city, though no one can find out the number.

The Russians have about 160 soldiers at this time at their Legation.

The British Representative, who dispensed with his guard when I did, has now ordered another.

John M. B. Sill

No. 201   Legation of the United States
                                                            Seoul Korea, March 2, 1896

Secretary of State

Sir:-

I have the honor to hand you enclosed confirmation of your telegram of Feb. 27, instructing me to report on Korean affairs. I have done so and now hand you enclosed this confirmation of my telegram.

My No. 200 of yesterday's date gives a detailed account of the situation at present. I have little to add to that account and to the telegrams herein confirmed.

I think I see plain indications that that present policy of Russia is to suggest the appointment of intelligent and reputable foreign advisers to the new government from nationals other than her own.

John M. B. Sill

Reading of Telegram from the Dept. of State.
Washington Feb. 27. 9. 25 P. M.

"Report on political situation in Korea. Is lurk (Russia?) practically governing the country through the King and abolishing reforms instituted by Japan."

Olney

Reading of telegrams to the Department of State
Dated Seoul Mch. 3, 1896.

"The King and cabinet are still at Russian Legation. No Japanese reforms have been abolished except hair-cutting is no longer compulsary. Speyer has gone to Japan to represent Russia there. Weaber is Minister Plenipotentiary here. No indications of material interference by Russia. Russian Minister earnestly disclaims such interference. English Consul is satisfied with Russias conduct so far. I only know that the King and cabinet defer to Russian opinion in matters of consequence. Russian Minister caused the American Legal adviser to attend all trials of suspected murderers of Queen, thus insuring fairness and thus avoiding customary cruelties. The King seems to govern with Russia behind the throne. Anarchy continues rampant in the provinces.

Sill

No 226   Legation of the United States
                                                            Seoul Korea July. 17, 1896.

Secretary of State

Sir:-

I have the honor to report the departure of the legation guard, and the present political condition of affairs in Korea as they appear to me.

On July 5th the guard of Marines from the U.S.S. "Yorktown" returned to their ship at Chemulpo. In reply to a note from Commander C.H. Stockton inquiring whether further attendance of the guard seemed necessary, I had said that provided a U.S. Warship should remain at Chemulpo to meet any sudden emergency, American interests would not, in my judgement, suffer by the removal of the guard, accordingly it was withdrawn. on the date mentioned above.

Experience has shown that the withdrawal could have taken place at an earlier date, but it required some time to convince myself and other Foreign Representatives that the Japanese Government would submit, without recourse to arms, to the sudden and complete overthrow of the predominance of its influence in this peninsula.

Several changes have taken place recently at the Japanese Legation. On May. 30. K. Komura. E.E. & M.P. left Seoul for Japan; M. Kato. Secretary of Legation remaining as Chargé d'Affaires ad interim. On July 7.th. S. Uchida, Consul, left on "Furlough", Mr Kato becoming consul in his place. Mr, Takashi Hara. H.I.J. M's. E.E. & M.P. arrived in Seoul recently and on yesterday he had an audience with the King. He has not yet announced that he has taken charge of the Legation.

It is understood that Mr. Colin de Plancy, the newly returned French Chargé d'Affaires, has secured a concession for the construction of a railroad from Seoul northward to Weiju, and that the Russian Minister has obtained a gold mining concession in the North-Eastern Province of Korea.

The French railway concession is granted on the same terms, as to all essentials, as those granted by the Korean Government to James R. Morse, except that it gives three years, instead of one, in which to begin construction and nine years after beginning, instead of three, for completion. It is however a much more costly road to build than the Seoul-Chemulpo one, and there must be much longer waiting for paying traffic.

The German Representative, F. Krien Esq. Consul. has been very urgent in his efforts to secure a mining concession for his nationals, but the fact that he conspicuously withheld any apparent sympathy at the time of the death of the Queen and during other times of misfortune and trouble, seems to make the Koreans indifferent to his urgent solicitations. Korean statesmanship is still, to a degree, in the personal stage.

The late Japanese Representative, Mr. Komura, before his departure, was endeavoring to secure for his countrymen the right to construct and operate a railway from Seoul south-east to the port of Fusan. There is a difference between the parties as to width of gauge, the Japanese desiring to build a narrow gauge, and the Koreans insisting upon standard guage. In my judgement the latter are making a mistake in so insisting, but they seem inclinded to be stubborn on this point.

As to the general situation, it may be said that the overthrow of Japanese predominant influence, brought about suddenly by the flight of His Majesty to the Russian Legation, seems, at the present moment to be complete and absolute. Whether it will be permanent the future will determine. At this moment nationals of any other Foreign Power could obtain from Korea, concessions upon more favorable terms and with less question and objection than Japan could obtain them. Russian policy seems to be to make the least possible show either of force or of prevailing influence. She keeps a comparatively small guard, sixty or seventy men, at her Legation in Seoul, and plenty of ships at Chemulpo and in neighboring seas. The indications are that, having come into possession, by the act of the King, of great power in Korean councils, she will hold with characteristic tenacity to what she has secured, making no exhibition of force unless she is compelled to do so.

His Majesty is still at the Russian Legation and though most of his people are anxious for his return to the Palace, there is nothing in sight to indicate that he intends an early return. I understand that, at the request of His Majesty, a considerable number of Russian Military officers are expected to arrive soon to train Korean soldiers, and it is generally believed that when they have trained these to a proper degree of efficiency His Majesty will go to one or another of his palaces under protection of an adequate native guard.

The Russian Representative, Mr. Waeber, says the King is his guest and that he will not suggest his departure from the shelter of the Legation, but that he is free to go whenever he deems it safe and advisable to do so, and it is definitely understood that Russia will not furnish a guard to protect him elsewhere. Meanwhile His Majesty feels a sense of personal security unknown to him since the seizure of the palace on July 23. 1894. until he sought and obtained his present Asylum on the 11th of February 1896. and I believe he will be slow to leave his present quarters until he has a sufficient native guard, satisfactorily trained and commanded, to protect him and his court.

This determination is not necessarily chargeable to timidity on His Majestys part, for his life will need special protection so long as the old Tai Won Kuhn, the abettor of those who murdered the Queen, and the author, during the last half century, of countless murderous intrigues, lives and is at liberty to plot and to conspire with others for the destruction of the present government. I understand upon excellent authority that he is in a great rage and eagerly awaiting a favorable opportunity to rally his formidable following for the murder of the King and the Crown Prince. The murder of the Queen in which he gladly acted a conspicuous though subordinate part has, it is said, made him more eager than ever before to put out of the way of his favorite grandson Ye Chun Yang, every obstacle to the Korean throne. There will never be peace in Korea until this incarnation of intrigue and remorseless cruelty takes final possession of the beautiful burial place which he has prepared for himself in a suburb of Seoul in sight of the Han river.

This city is now quiet and from the provinces we hear much less of disorder and organized robberies. Robbing and the desire to rove freely about abtaining food and other necessaries without actual labor in shops and fields, together with frequent promtings from the Tai Won Kuhn, seem to be the compelling motives of all these predatory bands though they usually attempt to cover their actual purpose by giving themselves a political or religious name. It must however be acknowledged that they have sometimes served a useful purpose by intimidating and. in many cases killing, some of the most cruelly oppressive of the local governors and magistrates.

We also hear little now of the attacks upon Japanese going about in the provinces, not because Korean hatred towards them is less intense and general, but because they have made their way to Japan or have come back under the protection of the still strong Japanese Legation guard in Seoul and of the more effective municipal police system that is in operation in this city.

It gives me pleasure to report some progress towards a better state of things in Korea. The Government has appointed a very competent Englishman, Dr. J. McLeavy Brown as a kind of overseer of the Treasury and money can now be drawn from it only upon correct vouchers and rigid investigation of the regularity of the order. Reports from the Korean Post Office Dep't show a steady increase in the use of mail facilities. The Government has nearly completed a telegraph line from Seoul to Weiju and the value of railroads is becoming generally understood. A Tri-weekly newspaper published by Dr. Jaisohn, half in English and half in Korean, is increasing a very considerable circulation. The Mayor of Seoul has recently published well devised, greatly needed, sanitary regulations for the City of Seoul and the police are looking to their enforcement. The City is also, as fast as the money at its disposal will allow, improving, widening, and draining the streets. and active interest is being shown in bettering the country roads. These are all new departures for Korea, but most conspicuous and important is the improvement in proceedings of the Courts.

Open courts in Korea wherein a Yangban (official) may be brought face to face with a wronged coolie; wherein witnesses are called upon to tell the truth without fear of torture, are new in Korea and cannot fail to contribute largely towards the overthrow of the miserable and utterly irresponsible tyranny of the Yangban class which has for centuries been allowed to bitterly oppress the lower caste men and women without fear of any accounting.

The beginning of this more humane policy dates from the opening of the examination into the circumstances of the death of the Queen, made by the Department of Justice shortly after His Majesty took refuge in his present quarters (see my No, 208 April 3. and enclosure) This was the first trial of importance in a Korean court in which there was freedom from danger of torture inflicted upon defendants and witnesses, and I am happy to say that this change was brought about mainly by the efforts of the present American adviser to the Department of Justice, viz, C.R. Greathouse Esq. formerly U.S. Consul General at Kanagawa, Japan.

Torture of defendants and witnesses survived the revision of Korean laws and rules of court procedure made by Japanese official advisers, and was in constant use until the investigation mentioned above.

It is notorious and not doubted here, that very severe torture was applied to the defendant in the trial of the grandson of the Tai Won Kuhn Prince Ye Chun Yang, in the early months of 1895, and in the trial of certain suspects in the abortive raid on the palace of Nov. 27. 1895 it was freely applied upon the persons of the accused. These trials were conducted by the Korean court but were under direct supervision of the Japanese advisers of the Department of Justice.

Within the last ten days there has been a striking illustration of the present movement in the line of progress and reform and of the danger to which a Korean administration has been constantly exposed and the resulting weakness and instability of any Korean cabinet.

It is the custom in Korea from time immemorial, that, theoretically any subject - even the meanest, and practically any Korean of the rank of Chusa, may memorialize His Majesty and accuse any officer, civil or military, with any crime or any form of disloyalty or treason, that the knowledge, malice or fancy of the memorialist may suggest. This memorial has also from ancient times been a privileged communication and there is no available remedy for the accused against any slanders that it may, and usually does, contain. Old custom has also made it the duty of the accused official, upon such accusation, to resign at once, go to his house and there await the pleasure of the King. The same custom makes it the duty of the King to consider the accusation and to refuse to accept the resignation and reinstate the officer, or to accept it and name a successor. It is therefore possible for anyone hostile to the Government or desiring to obstruct the administration, to procure the presentation of such a succession of memorials as would paralyze the Government for an indefinite period even in the midst of a crisis where interruption of its functions would be injurious to the last degree or even fatal to its existence.

Seeing danger in the continuance of such an absurd custom, His Majesty recently decreed that officials must not resign upon accusation by memorial, but must remain in office attending to duty unless he should request resignation or announce the dismissal of the accused.

A few days ago such a memorial (sang so) was presented to His Majesty by an inveterate office seeker and friend of the Tai Won Kuhn. It accused several members of the Cabinet and other eminent Korean Citizens of various crimes and misdemeanors. Instead however of following the ancient custom by resigning, the accused brought the memorialist before the Supreme Court of Korea to answer for libel and for damages if found guilty. As one of the plaintiffs was Dr. Philip Jaisohn. an American citizen, though born in Korea, and upon the invitation by the Korean Minister for Foreign Affairs, I attended the trial on 13th Instant. The complaint made against the memorialist has been sustained by the court and judgement including award of damages was given on the 18th Instant.

It is understood that the memorialist has yet to answer in the same court for lying to His Majesty.

The design of the plaintiffs was not to obstruct the ancient right to memorialize the throne but to hold memorialists responsible for false and slanderous utterances and also to establish a precedent for the reference by His Majesty of such accusing memorials to the Department of Justice for examination and report and to strengthen the decree of His Majesty mentioned above.

It seems almost certain that these results will be secured and that justice and the greater permanence of Korean administrations will be promoted by these trials.

John M. B. Sill

No. 231

Legation of the United States
Seoul Korea Sept. 1. 1896

Secretary of State

Sir:-

In my No. 226 of July 17. on page 6. I mentioned the efforts of the Japanese to obtain a concession for a railroad to connect Seoul and Fusan. I have now the honor to inform you that this has been definitely refused by the Korean Cabinet.

On page 15 of the above cited despatch, I spoke of a "better state of things in Korea". I regret to have to state that the tendency now seems to be to go back to the old condition of affairs prior to 1894.

There is a strong conservative element in the cabinet that seems to have great power with the King. They have instituted, to a large extent, the old order of oppressive extortion in the interior. And though Mr Waeber and Mr Brown, (see page 15 of above cited despatch) have protested against this and secured a Royal edict countermanding such extortion, I am assured that it is carried on without perceptible abatement.

Ye Wan Yong, the able Foreign Minister, seems to be the Chief object of the attack of this conservative party. It is too soon to predict the success or failure of the new movement, but it may cause Russia to assume a more vigorous policy than has seemed to be her intent thus far.

I may add that one of the acts of this conservative party was the selling of mining rights within the territory granted by contract to the American, James R. Morse, whereby 3000 miners were being employed by the Korean lessees. When knowledge of this was brought to the King by the Foreign Minister. His Majesty gave orders to have the work of the intruding miners stopped, but I am not yet in receipt of advices from the mines as to the result of this order.

These spurious leases were issued in the name of the Minister of the Household, - the same man who signed Mr Morses contract. He is one of the most reckless and energetic of the Conservative party. And his Department has control of these Royal mines.

It is the intention of His Majesty soon to remove to a reconstructed palace adjoining this foreign settlement. The remains of the Queen are to be removed to this palace in a few days, and workmen are laboring day and night to complete the buildings, as well as in building handsome broad roads leading to the new palace. In order to build these roads, hundreds of houses have been removed and much money is being expended. The general appearance as well as the sanitary condition of this part of the city will be greatly benefitted by these improvements.

John M. B. Sill

No. 239   Legation of the United States
Seoul Korea Oct. 13. 1896

Secretary of State

Sir:-
        In my No 235, Sept 28, informing you of the abolishment of the Cabinet, and the establishment of a council. I eroneously called this new body a Privy Council. It is instead, a Council of State, - a sort of parliament.
        I understand that the idea of establishing this body originated with the Russian Minister, who I am told drew up the regulations for its operations.
        I now hand you extracts from the Seoul Independent, being an Editorial (inspired I am told by the Editor) by the Russian Minister, followed by translations of the regulations for the Council. It is believed that the Council will be a good thing for the country.
        The difficulty of controlling such bodies in Korea is shown by the fact that about the first act of the President of this council was to memorialize the King against his further residence at the Russian Legation, and urging the necessity, or the advisability, of His Majestys speedy return to his Palace, at least to the Palace newly reconstructed in the Foreign Settlement here.
        Of course this may meet with Mr. Waebers approval, but the early presentation of such a memorial as one of the first acts of this council created by Mr. Waebers suggestion, seems strange to say the least.

H. N. Allen

No. 240   Legation of the United States
Seoul Korea Oct 27. 1896

Secretary of State

Sir:-
        I have the honor to inform you of the return to Korea of H.E. Min Yong Whan, who was sent as special ambassador to the Coronation of the Czar of Russia. With the Ambassador came Colonel Patiata, a surgeon, two Lieutenants, and ten non-commissioned officers from the Russian Army. These fourteen military officers are employed by the Korean Government to organize and drill the Korean forces. It is understood that as many more Russian officers are on their way to Seoul for the same purpose. The Russian Government also have a Military Agent here - Col. Strelbitzsky, and a staff of officers in charge of their Legation Guard. This guard is small. probably about 50 men. but by means of homing pidgeons and pre-arranged signals, the Legation can easily communicate with the Russian ships constantly kept at Chemulpo.

H. N. Allen

No. 243   Legation of the United States
                                                           Seoul Korea Nov. 4. 1896

Secretary of State

Sir:-

I have the honor to inform you that I am confidentially informed by the Korean Minister for Foreign Affairs that the Russian Government has agreed to loan to the Korean Government, a sum of money sufficient to pay off Korean financial obligations to Japan. The exact sum is not yet named, but will be determined by the Manager of the Russo-Chinese Bank, Mr. Pakatilow who has been here for some months closely investigating the finances of this Government.

It is the thought that this Mr. Pakatilow will have charge of the disbursement of this money. It is possible that he may take over and conduct a Korean Bank that is just now being started by influential Koreans.

H. N. Allen.

No. 245   Legation of the United States
                                                           Seoul Korea Nov. 13. 1896

Secretary of State

Sir:-

I have the honor to inform you that there is a change for the worse in the political situation here. Mr. Waeber, the Russian Minister at Seoul, has abstained from interfering in the details of Government as much as possible, and has given the conservative party so much liberty that they have now begun, through the King, to make changes in the Cabinet - a thing Mr. Waeber had declared he would not allow. Chyo Pyung Sik has been compelled to resign the post of Minister of Public Works Agriculture and Commerce. and Ye Yun Yong. has been changed to this vacant post. from that of Minister of War. While Min Yong Whan, the newly returned Ambassador to the Coronation of the Czar. was given the post of Minister of War. It is further confidently affirmed that Hong, the unpunished murderer of Kim Ok Kiun in Shanghai, in 1894, is to be made Vice Minister of Foreign Affairs. It is understood that all these changes, and others that are proposed, are objectionable to Mr. Waeber. and that they have been made against his urgent protest.

It seems to persons here that Mr. Waeber has not the full support of his Government in his plans and operations. Min Yong Whan brings back from Russia the news that a party in the Russian Government wish for Mr. Waebers removal and the appontment of a more vigorous representative in his place. Mr de Speyer now Russian Representative in Japan, is prominently mentioned for this post. The news of dissention among the Russians, brought by Min Yong Whan, and circulated here, who by certain Russians, is thought to be the cause of the sudden vigor of the Korean conservatives.

The Council of State organized by Mr. Waeber. - see my No. 239. Oct 13, is not working at all. About the only thing they did was to memorialize the King against his staying longer at the Russian Legation, and now Min Yong Whan, from whom Mr Waeber rightly expected suport, has sent in a similar memorial, and seems to have cast in his lot with the conservative and anti Foreign party.

There is also a move on foot to get rid of Mr. Brown. the Commissioner of Customs and gaurdian of the Treasury. He has done most excellent service in righting Korean finances. And though an Englishman, he is in active sympathy with Mr Waeber.

H. N. Allen

No. 258   Legation of the United States
                                              Seoul Korea Feb. 22. 1897

Secretary of State

Sir:-
     I have the honor to confirm my telegram to you of todays date as follows,
     "The King has moved from the Russian Legation to his Palace and guarded by his troops officered by Russia (ns). The move gives great satisfaction. All is quiet."
     In explanation of this I have the honor to inform you that for some time there has been a constant presentation of memorials from the official as well as from the unofficial classes, praying His Majesty to return to his palace, from the Russian Legation, where he took refuge on the 11th February 1896. Mr. Waeber, the Russian Representative, has not opposed the Kings departure though he has not advised it. I understandd that Col. Potiata, the Russian officer in charge of the Korean troops, did give the King assurance that he could protect him, and that he did this without first consulting Mr. Waeber. Mr. Waeber however placed no obstacles in the way of his going and on the 20th Instant - day before yesterday - His Majesty made a public procession and moved to the palace situated in this settlement, next door to the English Legation and near to our own.
     On yesterday I went with my colleagues to see His Majesty in his palace upon invitation, and took occasion to congratulate him on the peaceful conditions of his land that permits of his going in safety to his own palace. All is quiet and the move seems to give universal satisfaction.
     The palace is guarded by Korean troops officered by Russians, while the Russian Legation still retains its guard, as does also the Japanese Legation. These are the only foreign troops now in Seoul.

                                       John M. B. Sill

No. 263   Legation of the United States
                                              Seoul Korea March 18. 1897.

Secretary of State

Sir,-
     Referring to my No. 262, of the 11'th, instant I now have the honor to hand you an authentic copy of the memorandum written in English and signed at Seoul on May 14. 1896. by Messrs Waeber and Komura, - Representatives respectively of Russia and Japan.
     At the date of this document there were in Korea fully 5000 Japanese troops. Of these about 1500 were stationed at Seoul and Chemulpo - its seaport. Other bodies were stationed at Fusan and Gensan, at other points in the interior, and 600 soldiers were guarding the telegraph line between Seoul and Fusan, over which line the Japanese claimed ownership.
     Korean subjects, greatly enraged against all Japanese, were breaking said telegraph line whenever opportunity served and were killing Japanese subjects moving about in the interior without passports. whenever they were abel to overpower them. Nearly 50, had already been killed. The Japanese troops in Seoul were quartered mainly in barracks close in front of the Palace from which His Majesty had recently escaped when he sought and obtained asylum in the Russian Legation on Feb. 11. 1896.
     Up to this time it was expected that the King would, so soon as he could safely do so, return to his Palace, for as yet it had not been proposed to fit up for his occupation the new Palace, Kyeng Won; hence the Korean government was very urgent that these troops should be quartered elsewhere.
     The Japanese authorities promised to remove their troops from the Palace barracks, but showed no real disposition to do so. Other places affording sufficient and equally comfortable accomodation were proposed and offered, but objections were raised against every proposition. Three months had already elapsed since the escape of the King and there seemed to be no prospect that the troops would be removed to other quarters, or leave the city.
     The Japanese Representative, Mr. Komura, had expressed much impatience over the extended residence of the King at the Russian Legation, and had urged me to aid him in securing action by the diplomatic corps, condemning such residence as intolerable and equivalent to abdication. The Japanese news-paper publisher here advocated the same views with such similarity of argument and expression that

there could be little doubt of the source of ite inspiration, and Mr. Komura, desiring audience with His Majesty to advise him of his promotion to the rank of Envoy Extraordinary and Minister Plenipotentiary, was insisting that such audience should be granted elsewhere.

I make this brief review of the conditions in order that the importance to Korea of the "memorandum", may be better understood.

It will be seen that the memorandum forecloses Japanese objection to the residence of the King at the Russian Legation, until a time "when no doubt concerning his safety there (in his Palace) could be entertained"; settles the somewhat open question, so far as Japan was concerned, of the validity of the commissions of the Cabinet appointed at the said Legation; promises effective control of the Japanese soshi of whose efficiency as conspirators and assassins the Koreans had had abundant evidence in the brutal murder of the Queen on October 8. 1895; admits the right of the Japanese to protect their telegraph line from Seoul to Fusan but provides for the immediate withdrawal of four fifths of all their Army of Occupation and the ultimate withdrawal of their whole Army; the removal of such of their troops as were to remain at Seoul from the Palace gate to a place "near" their settlement; reduces the guard for the Seoul-Fusan telegraph line from 600 soldiers to 200 gendarmes having fixed location; and finally, evidently to save, in some measure, the "face" of Japan, provides that Russia may station troops identical in numbers and location, a provision of which Russia has not availed herself.

I enclose also a copy of the protocol signed June 9'th 1896. at Moscow by Prince Lobanoff and Marquis Yamagata, the translation of the same having been furnished by Mr. Waeber to the "Seoul Independent".

John M. B. Sill

P.S.

I also hand you enclosed a printed translation of the reply of the Korean Foreign Office to Mr. Kato, the present Japanese Minister here, when the latter forwarded copies of both the memorandum and the protocol.

No. 269   Legation of the United States
                                          Seoul Korea. May 8. 1897.

Secretary of State

Sir,-

In No. 240 of this series, Mr. Allen to Mr. Olney, the department was informed of the arrival in Korea of fourteen Russian officers for the purpose of drilling the Korean Troops, and it was intimated that "many more Russian officers" were expected to arrive for the same purpose.

There has been considerable excitement here for a few days past over the fact that the Minister of Foreign Affairs and one other Cabinet Officer had declined to agree to the employment of 168 more Russian officers in accordance with a request made by the King of Korea to the Russian Emperor through the former's Ambassador to the coronation ceremonies - Min Yong Whan. It seems this request was about to be complied with, but the necessary articles of agreement for the employment of these military people had yet to be signed by the Korean Council of State.

In illustration of the interest shown in this matter by the Japanese Government, I have the honor to hand you enclosed an extract from the Seoul "Independent" of today's date, showing that in consequence of vigorous inquiries instituted by the Japanese Government, the Russian Government has evidently given up the project.

Korean sentiment seems to be turning somewhat against Russia, probably from fear of absorption by their great neighbor. It is publicly rumored that Mr. Waeber, for many years Russian Representative at this Court, is now seeking with much difficulty to be taken on as adviser to the Korean Government, in view of his prospective early relief by Mr. de Speyer, present Russian Representative in Tokio. Mr. Waeber is under appointment as Minister Plenipotentiary to Mexico, but his interest in Korea is very great and his influence has been for good.

John M. B. Sill

No. 270   Legation of the United States
                                           Seoul Korea. May 10. 1897.

Secretary of State

Sir,-

I have the honor to hand you enclosed a confirmation of your telegram of the 8'th instant as well as of my reply of the same date, and to offer the following in explanation.

In my number 269 of the 8'th instant, I referred to the interest here in the proposed increase in the number of Russian military instructors for Korean troops, and to the fact that it has been understood from the first, that additional instructors would follow as there should be occasion to employ them.

On the arrival of the first installment of instructors, (See Allen's No. 240 Oct. 27. 1896) there was much interest here in noting how the Japanese authorities would view this new departure. This was months before the Russo-Japanese Convention and the memorandum signed reepectively in Moscow and Seoul had been made public, but, from the fact that said authorities made no objection, the belief became general that Japan, Russia, and Korea had come to an amicable understanding upon the matter of the training of Korean troops.

In March (See my No. 263. March 19) came to hand the full and authentic text of both the memorandum and the convention. There again arose much interest in the question whether Japan's interpretation of these documents would justify the plan which Russia and Korea were carrying out. This question was set at rest first by the acquiescence of Japan, and then by the action of Count Okuma, Japan's Minister for Foreign Affairs. Being sharply questioned in the Japanese House of Representatives, "He admitted that Russian officers were drilling Korean soldiers, but this was in deference to the request of the King and had no relations to diplomacy". Again also before the House of Representatives, he affirmed that this matter of training Korean troops had no relation to the Russo-Japanese undertaking and that "Russian officers appear to have been sent at the request of the King and no diplomatic question is involved" He also said "that it rested only with the King of Korea to appoint drill instructors of any nationality that suited him".

Under these circumstances I believed and had good right to believe, that in the matter of drilling of Korean troops by Russian drill instructors, Russia and Japan were in agreement. I had seen the acquiescence of Japanese authorities for half a year during which time the beginnings of this plan were in successful progress, in the training of a single regiment as a Royal guard. I had heard no word to the contrary, and in the absence of any symptom of objection, Count Okuma's deliverance on the subject seemed absolutely conclusive.

Ever since I have been in Korea, the country has existed in varying degrees of disorder. American interests here are now considerable, and they need peace and order above all other things, not only for the promotion of these interests but also for the safety of our comparatively large number of nationals, now that the finances of Korea are somewhat improved, its greateet need is a trained force sufficiently strong to police it effectively. The present troops available for this purpose are utterly incompetent to quell the constantly recurring insurrections. When they go out into the provinces for this purpose, they are, through lack of any discipline, vastly more dangerous to the safety of the country than the marauders against whom they march. To organize such an effective force is impossible without foreign aid. No one who knows Korea and Koreans will gainsay this for a moment.

When it became known a short time ago that it was proposed to begin the extension of the drill to soldiers outside of the Royal Guard, I was rejoiced to hear it, for I believed that such extension was vitally important for all concerned and, not for a moment supposing that I was antagonizing any interest, I spoke favorably of it, as occasion served. Learning that Mr. Ye Wan Yong, Korean Minister for Foreign Affairs, was hesitating about agreeing to the completion of a contract for additional instructors, drawn up at the King's request, I asked the Secretary of Legation to say to him that I regarded the matter an important one not only for Korea but for all who hold interests here, and that I hoped he would study the question in all its bearings, and, in view of the great need of a trained force to maintain order in the provinces, give the subject the grave consideration that its importance demanded.

The Secretary found him fixed in the opinion he had formed, and no more was said.

I did not hesitate to do this because Mr. Ye, a firm friend of America, and also His Majesty, have often asked me to advise them freely whenever circumstances would allow, and the welfare of Korea seemed to me to be at stake; and the advice was given while I had no thought that any interest could be prejudiced by my action.

This happened on April 23'rd. On the 27'th. I went to Chemulpo on official business. During my absence a messenger came to the Legation from the King, asking both myself and Secretary Allen to meet him on important business. Informed of my absence, the King still desired to see the Secretary, and, when His Majesty asked for an opinion on the matter of calling more military instructors, Mr. Allen declined to speak on the subject on his own behalf or on mine. On my return from Chemulpo April 29, I found that the audience of Mr. Kato, the Japanese Minister, with the King, held on the 26'th. was supposed to have been had for the purpose of objecting to the contract for additional instructors. This was my first intimation that Japan was interested in the defeat of the contract, and since that time I have been studiously silent on the subject.

On Wednesday May 5, Mr. Kato sent his interpreter and secretary to me to explain the attitude of Japan on this question. I stated to him the facts of my own attitude and willingly gave assurance's that I would do nothing that could prejudice the interests of Japan,.

Upon the arrival of your telegram, naturally taking it for granted that the Japanese Government must have obtained from its representative here the information on which this serious complaint against me was based, and feeling sure any misunderstanding on his part must have arisen from an imperfect rendering to him of what I said to his interpreter in my interview noted above, I went to Mr. Kato. He at once and most earnestly assured me that he had communicated nothing to his government on which such a complaint could be based, that he had not, during the pendency of present questions even mentioned myself or any one connected with this Legation to the Government of Tokio, that he had no knowledge of their information and that he knew no cause whatever of complaint ayainst me.

The whole matter is easily summed up. A plan was proposed which seemed to me the only solution at present in sight, of the most conspicuous difficulty under which Korea is now laboring. There was absolutely no indication that it conflicted with anyone's interests and indeed every indication pointed the other way. I believed it advantageous to American interests which are sensitive to disorder. I approved it and spoke favorably of it. Russia was connected with it but it was not easy to see that this would make against it if, as I believed, it antagonized no other power. Very soon I found that another friendly power conceived it to be opposed to her interests. From that moment I kept my own counsels.

The Secretary of Legation has had nothing to do with it, except with complying with my directions.

John M. B. Sill

Addenda.

Readings of telegrams

Readings of telegrams

Washington May 8. 1897.

"Japanese Government complains you and Secretary of Legation assisting Russian Minister in matter not concerning United States.

Department instructions positively forbid you to mix in internal affairs ot the country. Explicit compliance therewith expected."

"Sherman"

Seoul May. 8. 1897.

"Japanese Government is unjustly suspicious. Neither of us have meddled and will not. Minister from Japan denies knowledge of charge.

"Sill".

No. 286   Legation of the United States
                                                 Seoul Korea, September 9, 1897.

Secretary of State

Sir;-
         In my No. 277, July 13, I referred to Mr. Ye Wan Yong, then, and until a few days ago, Minister
for Foreign Affairs, as sturdily opposing and finally defeating the strenuous efforts of the Japanese
Representative to obtain recognition of validity for a temporary agreement made by Kim Yun Sik and Mr.
Otori in August 1894. This agreement gave to the Japanese the right to build, at a later date, the Seoul-
Chemulpo and the Seoul-Fusan Railways and provided for the opening of the port of Mokpo. It was made
and signed by the two gentlemen named above within a month of the taking of the Palace by force of arms
and while the whole Korean Government was under absolute duress by the Japanese Authorities. In this
despatch I showed also that Mr. Ye's course in the matter was of great advantage to American interests in
Korea.
         I have now the honor to inform you that Mr. Ye has finally been compelled to retire from the
Cabinet and has been relegated to the Governorship of the distant province of South Peng-yang. The
immediate pressure which drove Ye from the Foreign Office was applied by Mr. Waeber, the Russian
Representative, whose retirement from the Legation at Seoul, I recently reported. Mr. Ye had declined to
sanction the employment of additional Russian military drill-masters to train the Korean Army. Mr.
Waeber then went over the head of the Minister for Foreign Affairs, and negotiated more successfully with
the War Minister, Mr. Sim Sang Hun. But it was necessary that the final order should come from the
Foreign Office. So after much correspondence and successful negotiation with the War Office, Mr. Waeber
called on Mr. Ye as Foreign Minister to give effect to an agreement made without consultation with him.
This he squarely refused to do since he regarded the whole matter as belonging to his department and not
primarily to the War Office. Mr. Waeber then took the matter up vigorously and insisted upon, and easily
secured, Mr. Ye's removal.
         Mr. Ye's removal is a heavy loss to progress in Korea and disadvantageous to American interests
as well. He is a strong, consistent man, entirely fearless in the discharge of duty, and able to say "no"
when occasion requires and to stand manfully by his word. These are qualities that few Korean Statesmen
possess. I know of no one who can even approximately, fill the place which he has vacated.
         His successor is Mr. Min Chong Mook, who made haste to do what Mr. Ye refused to do.

                                                 John M. B. Sill

No. 8   Legation of the United States
                                                 Seoul Korea, October 1, 1897.

Secretary of State

Sir:-
         I have the honor to inform you that sometime ago I learned that the Russian Government had
applied for, and were about to obtain, a coaling station on Deer Island, in the harbor of Fusan.
         The Japanese have a coaling station on the same island as well as at Chemulpo and Gensan, and it
seemed not unnatural that Russia should ask for, and obtain, the same advantage.
         Later I learned that the Secretary of the Russian Legation had gone to Fusan, and in conjunction
with Russian Naval Officers, had selected 20 acres of land on the low lying western end of this large and
rocky island, at a point just opposite, and nearest to the large and ancient Japanese Settlement, and right in
the heart of the plot selected by the Korean Government at the suggestion of my predecessors, Messrs.
Heard and Sill, as well as other Foreign Representatives, for a site for the General Foreign Settlement of
Fusan.
         This is positively the only available site for this Settlement, which is granted and provided for in
the treaty between Great Britain and Korea, Article IV. Section I.
         I send enclosed a rough sketch of Fusan Harbor, showing that from the mountainous condition of
the main land and the most of the island, this low lying tract, near deep water and adjoining the Japanese
town of some 10,000 inhabitants, which has existed there for over 200 years, is the only suitable place for
the General Foreign Settlement.

It was so generally assumed that the Settlement would be laid out on this spot, that in 1894, at the request of the American, Russian and British Representatives, the Korean Government despatched its Chief Commissioner of Customs to Fusan to lay out the limits of the settlement on this place.

This was done and boundary stones were erected, enclosing an area of about 50 acres for a settlement proper, with ample ground around it for future use. The sudden taking off of the Queen and the consequent disorder, prevented a formal openning of this tract to settlement purposes.

This delay has been very annoying to this Legation, for we have several families living at Fusan in houses they have erected on ground for which they could not get proper title deeds, and we want this matter settled for their sakes. Also, two American firms of importance, have for some years been very anxious to open up business at Fusan, but could not do so until this settlement matter was arranged.

When therefore, I learned that we were likely to lose altogether the only available site, through this proposal of the Russian Government, I went to the Foreign Office on the 14'th. September, (the day after assuming charge of the Legation) and had a long talk with the Minister for Foreign Affairs. I told him that I had nothing to say as to the right or propriety of his Governments granting coaling stations to any power, but that I had learned with regret that he was thinking of granting to one country a large part of the site selected for a Foreign Settlement at Fusan for all the Treaty Powers: that a Settlement at Fusan was granted foreigners by treaty, and that the Korean Government had been repeatedly urged to carry out the treaty stipulations in this particular instance: that Americans and American interests had been really injured by this long delay, and that I could not see the only available site for settlement purposes otherwise disposed of without speaking: that I thought he should first fulfill the treaty obligations and lay out this Settlement, after which I would probably have nothing to say as to his disposal of the part of the large island still remaining.

He saw the point I was endeavoring to make, and assured me finally that he would do nothing in the matter without first consulting the Foreign Representatives, which was all I could ask.

I understand that the British, Japanese and German Representatives secured a similar assurance, though my action was entirely individual and had only to do with our own interests.

On the 22'nd. Sept. the Secretary of the Russian Legation had a long interview with the Vice Minister for Foreign Affairs, as a result of which he signed a "protocol" giving up all claim to this particular site, and agreeing to take another. See enclosure.

I may add that a few days later, this very excellent Vice Minister was transferred to the obscure Educational Department, and his former place given to a man said to be greatly his inferior in strength of character and general ability.

Horace N. Allen

No. 10

Legation of the United States
Seoul Korea, October 2, 1897.

Secretary of State

Sir:-

I have the honor to inform you that we are passing through another period of great excitement here. Suddenly yesterday afternoon, it was announced that the Cabinet had been changed by the dismissal of six ministers, the appointment of six and the retention of but two.

It was reported some days ago that theWar Minister, who has been in temporary retirement because of his refusal to sign the Russian Military Contracts, would soon be asked to resign, and it was also said that the Minister of the Household, having had a serious disagreement with the French Legation over Catholic lands in the interior, was expecting to be asked for his resignation, now that the French and Russian Legations seem to be in such perfect accord. But this wholesale change was entirely unexpected by most of the men dismissed, as well as by most of those appointed and by the City generally. I am informed by an officer who was at the Palace at the time, that the list of names of the new Cabinet was sent to the King night before last by Mr. de Speyer, the Russian Chargé d'Affaires, who insisted that the persons so named be appointed that night, and that if his advice was not at once acted upon he would be compelled to leave, - meaning presumably, that he would withdraw his guard from the Palace. It was done as he directed, during the night, and announced the next afternoon. The Cabinet now is composed of the following new appointee's, -

Justice Department	- Chyo Pyung Sik.
Household "	- Min Yung Kui.
Finance "	- Pak Chung Yang.
War "	- Ye Chung Kun.
Agriculture "	- Chung Nak Yung.
Education "	- Chyo Pyung Chik.
Those left over are, -	
Foreign Office	- Min Chung Mook.
Home "	- Nam Chung Chull.

Mr. Ye Wan Yong was removed from the position of Minister for Foreign Affairs some weeks ago at the instigation of the Russian Minister, as reported in Mr. Sill's No. 286, September 9. The present Minister was then appointed.

Of these new appointments there is not much to say, except in the case of the Minister of Justice, who will probably dominate and rule them all. Chyo Pyung Sik enjoys the most unenviable reputation of any public official in Korea. At one time he was very obnoxious to the French Catholics, and as the latter were under the care of the Russian Minister at that time, Mr.Waeber had a very disagreeable time with him. Last winter he secured the appointment as Minister of Justice, but owing to the opposition of the Russian Minister, he was not continued. He was in office enough however to make a desperate attempt to do away with his predecessor, who was an especial friend of Mr. Waeber's.

I send you enclosed a statement as to his career taken from the "Independent", a news-paper published in this City by Dr. Philip Jaisohn, a Korean who was naturalized in America. This statement was published at the time of the former appointment of Mr. Chyo, in December last, and regardless of the exact truth or otherwise of this report, we regretted exceedingly that it should have been published in a paper conducted by an American. While none of these charges have been denied, this Mr. Chyo has been embittered against all Americans and especially against Dr. Jaisohn and his Korean friends, who represent the party of progresss and independence in Korea. They will doubtless all feel the results of his illwill.

I am told that in one of his recent numerous memorials to the King, this Chyo urged the killing of all the wives and children and rear relatives of the refugee's in Japan, who were supposed to have been implicated in the murder of the Queen, and that he promised to do so if appointed to the Department of Justice. He will do this probably if not prevented. He has shown a most persistent intention of getting back, at any cost, the position he lost last winter through the opposition of the Russian Minister. He has been foremost in memorializing the King, urging him to take the title of Emperor: he is said to have made himself very agreeable to the French and to have promised the Catholic Christians great favors, though the French Bishop said to a friend of mine that he did not trust Chyo: he is known to have made strenuous efforts to become persona grata to Mr. de Speyer, but it was thought that a man with his record and one who had avowed the desire and intention to slaughter so many innocent people, would not meet with success in that quarter. He seems to have prevailed however.

The Koreans most interested in Korean Independence express themselves as feeling that the end has come. They will have to give up their "Independence Club" as a memorial has been presented against it, as well as praying for the suppression of the "Independent", the news-paper above mentioned. One edition of this is published tri-weekly in Korean and one in English, and the good it has done, and is doing, in enlightening the people is incalculable, and has been so expressed in published reports of the British Consul General to his Government, while foreigners generally express themselves in the same manner. Formerly this news-paper was much encouraged by the Russians, but of late I believe they have not considered it favorably. It early antagonized the French in some manner, - I am not quite certain just how.

I expect that we shall have to deal with quite an anti-American sentiment here for some time, though the King and many of his officials are our firm and warm friends.

Confidential.

I am today informed in strict confidence from the King, that he unwittingly consented to a private treaty or agreement with Russia ast spring, made through his Ambassador to the Coronation of the Czar. The paper, which was drawn up by Mr. Waeber, the Russian Representative here, binds Russia and Korea to the following: - Russia will drill, officer and control the Korean troops: Russia will control and regulate the Korean finances and the Customs; and Russia will protect the King and the Palace.

I knew something of this at the time as well as what is further told me now, that when in dire straits and virtual imprisonment under the Japanese-Korean Cabinet in the autumn of 1895, the King sent a telegram to the Czar through Mr. Waeber, asking for his protection, and that his escape to the Russian

Legation and subsequent events including the above mentioned agreement were the result of this cry of distress, the import of which he did not fully comprehend at the time.

This accounts for a remark of Mr. Waeber's to me that, "I do not care for the military contracts as we already have an ample agreement without that".

It accounts for Mr. de Speyer's remark to me quoted in my No. 9, of yesterday "that the King had asked for Russian advice and he intended to advise him", as well as for his statement to the King, as reported in my No. 3, Sept. 17, "that he must take Russian advice upon all matters and advise only with Russia; that Russia will see that he is not troubled, and that he will have ample funds for his enjoyment".

The British are greatly worried over the arrival of a Russian official M. Alexief who is supposed to be intended for the place of Mr. Brown, the Chief Commissioner of Customs and Financial Adviser, whose excellent work for the Korean Government has been frequently mentioned in this series. He has a five years contract and his removal may cause trouble.

M. de Plancy and M. de Speyer, the French and Russian Carge's d'Affaires; seem to be working together in perfect accord. None of the other Foreign Representatives are in their confidence.

Horace N. Allen.

No. 12   Legation of the United States
                                                          Seoul Korea, October 5, 1897.

Secretary of State

Sir:-
In continuation of my No. 10, October 2, I now have the honor to inform you that later and more complete reports confirm the statement that the recent change in the Korean Cabinet was due to the peremptory suggestion of the new Russian Minister. It is now learned that he made no objection to the appointment of three old gentlemen who are the personal friends of the King, but men of little strength, - the Ministers of Finance, Education and Agriculture, but that he insisted upon the appointment of the men of his own selection for the posts of Ministers of the Household, Treasury and Justice. The last named is said to have been the choice of the French Representative. I get this information from some of the Ex-Ministers and it is confirmed by conversation with my colleagues.

I have also to report the arrival in Seoul of M. Kir Alexeieff, Conseiler d'Etat. Agent du Ministére Imperial des Finances de la Russie, Seoul Corée'. This gentleman is attended by secretaries, and is to occupy one of several handsome brick houses that have been mysteriously built this summer, on land adjoining the Russian Legation, and which Mr. Waeber informed me privately, were being built for the King. They were probably a part of the general scheme that Mr. Waeber had been mapping out.

This Mr. Alexeieff, it is expected, will take the position now held by the Englishman, Mr. Brown, as Chief Commissioner of Customs, Adviser and virtual Comptroller of the Treasury. The great improvement in Seoul is due to Mr. Brown as well as the excellent condition of the Korean treasury at present. In conserving the revenues he has made many enemies among Korean Officials who were prevented from getting control of the funds of the Treasury, and he has stood in the way of certain Russian proposals, thus angering some Russian subjects toward their Minister, Mr. Waeber, to whom Mr. Brown owed this power over the Treasury. The latter has a five years' contract and some time ago his Representative told me that the British Government was much interested in Brown and his work and would in any event support him. This may have been premature for in conversation today, Mr. Brown told me that he would give up if things went on as at present. He said that he had felt for some time that his present work, in showing that Korea could be self-sustaining and able to stand alone, was really an injury to the country at large, since it simply served to bolster up the present "corrupt" Government from which the country could expect no good whatever. That if a strong power would come in, able and willing to enforce order throughout the land and put down squeezing and other corruption, the lot of the people would be vastly improved and the country would undoubtedly prosper. He said that, looking far ahead he felt sure that Korea must in time go over to Russia, since Japan, the only one interested in preventing this, was impotent in the matter, therefore he felt no inclination to place obstacles in Russia's path now.

It is repeatedly said that had Mr. Brown remained in the British Consular service, instead of leaving it for the Chinese Customs, years ago, he would now be British Minister in Peking. He is regarded by Englishmen in the East as one of their best and strongest men, therefore I have reported his remarks on this subject.

The German Consul, who has been for ten years the Representative of his country in Korea, said to me that he was asonished that Mr. de Speyer should reverse the policy of Mr. Waeber and at once affront Americans by persecuting Korean Officials for being friendly to the United States; that Mr. Waeber had appreciated the friendship of Americans and had made the most of it: that the progressive party and the sometimes so-called American party were the same, and that but for them there would now be no schools in Korea, there would be no such developments as the Mines and Railroad, and that this change in policy seemed to indicate that Koreas new masters cared not for the development of the country.

Korea must evidently have some stronger nation as her over-lord. China was not equal to her great opportunities, Japan failed, England evidently does not care to assume the responsibility, and it seems to fall naturally upon Russia. With a strong Government, the general condition of the country must improve, as mentioned in the remarks reported above. Our interests can hardly be interfered with. Our Government does not want its citizens to meddle in politics here, and I shall see that its instructions are carried out to the best of my ability. Our financial enterprises as represented by the Mines and Railroad should not be obnoxious to Russia, as they were obtained with the knowledge, and in the case of the Railroad, the consent of the Russian Minister, and from Mr. de Speyers talks with me, I infer that he is interested in seeing the Railroad completed.

Aside from kerosene, our trade does not interfere with that of Russia.

It is supposed by many, including some Russians, that much of Mr. de Speyers course is actuated by his opposition to his predecessor, and a desire to reverse the policy of Mr. Waeber.

Horace N. Allen.

No. 17   Legation of the United States
                                                                         Seoul Korea, Octobed 9, 1897.

Secretary of State

Sir:-

Referring to my No. 12, Oct. 5, announcing the arrival of Mr. Alexeieff to take charge of Korean finances, I have the honor now to inform you that on the 6'th. instant Mr. de Speyer informed the Foreign Office of the arrival of this gentleman and the circumstances connected with his coming, and desired immediate information as to when he should assume his duties. I am able to send you enclosed a translation of this letter from Mr. de Speyer to the Foreign Office, and you will notice that in it this Mr. Alexeieff is mentioned as "Resident", which, I am informed is the same Chinese character as is used in designating the British Resident in India. You will also see that the letter contains an allusion to the secret arrangement made between the Korean Ambassador to the Coronation, and the Russian Government, referred to at length in my No. 10, Oct. 2,. In talking with Mr. Ye Wan Yong, late Minister for Foreign Affairs, about this agreement, he said that while his name was apparently attached to the document, he had not signed it and did not know of its existence till recently. I am told the document bears no seals, which are considered so necessary in Korea for the authentication of any document.

Upon hearing of Mr. de Speyers despatch to the Foreign Office, virtually asking for the removal of Mr. Brown, the Englishman now in charge of Korean Customs and Finance, Mr. J.N. Jordan, H.B. M's. Consul General, asked for an audience with the King to protest aginst this course. An audience was promised but was later declined on the ground of illness of the King, which Mr. Jordan claims to know was a mere pretext. He has telegraphed his Gov'mt in addition to other particulars, that he has been refused an audience.

Mr. Pak Chung Yang, the newly appointed Minister of the Treasury, (one of the three old gentlemen, personal friends of the King, who were allowed to enter the new Cabinet, see my No. 12, Oct. 5) has sent in his resignation because of this request for the removal of Mr. Brown, which falls to him to do. The resignation has not yet been accepted, but this display of courage is quite surprising to all.

I am told that the King is so hedged in by the Russian party as to be unable to speak privately to his friends. A Korean friend of mine tells me that the King sent for him several times but was unable to converse with him because of the constant presence of one of three Russian Interpreters, who are said to be on duty in the Kings rooms all the time. I should add that the whole situation is practically in the hands of the Russian Chief Interpreter, owing to the absence of a knowledge of the Korean Language, of Korean affairs and persons, on the part of the new Representative and his staff. The Assistant Russian Interpreter has just been appointed Vice Minister of War.

Mr. Waeber, lately Russian Representative here, assured Mr. Brown that this Mr. Alexeieff was intended as adviser to the Household Department, and would not supplant him (Brown). Mr. de Speyer now states that the matter is not one for discussion, that at the request of the King Mr. Alexeieff was sent here to take charge of Korean Customs and Finance and there is no further use for Mr. Brown.

Mr. Jordan informs me today that he has had no reply to a second request he made for an audience, and that he thinks one will not be granted. He also tells me that Mr. Kato, the Japanese Minister here, has informed him that he has been instructed by his government to cooperate with him in attempting to prevent the removal of Mr. Brown.

Horace N. Allen.

Copy of a translation of a letter from the Russian Chargé d'Affaires - de Speyer, to Min, Korean Minister for Foreign Affairs, Dated October 5 (?) 1897.

The King of your honorable country, at the time of the coronation of the Emperor of my country, sent a Special Ambassador to Moscow and instructed that Special Ambassador to express in writing the strong wish of the King that the Government of Russia should send an official from the Finance Department to Korea, stating clearly to Our Government that that official would examine into and control all the revenues of Korea, whether customs or internal revenue.
In consequence of this request of the King, the Emperor was already graciously inclined to select from the staff of the Finance Department, a councilor of State to reside in Korea as a "Resident" and directed him to proceed to Korea for the purpose stated.
This official's name is Alexeieff, and he arrived a few days ago in Seoul.
I have therefore the honor to request Your Excellency to be so good as to inform me the official's concerned, of his arrival, and give me immediate information as to when he shall take charge of his duties.

Min sent this at once to the Treasury with a note saying "Be good enough to examine into this and give me a prompt reply for translation."

No. 22   Legation of the United States
                                              Seoul Korea, October 16, 1897.

Secretary of State

Sir:-

There are so many reports current here of the strange antagonistic attitude of the new Russian Representative toward Americans, and of his remarks regarding them and their Korean friends, that I deem it my duty to call your attention to the conversation I had with him, as reported in my No. 9, Oct. 1, and to now hand you enclosed, noted of a further talk I had with him at my house on the evening of the 14'th instant, after a dinner given in his honor.

I wish especially to call your attention to his remarks regarding Ye Wan Yong and the "Pro-American" party, - "That man: He is the worst I have known. I have put a cross on his name and he shall not hold any office in Korea while I am here. He is the head of this Pro-American party what is all the time crying 'Independence' 'Independence'. You shall see I will put that party out of Korea, it shall not exist". I will refer you to Mr. Sills No. 286, Sept. 9, for a description of this Mr. Ye, who I can assure you, is the finest type of a broad minded, high character Korean I have known in 14 years here. He was Secretary of Legation to the first Korean Minister to Washington, and became much impressed with American institutions. He has devoted himself largely to Educational work and was Minister of Education for a time. He had the high respect of all foreigners here, and was the respected friend of the former Russian Representative, Mr. Waeber, but when he displayed such unexpected strength in refusing to sign the Russian military contracts, Mr. Waeber had him removed from the position of Minister for Foreign Affairs. He was in that position however when the American Railway Concession was signed and had much to do with it, as had Mr. Waeber as well. I am told that Mr. de Speyer is very bitter against his predecessor and this Mr. Ye, for having allowed this concession to go to Americans.

I also call your attention to Mr. de Speyers remarks regarding Mr. Waeber, - "Ah, Mr. Waeber, but I do not approve of Mr. Waeber. I like not many things he has done. You will find me a true Russian.

Mr Waeber is not a true Russian". Mr Waeber is an old, experienced and highly respected official of gentle but firm bearing; his success as a diplomatist can be seen by what he obtained for Russia from Korea.

As to what Mr. de Speyer says of American Missionaries opposing the military contracts, I feel perfectly sure that they had not the slightest thing to do with it one way or another. We have several Americans in the employ of the Government as Advisers and I know that one of them - C.R. Greathouse, very strongly favored the matter and urged the Foreign Minister (his chief) to sign the contracts, while another adviser Philip Jaisohn, - a Korean naturalized in America - took the opposite side. They were each entitled by their positions to give advice. I myself was personally asked by the King for an expression of opinion on the subject, but I strictly declined to express any opinion, see Mr. Sill's No. 270, May 10.

While Mr. de Speyer seems to take himself very seriously, and speaks his mind very freely, and in a manner not altogether agreeable at times, I do not think that he will attempt to interfere with the legitimate pursuits of Americans here, or that he will interfere with vested American rights in Korea, beyond his present avowed intention to destroy American influence. In this I do not think he can be entirely successful, owing to the deep regard entertained by the King and the better officials for America as the true and disinterested friend of Korea. But he can certainly make it unpleasant for us, especially by the appointment to office of men whom he can trust to annoy us as much as possible, - a course that will be comparatively easy now that we have such large interests as the Mines and the Railway.

I enclose a copy of the circular referred to in both of the conversations above mentioned, and which Mr. de Speyer stated to me he had been the means of having issued, through our Minister to Japan, Mr. Dun.

Horace N. Allen

No. 27   Legation of the United States
                                                         Seoul Korea, October 25, 1897.

Secretary of State

Sir:-

I have the honor to inform you that there seems to be a lull in the political agitation here just now. On or about the 21'st. instant, Mr. de Speyer, the Russian Charge d'Affaires, again sent a note to the Foreign Office, said to have been couched in very strong terms, regarding Mr. Brown, the Englishman in charge of Korean Finances. See my Number 19, Oct. 14. That same night the Korean Interpreter of the Russian Legation is said to have used very strong and abusive, as well as threatening language, to His Majesty, so that the latter gave way entirely and ordered the Foreign Office to dismiss Brown. The Foreign Minister while he is supposed to be willing enough to serve Russia, seemed not to care to take the responsibility of doing this unless His Majesty would recall his decree placing Brown in this position of virtual Comptroller of the Treasury. His Majesty would not allow the mention of his name in the matter, it is said, so the Foreign Minister sent another note to the Minister of the Treasury, asking him to dismiss Brown. This he declined to do in the face of the Royal Decree above mentioned, as well as the formal contract in Brown's favor, and there the matter rests. Mr. Jordan, H.B.M's. Consul General, tells me he is authorized to sustain Brown, and if the latter will stand firm, nothing but force will succeed in expelling him.

I am confidentially informed by a member of the Russian Legation that on or about the 22'nd. instant, Mr. de Speyer received a very severe telegraphic reprimand from his Government, which may account for the present lull.

At one time, see my No. 20, Oct. 14, it seemed that we were on the eve of an insurrection of the Korean troops against their Russian instructors. This has also quieted down, due largely, I am told, to advice given by the Japanese Legation here. Koreans inform me privately, that the Japanese Legation has advised the "hot-heads" to do nothing at present, but wait a little and Japan will assist them. Whether this means that she will assist them by the use of diplomacy at Petersburg or by force here, does not seem clear.

I do know that while Mr. Kato, Japanese Minister Resident here, knows all about the secret convention between Korea and Russia, as well as the violent control taken of Korean affairs here by Mr. de Speyer, no hint of these things appears in the Japanese papers, whose correspondents here are always first to report such matters. On the contrary, articles appear in these papers seeming to give the impression that the recent Cabinet changes here were due to an "Anti-Russian" sentiment, as will be seen by the News-paper clipping I enclose. Later papers are no clearer on the subject.

It would seem from this that the Government of Japan does not care at present to brave the violent public outburst that the full knowledge of the facts would doubtless cause among the excitable people of Japan. I am told however, by the representative of a business firm in Japan, that the Japanese Cabinet had a three days council with the Naval and Military authorities over Korea, on about the 5'th. October.

Any decisive action that Japan may be contemplating will doubtless be delayed, pending the arrival of the two magnificent Battle-ships now en-route to Japan from England, and expected within a few days. I send a clipping descriptive of these ships, as well as one descriptive of their management.

At present it would seem that Russia is unprepared for a conflict in Asiatic waters, as she is supposed to have but 20,000 soldiers at Vladivostock, which port will soon be closed by ice, while her coaling stations in these waters are still a matter of the future.

The proposed coaling station at Fusan, see my No. 8, Oct. 1, and my No. 16, Oct. 8, is a direct menace to Japan and is looked upon by the Japanese Legation here as such in the fullest degree. I enclose a news-paper article on the subject, written in very mild terms.

I have not thought it best to make further protest in regard to the use of the Foreign Settlement site at Fusan for this purpose - a coaling station, lest I be regarded as throwing my influence on the side of Japan, in what seems to be, a coming struggle. I could not do much anyway, and I know the desire of the Department that I should keep clear of any such entangling alliances.

Were it not for the case of Mr. Brown, England would probably not take such a pronounced stand against Russia in Korea as she is now forced to take, and for Russian purposes in Korea, the forcing of this issue in such a violent manner at present, has been decidedly inopportune and unstatesmanlike. The former Russian Minster would doubtless have followed out his avowed intention of placing the Russian Financial Agent in charge of the Household Department, which is now the most important of the Korean Departments, and to which all the revenues could have been gradually diverted, until Mr. Brown would have been compelled to resign out of self-respect, as his power and influence would all have disappeared. As it is, public sentiment, regardless of nationality, is all with Brown. I enclose a clipping illustrating this.

The British Representative here, says that while he cannot believe that his Government would openly join Japan against Russia at this juncture, he is quite sure that if Japan were to strike a blow now while England is irritated she would receive at least the passive support of the latter.

I am repeatedly asked for advice by the Koreans at present, but I have abstained and shall carefully abstain from giving advice, or from mixing up in these matter, and shall confine myself strictly to the protection and furthering of our own considerable interests.

Horace N. Allen.

No. 29   Legation of the United States
                                                 Seoul Korea, November 7, 1897.

Secretary of State

Sir:-

Referring to my No. 27, Oct. 25, regarding the matter of the dismissal of Mr. Brown from his position as Adviser to the Financial Department and Chief Commissioner of Customs, I now have the honor to inform you that the matter is closed in favor of Russia, and to give you the details of the conclusion, which I am sure you will find to be of interest.

On Oct. 26, Mr. Jordan, H.B.M's. Consul General here, received a despatch from the Korean Foreign Minister announcing the appointment of Mr. Alexeieff in the place of Mr. Brown, and stating that "in regard to the dismissal of the present Adviser to the Finance Department and Chief Commissioner of Customs, I will be glad to see you and discuss the terms". Mr. Jordan promptly returned this despatch with the statement that he had nothing to discuss with him in the matter.

The Foreign Minister then telegraphed to Sir Claude Mc'Donald, H.B.M's. Minister at Peking, who has credentials for Korea as well, stating that he had addressed Mr. Jordan upon the matter of the dismissal of Mr. Brown, but that Mr. Jordan had returned the despatch without explanation, The next day he received a reply from Sir Claude to the effect that Mr. Jordan was acting with his entire approval and that the dismissal of Mr. Brown was altogether unwarrantable. See enclosures.

In my No. 27, Oct. 25, I pointed out that while the Minister for Foreign Affairs owed his appointment to the influence of the Russian Legation, he was not as energetic as they seemed to desire him to be, and Pak Chung Yang, the Minister of the Treasury, was showing very unexpected strength in flatly refusing to dismiss Brown while his contract and the Royal Decree placing him in charge of the finances were still in force. There seemed to be a lull in the agitation and on Nov. 3, Mr. Jordan informed me that the British Chargé d'Affaires at St. Petersburg, Mr. Goshen, had had an interview with the Russian Foreign Office official in charge of Asiatic matters on the subject of the removal of Mr. Brown, in which this official had stated that Mr. de Speyer was acting entirely upon his own initiative: that the Korean Government had asked the Russian Government for financial experts, and one such had been sent, "but we have absolutely given no instructions to our agent in Korea regarding the removal of Mr. Brown." Mr. Goshen then suggested the sending of a telegram to Mr. de Speyer asking him to delay further action pending the receipt of instructions, and the official agreed to consult the Minister for Foreign Affairs on the subject.

On this same day, Nov. 3, every one here was much surprised by the removal of Min Chong Mook, who had been apointed Minister for Foreign Affairs at the instigation of Mr. Waeber, late Russian Representative here, in place of Ye Wan Yong who had refused to sign the Russian Military Contracts. (See Mr. Sill's No. 286, Sept. 9.) Min was known to be altogether pro-Russian, but he is a timid man and disinclined to assume responsibility; he was replaced by Chyo Pyung Sik, who is also Minster of Justice and President of the Council of State. I wrote of him fully in my Number 10, Oct. 2, Page 2.

The general impression was that as matters were progressing slowly a more vigorous minister was desired who would assume all responsibility and not call upon his colleague of the Treasury to do what might as well be done at the Foreign Office. Results seem to have borne out this inference, for on the 4'th. it was known that the contract for the Russian Financial Agent was prepared, and on the 5'th. Nov. it was signed by the Russian Chargé d'Affaires and the Korean Minister for Foreign Affairs, Chyo, it being rather a treaty or agreement between the two Governments than a private contract. I am able to hand you a most careful and exact translation of this document, and you will see that it places Russia in entire control of Korean finances: no new financial scheme such as the raising of a loan or even the paying of a debt, can be attended to without Russian consent: nor foreigner of another nationality can hold the position thus given to a Russian, and no time limit is given to the agreement which is to be perpetual. In order to make this arrangement effectual, Russian agents will have to be stationed all through the interior for the proper collection of the revenues, and with the Korean army in Russian hands as it now is, these agents will be furnished with a very efficient police force. The condition of the people cannot be worse than it is now, and they will doubtless welcome such a system of control.

The King professes to be in utter dismay over the situation, but he receives little sympathy, as it is due entirely to his weakness and desire for his personal safety that the present state of affairs was brought about.

I enclose a clipping from the Seoul Independent of Oct. 30, giving a resume of the proceedings connected with the dismissal of Mr. Brown, as well as an item as to the intentions of Mr. de Speyer toward the Missionaries. It is not unlikely that he may attempt to interfere with our missionaries, but he will be hampered by the fact that the French Catholics, whom he will hardly care to molest, enjoy so many more privileges than do our people, that in claiming equal rights for Americans our people will have all they can desire.

I also enclose a clipping from the same paper showing something of the remarkable work Mr. Brown has been able to do in conserving the revenues of this country, which, until he took charge of the Treasury a year and a half ago, was without funds, without credit, and the foreign merchants would not take the smallest Government order without being paid in advance. During this time Mr. Brown has enabled Korea to pay off 2,000,000 yen of the debt to Japan of 3,000,000 yen: he has paid such sums as 100,000 for a cemetery, 100,000 for the Imperial Coronation: he has made beautiful broad, clean, avenues of the dirty lanes of Seoul: he has made possible the most unprecedented building of palaces, temples, etc., and he has a reserve fund of 1,200,000 yen, to hand over to his successor.

Mr. Brown tells me that his relations with Mr. Alexeieff are quite amicable and that the latter has requested him to remain, but that he cannot do so.

In conclusion I wish briefly to sum up the situation and enumerate the steps by which Korea has found her way to a virtual Russian Protectorate.

Ten years ago, while in the service of the Korean Government, I had occasion to make a public statement to the effect that Korean independence was practically assured for the time by her geographical position; that China then claimed suzerain rights, but that she could not absorb the country without a conflict with Japan which she did not seem to court; that Japan cast longing eyes upon the peninsula but that she could not hope to take it without a struggle with China, which, as the latter was backed in her claims on Korea by England, she would hardly dare precipitate; that Korea must eventually fall more or less under the influence of Russia with the completion of the Siberian Railroad, since Vladivoskock - the

Eastern terminus of that road - is effectually blocked by ice in winter, and a port to the south on the Korean coast would be an absolute necessity.

This statement was much resented at the time by the then Russian Representative - Mr. Waeber, who assured me that with new and improved ice-breaking machinery, Vladivostock would be kept open. He voluntarily admitted to me last summer that this was impossible bacause the weather is so severe that even with a more or less open way, the ships could not with safety brave the storms of sleet and the dangerous navigation in winter necessary to reach that port.

In 1893 the then Russian Representative here, said to me that the Siberian Railroad would be completed in six years, and later on in a burst of confidence, he said that Russia wanted nothing in Korea at present, "but after six years, then you will see".

The Japan-China war undoubtedly precipitated matters, and compelled Russian action before the contemplated time. China, not receiving the assistance from England she had been led to expect, fell as easy prey to Japan, and in 1894 the latter at last gained control over Korea. She very wisely sought only to assure the independence of Korea with Japanese influence paramount, but Japanese blundered most astonishingly in arranging and carrying out the details and instead of improving their opportunities here they lost their influence entirely upon the murder of the Queen, which made Korea ripe for falling into the hands of Russia.

While a prisoner in the hands of the Pro-Japanese Cabinet, formed after the removal of the Queen, the King, through the Russian interpreter, was induced to ask the protection of the Czar, which request was more formally stated by the Korean Ambassador to the Coronation, and resulted in the private agreement between the two powers, granting Russia control over Korean financial and military matters in return for the protection of the King and the palace.

All this was done in a most gentle and persuasive manner by the recent Russian Representative here, Mr. Waeber, and had he remained, the execution of these well laid plans would doubtless have gone on in the same quiet and unalarming way. The recent sudden and peremptory changes do not seem to be in the usual style of Russian diplomacy.

I do not think that Russia desires to make Korea an integral part of the Czar's dominion. It would be too much trouble and expense to protect it, while Korea independent will serve as a useful buffer between the real Russian domain and the rising and warlike Empire of Japan.

It was the carefully pursued policy of the late Russian Representative, Mr. Waeber, to abstain from all appearance of meddling in Korean affairs, often going to the extreme of allowing certain abuses to continue rather than speak, when a word of rebuke from him would have had much, if not a conclusive effect. In this way he was able to control Korean affairs so far as he desired without seeming to work against, or weaken, the pet idea of independence, so dear to the better Koreans. His successor has taken a directly opposite course, and his first two months service here have been very stormy, but successful in a way.

Horace N. Allen.

No. 39   Legation of the United States
                                                                   Seoul Korea, November 27, 1897.

Secretary of State

Sir:-

I have the honor to inform you that on the 21'st. and 22'nd. instants, the long talked of funeral took place of the late Queen of Korea who was murdered on October 8'th. 1895. It was rather a funeral in her honor than of her remains, as I understand that only one of the small bones of the finger was rescued from the fire in which her murderers attempted to hide their guilt. Having been given the post-humous title of Empress, she was buried with Imperial ceremonies.

As the Korean Government had sent a Special Envoy to be present at the funeral of the Dowager Empress of Japan last year, the Japanese Government appointed their Minister to Korea to represent them officially at this funeral as Special Envoy.

It was decided at a meeting of the Foreign Representatives, that we should accept the invitation of the Household Department and be present with His Majesty through these funeral ceremonies.

We began by repairing to the Palace before dawn on the 21'st. where after a long and tedious wait in the cold, we saw the bier leave the Palace and then paid our respects to His Majesty. The procession then slowly found its way to the Cemetery, six miles east of the City. It showed lavish display of money, but to Foreigners the features would seem chiefly to be grotesqueness and lack of order. I enclose an extract from the Seoul "Independent" of the 25'th instant, descriptive of the event.

At 2 P.M. of the same day we went to the Foreign Office to join the procession of His Majesty to the grave, but the latter feeling chagrinned at the long delay he had caused us in the morning, started off an hour earlier so as to be on time. Not knowing of this change we were spared the necessity of making a part of the procession.

Arriving at the cemetery we were quartered in neat little 8x8 foot paper rooms, each containing a narrow cot and each room having to do duty for four persons. We were served with dinner, at which occasion, owing to the lack of order and arrangement, the Japanese Envoy was placed in such an undignified position that he had to complain of it.

At 3 A.M. on the 22'nd. we attended the King and bade adieu to the bier. At 7 A.M. the internment took place, and at 10 A.M. we had a formal audience with His Majesty, after which I made my excuses and returned home as I was quite ill from exposure and was confined to my bed for several days. The other Representatives waited and returned to the City in the evening (22'nd) with His Majesty.

His Majesty had implored me to get up a guard to accompany him, as was done by my predecessor in 1890, at the time of the funeral of the Dowager Queen. When I had kindly, but firmly shown him that this was impossible, he urged me to at least get up a guard for the Legation, which I also politely declined to do on the ground that there was no adequate cause for so doing. My reasons were briefly that an American guard could only be summoned for the protection of American lives and property; that it could not be used off American property, nor could it be brought here when there was no sign of any danger to American lives or property.

At his most urgent request, I extended an invitation to such of the officers of our ship at Chemulpo as should care to see the ceremonies, to come and be my guests, and Captain Wildes of the "Boston" sent six officers who accompanied me through all the ceremonies, in full uniform. Many American citizens were also present, a house having been prepared for the entertainment of non-official guests, and Americans had been especially invited by the Household Department.

One notable feature of the occasion was that four Russian non-commissioned officers constantly remained by His Majesty's chair and no one was allowed to approach without permission.

The obsequiousness of the officials in charge toward the Russian and French Representatives was very conspicuous. Much of what may have seemed to be neglect of others however, may be charged to the general lack of order and system on the part of the natives, and to the keen desire of time serving officials to make themselves secure with the party in power. A short time ago, we saw the matter reversed, and the Russian Representative was neglected by these same officials, who then devoted themselves to the Japanese Minister quite as enthusiasticaly as they waited upon the Russian Chargé d'Affaires at this funeral.

Horace N. Allen.

No. 41   Legation of the United States
                                                         Seoul Korea, December 1, 1897.

Secretary of State

Sir:-

Referring to my various despatches regarding Russian aggression in Korea, ending with my No. 36, Nov. 19, I now have the honor to inform you that Mr. de Speyer, the Russian Chargé d'Affaires here, whose peculiarly vigorous measures have caused such general surprise, has been appointed Russian Minister to China. The Appointment of his successor has not yet been announced. He expects to remain here some months still.

In discussing this apointment with me yesterday, Mr. de Speyer showed evident pleasure at the marked promotion, though it is generally believed to be in line with the rebuke he received from his Government, mentioned in my No. 27, Oct 25, Page 2, as well as with the statement of the Russian Foreign Office, that he was acting upon his own initiative. See my No. 29, Nov. 7, Page 2. While the appointment is a distinct promotion, it seems to indicate a modification of Russian policy in Korea.

In this connection I may add that Mr. de Speyer has given up expressing himself violently against Americans and their Korean friends, as was noted in my No's. 9, Oct. 1, and 22, Oct. 16, and has of late shown a very friendly and conciliatory spirit.

Horace N. Allen

No. 48   Legation of the United States
                                                    Seoul Korea, December 20, 1897.

Secretary of State

Sir:-

I have the honor to report to you upon several matters, chiefly relating to Russian movements in Korea; none of which seem to merit a special despatch.

The long expected Russian fleet put in to Chemulpo some days ago, and the Admiral made a short visit to Seoul, where he had an audience with His Majesty. Koreans inform me that the usual formalities were not observed in obtaining this audience, but that the Admiral entered the Palace unannounced. They also assure me that the Admiral made a peremptory demand for the coaling station at Fusan, mentioned in my No's 8, Oct.1: 16, Oct. 8: 27, Oct. 25 - Page 3. When His Majesty said that he would confer with his Foreign Minister on the subject, the Admiral is said to have declared that to be unnecessary, as he (H.M) was the ruler and the one through whom he would treat. Thereupon His Majesty is reported to have given his assent. I asked the Minister for Foreign Affairs, a few days ago, if it were true that this coaling station had been given to Russia. He said it was true, but that the formalities had not yet been gone through.

There has been much comment here of late over the report that the Russian Government was acquiring a very large portion of the ground allotted to the General Foreign Settlement at Chenampo. I was fortunate enough to see the plan of this land, made for Mr. de Speyer by a Russian officer, and saw for myself, that while they have acquired a tract of land just outside the Settlement limits but within the treaty area, larger than the Settlement itself, their purchase within the Settlement limits is not greatly in excess of that of the Japanese, though both are larger than the Municipal Council will probably care to allow.

The firm of Townsend & Co. who do a large rice mill buisness at Chemulpo, had acquired a piece of ground for a rice mill, just about in the middle of this tract now purchased by the Russian Government, and Mr. de Speyer was very anxious to secure this land from this American firm. It was in this connection that he showed me the above mentioned plan. I represented the matter to Mr. Townsend, who as a business man did not care to antagonize the Russians, and sent me his deeds to hand over to Mr. Speyer for the cost of the land, or in exchange for another site; the last named offer will probably be accepted as it is more satisfactory to both parties. This incident seems to have given much satisfaction to the Russian Legation.

Rumors have been current here of late that Russia was about to loan Korea a sum of money variously estimated at from three to ten million yen. I cannot get confirmation of this, but I am sure a loan will be made. An agent of the Russo-Chinese bank is now here in this connection.

A loan was promised Korea by Russia about a year ago, See my No. 243, Nov. 4, 1896, but it was given up for some reason.

Korea will soon be in urgent need of funds. Since Mr. Brown was removed from the Treasury, the native officials have been able to get at the reserve, which I hear, has entirely disappeared. A short crop of rice this year will give them less revenue than they had last year.

The Russians censure Mr. Brown for paying the second million yen on the debt to Japan, which money they claim, was needed in Korea and Japan did not wish to have it repaid, while the only good it could do was in showing what Mr. Brown could do with Korean finances. Mr. Brown himself said to me that he thought it was a mistake, and that, had he known how things were to go, he would not have made the second payment of a million yen.

Mr. Brown, though out of the Treasury, which is now in the hands of Mr. Alexeieff, still holds his place in charge of Maritime Customs, and England seems to be about to make a demonstration in his favor. British ships have been seen about Port Hamilton so frequently of late, that I took occasion to ask Mr. Jordan, H.B.M's. Consul General here, if his Government were intending to retake the place. Rather to my surprise he was unable to give me a definite reply, but thought he would be able to do so in a few days. I believe they will at least occupy the port.

Port Hamilton is a group of islands off the southern coast of Korea in about Latitude 34 by Longitude 127-3. It was offered to us through Admiral Shufeldt - so I was told by the latter. England occupied it in 1885 to prevent its occupation by Russia. She gave it up soon after, at the solicitation of China, and upon the latters promise not to let it pass into the hands of any other power. Russia agreed at the same time that she would not occupy Korean harbors or territory. It is this agreement on the part of Russia to which Mr. Curzon refers in his remarks made in Parliment, see my No. 31/3. Nov. 10.

The French Representative seems to be almost as influential here as is the Russian. They seem to work together very harmoniously. It has been stated by Mr. de Speyer, that a Frenchman will be placed in charge of Korean Customs, and a French Industrial School is about to be established here. The French are making a persistent effort to have their language supersede English in Korea and they are succeeding with the help of the Russians, who use French mostly. There are several teachers of French now in Seoul, and Mr. de Plancy, the French Chargé d'Affaires, has declined to sign documents in English, having a French translation made, to which he attaches his signature.

Germany seems to be more in favor here in Korea, since her occupation of Kaiu Chow Bay, which for some reason seems to please the Koreans, at least certain Cabinet Ministers have so expressed themselves to the German Consul.

The lot of the Japanese in Korea is not very pleasant to them at present. The Koreans seem inclined to make the most of the weakness of their old enemy. Mr. Kato, the Japanese Minister, told me the other day that the Korean Government had declined to allow the Japanese to fill in the fore-shore in front of their settlement at Chemulpo. This was agreed to by the Foreign Representatives, see my No. 37, Nov. 27. It is a work that is manifestly for the good of the port, and the Korean Government had assented long before. They now withdraw their consent as the work was not put through when it was formerly agreed upon.

His Majesty fears a conflict between Russia and Japan, in which he will be in worse condition than he was in the Japan-China war. He bases his fears on confidential reports from his Minister in Tokio.

I am refraining from mixing in any of these matters, and as Americans we are strictly attending to our own concerns.

Horace N. Allen

No. 51

Legation of the United States
Seoul Korea, December 27, 1897.

Secretary of State:

Sir:-

I have the honor to hand you, appended to this despatch, confirmation of my telegram of yesterday, and to offer you the following explanation of the circumstances that led to my sending it.

Of course there is much excitement here over the taking of Port Arthur by the Russians, and the reported occupation of Chusan and Port Hamilton by the English. The Koreans and some foreigners think that Japan may strike a blow for the recovery of Korea, now that Russia is engaged, especially so in case England and Russia should come into open conflict - an event that has been made to seem probable by the action of the fleets of these two countries and the statements of the Russian Representative here.

On the night of the 24'th. instant, His Majesty sent his most trusted Eunuch to me with the information that Russia was about to send soldiers here for his protection, and asked me what he should do. Mindful of the secret convention by which Russia had agreed to protect the King and the Palace, (see my Number 10, Oct. 2, Page 4), and knowing that the Russian fleet was pretty well engaged elsewhere, this did not seem strange to me, and I had to reply that under the circumstances I had no advice to offer. He then went on to say that the Japanese were intending to send soldiers as well, and that in such case, His Majesty's life would be in danger. I replied that I thought not, but he went on to say that they understood that England and Japan had united, and if the former should keep Russia engaged, the latter could work her will in Korea, and he plainly suggested assylum at this Legation for His Majesty. I very promtly replied that that would be the worst thing for him; I could not invite him here; I could not protect him if he came, and even if he should succeed in getting inside our gates, I would be unable to keep him long, and his condition after such an attempt would be worse than before; he had asked for Russian protection and it was for their interests to see that he got it, and while we entertain the kindliest feeling toward His Majesty we would deeply regret being in any way instrumental in making his condition any worse than it now is.

He then asked me to convey to Mr. Kato, the Japanese Minister, some very flattering messages from His Majesty as a sort of peace offering. Without giving offense, I was able to show him that I could not well carry such messages, as if known, such action would surely give offense to Russia; that I must remain strictly neutral and, as a friend to all parties, I might later on, with the consent of my Government, assist in bringing all to an understanding. This seemed to him very satisfactory. I agreed to say incidentally to the Japanese Minister, if occasion offered, that I understood His Majesty entertained a very high opinion of him personally. I shall probably not even do this now.

The wisdom of abstaining from any interference in these matters was shown me on the 26'th. when the same messenger came to inform me that His Majesty was now in secret conference with Mr. Kato, through a trusted Korean, and was about to conclude a secret agreement with Japan for protection. I asked him if it were true that Mr. de Speyer had induced His Majesty to ask for Russian Military protection, and he admitted that he had yielded to the urgent recommendation of Speyer that such protection should be asked, and that about 3000 soldiers would probably come here from Vladivostock.

This duplicity may very likely bring on a conflict, and I thought best to telegraph you at once. I appreciate the confidence of His Majesty, which enables me to get early information of these matters, and I therefore mentioned the fact that the information was confidential.

My own course is, and shall be, strictly neutral and confined to the protection of our own interests, which is now a somewhat difficult matter, as, owing to Russian suggestion, the Korean Foreign Office is attempting to summarily dismiss certain of the American employes of this Government, who have contracts still in force.

I think I will succeed in bringing these matters to a satisfactory settlement without the necessity of referring them to the Department, and will make the matter the subject of a special despach later on.

Horace N. Allen.

No. 69   Legation of the United States
                                   Seoul Korea, January 30, 1898.

Secretary of State

Sir:-

Referring to my No. 67, Jan. 21, in which I allude to the evident desire of Russia not to irritate Japan unduly, at present, and the fear of the Russian Representative that Japan might demand a concession for the long talked of railroad from Seoul to Fusan, in consequence of which fear, he had induced the issuance of a decree to the effect that hereafter no concessions for mines or railroads would be granted to foreigners by the Korean Government: I now have the honor to inform you that I learn on good authority that on yesterday, the Japanese Minister formally requested, or demanded, the above named concession, and, as the evident support given to Japan by England as shown by the apparent cooperation of the two fleets, as well as the hourly expected arrival of the Japanese fleet at Chemulpo, has so influenced this Government in favor of Japan, that this concession will probably be granted in spite of the decrees to the contrary, unless Russia can frighten the Koreans into refusing the same.

Horace N. Allen.

No. 86   Legation of the United States
                                   Seoul, Korea, March 14, 1898.

Secretary of State

Sir,

Referring to my No. 76, February 24, I have the honour to inform you that the settlement of the matter of the attempt on the life of the Interpreter of the Russian Legation is causing much commotion here.

In the above cited despatch, I referred to the arrest of Prince Ye Chai Soon; this arrest was resented by the Imperial family as it was done by the Chief of Police without the Imperial order which must precede the arrest of a prince. The well known hostility of the Russian Interpreter for Prince Ye Chai Soon, and the contempt in which this Interpreter is held by the official class, made the matter worse. The Interpreter is a very common and uneducated man, unable to read or write the official Chinese character used in Korea, but, having born near the border, he speaks Russian. His corrupt dealings in money matters are much complained of by Koreans. Both Mr. Waeber and Mr. de Speyer have said to me that they had no doubt he made more or less personal gain from his position, as that was very common in Korea, but he has always been sustained and supported in his acts by each of these gentlemen.

The attempt on this man's life was simply a clumsy resort to ancient methods by these people, who saw their Government irrevocably slipping out of their hands and despaired of any other kind of help. None of the Russians here speak Korean, so this Interpreter becomes the mouthpiece, counselor, and general informant of the Minister as to things Korean, and to him, because of the violent and threatening language he uses to His Majesty, the officials ascribe much of their ill-fortune.

The Chief of Police was dismissed for making this illegal arrest, and Mr. de Speyer began at once to press the Emperor to appoint this ex-official as Minister of Justice, - the man at the time had taken refuge in the Russian Legation.

This excited and alarmed the better classes, and the "Independence party" became more conspicuous. I sent you a copy of a memorial of this Independence Club in my No. 76, February 24, Enclosure 1; I now have the honour to hand you enclosed an extract from the "Independent" of the10th. instant, being another memorial sent from another quarter. It is entirely confined to denunciation of this Interpreter Kim.

Each Korean Nobleman of a certain class has several hundred followers at his country place, and such large bands of these countrymen are now coming to the city that it is thought the nobility is about to stand for its rights with all the force it can muster. The Russians are finding the Koreans very difficult to handle, as did the Japanese. Kindness will accomplish much more with them than harshness, but above all strong measures must be backed by ample force. At present the Russians have only 100 marines hers, against the Japanese 200 regular troops, with 500 police, gendarmes and citizens capable of service. An uprising, such as seems not to be improbable, would result in temporarily driving the Russians out entirely with great loss of life, and the Koreans would be foolish enough not to count the cost, and attempt some such course.

Some of the Russian advisers here blame their Representative severely for the unnecessarily harsh measure he has adopted which have brought about, very largely, the present state of affairs.

Horace N. Allen

No. 89   Legation of the United States
                                                                 Seoul, Korea, March 19, 1898.

Secretary of State

Sir,

      I have the honour to inform you that affairs between Korea and Russia have come to a crisis, and to confirm my telegram of the 17th. instant upon the subject. - Enclosure 1.

In his attempts to secure coaling stations at Fusan and the new ports, Mr. de Speyer, the Russian Representative has caused sudden and peremptory changes in the Cabinet, see my No. 87, March 14, and has so outraged the feelings of the better class of Koreans as to cause them to rise in protest, and Seoul has witnessed recently the novel sight of large mass-meetings of well behaved, orderly citizens of the better classes, addressed by native Koreans upon the subject of their independence.

This opposition has been a great surprise to those who have known Korea longest,; There is no doubt, apparently, that the concessions desired by Russia could have been obtained without difficulty, had harsh measures not been adopted from the very beginning. of the discussion of the case last September.

The attempt on the life of the Interpreter of the Russian Legation brought about very strained relations between that Legation and this Government. In the conversation he had with me at my house on February 24, (see my No. 77, Feb. 26) Mr. de Speyer said to me: "Two very pleasant things occurred to me on the same night; one, the death of the Emperor's father removed an enemy, and the other, the attempt on the life of my Interpreter, places this Independence party right in my grasp. I will push this matter to the farthest limit."

This he has done. (See my No 86, March 14th.). It seemed for a time that we were on the eve of a serious conflict here over this matter. This was the view also taken by the Japanese Minister, Mr. Kato, who informed me that he had telegraphed fully to his Government and informed them of this fears that a conflict was probable, and that Baron Nishi, Minister for Foreign Affairs, had consulted with Baron Rosen, the

Russian Minister at Tokyo, who had referred the matter fully to his Government by telegraph. Mr. Kato further informed me that a reply had been received by Baron Rosen, conveying the assurance that the Russian Government did not intend to let matters in Korea proceed so far as to involve a conflict.

About this time we were greatly surprised here by a sudden change of policy by the Russian Government in direct opposition to that pursued by the Russian Representative here. On March 7, Mr. de Speyer forwarded to the Korean Government a communication from the Emperor of Russia to the Emperor of Korea, being a direct request for a plain expression of the desires of the latter in regard to Russian assistance, and offering, if such assistance were not desired, to remove the Russian Financial Advisers and Military Officers at once. See enclosure 2, from the Seoul "Independent" of March 12,

While this letter was under consideration by the Council of State, a mass meeting of citizens was held, at which, after speeches were listened to, a memorial was drawn up praying for the acceptance of the offer of the Emperor of Russia. I enclose an extract from the Independent of March 12, giving an account of this meeting and a copy of the memorial. After due deliberation by the Council of State, a polite reply was handed to Mr. de Speyer, accepting the offer to remove the Russian officials. Encl. 4. I am informed on good authority, that Mr. de Speyer did all in his power, even using threats to secure a rejection of this offer by the Korean Government, and later to have the letter of acceptance withdrawn personally by His Majesty. Failing in this, he telegraphed the Korean reply to St. Petersburg, and on yesterday, he handed to the Korean Foreign Office the final reply of his Government, and the announcement that he had made arrangements to withdraw his people.

I enclose copy of this letter from the "Independent" of today.

In telling me of this matter, Mr. de Speyer infomed me that the military officers would be retained with his Legation guard, which has just been reinforced. It now numbers about 150 men.

Mr. de Speyer does not conceal his bitterness over this ending to his strenuous efforts here. As I informed you in my No. 67, Jan. 21, p.2, he assured me that he had not only acted all through his course without instructions, but in the face of urgent telegrams from his Government to be cautious, and avoid creating difficulties. He said he was conscious that he would be made to suffer if he failed, but that he could not fail. His failure has apparently caused him to suspect every one; he has spoken to me so bitterly of every Representative here except our French colleague, that I have had to decline to listen to his remarks. He again brought up the subject of American Advisers and American missionaries yesterday, in telling me of the above matter, and claimed that American missionaries were present at the mass-meeting above referred to and were advising the speakers as to what to say. I assured him that he was entirely mistaken as I had sent my Interpreter to report on that meeting, ad and from him as well as from others, I was positive that no American could be charged with any such thing. He then claimed that students of the American and English schools were of the speakers. This I had to admit. But I had learned that they were there without the knowledge of the American teachers, - who could not have restrained them had they known of their intentions.

He made other vague charges against Americans for expressions used in their sermons, which I declined to admit unless he would frankly state the facts in each case.

I mention this to assure you that our people have not had the slightest connection with this Anti-Russian agitation, which is due entirely to the harsh measures of Mr. de Speyer.

Mr. de Speyer complained much of certain American Advisers, and these complaints I had to admit. I claimed however, that as these men were employed by the Korean Government without any recommendation of, or connection with our own Government, it was not for me to dictate to them the kind of advice they were to give; that if the Korean Government did not approve of their acts or advice, it could give them instructions to the contrary, which I felt sure they would obey.

His chief complaint is against Dr. Jaisohn, the editor of the "Independent". Dr. Jaisohn agreed to surrender his contract on being paid what was still due him, and to leave the country. This proposition was accepted, but so many Koreans desire his presence that the money has never been paid him. I understand that some, or all of the American Advisers will be asked to surrender their contracts on the same terms.

Horace N. Allen.

No. 111   Legation of the United States
                                               Seoul Korea, June 3, 1898.

Secretary of State

Sir:-

Referring to my No. 8, Oct. 1, and my No. 16, Oct. 8, in regard to the matter of the proposed Russian Coaling Station on Deer Island in the harbor of Fusan, Korea, I now have the honor to inform you that this question has been settled by the allottment of 900,000 square metres of land on this island, including the proposed site of the Russian Coaling Station, for a General Foreign Settlement.

This action was the result of a conference held by all the Representatives except the former Russian Chargé d'Affaires, Mr. Speyer, who, though he did not attend the meeting, ratified, or sanctioned, the proposals there made, to ask for the whole low-lying end of this island for the Settlement allowed by treaty.

This arrangement seems to be a satisfactory one, as it finally defines the Settlement area at Fusan, and the limits are ample to allow of the Coaling Station and yet furnish ample room for all probable comers.

The proposition to take this whole end of the island for settlement purposes, was my own, and I secured the approval of the Russian Representative, Mr. de Speyer, to the proposition. As all ground within these limits will be subject to Municipal Regulations, it seemed to offer the best solution of a vexed question.

                                               Horace N. Allen.

PERIOD OF EQUILIBRIUM
AND DE FACTO KOREAN INDEPENDENCE

Independence Arch constructed in 1896 by the Independence Club

Reprinted from Allen D. Clark and Donald N. Clark, *Seoul: Past and Present, A Guide to Yi T'aejo's Capital* (Seoul: Royal Asiatic Society, Korea Branch, 1969), following p. 178.

No. 33

Legation of the United States
Seoul Korea, November 13, 1897.

Secretary of State

Sir:-

I have the honor to inform you that on the 11'th. instant, the Korean Independence Club gave an entertainment, at its club house in honor of the adoption of the name of Tai-Han for this country.

This entertainment was given at the request of His Majesty, hence many of the participants were of the factions that have been inclined to keep aloof from this association.

I had intended to be in Chemulpo on that date attending to some consular work, but at the earnest solicitation of the members of the club, I postponed my visit on the express stipulation that I should not be called upon for a speech at the celebration. The Japanese Minister was the only other of the Representatives present.

I hand you enclosed a clipping from todays "Independent" giving an account of the meeting.

I may add that at a recent meeting of this society, the actual members, after some most stirring speeches in favor of Liberty, voluntarily released all their slaves. The club is composed of the best element among the Korean Officials and will undoubtedly continue to do a great deal of good for the country if unmollested. The members seem all to have taken America as their model and this is not altogether relished by some of the foreign element in Seoul.

Horace N. Allen.

No. 77

Legation of the United States
Seoul, Korea, February 26, 1898.

Secretary of State

Sir:

Referring to my No. 76, February 24, handing you copy of a Memorial presented to the Throne by the Independence Club of Seoul, and directed against foreign (Russian) control of Korea, I have now the honour to inform you that on the 24th. instant I had a long visit from Mr. de Speyer, the Russian Representative, who complained that among those known to him as implicated in instigating this attack upon his Government, were three Americans, Dr. Jaisohn, General Legendre, and Colonel Nieustead.

I expressed my profound astonishment at the mention of the last two names, and explained that as Colonel Nienstead had been long confined to his house by what is pronounced to be a fatal illness, I could not see how he could be so accused. After some discussion he decided to drop the name of Colonel Nienstead, but was very strong in his accusations against the other two. As to General Legendre, I explained that being a Frenchman by birth and education, and having lived but a few years in the United States, where he was naturalized, he had affiliated more with the French and Russian Legations here than with our own, and that he owed his reappointment as adviser to the Korean Government entirely to the French and Russian Legations, where he had been a frequent visitor, while, until recently, he had only appeared at this Legation on formal occasions, and when he wished to sign his pension papers. Mr. de Speyer admitted all this, claimed that he and M. de Plancy had discovered General Legendre to be untrustworthy and had dropped him, and that he would certainly use the fact of his naturalization to apply to me for protection, to which I replied that he would most certainly obtain it and I would see justice done him, but that it seemed strange to me that his name should be mentioned in connection with the Independence Club, with which I had supposed that he was not in sympathy. (Note: Gen'l Legendre denies these charges in toto).As to the case of Dr. Jaisohn - a Korean by birth, but naturalized in America - I freely admitted that as he was Editor of the "Independent" and prominent in the Independence Club, and as he had announced in his paper (see enclosed extract in my No. 76 above-cited) - that he was in sympathy with the memorialists, I was not surprised, but I could do nothing more in his case than I had already done. The Korean Government having expressed a desire through the former Minister for Foreign Affairs, Chyo Pyeng Sik, to dispense with Dr. Jaisohn's services, I had arranged that they might do so on paying him in full for the amount of the unexpired term of his contract, no fault being found against him. That this arrangement was satisfactory to both parties, but that the money had not yet been paid. I further explained that as these gentlemen were all advisers in the Korean Government, they were free to advise, and I was not to be the judge as to the character of the advice they might see fit to give.

Our conversation was entirely friendly, and Mr. de Speyer quite agreed with me as to my position He volunteered much other information, which will appear in other despatches I am about to address to you. I wish to make it plain to the Department that my relations with every Legation in Seoul as well as with the Korean Government are most cordial and all that could be desired, while the relations existing between some of the other Representatives are quite strained. We have no difficulties on hand, and in the midst of the general turmoil, we get the substantial benefits, as, for instance, the contract for Electric Street Railroads and Lighting, as noted in my No. 73 of Febr. 15.

I must add that Mr. de Speyer insists that the attempted assassination of his Interpreter is due to the spirit evoked by the above cited memorial, I enclose extracts from today's "Independent": The Imperial reply to the above mentioned memorial; The letter from the Russian Representative concerning the attempted assassination; the Imperial Edict in reply to this demand of the Russian Representatives for justice, and the notice of the arrest of a suspect. This arrest seems to have been on a false charge, and it is my painful duty to state that last night Prince Ye Chai Soon was arrested as chief instigator in this cowardly attack, while other ex Cabinet Officials are mentioned as being implicated in the affair.

Ye Chai Soon is a nephew of the late King, and one of the first nobles of the Empire. He was made Minister of the Household when His Majesty fled to the Russian Legation. He was a firm friend of Mr. Waeber, the former Russian Representative. When Mr. de Speyer arrived, His Majesty, not liking the domineering ways of the Russian Interpreter, had Ye Chai Soon inform Mr. de Speyer that he would prefer the services of another interpreter. Mr. de Speyer resented this, as did his Interpreter, and His Majesty fearing trouble, denied having given the instruction. A feud arose between Prince Ye and Interpreter Kim, which resulted in the attempt upon the latter's life.

As this will be a serious matter, I have dwelt upon it at length.

Horace N. Allen.

No. 116   Legation of the United States
                                                      Seoul Korea, June 24, 1898.

Secretary of State

Sir:-

Political Affairs in Korea have been very quiet since the withdrawal of the Russian Advisers: Military officers, and bank, and the departure of Mr. de Speyer. The present Russian Chargé de'Affaires, Mr. Matunine, abstains from all interference in Korean political affairs, and the Japanese, if active at all, are not so in a manner to cause comment. The latter retain in Seoul their garrison of 200 soldiers. The British have had a guard of marines at their Legation for some time, but they have recently been removed for service with the fleet. Mr. Jordan thinks a small permanent guard may possibly be sent him from England. The Russian Legation has a permanent guard of 20 men and an officer, ordered to this duty from St. Petersburg. Mr. Matunine asked me to request a permanent guard for this Legation, from my Government, but I declined.

There has been quite a demand of late for concessions from the Korean Government, which the latter has shown great persistence in refusing to grant. The Russian Gov'mt were refused an island in the harbor of Mokpo: The French were unable to obtain the fulfillment of a mining clause in their concession for a Railway from Seoul to the northern border: The Japanese have been unable to secure the concession for a railroad from Seoul to Fusan, and the British, who have received no such concessions as have all the other countries represented here, were met with a flat refusal when they asked for a coal mining right. Mr. Jordan was however, able to make such representations as to the disappointment and possible resentment of his Government at such unfair treatment, that last night the Council of State passed a resolution to grant the English Company a mining right.

The matter of the holding of large tracts of land at the new ports, by Foreign Governments to the detriment of the settlements proper, has been settled by Russia's decreasing her former excessive demands, to very resonable ones.

Affairs in the Interior are not promising. Magisterial corruption is very common, and reports of oppression, extortion, and possible uprisings in consequence, are very frequent. In some cases, where the Christian converts of our Missionaries were being brutally ill-treated for purposes of extortion, I discussed the matter informally, and unofficially, with the Minister of the Interior, and without in any way violating my instructions, I was able to bring relief to our people and their followers.

The Minister for Foreign Affairs, Chyo Pyung Chick, has been made Minister of Justice, and Mr. You Key Whan, the Vice Minister, has been made Acting Minister for Foreign Affairs.

The disposal of the Seoul-Chemulpo Railroad on completion, by the American concessionaire, to a Japanese syndicate, has not caused much comment here among Koreans. It seems however to have given offence to the Germans, if I may judge by the remarks of my German colleague and the acts of his countrymen here. It is quite probable that the Koreans may in consequence, be led to look upon the matter in a manner unfavorable to Americans.

Horace N. Allen.

No. 131

Legation of the United States
Seoul Korea, August 4, 1898.

Secretary of State

Sir:-

I have the honor to acquaint you with certain facts concerning the present political situation in Seoul.

The Acting Foreign Minister, Mr. You Key Whan, has been released from office, and a former Minister, Mr. Ye Toh Chai, has been made Acting Foreign Minister.

This change is explained to me to be in consequence of the recent difficulty between Acting Minister You, and the German Consul, Mr. Krien; See my No. 120, July 8.

It was reported to me that Mr. Krien had sent his interpreter to the palace with the statement that Prince Henry, who is now at Fusan, could not come to Seoul while "such a man as You is Foreign Minister". Mr. Krien admits sending a message similar to this, but says that he thinks the real reason for the Prince's not coming to Seoul, is that Germany has not recognized the Imperial title of His Majesty, which would make such visit somewhat awkward under the circumstances. He also said that he thought the unpleasant notoriety given him (Krien) by the newspapers in Japan, over his encounter with the Korean Foreign Minister, may have something to do with the Prince's non-arrival here at this time.

The Independence Club has of late assumed great importance and is in danger of losing all control over its more fiery members. So that it is now regarded as a menace to the peace of Seoul and the country.

In my No. 127, July 26, I showed how this Club had succeeded in ridding the Government of the obnoxious Chyo Pyung Sik. They are now endeavoring to drive out of office the companion of Mr. Chyo, the Ye Yong Ik, mentioned in my No. 125, July 18,.

I enclose an extract from today's "Independent" giving an acount of a conference held on this subject between a committee of the Club and several Cabinet Ministers.

I also enclose copy of an editorial from the same issue of the "Independent", being an admonition to the Club to be more cautious in their deliberations.

In this connection I hand you enclosed a translation from a Seoul news-paper, published in the native character, purporting to be a synopsis of a speech delivered before this Independence Club, by one of the American Advisers to the Korean Government, Mr. C. R. Greathouse. I send this translation, because of the fact that the speech has caused much comment and my attention has been called to it by two of my colleagues, the Russian and the German Representatives. I may add that Mr. Greathouse says the speech is not rightly reported. He is in the employ of the Korean Government and was asked to do something in regard to the Independent Club, his course being left to his own judgement. He thought it best to make this speech, and I do not know that the Korean Government has objected to it.

Horace N. Allen.

No. 96   Department of State
                                            Washington, September 22, 1898

Horace N. Allen

Sir:
    I have to acknowledge the receipt of your No. 131, Diplomatic Series, of the 4th ultimo, reporting on the political situation in Seoul.
    With reference to the speech made by Mr. Greathouse before the Independent Club, a translation of which from the "Independent" of August 2, 1898, you enclose. I call your attention to Mr. Olney's instruction No. 132 sent to your predecessor on January 11, 1896, wherein Mr. Sill was enjoined to caution all Americans resident in Korea to strictly refrain from any expression of opinion, or from giving any advice, concerning the internal management of the country, or from an intermeddling in political questions. American citizens in Korea should remember, that the obligations of friendly neutrality are no less morally incumbent upon the individual citizen than they are, as a precept of international law, binding on the Government to which the citizen owes allegiance and whose protection he may claim in case of need.

                                            Alvey A. Adee

No. 145   Legation of the United States
                                            Seoul Korea, September 17, 1898.

Secretary of State

Sir:-
    Referring to my No's. 137, Aug. 23 and 124, July 12, regarding a conspiracy to depose the Emperor of Korea, I have now the honor to inform you that an attempt was made on the night on the 14'th. instant to poison His Majesty and the Crown Prince. A substance, supposed to be crude arsenic was placed in the coffee they were to drink at a late supper. It is reported that the poison, instead of being placed simply in the two cups intended for it, was placed in the coffee pot, thus affecting the whole company but proving fatal to none. All were made quite sick and the Crown Prince was reported to be in a critical condition for some time. All have now recovered.
    In my No. 141, Aug. 27, I informed you of the arrest and banishment of the former interpreter of the Russian Legation. A palace servant has now confessed to having placed this poison in the coffee at the solicitation of the family of this banished ex-interpreter. The family of this man have therefore been arrested and the man himself will be brought from exile for punishment.
    His Majesty seems to consider his position so unsafe that he recently commissioned one of the American advisers Mr. C. R. Greathouse, to proceed to Shanghai and secure for him a guard of thirty foreigners. These men have now arrived in Seoul. They are such men as might be expected to be found in a foreign port, willing to engage in some novel enterprise, even though the pay might be small as in this case. They are to receive the equivalent of $35. gold and board themselves; quarters and uniform to be furnished. Several nationalities are represented, there being 9 Americans; 9 British; 5 French; 5 German and 2 Russians in the number.
    I knew nothing of this project till Mr. Greathouse was well on his way. No one outside the palace seems to have known of it. Once before when the employment of a lot of Americans for such a purpose was proposed, I opposed it strongly on the grounds that the presence of such a body of unorganized, undisciplined and uncontrolled men would be a grave source of danger, and I could not allow my countryment to be introduced for such purpose without protest. The matter was given up, but in this case I was intentionally kept uninformed of the measure.
    All my colleagues, with myself, are much annoyed by this action and Mr. Greathouse is severely blamed. I am pretty sure I am blamed for allowing it, but I was not aware of it and am not in any way responsible.
    These men in the absence of all proper control, will surely be a danger to the peace of the City, and as they are only amenable to their own Consular authorities, each Representative expects to have more or less trouble with them.

I trust the Department will act promptly upon my request to be supplied with a jail and the necessary paraphernalia of a Consular Court. See my No. 121 July 9, and No. 17 Consular Series. I now have a murder case on hand in which the one to be arrested bids fair to be an American, and with the rough element we are getting here, we will be frequently called upon for similar services hereafter.

Horace N Allen

No. 108

Department of State
Washinton, November 14, 1898

Horace N. Allen:

Sir
I have to acknowledge the receipt of your No. 150, Diplomatic Series, of the 7th ultimo, in which after referring to an attempt to poison His Majesty the King, and the Crown Prince, and the rumored efforts to obtain by torture the confessions of certain persons suspected of the crime, you state the action of the diplomatic body in sending a joint note to the Korean Foreign Office protesting against the use of torture, and asking for the removal of the law minister from office - You did not join in the signature of this note, but your did, on September, 30, send to the Korean Foreign Office your individual protest.

The humanitarian motive which promted yor communication is appreciated, although it is thought that your representations might have taken a form less likely to suggest concerted action with your colleagues to press upon the Korean Government a matter growing out of the unhappy political condition of the country.

It is moreover appropriate that I should comment, although in no spirit of censure, upon the manner and form of your concluding paragraph, where, after characterizing the the practice as repugnant to modern rule and usage, you say that you "cannot but protest against its reinforcement."

This appears to assume as a fact, what you were careful to describe as being merely "persistently rumored", and later to regard as credible, because your Russian colleague was not afforded an opportunity to disprove it.

Moreover you were unfortunate in using the word "protest", which in diplomatic usage, has a well defined and extreme sense, indicating the sovereign right of the protestant power to lodge a remonstrance, and, if unredressed, to seek a remedy for its grievance. Neither phrase of right pertains to any representation you might make on a subject of the internal administration of Korean affairs, unless the application thereof should injure the person, or invade the rights of an American citizen. Had your communication taken the form of inplied remonstrance and strongly expressed hope that no intention of restoring the abolished practice of torture had been or was now entertained, it would have received the unqualified approval of the Department.

Korea having won the respect and sympathy of many nations by her earnest efforts to attain a higher plane of action comporting with modern civilization and progress, any indication of reversion to admittedly reprehensible and barbaric usages on her part could not but cause a most painful impression in quarters where the only impulse is our friendly interest in the Korean desire for material and moral advancement.

In this connection, I also acknowledge the receipt of your No. 152, Diplomatic Series, of the 13th ultimo, reporting the hanging of three of the suspected persons, and the mutilation of their bodies, leading to the dismissal from office of the Minister of Law, his Vice Minister and other officials obnixious to the people, and the formation of a new cabinet.

John Hay

No. 152   Legation of the United States
                                                     Seoul Korea, October 13, 1898.

Secretary of State

Sir:-

I have the honor to inform you that this city has just passed through a period of intense excitement. A peaceful revolution has taken place, and at the demand of the masses, almost a complete change of cabinet has been made. Such cabinet changes took place when, in 1894 the Japanese took practical possession of Korea, and again in 1896 when His Majesty took refuge in the Russian Legation. The latter event witnessed the brutal murder of three cabinet officers. There seems to be no likelihood of any such occurence in this instance.

In my No. 150, Oct. 7, I informed you of the attempt on the part of the Minister of Law, Sin Key Sun, to have the old laws relating to torture, mutilation of the bodies, and destruction of the families of "traitors", reenacted. I sent you as enclosure /1 in that despatch, the memorial of this officer upon that subject, and noted my refusal to join with my colleagues in asking for his dismissal. Such joint action on our part would have placed us too much in line with the Independence Club, and I think now that we are all glad we did not take such action.

This Independence Club has grown till it now represents the mass of the Korean people. Once before they compelled the dismissal of two notoriously corrupt officials, see my No. 131, Aug. 4 and No. 127, July 26. Now they have compelled the dismissal of the Minister and Vice Minister of Law, and the resignation of the Ministers of the Household; Finance and War, and the appointment in their stead of some of the best men in Korea.

The incident is the direct outcome of the banishment of the once all-powerful interpreter of the Russian Legation, Kim Hong Youk, - A man most hateful to the Independence Club, but for whom they demanded a fair trial, but in vain. Later this Kim was accused of the attempt to poison His Majesty in the so-called "coffee plot"; see my No. 141, Aug. 27 and No. 145, Sept. 17. The evident fact that torture was being applied to these suspects, whom many people firmly believe to be innocent, but so accused to shield the real culprit, caused the Foreign Representatives to enter a protest against such torture: see my No. 150, Oct. 7.

This ex-interpreter Kim, was brought from banishment, arriving in Seoul on the night of Oct. 7. He is said to have confessed to being guilty of the attempt at poisoning, and the Koreans generally believe that this was due to unbearable torture. The request of the Russian Chargé d Affaires, to be present at the trial, was ignored. The man with his two chief "confederates" who were both former employees of the Russian Legation, were hung on the evening of Oct. 10. The Minister of Law insisted that the bodies be mutilated and laid in the streets, but His Majesty refused permission for this barbarous course. The refusal was apparently ignored, for the bodies were given to the mob, and by them were dragged about the streets and abused. They were seen during the night lying naked on the public street, by a foreigner, A. B. Stripling.

The wife of Kim Hong Youk, being heavy with child, was not killed, but was beated with 100 blows and then banished.

For disregarding the instructions of His Majesty regarding the treatment of these bodies, the memorial of the Independence Club was received and in accordance therewith the Minister of Law and his Vice Minister were summarily dismissed from office.

Meantime, for days this Independence Club, to the extent of several hundreds, sat day and night before the palace, demanding by memorial, the dismissal of the other obnoxious officials. The people of the city contributed money for their support and the shops closed their doors as a mark of sympathy with the memorialists.

It was such a demonstration as Korea has never known before. All was done quietly and in an orderly manner, but a determination was shown that would brook no interference.

The President of this Club, or party, is Yun Chi Ho. He was the first interpreter to this Legation (1883-4). He afterwards spent some ten years at school in America, where he became an enlightened Christian gentleman. He publishes the Seoul Independent News-paper, and some of his editorials would do credit to any college-bred American. In his life he is entirely consistent with the high standard he took for himself in America. He does not bother this Legation, and has the courage of his convictions, though he confesses that it is difficult to hold his party within bounds.

It was rumored that this Mr. Yun was to be arrested and thrown into prison for disturbing the peace. This caused great excitement and it looked for a time as though bloodshed would ensue, as would have been the case had not better counsels prevailed to prevent any such arrest.

The women of Korea are most carefully secluded; never going out without being heavily veiled or in a closed chair. They are never mentioned, much less heard, in public. Yet the recent movement was so inspiring to all classes, that some hundreds of Korean ladies met and drafted a memorial asking to be provided with schools for themselves and their daughters, and fully indorsing the petitions of the Independence people. This memorial was brought to the palace by a delegation of women, and it must have had much to do with convincing His Majesty that it would be useless to further disregard the voice of the people.

The memorialists were finally successful and last night the removal of the obnoxious officials was announced, and this mornings official gazette announces the formation of the new cabinet, which is as follows: -

Prime Minister (Acting), Pak Chung Yang.
Foreign Minister, Pak Chai Soon, -lately Acting Minister.
War Minister, Min Yung Whan.
Finance, Chyo Pyung So.
Interior, Ye Kun Myung.
Education, Ye Toh Chai, Retained.
Law, Soh Chung Soon.
Household, Yun Yong Koo.
Public Works, Agriculture Commerce and Posts and Telegraphs. Minister - Min Pyung Suk.
Vice Minister - Min Sang Ho, who will have practical charge of Posts and Telegraphs.

Korea has never before had such a high class cabinet, it is claimed, and it remains to see how long a high class official can retain his office.

Of these new cabinet officers, Pak Chung Yang was the first Korean Minister to Washington, and was most falsely accused and unjustly imprisoned last summer, see my No. 124, July 12. Min Yung Whan ("The Good Min"), has just returned from a sojourn to Washington, where he stopped on his way home from his post as Ambassador to Russia, because of some difficulties connected with his mission. Col. Min Sang Ho, has also just returned from service at Washington in connection with the Universal Postal Convention. These three appointments give great general satisfaction to the Independence Party.

I hand you enclosed an extract from the Seoul Independent, giving, editorially, the memorial of the Independents.

Horace N. Allen.

No. 154

Legation of the United States
Seoul, Korea, October 27, 1898.

Secretary of State

Sir,
Referring to my No. 152, October 13, wherein I gave a detailed account of the action of the Independent Club, in compelling a complete revision of the Korean Cabinet, I now have the honour to inform you that they have succeeded in obtaining a decree granting freedom of speech, and they have practically succeeded in securing a sort of popular assembly which, it is thought, may lead to the establishment of a legislative body by popular election. After the successful movement to compel the dismissal of the objectionable members of the Cabinet, as cited in the above named despatch No. 152, this Club made a demand for a reorganization of the Privy Council, to be compossed of members, half of whom should be appointed by the Indepence Club, which Club would further take the lead in drawing up regulations to govern the actions of the Privy Council. An answer was promised to this petition within a week.

I enclose an editorial from the Seoul Independent of October 18, giving a translation of this petition.
In reply to this last demand of the people through the Independence Club, the Club's President, Mr. Yun Tchi Ho, (T.H. Yun), was made Vice President of the Privy Council, which was to be composed of fifty one members as follows: seventeen from the Government, seventeen from the Independence Club, and seventeen from the Imperial, or "Pedlars'"" Club. The latter is a reorganization of an ancient guild

composed of all the thousands of pedlars in Korea - an association that became so powerful that it had to be suppressed. It is now being operated by bad men, in opposition to the Independents. Its President is the man Hong, who murdered the political refugees, Kim Ah Kiun, in Shanghai in 1894.

The association of these seventeen men from the Pedlars' Club with those from the Independence Club, angered the latter, and they met in the city to protest against it. The Emperor issued a decree forbidding such meetings in the city and ordering them to disperse. They did not obey, but went in a body to the Police Department and asked to be arrested as they were there in violation of His Majesty's orders. Three hundered of the most popular men in Korea could not well be arrested, so they were again ordered by Imperial Decree to disperse. This they refused to do until they had been granted freedom of speech. After several days of delay, during which the Independents remained encamped before the Police Department, His Majesty granted their prayer, and I now enclose a memorial from today's Seoul Independent setting forth the facts of the case.

Mr. Yun Tchi Ho has declined to act as Vice President of the Privy Council composed as it is, with the seventeen men from the Pedlars' Club.

Horace N. Allen.

No. 161   Legation of the United States
                                                               Seoul, Korea, November 14, 1898.

Secretary of State

Sir,

       This city has again been experiencing one of those unhappy agitations for which it seems to have a well merited reputation, and I have the honour to briefly narrate the principal circumstances.

       On October 26, last, a most remarkable mass-meeting took place in the centre of Seoul, being a futher demonstration by the people, headed by the Independence party, of their determination to interfere in the conduct of the Government.

I have the honour to hand you enclosed an extract from the Seoul Independent of November 1, giving an account of this meeting, which, by the way, was attended by a Committee of thirty ladies from the women's club, - a most remarkable occurrence in this land of female seclusion.

Mr. T. H. Yun, (Yun Tchi Ho), in accepting the chairmanship of this meeting, insisted upon certain rules of respect to His Majesty; to Foreign Powers represented in Korea, to the setting aside of selfish personal aims, and to the avoidance of the discussion of such trivial matters as the change of the national costume.

The result of the deliberations of this gathering was the drafting of a Memorial asking that no foreign (military) aid be asked to uphold the Government; that concessions and such like documents be signed by the whole Council of State, instead of by an individual Minister; that fair trials be granted; that the Cabinet have a voice in the appointment of high officials; that taxes be placed under the control of the Finance Department alone, and that existing laws be enforced.

These demands were granted a few days later by Imperial Decree, at the suggestion of the best of the high officials.

A few days after the publication of this Decree, certain evilly disposed men, headed by the notorious Chyo Pyung Sik, who had just returned from banishment, persuaded His Majesty that the real object of this movement was to force a Republic on Korea. I am told that these men agreed to break up this popular movement and to take upon themselves the responsibility for the consequences. They produced a bogus placard which, they claimed, came from the Independence party, calling for the election of a President of Korea, mentioning the names of Pak Chung Yang and T. H. Yun, as President and Vice President. While those who know Korea and the motives of this popular movement are perfectly certain that this idea of a republic was a mere invention of the evil disposed, it had its effect, and His Majesty promply dismissed the very excellent Cabinet I had occasion to mention in my No. 152, October 13, and took as his Prime Minister the corrupt and unscrupulous Chyo Pyung Sik, whose doings have necessarily formed a considerable feature in this series of despatches.

Another man of very questionable reputation, - Min Chong Mook, was made Foreign Minister.

These appointments were made in the night of November 4, and before morning the arrest of nineteen of the leaders of the Independence party was ordered. Seventeen were promptly arrested, and two escaped, one of whom was the President of the party, T.H. Yun.

This caused the most intense excitement in Seoul, and thousands of people collected before the prison, where they remained day and night asking to be arrested with their leaders.

On the 6th. instant I was informed by Americans resident in Seoul, that they were in great fear for their lives, as it was generally reported on the streets that the military would fire into this crowd to disperse them, and that such action would cause a general riot in which the Americans living in widely separated localities in Seoul would be in great danger from a lawless mob.

Mr. Jordan, my British colleague, came in, in the evening, greatly alarmed over similar reports from his own people and together we went to see Mr. Matunine, the Russian Chargé d'Affaires, who was supposed to be well posted, since Chyo Pyung Sik the Premier, and Min Chong Mook, the Foreign Minister, were strong pro-Russian officials, and had endeavored the night before, to have a concession signed granting to Russia all the coal mines of Korea, and the much talked of coaling station on Deer Island. While this scheme had fallen through, we were aware that Russian influence was, for the time, paramount.

Mr. Matunine seemed worried, and while he said he did not object to the use of force in dispersing the crowd in front of the prison, he would deprecate the shedding of blood, and authorized me to say as much for him to the Foreign Minster. - I happen to be Dean of the Foreign Representatives at present.

Learning that the Foreign Minister was then at the British Legation, I went there with Mr. Jordan, and delivered this message, receiving the assurance that force would not be used against the crowd, at least, not before sufficient notice had been given, so that I could arrange for the protection of American lives and property. Three days later, I learned that a certain man of no military knowledge had been appointed from a Judgeship to be Colonel of the First Regiment in order that he might fire on the crowd, and I was credibly informed from the Palace that the Foreign Minister had falsely reported me to His Majesty as being entirely in favour of the use of force. Mr. Jordan having heard similar reports called upon me to ask that I assemble the Foreign Representatives for a meeting, that we might demand an audience with His Majesty to protest, in the interest of our defenceless citizens aginst this proposed bloodshed.

I declined to do this at his request, which was with the sanction of the Japanese Representative, as I did not wish to be ranged on one side with these two Representatives as against those of Russia and France on the other. I stated that I would ask for an audience for myself personally, to explain my own previous statment to the Foreign Minister, and that I would send a Circular to my colleagues telling them of my proposed action, so that they would be prepared in advance to take such steps as they might desire.

This I did and I send you enclosed, copies of my circular and of my letter to the Foreign Minister.

The latter despatch had the effect of bringing the Foreign Minister at once to my house, where he spent three hours in the evening, and gave me such strong assurances, that I agreed to let the matter of an Audience lie in abeyance pending results. Mr. Jordan, who had also asked for an audience did the same.

His Majesty, learning incidentally, the next day, that these requests had been made but had not been submitted to him, and learning further that while this coterie of officials about him had assured him that the crowd of people before the prison numbered between 30 and 100, there were really thousands there, supported by the whole populace, he promptly dismissed the Foreign Minister and reappointed Pak Chai Soon, who had been relieved a few days before.

He had the seventeen arrested people dismissed with nominal punishments, and all might have been well had the people dispersed, but the movement had gone beyond the control of the leaders, and the people remained, demanding the names of the persons who had got up the bogus placard about the formation of a republic,

Serious trouble may yet result, since the evil disposed officials, though dismissed, are still refugees from the people, in the Palace, where their unwise counsels may yet prevail upon His Majesty.

I send you a further clipping from the Seoul Independent of Nov. 10, descriptive of the above demonstration. I may mention in this connection, that one of the seventeen arrested men was taken from the house of an American. The house was used as a chapel, or school, and its foreign ownership may not have been known to the police. Upon my representations and demands, the man was placed back in the house whence he was taken, and I was asked officially to surrender him, but before I could take action the man had voluntarily gone to the police court, and given himself up.

Horace N. Allen.

No. 162   Legation of the United States
                                               Seoul, Korea, November 28, 1898.

Secretary of State

Sir,

      In my No. 161, November 14, I had the honour to inform you of the serious agitation then in progress in this city, between the people and the Government. I informed you of my prompt protest, in the interest of American lives and property, against the shedding of blood in dispersing the peoples's meeting, and that, as a probable result of this protest, the newly appointed coterie of officials whose advice had caused this difficulty, were dismissed, but were supposed to be in hiding in the Palace, since an order for their arrest could not be executed.

Subsequent events prove my fears to have been well grounded. Force was used, and the city was, for days, in the hands of an infuriated mob.

The soldiers of Seoul, some six thousand in all, with eleven hundred policemen, were in more or less open sympathy with the people; members of their own families being associated with those who were gathered in the street to memorialize the Throne. It was therefore thought to be useless to attempt to disperse the memorialists by using the troops or the police. From ancient times the Pedlars' Guild in Korea has been a very powerful organization. They are packers, as well as pedlars, and, numbering thousands, they travel all over the peninsula, and are very clannish. This guild was deprived of its charter during the reform movement that followed the Japan-China war in 1894, but they have held together just the same. Finding that the troops could not be depended upon to attack the people, His Majesty was induced to send for the Pedlers to come to his assistance on the promise of a renewal of their charter, and a good daily wage for their service. They came, and being comparative strangers in Seoul, they could be relied on to attack the people. On the 21st. instant, a few hundred pedlars armed with clubs marched past the gates of the foreign Legations to the Palace near by, and attacked and quickly dispersed the few hundred memorialists sitting there, but they were later attacked by the people, and several were reported to be killed.

The next day the people went out of the city by thousands to meet the pedlars, who had been largely reinforced. The latter were well organized, while the people were a mere mob, which was speedily sent flying back to the city gates after the pedlars had killed a few of the attacking party. This so angered the populace that they began to destroy the houses of the officials who were supposed to be in sympathy with the pedlars. The latter threatened to enter and destroy the city, and it seemed that no one would be able to preserve order.

The Japanese have a regular guard of 200 soldiers stationed in Seoul, besides a large and efficient police force. The Russians have a guard of twenty mounted cossacks, with an officer. The British Representative telegraphed for a ship, and got up a small guard of marines. I was strongly urged to ask for a guard, but declined to do so. We have so many Americans here, living in all parts of the city, that a guard would only be of use to protect them after I had called our people into the Legation, and if I should do that, the American men themselves would serve as an efficient guard, whom I could arm with the rifles I have been supplied with. Knowing that a request for a guard might embarrass our Naval Authorities, I declined to ask for one. I felt safe in taking this course, as I was well aware that neither the pedlers nor the people were at all opposed to or unfriendly to foreigners. It was purely a Korean affair. Also, with the Secretary of the Legation, my two sons and the constable, all accustomed to the use of fire-arms, we had an efficient temporary guard to hold the gates of the Legation. I wish, in this connection, to point out the great usefulness of the constable, or jail keeper, since, by his presence at the gates, I was enabled to refuse to admit any of the numerous refugees who were so anxious to get to this Legation for protection/

      The foreign Representatives were invited to an Audience at nine o'clock A.M. on the 22nd,; we went and were received singly, which kept us there all morning, and, as the foreign Advisers were asked to Audience in the afternoon, this kept a body of foreigners near the Emperor all that day. Before going to the Audience, we felt that it was but a ruse to secure the protection of our presence. His Majesty asked for advice from each Representative; I of course, declined to advise him, though I did protest very strongly against the endangering of the lives and property of Americans by calling in hired mercenaries to attack the people.

On the 23rd. instant, the Cabinet all resigned, and His Majesty was left to the counsels of the refugees in the Palace, who had brought on the whole trouble. The situation became so grave, that on the 26th., we were again asked to an Audience, at which time his Majesty was to personally address the people and the pedlars separately with the intention of inducing them to disperse.

We declined to attend, until we had been assured from the Palace as to what His Majesty intended to say, and that we would not be held responsible for anything that might be said or done on that occasion.

We all attended this Audience with the exception of Mr. Matunine, the Charge d'Affaires of Russia, who unexpectedly declined to go, at the last moment. The interview was entirely successful. His Majesty granted the demands of the people, as embodied in the six articles I handed you with my No. 161, of November 14. He also renewed the charter of the Independence Club, and agreed to have brought to trial the five officials who had caused the arrest of the seventeen members of the Club. (See above-cited despatch). Upon these premises, the people dispersed. To the pedlars, His Majesty made a little speech asking them to disperse, and declining for the present to renew their charter.

All seems quiet now, though the disturbance has caused the destruction of seventeen houses of officials; the death of a number of people, - not more than twelve, I believe, and the wounding of many others. Both the Japanese and the Russian Representatives have been very careful not to violate the terms of the Lobanov-Yamagata Convention by which each country agrees not to interfere singly in Korean matters, but each of these Representatives was apparently keenly on his guard to detect any violation of this convention by the other.

This was the first purely Korean disturbance of any importance ever witnessed by foreign Representatives, none of whom interfered. It was settled by the Koreans, in their own way. It is, however, in all probability, the precursor of furthur outbreaks of a similar nature.

Horace N. Allen.

No. 167

Legation of the United States
Seoul, Korea, December 23, 1898.

Secretary of State

Sir,

In my No. 162, November 28, I concluded my account of the agitated state of affairs in Seoul by a reference to the open air meeting in which His Majesty promised the people in the presence of the Foreign Representatives that he would carry out the reforms he had already promised. This pledge was not fulfilled, and the people began again to hold public meetings.

This time the Christians taught by the America missionaries were brought into participation in the agitation. As threats were made against American property, I had to take the matter up, as will be seen in the enclosed correspondence which I forward as a matter of record, and which resulted in inducing the Christians to abstain further from such participation.

1/ Translation from a forged letter from the Pedlers Club threatening American property, and a true rejoinder from the same club.

2/ Two letters from myself to the Foreign Office calling attention to the above threats. The second one of which embodies the Foreign Office's reply to the first.

3/ Two letters from myself to the Rev. Appenzeller, urging compliance with the Department's circular of May 11, 1897. During the past fortnight or so, there has been, practically, no central Government in Korea. Every day has witnessed the appointment of Ministers of State only to be discontinued the next day. The departmental offices have been closed, and public business stopped, and the city practically turned over to the agitators. There has been no disorder of any great consequence since the attack upon the people by the pedlars, and the consequent destruction of property as described in my above cited despatch No. 162.

Absolutely no taxes come in from the country, and the treasury is entirely exhausted. There being no money to pay the soldiers and officials, it is thought that the former may create great disturbances.

There are wise and upright officials in Seoul who could bring order out of this chaos, but they seem not to be in the confidence of His Majesty, who is said to be largely under the influence of Madam Om, the mother of his youngest son who is believed to entertain hopes of becoming Empress throught the assistance of those who have the credit of originating the present disturbance.

Many Koreans credit the Japanese with a desire to see His Majesty persevere in making himself so objectionable to the people that they will be compelled to rid themselves of him and recall the princes who are sojourning in Japan as refugess. I can see nothing, as yet, to support this view unless it be that the popular movement seems to have the sympathy, if not the actual support of the Japanese Legation. On his return from Japan, Mr. Kato, who was recently promoted from Minister Resident to be His Imperial

Majesty's Envoy Extraordinary and Minister Plenipotentiary to Korea, had a long audience (Dec. 15,) in which, as he voluntarily told me, he had advised against the use of force to disperse the people, until His Majesty shall have carried out the solemn promises he made them. He says also that he gave ample and most appreciated assurances that the princes and others refugees in Japan would not be allowed to return to Korea at present. In this connection I enclose a clipping from the Japan Mail of Dec. 5, descriptive of the surveillance exercised over these men by the Government of Japan.

One of these men, Prince Pak Yong Hio, who is described in my No. 122, July 11, was reported to have arrived at Chemulpo a few days since, and as he is known to be a patriot and an able man, the people memorialized the Throne in his favour. Orders are now issued for the arrest of those who signed and favoured this memorial. The Japanese insist that he did not arrive.

While in Japan, Mr. Kato was interviewed by the representative of a liberal newspaper, and I enclose a clipping from the Japan Mail of Dec. 6, giving an account of this interview, which I commend to your attention as presumably illustrative of the sentiment of the Japanese upon this, to them, important question of Korean matters.

The Russian Charge d'Affaires, Mr. Matunine, has freely expressed his great dissatisfaction with the Lobanoff-Yamagata Convention, made at a time when Russia was under no necessity of making any such agreement, and by which either party is now prevented from singly interfering to restore order in Korea. He has seemed anxious for some opportunity of disregarding this convention, but Mr. Kato says he has declined even to represent such a course to his Government at Tokyo, and the existence of this agreement seems now to be especially agreeable to the Japanese. With the large community of Japanese in Korea, protected by an ample guard, and with a considerable following among Korean officials, the Japanese may be able to quietly influence public affairs so as to restore order and at the same time strengthen their position here. It seems evident that the Koreans must lean upon and advise with some foreign power. They have gone steadily from bad to worse since the complete withdrawal of Russian influence last spring, which was followed by the substitution of no other overpowering outside influence. His Majesty is kind and affable to a fault, but very easily influenced, and since the unfortunate death of his Queen who was one of the strongest personages in asiatic politics he seems to be without any settled policy and simply shifts from one thing to another under influences which seem to be the worst that could be brought to bear upon him.

Horace N. Allen.

PERIOD OF MUTUAL ANTAGONISM AND AGGRESSION

"Shibusawa Money" Used by the Dai Ichi Ginko in Korea

Reprinted from *Pictorial Chosen and Manchuria* (Seoul: compiled by the Bank of Chosen in commemoration of the bank's decennial, 1919), 58.

A. Increasing Japanese Interests

No. 144

Legation of the United States
Seoul Korea, Sept. 13, 1898.

Secretary of State

Sir:-

I have the honor to inform you that the long talked of concession for a railroad to connect Seoul with the extreme southern port Fusan, was granted to the Japanese of the 8'th. instant.

It is supposed that the unofficial visit of Marquis Ito to this Capital which took place a few days ago, had something to do with determining the final action upon this matter. The subject has been prominently discussed for four years, and it has of late seemed to be the thing most desired by Japan from Korea.

The Japanese desired the concession for the road to connect Seoul and its port, Chemulpo, 25 miles distant. This went to an American - J. R. Morse, who, becoming involved in financial difficulties, transferred his concession to a Japanese Syndicate of which he is a member. This transfer gives the Japanese the only railway that can hope to be made immediately profitable here, and in connection with the new concession, it becomes even more valuable than before, being the outlet for all future railroads to be built in Korea.

The Seoul-Fusan concession, which was based upon the Seoul-Chemulpo one, compels the commencement of work within three years from the date of signature, and the work must be completed within ten years of its commencement. The Korean Government may buy the road and its properties at the expiration of ten years from the completion of the same, and it cannot be sold to other than Koreans. The Korean Government furnish a free right of way and terminal facilities.

The length of the road will be about 400 miles and it is estimated that it will cost 25 million yen ($12,500,000 gold), but judging from the cost of the Seoul-Chemulpo road, this more difficult one cannot be built for less than 40 million yen or 20 million gold dollars.

It was at one time supposed to be of great strategic importance and as it cannot well be made to pay a profit on the investment for many years to come, it is supposed that the strategic value is still the chief feature considered. This seems to be a mistake under present conditions however, for troops could now be thrown into Seoul from Port Arthur before they could be brought here from Japan, even if the railway were well protected and in good working order.

There seems to have been no foreign opposition to the granting of this concession at this time, though by reference to my No. 67, Jan. 21, and No. 69, Jan. 30, you will see how actively the then Russian Representative, Mr. de Speyer, was opposed to the measure.

Horace N Allen

No. 153

Legation of the United States
Seoul Korea, October 20, 1898.

Secretary of State

Sir:-

I have the honor to hand you enclosed, an extract from the Seoul Independent of todays date, giving a translation of a memorial from the Independence Club, relative to and protesting against the gradual absorption of Korea by the Japanese, who are complained of as living all about through the interior, contrary to treaty stipulations, and engaging in trade.

It is generally believed that the steady influx of Japanese into Korea, and their rapid scattering about through the whole interior, is due to a well devised plan for a kind of peaceful absorption of the country.

With thousands of Japanese resident at Chemulpo, Fusan Gensan and Seoul; with a rapidly growing settlement at Mokpo and the other new ports as centers, this occupation of the interior is comparatively easy, and the Korean trader is unable to compete with the strangers.

Koreans complain bitterly that they cannot get justice before a Japanese Consul, and this complaint is also made by Chinese and Western Foreigners, some glaring cases of injustice having recently occured in which Chinese were the complainants with the British Representative assisting them. The Koreans are often brutally treaty by the Japanese and it is not unnatural that they detest and fear them.

Horace N. Allen.

No. 272

Legation of the United States
Seoul, Korea, August 23, 1900.

Secretary of State

Sir:-

I have the honor to hand you the following account of the situation in Korea.

In my No. 252, of May 30, 1900, I informed you regarding the sudden execution within a few hours after the close of a perfunctory trial, of the two Korean political refugees who had recently returned from Japan, upon a promise in the case of one of them, made by the Emperor of Korea, to the Minister from Japan, that no torture should be used at the trial. This promise was apparently taken to mean that justice should be done.

Fearing the consequences of this act, the Emperor of Korea claimed that it was done without his knowledge, and he banished the judges for a term of years in consequence. The Chief Judge who was responsible for the execution of the refugees was secretly brought back to Seoul immeditely and remained in hiding in a house of the Governor of the city adjoining the compound of the American employees of the Seoul Electric Railway Co., of which Company the Governor was the President until his sudden death on the 16th instant. After a few weeks of quiet this Judge was formally pardoned and is now mentioned in connection with certain high office.

The Korean Minister at Tokyo finding it possible to smooth matters as he was instructed to do, was summarily recalled and has returned to Seoul. From this gentleman, Mr. Ye Ha Yong, who was at one time Korean Chargé d'Affaires in Washington, I learn that the killing of these refugees caused intense excitement in Japan and that he fully expected from the many threats he heard and from the attitude of the Japanese Government that Korea would be held to a strict accounting therefor, when the sudden rise to such alarming proportions of the Boxer movement in China caused the Korean incident to sink into insignificance.

Notwithstanding the fright Korea had experienced she still kept on in her mad career of persecution of all suspects in connection with the murder of the Queen in October, 1895. This course became so alarming that Mr. Hayashi, the Japanese Minister, spoke to me upon the subject and asked if I could not induce the Emperor to drop the matter in the interests of the peace of the country. I made the attempt successfully as I informed you in my No. 264, of July 17, 1900, and was heartily thanked by my colleagues.

It now appears however that the assurances I obtained were a mere blind, for the appointment as Minister Plenipotentiary to Japan of Chyo Pyung Sik is officially announced. This corrupt and inhuman official has been the subject of frequent despatches from me to the Department, notably No. 125, of July 18, 1898. I now hear privately that he obtained his appointment upon his promise to secure either dead or alive the Korean refugees still remaining in Japan. This information seems to me to be true as it comes from a Korean official who should know. I am told however by Col. Min Sang Ho, the Vice Minister of Commerce and Communication, that the ostensible reason for Mr. Chyo's appointment is in order that he may call upon the various Foreign Representatives in Tokyo and may induce them to approach their Governments with a view to securing an international agreement guaranteeing the independence of Korea. Col. Min was appointed as Secretary to Mr. Chyo and should know whereof he speaks. He is one of the most enlightened Korean officials, was educated in America and is an able young man. He declined the appointment and was relieved. He speaks of this attempt as a farce, but says that the proposition has the support of a special commissioner from Japan to Korea who is reported as being now in Seoul, and says it originated in the rumor that the Foreign Representatives at Tokyo are advising their respective Governments on Far Eastern matters in connection with the current disturbances in China. I hear also that the Secretary of the Japanese Legation at Seoul had a three hours audience with His Majesty a few days since after which he left immediately for Japan.

The impression is gaining ground in Seoul that Korea must come under Japanese influence as a result of the present crisis in China. It is believed also that Japan would not care to court the difficulties that would beset her if she should actually take the peninsula. It would seem to be better for her to content herself with securing an agreement whereby she might maintain a sufficient force in the country to preserve order, which would give her virtually the power of a dictator with the happy illusion of independence still maintained.

If I may judge by recent utterances of Mr. Pavlow, Russian Chargé d'Affairs here, I conclude that something of the kind may be contemplated by Russia in view of her extensive operations in Manchuria which bid fair to occupy all her attention for some time.

I have in my No. 256, of June 6, 1900, and the previous despatches to which that one refers, acquainted you with the negotiations between the Korean Government and Messrs Leigh Hunt and J. Sloat Fassett concerning a loan to be made by these gentlemen, to be secured by the mines of the Imperial Household Department: of the non-alienation promise claimed by the Russians covering these mines, and of Mr. Hunt's negotiations with the Russians looking to the removal of this so claimed promise: which negotiations progressed satisfactorily until Mr. Hunt had been made to more or less commit himself to a recognition of the Russian claims, when negotiations were summarily closed without reason and Mr. Pavlow promptly changed his tone with me and announced that his Government was opposed to the Koreans securing any loan whatsoever. See my No. 228, of February 15, 1900.

The Japanese Legation at Seoul has been for some time supporting a demand for a concession from the Korean Government to a Japanese syndicate for one group of these Household Mines, known as the Chick-san Mines. I have not attempted to interfere with the granting of this concession, though it is for mines now under negotiations with the Americans, for I realize that the grant of these mines invalidates the claim made by the Russians. I am supported in this by Mr. Hunt.

It was reported recently that the concession has been, or was about to be, granted and I hear that Japanese are now actually at work on the property. Learning this I saw Mr. Pavlow and the matter was incidentally mentioned. I asked him if he realized that this grant did away with the so-called Russian claim, and he replied that he did not care if it did: that he had other matters of greater importance on hand in connection with the Chinese situation, and intimated that these Korean matters could be adjusted in the future.

It reminded me of a statement made to me by Mr. de Speyer, former Russian Representative in Seoul, at the time of the sale of the American Seoul-Chemulpo Railway to the Japanese, that it would all come back to Russia in time. See my No. 67, of January 21, 1898.

Evidently the Russians feel that they must acquiesce in letting Japan control Korea for the present, but it seems equally true that they have intentions regarding the peninsula for the future when Russian communications with these parts are perfected. I cite in further evidence of this the extensive purchase recently made by Russia at the new Korean ports, Masampo, Mokpo, and Chenampo, (See my Nos. 81, of March 7, 1898: 245, of April 21, 1900: 250, of May 16, 1900: 257, of June 8, 1900) and the fact that they usually ask for everything desirable in the form of a concession with the apparent intention of giving it up in exchange for a "non-alienation clause" which will prevent the grant to anyone else. See the incident of the Kojay Do island at the harbor of Masampo, in my No. 245, of April 21, 1900.

Matters in Korea itself are not unusually disturbed. His Majesty is evidently extremely desirous of making it plain that he is in full sympathy with the Allied Forces in China, as against the Chinese, and to this end, in addition to the personal telegrams he sent to the Rulers of the Treaty Powers, he sent a consignment of flour, rice and cigarettes to the force at Taku the other day by one of his steamers.

Intelligent Koreans are aware that they are drifting towards Japan however. Official corruption is as common as heretofore and the Emperor seems powerless or indisposed to correct such abuses. He recently at my suggestion called in the secret officials known as "Ussa", see my No. 264, of July 17, and No. 267, of July 22, 1900, and at about the same date he dismissed nine governors at one time for "squeezing", but I am assured this wholesale dismissal was for the purpose of selling the offices to new men and that thus he realized a handsome profit from his act of reform, while the Ussas have been replaced by "Law Officers" who, it is said, will be quite as bad as were the men they have replaced. This being the case the opportunity for Japan to step in will soon be ripe, provided she can do so without danger of immediate complications with Russia.

In view of this, which seems to me inevitable, I regret exceedingly that Americans should seem to be antagonistic to Japan. I refer you to some correspondence I had with the Department regarding unfounded charges unnecessarily made by Mr. Sands to the Japanese Foreign Office last autumn regarding Japanese and the Japanese Minister in Korea, (See my No. 222, of January 5, 1900 and No. 255, of January 30, 1900.) which cannot but have left an unfortunate impression.

Considering the smallness and poverty of this Empire, and compared to the interests of other peoples, Americans are much in the lead in financial interests. We have the extensive and successful gold mines of Messrs Hunt & Fassett: the Electric Company of Messrs Collbran & Bostwick, which is now putting in an eighteen mile extension of their railway line and an extensive electric light plant, as well as being now in negotiation for the loan of sufficient money to Korea to cover the erection of a water-works for which the Company has an agreement covering construction. They also propose loaning American capital for the organization of a Bank for which they have secured a charter and money to erect a handsome building. Furthermore we have one extensive commercial firm doing the largest single importing business in Korea, besides many particularly successful missionaries scattered throughout the country.

Much friction may be caused the operations of these people in the event of Japan becoming all powerful in Korea, for the Japanese deeply resent and openly deny the growing commercial interests of America in Korea. It is my constant endeavor, therefore, to promote a friendly feeling between the two countries and the relations existing between the two Legations are most cordial. There are influences at work, however, which are very disagreeable to the Japanese and of which I may have to report to you in a later despatch.

Horace N Allen

No. 289   Legation of the United States
                                                          Seoul, Korea, October 19, 1900.

Secretary of State

Sir:-

I have the honor to report, as another indication of the influence Japan is exercising in Korea for the moment, that upon the 3d of this month, by the interchange of diplomatic notes, a concession of a fishing monopoly off six districts of the province in which Seoul is situated, was granted to the Japanese by the Korean Government. The Koreans are to enjoy the same rights of fishing off the coasts of Japan, but they are not likely to avail themselves largely of the privilege. Japan acquired the right to fish off the East and South coasts of Korea some years ago.

The grant of the fishing concession and of that of the ginseng, reported in my despatch of August 31 last, No. 275, are thought to be related. The handling of the ginseng, whether it has been by Europeans or Japanese, has always be seriously hampered by thefts of the root by Japanese subjects. The Japanese Minister has promised that these thefts shall be prevented this year and that the entire crop shall be manipulated by the persons who have received the concession.

Horace N Allen

No. 301   Confidential.   Legation of the United States
                                                          Seoul, Korea, November 23, 1900.

Secretary of State

Sir:-

In my despatch No. 282 of September 25th last, and the despatches which preceded it, I mentioned the negotiations between the Americans, Messrs Hunt and Fassett, and Collbran and Bostwick, regarding loans to be made to the Korean Government. I have now the honor to inform you that Baron Shibusawa, President of the First Bank of Japan and of the Seoul-Chemulpo Railway Company, as well as of the syndicate of the Seoul-Fusan Railway, has just made a short visit to Seoul for the ostensible purpose of attending the formal opening of the Seoul-Chemulpo Railway, which took place on the 12th instant, though the road has been in partial operation for over a year and in complete operation since the bridge over the Han river was finished in July last.

Baron Sibusawa's real object in visiting Seoul, however, was known to be in connection with a loan to the Korean Government. I am not yet fully acquainted with the details of the loan negotiations; the Koreans say that a loan of Yen 5.000.000 was effected, but Mr. Hayashi, the Japanese Minister, intimated to me that it was but Yen 1.000.000, secured upon the Custom's revenues. I think the latter is true.

This money is expected to be used in establishing a currency system for Korea, which has long been a pet scheme with Mc Leavy Brown, the Chief Commissioner of Customs, who received an Imperial Decree on October 23, 1899, authorizing him to negotiate a loan for this purpose to the extent of Yen 5.000.000 by pledging the custom's resources. This decree antidates anything bearing on the subject that Americans have received and this Japanese loan will probably prevent the acceptance of a loan upon the Customs from Messrs Collbran and Bostwick for the establishment of a Korean-American Bank. It should not prevent this firm from making a loan for the construction of a system of water-works for the city of Seoul, however, for which they hold an agreement.

I am confidentially informed by the chief eunuch officer of the Palace, that Baron Shibusawa also offered His Majesty a present of Yen 300.000, for which he desired a new concession in connection with the Seoul-Fusan Railway, namely, the right to establish fifty stations on the line of this railway, between Seoul and Fusan, where Japanese citizens to the number of "one hundred households" may reside and carry on business of all kinds including farming. This seems to accord with the so-named "Korean colonization scheme" of the Japanese Government, and as the line of this proposed railway winds through the richest agricultural district of Korea, the presence of these large Japanese communities through this region would give Japan virtually the control of the whole South of Korea. Of course the term "one hundred households" is very elastic and could well be made to cover some thousands of individuals. I do not suppose that any nation but Russia and her immediate followers would seriously object to this plan, which would doubtless work to the preservation of order in Korea, while the "most favored nation clause" would make the provisions operative to the subjects of the other Treaty Powers.

In my No. 290 of October 20th, in writing of the important audience accorded Mr. Pavlow by His Majesty, I mentioned as one of the subjects brought forward by Mr. Pavlow, a recent order for arms and ammunition given through Mr. Brown to English parties. Mr. Pavlow said he supposed this referred simply to an order for twenty six Maxim guns. I am now confidentially informed that it referred to an order for machinery and workmen for an arsenal, the initial cost of which is to be Yen 700.000, which is also to be secured on the Custom's revenues.

I am unable as yet to verify this report which comes to me from Korean sources. If it is true it would seem to be opposed to the proposed international agreement against the importation of such war material into China, since it would be a simple matter to export any such material from Korea into China. I believe also that the proposals of the French Government against the importation of such material into China includes the adjoining countries as well. In this connection I may mention that Mr. Gubbins, H.B.M's Charge d'Affaires during the past few weeks, informed the Korean Government of his Government's intention to prohibit the export of arms to China. This caused some comment at the time, as the other Foreign Representatives could not understand the reasons for his making such an announcement. It may well have been for the purpose of bringing to a settlement the negotiations for the prompt placing of this large order for war materials soon to be prohibited.

Money is very scarce in Korea and salaries have not been paid for over two months. I am now at work upon a report in connection with the recently announced budget of Korea and I will try to arrive at some approximate estimate of the actual revenues of the Empire. It was recently resolved to increase the land tax from Yen 6.00 per measure to Yen 10.00. This increase cannot but cause disorder, as the people already pay all they possibly can. Considerable increase is contemplated in the military expenditure, and a large amount of money is urgently needed to meet the heavy demands due to the extensive work in new roads, improvements and temple buildings upon which His Majesty is engaged. Owing to this great demand for ready money, the proposition of Messrs Hunt and Fassett to loan Yen 5.000.000 on new mining concessions, has again been taken up, and the agent of their Company is now in telegraphic communicaiton with Mr. Hunt in New York on the subject. The chances are favorable for the success of the negotiations, providing Messrs Hunt and Fassett are willing to accept the terms proposed by the Koreans.

Horace N Allen

No. 476   Legation of the United States
                                               Seoul, Korea, June 20th, 1902.

Secretary of State

Sir:-

I have the honor to hand you enclosed an extract from the Kobe Chronicle of June 9th, purporting to be a copy of certain recommendations said to have been made by the Japanese Minister at Seoul, Mr. G. Hayashi, to his Government, relative to measures Japan should adopt in Korea.

He is said to have proposed, with the sanction of the British Minister, that the Japanese and British Governments should decide all important questions for Korea concerning home and foreign affairs; that a loan to Korea should only be made by England, Japan or the United States; that the employment of foreign advisers should be discouraged, and that unity should be promoted between the Korean Court and the Korean Government.

I have spoken to Mr. J. N. Jordan, the British Minister, about this, and he says that there is no truth in the report so far as he is concerned.

Some such proposition seems to be of a timely nature. As I attempted to show in my despatch No 470 of May 31. Confidential, there practically is no government here. The country is exploited for the benefit of the Palace, that is the Emperor and his satellites. Offices are sold to the highest bidder for increasingly high sums, which results in the most awful oppression of the people. This cannot go on much longer without causing a revolt of the people which will call for foreign intervention. Practically the same conditions prevailed in the years immediately prior to 1894, when Chinese influence was paramount and office selling was allowed to procede to excess. This resulted in the Tong Hak uprising, which induced China to send troops to put down the disturbances and thus brought on the Japan-China war.

My Russian colleague, Mr. Pavlow, in talking with me recently on the subject, expressed himself as of the opinion that the country could endure the present condition for one year more, especially as the crop prospects are now improving. He thought that by that time the rapacity of the government in selling offices would so alarm possible purchasers that there would be few if any sales, and the Palace people would loose their revenues while the overtaxed people would be forced by that time to revolt.

Unless some strong power or powers take it upon itself or themselves to compel the Emperor to accept and follow sensible advice, disorder is sure to ensue from the present course, and as the so called Korean Army would be powerless in the face of such a contingency, self protection or the protection of interests will bring about foreign intervention.

                                               Horace N Allen

No. 516   Legation of the United States
                                               Seoul, Korea, October 17, 1902.

Secretary of State

Sir:-

I have the honor to advise you in regard to some little difficulty now being experienced between the Korean Government and the Japanese Authorities in connection with the so-called "Shibusawa Money".

The branch banks of the Japanese banking corporation known as the Dai Ichi Ginko, or First Bank of Japan, do the principal banking business in Korea. Baron Shibusawa is at the head of this banking corporation.

Since Japan adopted a gold standard the old silver one yen pieces have been withdrawn from circulation in Korea, where they had become the standard money. Silver half-dollars were issued in their stead but the amount seems to be insufficient for the demands of trade. One Yen paper money has at times been quite scarce also.

In order to meet the requirements of trade the First Bank decided to issue notes of their own for circulation in Korea alone, to be redeemable in Japanese gold yen at its equivalent, at any of the branches of the First Bank in Korea. It was at first announced that these notes would be for one yen, and it seemed that the issue would work for the convenience of the public. They were to be simply a promise on the part of the bank to pay, and were of the nature of a private obligation.

These notes were put into circulation in May last and met with a ready reception.

Now however, the Dai Ichi Ginko is issuing five and ten yen notes and propose to issue notes of the denomination of twenty yen. This has alarmed the Korean authorities and some foreigners have taken up the matter. The Russian Chargé d'Affaires, ad interim, Mr. Stein, having advised the Korean Government that the Russian subjects in the employ of the Korean Government will not accept these notes in payment for sums due them from their employers.

I had some conversation with the Acting Foreign Minister yesterday, of his own seeking, and later I spoke with Mr. Hayashi Japanese Minister, on the subject.

The Foreign Minister informed me that his Government was very much opposed to the issue of these notes in such large amounts: that they had given no consent for the issue: that they feared they might be suddenly called in and considerable sums be thus left with the ill-informed natives, and that he had asked the Japanese Minister if his Government would guarantee the payment of the notes but he had received a reply in the negative.

Mr. Hayashi informed me that permission to issue the notes had been granted to the Bank by the Japanese Department of Finance: that their issue was a matter of convenience to trade: that the Finance Department of the Japanese Government required the Bank to keep a reserve to the amount of the whole issue at first, but that later on the reserve could be cut down to one half the amount of the issue: that the issue at present was between Yen 150,000 and Yen 160,000, and that the amount of the issue was not yet limited though the Finance Department of Japan might limit it later if they thought best to do so. He explained that as a measure of safety the Japanese Consuls at the Korean ports would be required to make a semi-monthly examination to ascertain if the required reserve was on hand for the redemption of the notes, and that a quarterly statement would be issued showing the number issued and the power of redemption.

The Dai Ichi Ginko has a capital of	Yen	5,000,000
with a reserve of	"	1,000,000
Their profits for the half of last year	"	1,555,245-
After deducting for general expenditures		1,151,254-
they had a net profit for the half year of		403,990-.

The Bank is considered as being the strongest in Japan, and Baron Shibusawa is regarded as the chief financier of that country.

Evidently there is not great chance of loss to the holders of the notes, but the Korean Government is objecting so strongly to the issue that they have instructed the local officials at the ports to refuse to accept the "Shibusawa Money", this has caused a very heated discussion between the Korean Foreign Office and the Japanese Legation, into which the Russian Legation seems to have been drawn by the action of the Chargé d'Affaires ad interim, in announcing that Russians would not accept this money.

Americans are not interested in the discussion so far.

I hand you enclosed a copy of one of the one yen notes in question, unsigned, and a copy of the last obtainable report of the Dai Ichi Ginko.

Horace N Allen

No. 580

Legation of the United States
Seoul, Korea, February 13, 1903.

Secretary of State

Sir:-

Continuing the subject of my despatch No. 575, of the 8'th, instant, regarding reprisals about to made upon Korea by the Japanese Government because of the action of the former in opposition to the "Sibusawa Notes", I now have the honor to inform you that Mr. Hagiwara, the Japanese Charge d'Affaires ad interim, told me last evening that the matter had been satisfactorily settled, by the Minister for Foreign Affairs, at the order of the Emperor, giving him on yesterday, in the presence of Mr. Jordan, the British Minister, a solemn promise that the violent proclamation of the Governor of Seoul - mentioned in my No. 575 - would be replaced by one instructing the people to freely receive and use these notes; that this proclamation should also be made at the ports, and that the letter of the former Minister for Foreign Affairs withdrawing objections to the issue of these notes, should be published as the fixed policy of the Government. This letter is the one of which I wrote you in my despatch No. 571 of the 2'nd. instant. It was said to have been obtained by questionable means and in consequence thereof the Minister for Foreign Affairs and his Vice Minister, were dismissed from office.

Mr. Hayashi, the Japanese Minister, was due two days ago on the Cruiser "Takasago" but as the latter was delayed to "take on heavy material", he is not due to arrive until today.

A significant incident in conection with this affair is the unwarranted action of the Seoul-Chemulpo Railway Company in laying down a temporary track over the bund road of the Municipality of Chemulpo, for the purpose of "landing heavy material". The Company will doubtless apologize for having taken this action without first asking permission. At the time of the Japan-China war, in 1894, the rights of the International Settlement were disregarded by the Japanese. Evidently the Japanese were found to be in earnest regarding the matter of reprisals, hence the prompt settlement made by the Koreans.

Mr. Hagiwara told me that he considered Ye Yong Ik as the prime mover in this opposition to the notes and he felt sure he had the support of the Russians. He said that as Ye was still bent on an extensive banking scheme - which I explained in my No. 567 of January 22 - he did not consider the present matter entirely closed. He also told me that the Russians were conducting some very secret negotiations through Ye Yong Ik, in regard to the southern port Masampo. I have heard no inkling of any such negotiations and from all I can learn the Russians seem to be very well satisfied with what they now have there, especially since they obtained the non-alienation agreement mentioned in my No. 525, Nov. 6/02.

Horace N. Allen.

No. 589   Confidential.   Legation of the United States
                                       Seoul, Korea, March 18, 1903.

Secretary of State,

Sir:-

Continuing the subject of my despatch No. 588, of the 15'th. instant, it now seems probable that the Japanese will arrange with Ye Yong Ik to establish a Korean bank and issue a paper currency, in connection with the First Bank of Japan, which now has branches in Seoul and the open ports of Korea. This banking and currency scheme has long been a pet project of Ye Yong Ik, and it was for that purpose that he desired to make a loan from Belgium. The loan having failed of completion, Ye seems now to have gone over to the Japanese with his project. He is said to have ¥3,000,000 now on hand, and ¥2,000,000 in sight, though the salaries of Korean officials have not been paid for the past two months. If he turns this fund over to the First Bank, - Dai Ichi Ginko - and uses the Shibusawa notes as his paper currency, it will probably be a successful enterprise and work for the betterment of commercial interests in Korea. At the same time, it will place Korea very much in the hands of the Japanese, who have of late assumed a much more agressive attitude here than formerly.

The Russians are showing much evidence of concern over this new departure, and Mr. C. de Weaber, Special Envoy from Russia, leaves for Port Arthur tomorrow to confer with Governor Alexeieff.

Horace N. Allen

B. Attempts to Secure an International Guarantee of Independence

No. 278   Legation of the United States
                                    Seoul, Korea, September 10, 1900.

Secretary of State

Sir:-

Referring to my confidential despatch No. 275 of August 31, I have now the honor to inform you that His Majesty the Emperor of Korea sent a confidential message to me through Colonel Min Sang Ho, who appears to head the pro-American party at Court since the death of Ye (part of the name is missing) Yun, late Governor of Seoul, to the effect that, though he had instructed his Minister in Tokyo, Mr. Chyo Pyung Sik, to do nothing regarding the matter of an international guarantee of Korean independence, the latter had telegraphed him that Japan was willing to take up and propose it providing Korea would establish a standing army of 50.000 men. Chyo said he replied to this proposition that the revenues of Korea would not admit of the increase unless the land-tax was doubled, and the Japanese Minister of Foreign Affairs answered that the means "would be provided".

I was asked for my opinion and replied that as the present revenues were insufficient for the expenses of the Government I did not see how Korea could contemplate any such great increase in her budget, while a doubling of the already burdensome taxes would certainly result in internal disorders of a serious nature. I was thereupon told that the French Acting Chargé d'Affaires M. Lefevre, had suggested that the question be laid before the Russian Representative and I was asked my opinion as to whether or not this was advisable.

I replied that I could not advise His Majesty as to that matter. The question of an international guarantee of the independence of the country was one that would have to come before all the Powers interested; I could not understand therefore, why it should be kept from any of the Foreign Representatives at Seoul. It was decided apparently that the question was one the settlement of which immediately was not of vital importance and I believe it was determined that the matter should be held in abeyance for the time being.

You will remember that this proposition for an international guarantee came from the Japanese themselves and that Mr. Chyo was sent to Tokyo upon the suggestion of the Japanese officials here. This condition as to a large standing army seems therefore to be a somewhat suspicious one to be brought up at this time.

Horace N Allen

No. 284

Legation of the United States
Seoul, Korea, October 2, 1900.

Secretary of State

Sir:
In my despatches No. 272 of August 23, page 3, and No. 275 of August 31, page 2, I explained the mission of the newly appointed Korean representative to Japan, Chyo Pyung Sik, which had in view the securing of an international guarantee of the independence of Korea, which was to be obtained through the intervention of Japan. In my No. 275 of September 10, I informed you of the condition made by Japan calling for the establishment of a standing army of fifty thousand men by Korea, and in No. 282 of September 25, page 5, I informed you that it seemed probable that His Majesty would accept a Japanese loan of Yen ten million for the purpose of establishing this military force.

I have now the honor to inform you that these projects appear to have fallen through.

M. Pavlow, the Russian Chargé d'Affaires, has been more active than usual of late and has had one or more long private audiences with His Majesty. As an apparent result of this increased activity the officials who have been most prominent in promoting Japanese influence are reported as being much more cautious than they were, while the matter of the loan seems to have been dropped, accordig to unofficial reports that come to me from the Palace.

In this connection I may add that on yesterday His Majesty informed me through a chamberlain, who was specially sent, that Chyo Pyung Sik was about to return to Seoul from Tokyo and that three days ago Mr. Chyo had telegraphed that The American Minister at Tokyo had told him it would be impossible for him to get this guarantee through the Japanese Government, but that it would be much better for the United States to propose it, and that as he (the American Minister) was about to return to the United States on leave, he would agree to speak to the President about it." I hand you enclosed a copy of a letter regarding this communication I have sent to Mr. Buck.

If the rumor is true -- and it appears to be implicitly believed in the Palace, so that any injury that might be done has already practically resulted by the raising of hopes that bid fair not to be realized -- I think it a thing to be seriously regretted. Such an international guarantee as would protect the Koreans from all outside interference and allow them to "stew in their own juice", has long been a cherished object of the present Ruler. He has repeatedly suggested that the United States should propose something of the kind to the other Powers. My predecessors and myself have always avoided allowing the matter to come to an official request and have been able to put it aside without giving offense. Before leaving for America in the Spring of 1899, at an imformal interview accorded me, His Majesty called my attention to a newspaper report to the effect that Mr. Conger had announced that the United States "Would maintain the integrity of China", and asked that I obtain a promise of the same kind for Korea. I very strongly expressed my disbelief in the truth of the statement made by the newspaper, but agreed to speak to the President upon the subject. It was for this reason that I went to Lake Champlain, where I had the honor of mentioning the matter to President McKinley and yourself. You assured me promptly that there was nothing in the report and the President heard me patiently and told me to make a negative reply in suitable form. Fortuitous circumstances enabled me to do this on my return in such a manner as to leave a pleasant impression and to cause no ill feeling or injury to American interests. Having quieted the matter in this way I regret that it should be raised again unnecessarily lest failure may cause injury to the growing American interests I have to protect here.

I assume of course that our Government would not care to take upon itself such complicating negotiations, which would almost necessarily compel the sponsor to see that such an agreement was carried out even to the probable necessity of an exhibition of force.

Horace N Allen

No. 286   Legation of the United States
                                                                          Seoul, Korea, October 9, 1900.

Secretary of State

Sir:-

Referring to my No. 284 of October 2, regarding the impression that Koreans have obtained from United States Minister Buck of Tokyo, that the United States might undertake to secure an international guarantee covering the independence and neutrality of Korea, I have now the honor to report that I received a visit on yesterday from M. Pavlow, the Russian Chargé d'Affaires here, who asked me whether the United States had any such intention. He explained that he inquired in order that he might report to his Government whether or not this action was contemplated by the Government of the United States and what he considered the gravity of the proposition and how he believed it could but work to the discredit and injury of Korea by removing from her the restraining fear that now serves as some slight check upon her unruly tendencies. He explained further that he had received telegraphic advices from the Russian Minister in Tokyo, who had mentioned the matter of neutrality to Mr. Buck and who had been informed by the latter that he had said simply "any such thing would have to be decided in Washington". M. Pavlow affirmed, however, that the Koreans appeared confident of the assistance Chyo Pyung Sik had led them to believe would be rendered by the United States.

In reply I stated that I knew absolutely nothing about the affair except that a chamberlain had called on me and reported it without asking my opinion. I had not telegraphed Mr. Buck as I could not fully explain the incident by telegraph and as I was able to catch an early steamer with a letter, to which I expected shortly to receive a reply. I added that I felt confident that the remark attributed to Mr. Buck was merely an off hand one and that I had no information to lead me to believe that my Government would ever consider the matter of neutrality; that the proposition was not a new one but had been proposed frequently to my predecessors as well as to myself and that we had always tried to discourage it and to prevent its coming to an official request.

M. Pavlow seemed much relieved to find that I had no information on the subject. He told me he had reason to believe that it was part of a plan arranged by the Japanese (of which the newspaper rumor that Russia and Japan intended to divide Korea, mentioned in my No. 280 of September 12, was a part), and that Japan had hoped to obtain an agreement with Korea whereby she should consent to allow Japan to preserve Korean neutrality with a large Korean army under Japanese control.

I hand you enclosed a copy of a letter I have sent Mr. Buck.

Horace N Allen

No. 287

Legation of the United States
Seoul, Korea, October 11, 1900.

Secretary of State

Sir:-

Referring to my No. 286 of October 9, regarding assistance expected by the Korean Government from the United States Government in securing an international agreement covering the neutrality of Korea, I have now the honor to hand you enclosed a copy of a letter I have received on yesterday from Minister Buck upon the subject, dated October 1, the date on which His Majesty telegraphed his minister in Tokyo, Chyo Pyung Sik, to accept Mr. Buck's reported offer of assistance. This letter is in reply to one from me, dated August 25, informing Mr. Buck of the appointment and reported mission of Mr. Chyo.

Mr. Buck states in his answer that he gave Mr. Chyo

"no assurance that I would take the matter up with the State Department and while expressing my kind feeling and that of the United States toward Korea, I gave him to understand that it would not be proper for me to do so: suggesting that, if the Korean Government desired to accomplish the ends he had in view, it could approach my Government on the subject through its representative in Washington"

Evidently Mr. Buck's reply was not properly interpreted and Mr. Chyo's desires may have led him to accept the translation most agreeable to himself. I shall make use of this statement from Mr. Buck upon the first opportunity and shall endeavor to correct the impression given out by Mr. Chyo with as little annoyance to the Court as possible.

Mr. Chyo informed Mr. Buck that he did not mention the matter to me for the reason that I was "absent when he left". The fact is that the matter was kept a great secret and I only learned it incidently through Col. Min Sang Ho, who declined to accompany Mr. Chyo as Secretary. I have not been absent from my post. I have spent the Summer at Chemulpo, twenty five miles distant by rail, with telegraphic and telephonic connection. I have been at the Legation office as often as necessry and have always been ready to go when it seemed at all desireable. Mr. Chyo did not wish to consult with me and evidently merely jumped at the proposition to lay the blame of the refusal of assistance in this matter on the United States, when he found he could not succeed with Japan except at too great a cost.

Horace N. Allen.

Copy of a letter from Minister Buck at Tokyo to Minister Horace N. Allen at Seoul, Korea.

No. 479.

United States Legation,
Tokyo, October 1, 1900.

Hon. H. N. Allen,
United States Minister, Seoul, Korea.

Sir:-

Referring to your official communication respecting the appointment Chyo Pyung Sik who has recently come to Tokyo as the Korean representative to Japan, who would attempt to accomplish certain ends, among which you mention was to secure through the co-operation of the Foreign Representatives here from their respective Governments some international agreement by which Korea might be assured of independence and immunity from aggression, I desire to state that he has visited me among others and expressed his desire on that subject. It seems that he wishes that Korea be regarded as neutral and inviolate territory like Switzerland : that a guarrantee of all the great Powers may be given of independence and security from all invasion or interference. He has solicited my efforts in that direction, as I understand he has others. Of course I could give him no assurance that I would take the matter up with the State Department and while expressing my kind feeling and that of the United States towards Korea, I gave him to understand that it would not be proper for me to do so : suggesting that, if the Korean government desired to accomplish the ends he had in view, it could approach my Government on the subject through its representative in Washington. On asking him if he had seen you respecting this matter, he said he had not, as you were absent when he left.

Mr. Chyo seems to be a bright, active old man. He appears to be in great fear of future troubles between Japan and China, and that Japan has a purpose to absorb Korea, and of trouble soon between Japan and Russia.

I am a little interested to know who is this Chyo and what his standing and consequence is in Korea : also whether he has been sent to reside here as the representative of his country, or specially sent for the purpose you indicate, to remain temporarily only.

Anything you can give me on these maters will be appreciated.

(signed) A.E. Buck.

No. 290   Legation of the United States
                                                     Seoul, Korea, October 20, 1900.

Secretary of State

Sir:-

Referring to my No. 287 of October 11, regarding the matter of an international guarantee covering the independence of Korea, I have the honor to inform you that Mr. Pavlow, the Russian Chargé d'Affaires, had an audience with the Emperor of Korea last evening at which this matter was discussed.

Shortly after the audience His Majesty sent a confidential message to me by Col. Min San Ho, Chief of the Bureau of Communications, who gave me the following account. Mr. Pavlow is said to have told His Majesty that he had heard of the mission of Chyo Pyung Sik through the Russian Minister in Tokyo: that he had telegraphed the information to St. Petersburg and the Czar had instructed the Russian Foreign Minister to telegraph him instructions to see His Majesty at once and explain to him that under no circumstances would Russia consent to any diplomatic or political arrangements between Korea and other powers that were not first submitted to Russia: that any proposed political changes must first be submitted to the Russia Government, for which reason His Majesty should call him (Pavlow) frequently to the Palace and advise with him fully and frankly: that Russia was the only real friend of Korea and the only one that stood ready to come forward and protect her: that Japan was simply talking and attempting to put through underhand tricks that would eventually injure Korea, and that the American Government was now playing with the Japanese Government and anything proposed to or through the United States would be the same as though it were proposed directly to Japan: that Japan was protecting the Korean refugees, who were plotting against the Korean throne, and that the next place of refuge for these traitors would be the United States.

He demanded of the Emperor also, who had by this time become seriously alarmed, whether or not it were true that Korea was buying arms and ammunition through McLeavy Brown, the Chief Commissioner of Korean Customs. His Majesty admitted that it was true and Mr. Pavlow demanded copies of the contracts, for which he was referred to the War Department. His next demand was that Kim Yong Chun be continued permanently in charge of the Finance Department -- a position he has held temporarily during the absence of Mr. Chyo Pyung Sik. This official is the one mentioned in my despatch No. 229 of February 16, 1900, and who appears to have made successful overtures to Russia.

I have no doubt of the truth of this report. It came to me at once, presumably because of the assistance Mr. Chyo promised would be granted by the United States in securing the proposed neutrality agreement. Mr. Pavlow may have received some word from his Government, but I am inclined to think, from what I know of him, that he made the most of any instructions he may have had. In my No. 286 of October 9, I informed you of Mr. Pavlow's visit to me on the 8th instant, during which he asked me and for his Government if the United States Government had proposed to act in regard to the neutralization matter.

I feel sure that a report similar to the one brought me has been, or will be made to my Japanese colleague and may lead to inquiries of the St. Petersburg Government. I had already sent His Majesty the substance of the information contained in Mr. Buck's letter, of which I sent you a copy in my despatch No. 287 of October 11, and I took occasion to express it as my opinion that Mr. Chyo had telegraphed regarding Mr. Buck's reported proposals as the result of a faulty interpretation of an ordinary social conversation.

The information contained in this despatch came to me confidentially, as you will see, but as the Korean Foreign Minister was present at Mr. Pavlow's audience I suggested that he inform me of the matter officially so that I could publicly inform my Government.

Horace N Allen

No. 292   Legation of the United States
                                                                   Seoul, Korea, October 29, 1900.

Secretary of State

Sir:-

Referring to my Nos. 284, 286, 287, 290 and 291 of October 2, 9, 11, 20 and 24 instants, regarding the subject of the proposed scheme for the neutralization of Korea, I have now the honor to inform you that this incident is practically closed, owing to the demands of Japan in connection therewith, as well as to the opposition of Russia as mentioned in my despatch No. 290 of October 20, relating the main points of an interview between the Korean Emperor and the Russian Chargé d,Affaires.

Mr. Chyo Pyung Sik has returned from his mission to Japan quite disheartened by his failure either to secure the extradition of the Korean refugees there or to obtain the voluntarily proposed assistance of Japan in securing the desired neutralization guarantee. See my despatch Nos. 272 and 275 of August 23 and 31 last, announcing Mr. Chyo's departure and mission. The Japanese newspapers stated that Mr. Chyo had been recalled in consequence of certain cabinet changes being made here and that he would be given the office of Premier. The cabinet changes were not of sufficient importance to report and instead of Chyo being given the post of Premier he is for the time being out of active official life.

The interview between His Majesty and Mr. Pavlow, described in the above cited despatch No. 290 of the 20th instant, has assumed greater importance than the mission of Mr. Chyo. In accordance with my request that the communication regarding the same be made to me by the Foreign Minister without any charge of secrecy, His Majesty ordered a council to decide if this should be done. It was decided that a draft of the conversation should be made, submitted to Mr. Pavlow for approval, and then a copy should be given to each of the Foreign Representatives. When the draft was submitted to Mr. Pavlow, however, he is said to have announced that it was entirely wrong owing to misinterpretation. He had at the audience nevertheless his own interpreter who is a native Korean naturalized in Russia. I do not know what other communications passed on the subject, but I do know that when my German colleague Dr. Weipert, (who had heard of this matter from the Japanese Minister) asked the Minister for Foreign Affairs as to the matters discussed in his presence at the audience of Mr. Pavlow, the Foreign Minister firmly denied that anything of importance was discussed and proceeded to deny each subject specially. You will have noted from reading my despatch No. 291 of October 24th that Mr. Pavlow was apparently very desirous of convincing me of the unimportance of his remarks at the audience in question. Evidently the interview had an effect opposite to that he had intended. One indication of this result is that the man Kim Yung Chun, whom Mr. Pavlow was stated as having proposed at the audience as permanent Finance Minister, has since been dismissed from office entirely and is for the time out of favor, presumably because of his supposed intimate relations with the Russian Legation.

While Mr. Pavlow seems to have gone too far in this instance, yet his refuted declarations at that interview will have an effect in the direction he appears to have desired, for the question of the neutrality of Korea will probably not come up soon again, and His Majesty will have in mind the fact that Russia is prepared to object to changes which she has not first approved, even if the objections have to be modified later.

There seems still to be some probability that Japan may make a private loan to Korea for the purpose of increasing the Korean army, which will in that case presumably come under Japanese control more or less openly. This proposition was a result ot the neutralization suggestion and was probably had in mind by the Japanese when they are said to have proposed the mission of Mr. Chyo in connection with the neutralization scheme.

Horace N. Allen.

C. Treatment of Korean Refugees

No. 122

Legation of the United States
Seoul Korea, July 11, 1898.

Secretary of State

Sir:-

I have the honor to inform you that there is much excitement in Seoul at present over a reported attempt to overturn the Government and cause the abdication of the Emperor. The name of Prince Pak Yong Hio is connected with this conspiracy. It is supposed that he intends to attempt to place on the throne, Prince Wui Wha, who has recently returned to Japan from a year's absence at a school in Washington.

Prince Pak Yong Hio has been a refugee in Japan most of the time during the past fourteen years, since his connection with the bloody emeute of 1884. He was brought back to Korea by the Japanese after the Japan-China war, and forced into high office. He did well and seemed to have the best interests of his country at heart. He fled to Japan again, however, after the flight of His Majesty to the Russian Legation in February 1896. I believe he went to America during his present exile. He is now reported to be on his way back to Korea from Japan, in company with Prince Wui Wha.

A number of arrests were made night before last in connection with this reported conspiracy. Chief among those arrested are, Kim Chai Pung, Ex. Police Inspector; Ye Chung Goo, also an Ex. Inspector of Police, and Kim Chai Un, a Colonel in the Korean Army. General An Kyung Soo has taken refuge in the Japanese Settlement at Seoul.

The last named gentleman is one of the wealthiest, most influential and enlightened of Korea's prominent officials. He has been General of the Army: Cabinet Minister and Governor of a province. Of late he has been prominent in the deliberations of the Independence Club. Most people are surprised at the connection of his name with the present reported conspiracy, and it is thought that his flight was more a measure of precaution than a confession of guilt. For no matter how innocent a man may be, it is too often the case that Korean justice is only meted out to such suspects after they have been summarily dealt with, and are unable to profit by an acquital.

General An has had much experience in such matters, having once been paraded through the streets of Seoul with a cangue about his neck, and barely escaped with his life, to be promoted to very high rank shortly after.

It is pretty generally believed that this reported conspiracy is but the concoction of some mischief making Koreans who have hopes of gain to themselves through the resulting disturbance. The effects however, may be quite as serious as they would be if the matter was founded entirely upon fact.

Horace N. Allen.

No. 228

Legation of the United States
Seoul Korea, February 15, 1900.

Secretary of State

Sir:-

Referring to my No. 214, Nov. 18, 1899, Confidential, I now have the honor to inform you that the Representatives of Russia and Japan therein mentioned, have each returned from leaves of absence in their respective countries. They met and had a conference in Tokio, moreover, the object and result of which is unknown to me, but may have been communicated to you by Minister Buck.

Mr. Pavloff, Russian Chargé d'Affaires, remained two weeks in Seoul before seeing His Majesty. His audience took place on the 12'th. instant and lasted for two hours. I am informed that he used very strong language in demanding that the matter of the purchase of ground at Masampo by Japanese, which ground he had selected as a reserve for Russia, be cancelled. See above cited despatch.

In the meantime, Mr. Hayashi, Japanese Envoy Extraordinary and Minister Plenipotentiary, has brought back to Korea General An Kyung Soo, a Korean who has been for two years a refugee in Japan because of his alleged connection with a plot to overturn this Government and place a new ruler on the throne. See my No. 122, July 11, 1898.

An armed Japanese is said to remain in the prison with General An, and at his audience, Mr. Hayashi secured a promise from the Emperor that General An would have a fair trial and that torture would not be used.

It is expected that the trial will not amount to much and that this protegee of Japan will be soon relieved of all charges against him and be given high rank. He will, in that case, be a very powerful personage here and it is a great coup for Japan. It is further supposed that the favorable result expected from this trial, under Japanese auspices, will induce the numerous other Korean refugees now in Japan, to return to their country and assume more or less control of affairs. While this may not be a good thing for Russian designs, it cannot be bad for Korea, since these men, however misguided they may have been, are enlightened and in favor of progress, they are more of the nature of patriots than most Koreans and while they should of course be especially favorable to the Japanese, I know that quite a number of them are most favorable to the United States, so that American interests will probably not suffer from their return.

In my No. 214, above cited, I mentioned the matter of the loan and mining concession of Messrs Fassett and Hunt, which was prevented of consummation by a foolish promise previously made by the Koreans to the Russians, but which it was expected would be waived in favor of the Americans for a consideration. I informed you that Mr. Hunt was en route to St. Petersburg on a mission to arrange for the removal or purchase of the Russian claim. When in Paris on the 9'th. instant, he telegraphed his agent here that negotiations were broken off and intimated duplicity on the part of the Russians and the international complications, as the cause.

Just prior to receiving this word I had had some conversation with Mr. Pavloff and was greatly surprised to find that his attitude was entirely changed. Instead of favoring the American proposition he bluntly stated that he was opposed to Korea's obtaining a loan from anyone and he said he thought his Government would view the matter in the same light.

I had experienced much difficulty in keeping off certain Englishmen who with Japanese support, were trying in an unfair and underhanded manner to secure this particular concession while Messrs Hunt and Fassett were away attending to negotiation thereupon, and having succeeded in that mattter in a fair and open manner, it is discouraging to find Russia acting in this trully "dog in the manger" manner. As it stands the Russians have a foolish promise from the Koreans that while they will not let the Russian applicant have the concession in question, they will not give it to any other foreigner than Russian. This concession covers all the mines of the Household Department, which practically includes all the known mines of every description in Korea, therefore this promise if adhered to will effectually prevent the development of the very rich mineral resources of this peninsula, for the Koreans cannot do the work themselves and they will not give it over the the Russians.

The demand for mining concessions in Korea is so very great that some new arrangement will probably have to be made offsetting this promise. In the meantime the Japanese have applied for five mining districts covered by this promise; the Germans and English have each applied for a new district in addition to what they have, and the English firm, Pritchard-Morgan & Co. on direct advices from Lord Salisbury, have forcibly taken the richest one of these Household Mining districts by virtue of a concession given before the promise was made to Russia. This was against Russian instructions - (very strong advice).

Horace N. Allen.

No. 252

Legation of the United States
Seoul, Korea, May 30, 1900.

Secretary of State

Sir:-

I have the honor to hand you enclosed confirmation of my telegram of yesterday regarding the sudden conviction and hanging of the Koreans who had been political refugees in Japan until their recent return to Korea. My reason for incurring the expense of this telegram is that the matter bids fair to lead to serious international difficulties.

By reference to my despatch No. 228, of February 15 last, you will see that one of these refugees, General An Kyung Soo, was recently brought to Korea from Japan, upon a guarantee of the Emperor of Korea given personally to the Japanese Minister, Mr. Hayashi, that An would have a fair trial and not be tortured. My letter of July 11, 1898, No. 122, fully explains the trivial nature of the charge against General An. During his trial he confessed to having been favorable to the plan of retiring the Emperor and having the Crown Prince rule, but disclaimed any desire to use violence in attaining this object, as he had expected to accomplish the change by persuading the Emperor to consent to it in the interests of the empire.

In my No. 250, of May 16, 1900, I informed you of the arrival of another of these refugees from Japan, a man named Kwan, who was a police commissioner at the time of the murder of the Queen, October 8, 1895, This man confessed that he knew of the events of that date, but that he was not guilty of complicity in the murder. It was reported that an armed Japanese remained in the prison with General An. This man proved to be a Korean dressed as a Japanese, however, and he was removed.

About a week ago the Japanese Minister, Mr. Hayashi, was reported to have sent a suggestion to the Emperor that he call back the second Prince, Wui Wha, who is also a refugee in Japan. See above cited letter, No. 122. This convinced the Koreans that the return of these refugees was part of a general plan of the Japanese to secure control of the Korean Government through these men of pro-Japanese sympathies. As a result it became evident that the two refugees in prison in Seoul were to be examined very strictly. On the 25th instant it was reported that General An had died in the court room the evening before, as the result of severe torture applied. I looked up this rumor and learned that he had merely fainted and lost consciousness for a time owing to threats of torture and the bringing before him of the appliances for torture, as though they were about to be applied.

Mr. Pavlow, the Russian Chargé d'Affaires, left suddenly for Port Arthur on a gunboat, upon the 25th. I merely mention this as a coincidence, not that I have any reason for thinking Mr. Pavlow had anything to do with this case, although he cannot have regarded the return of these refugees under Japanese protection with favor. On Sunday the 27th, these men were again tried before the Commissioner of Police as Chief Judge. The interpreter of the French Legation and a young and insignificant English-speaking Korean, named Chang Bong Whan, acted as Associate Judges. The last named was at one time Secretary of the Korean Legation at Washington. At four P.M., Sunday the 27th, the two refugees were found guilty of treason and they were hung to death that night. The Korean law requires that the verdict and sentence in such cases be read to His Majesty and receive his sanction before the execution takes place, unless there seems to be danger of the men escaping or being rescued, under which circumstances the execution may take place without being referred to him. It is claimed that this course was followed in this case, and the Chief Judge has placarded the city with a notice to the effect that he and his Associated Judges ordered this execution without the Emperor's knowledge. See enclosure No. 2. No one will believe this, however, for one of the curses of this country is the practice of referring everything to His Majesty, however trivial it may be, so that it is impossible for anything of this kind to be done without His Majesty's knowledge. In support of the theory of ignorance on his part, he has sentenced the Judges to banishment, but the Council of State has presented a very strong memorial against such action and the order of banishment may be recalled.

The Japanese Minister on hearing that torture was being applied to these men in violation of the agreement between the Emperor and himself, attempted in vain to obtain an audience on the 26th and 27th instants, and his attempts were supposed to have hastened the end, since it was feared he would try to rescue the men. I was told by the Governor of Seoul that the soldier who conveyed the prisoners from the Court to the jail and superintended the execution had orders to shoot any foreigners who should attempt to interfere with them. I also heard from the same source that within a half hour of the execution, a large party of Japanese in civilian dress broke into the prison to rescue the men, but were too late. Mr. Sands, the American advisor to the Korean Household Department, had the bodies of the executed men examined, but found upon them no traces of torture having been applied. I hear that Mr. Hayashi is taking vigorous measures in view of the violation of the Emperor's agreement that torture should not be applied. The Koreans hope to prove that torture was not applied and that a fair trial was had and that they were justified in the hasty execution.

It seems probable that serious difficulty will result from this action. The Japanese influence has been growing more and more strong of late, but this will almost entirely break it down, since no Korean official will care to work with or for them when it is shown that they can offer no better protection than was afforded to these men who returned to Korea under assurance of ample security from the Japanese. Japan will have to assert herself most forcibly and at once, or "lose face" and see the Koreans go over to the Russians once more.

In view of all this I thought it best to send you the facts by telegraph, as everthing points to serious and immediate international complications. The Japanese happen to have a considerable force of soldiers here just now. One guard is leaving and its relief has just arrived, making seven hundred and fifty regular soldiers in all, with a very large staff of officers. Large numbers of Japanese so called "railroad coolies" have been arriving during the past month. These men, whether disguised soldiers, as is reported, or not, are good material out of which to compose a military force in connection with regulars already here. It is supposed that in this way a force of some three thousand could easily be organized, and as they are present in Seoul, a disturbance in the city would permit their use for the protection of Japanese interests, without directly violating the agreement of non-interference between Japan and Russia.

Horace N Allen

Translation of the Proclamation of the Judges, issued on the morning of May 28, 1900, in which His Majesty is exonerated from all blame for the execution of the refugees from Japan.

A Proclamation.

How can there be any one in the world who does not call for vengence for the murder of his mother while he is her child!

There is no dynasty where there are not traitors. But alas! As to the trouble of the year Ul Mi -- (1895, that of the murder of the Queen) -- it was such a terrible and outrageous one that the like of it was never heard of in the olden time, under the Heavens and upon the Earth. The people of this country, subjects and children of His Majesty, who could not die with her on that day when she was murdered, still grope along with the thread of life, and when they look toward Hong Nung -- (the Queen's tomb) -- their eyes are filled with bloody tears, which obscure the light of the sun and cause even the grass and trees to have a sad and sober appearance.

Now the arch trators, An Kyung Soo and Kwan Yung Chin, dared to return to this country fearlessly. They confessed to the crimes they had committed, and they were to be executed according to the provisions of law, but if they should be executed in the regular manner it would cause delay, and we cannot bear to stand with them under the same heaven even for one or two days. Angry blood is boiling in our veins and we ourselves hung them before the matter was referred to His Majesty

In this manner we inform the soul of Her Majesty in Heaven, and condole with our brothers in this country below.

No. 255   Legation of the United States
                                                 Seoul Korea, June 4, 1900.

Secretary of State

Sir:-
Referring to my No. 252, of May 30, regarding the trial and execution of two refugees recently returned from Japan, I have the honor to inform you that the Japanese seem to have developed a very surprising weakness regarding that mater. The Japanese Minister Mr. Hayashi seems to confine his efforts to an attempt to secure an official acknowledgment that torture had been applied to these men. Two of his phisicians who reported upon the case declared that torture had been used, while three other physicians of high repute, namely a Russian, an English, and an American physician each declared that the bodies showed no signs of the application of torture. Torture evidently was not resorted to and the Koreans stick to that one charge, upon which they are safe. Mr. Hayashi has tried to obtain an audience with the Emperor of Korea, but in vain. He is said to have used very strong language to the Korean Minister for Foreign Affairs and to have accused His Majesty of falsehood and of breaking his promise to him that no torture would be used upon Gen'l An Kyung Soo. At last he is reported as having asked an audience because of telegraphic instructions he had received from his Government, whereupon the Korean Government telegraphed to its minister at Tokio that no audience could be granted to Mr. Hayashi because he had insulted the person of His Majesty by accusing him of falsehood and breach of faith. I am told that then Mr. Hayashi approached the Foreign Minister in a most conciliatory manner and tried to induce him to officially admit that torture had been applied as that would end the matter once and for all. His prayer was denied.

The whole matter is most unfortunate. Public men in Japan such as Count Inouye, have announced in public that it would be a mistake to return these refugees to Korea under the present Government as it would only cause trouble and excitement, they were however returned and the responsibility must lie with the Japanese Government under whose protection they lived and moved about.

They were under strict police surveillance all the time and could not have returned without permission. General An actually returned either with or about the time Mr. Hayashi returned from a hurried trip to Tokio at the beginning of the year. If the latter had a plan in bringing An back, he was mistaken in contenting himself with the mere promise that torture would not be used.

It is one of those blunders so common to Japan in her dealings with Korea. She has now the contempt of the Koreans, who having had a taste of blood, are anxious to get back the other refugees to treat them in the same manner. Russia has scored heavily in the matter, while the Koreans themselves will be harder to deal with than they were before.

As an act of propitiation, the Judges who sentenced the men, were banished one day and allowed to come quietly back to the city the next day. The whole thing was a grand farce and a most violent affront to Japan. When I cabled you the facts I could not suppose that the Japanese would take the matter so mildly.

Horace N Allen

No. 260   Legation of the United States
                                                           Seoul, Korea, June 15, 1900.

Secretary of State

Sir:-

Continuing the subject of my despatches numbered 252 of May 30, 255 of June 4, and 258 of June 8 last, regarding the killing of the refugees An and Kuan, I have now the honor to inform you that that matter appears to be settled at least for the present.

By enclosed extracts from the "Japan Daily Mail", of June 4 and 8, you will see that Mr. Hayashi seems to be blamed for his handling of this matter. I also enclose another extract from the same newspaper, of June 9, treating editorially of the refusal of the Korean Government to grant the Japanese Minister an audience. When matters seemed to have reached a critical stage because of this refusal, Mr. Pavlow, the Russian Chargé d'Affaires, called upon the Korean Foreign Minister and told him that he had better grant Mr. Hayashi an audience and asked for one for himself. The Foreign Minister then saw Mr. Hayashi and informed him he would have to grant the audience but that he much preferred that the latter should apologize for his charge that torture had been used in trying the two refugees and that such was a breach of faith on the part of His Majesty, as they could then grant the audience upon that ground rather than upon the request of the Russian representative. The Foreign Minister informed my interpreter that some sort of apology, either real or implied, had been made, though I am not certain as to its exact character. The audience was therefore accorded on the 14th instant, after Mr. Pavlow had had a long and confidential one the day before. I am told from the Palace that Mr. Pavlow claimed credit for arranging this difficult matter satisfactorily and also that he complained of a "Secretary of a Foreign Legation" who had been giving unwise advice in this matter. This was taken as referring to Mr. Sands, formerly Secretary of this Legation, who is unpleasantly mentioned in this connection and who is represented in the public press in Seoul as having memorialized the throne in favor of the confiscation of the property of the executed men, thus seeming to support the current rumor that he favored, if he did not advise, the action of the Government in dealing with the two refugees. As Mr. Sands is an adviser to the Korean Government and inclined to act in an entirely independent manner, and considering his recent connection with this Legation, I have thought it best not to seek to know from him anything in regard to his plans, and when the subject is mentioned to me, as it frequently is, to disclaim all knowledge of, or responsibility for, his acts.

I do not know what took place at the audience granted Mr. Hayashi other than that it is generally understood that nothing disagreeable occured: that Mr. Hayashi has apparently given up the claim that torture was used on the refugees, and that satisfactory relations between Korea and Japan are once more established.

Mr. Hayashi's mistake was in basing his whole case upon the use of torture, which claim he failed to sustain. Through this mistake the Koreans were able to evade the consequences of their acts, at least for the immediate present.

I also enclose a translation of the Judgment delivered in the case of the two men An and Kuan.

Horace N. Allen.

*Enclosure No. 3, with despatch No. 260, of June 15**

Judgement vs Kwon Yung Chin and Kiung Soo

Accused Kwon Yung Chin, in the 7th, moon of the year Kapo (1894), was invited by Ye Chun Yong (Tai Won Kun's grandson) and when he went to his house Ye Chun Yong told him that Her Majesty the Queen would get the Mins who lost their powers, to make up a trouble and till all the members of Kui Moo Chur (Cabinet Member), and that therefore it would be far better to weed out the roots of the bad grass when they mow it down. Accused asked him who the root was, and Ye assured him that Her Majesty was the root, saying that as long as the queen would live in the world, no reformation could be made although they were trying so hard; that when one weed out the the bad roots, leaving some alone, it would cause a trouble all the same, so that if they could also get rid of the Crown Prince and Eui Wha Prince, there would not be any danger. He heard and knew the traitorous plan which never was in oldern times, but did not inform to the Government.

He also on the day before the queen was murdered in 8th. moon of Ul Me year (Oct. 7, 1895) was sent for by the Japanese Secretary and went to him with Choh Hui Yun and Ye Too Whang and heard from there the plan of killing the queen the next morning, and sent his younger brother Kwon Tong Chin with Choh Hui Yun's cousin Choh Hui Moon to the Palace on the morning the queen was killed, He ran away to Japan for some years and he came back for the punishment as he knew his crime was very serious.

Accused An Kiung Soo went to Ye Chun Yong's house in the 7th. moon of Kapo year (1894) on the latter's request, Accused found Yu Kil Chun and Pak Chun Yang were also there. Ye Chun Yong told him that he and others would all be killed. When accused asked him the reason he said as the queen was trying to kill all the cabinet members, they had better get rid of the roots when they mow off the weeds, to which the accused answered that if one was guilty he would die for it, but how could he try to do such an affair. Ye Chung Yong wanted him to go and consult the matter with the Japanese Minister, he went because he could not refuse to do so to his face, and had some other talk with the Japanese Minister and did not mention any word about the matter, but on coming back to Ye Chun Yong he told him falsely that the Japanese Minister refused to do that.

The accused also in the 4th. moon of the year Moo Sool (1898) tried to engage the military officers to ask H.M. to abdicate the throne to the Crown Prince, keeping a strong guard at the back of the Russian Legation. In case H.M. refuse to do so, they would make him do it, but when he heard of the order to arrest him he fled to Japan. But he thought he had better to be killed or not according to the Korean law, and he surrendered himself up. It is so clear according to their testimony and confession they be put to the punishment of hanging, according to the law against the traitorship.

Judges' name.

No. 455   Legation of the United States
                                                               Seoul, Korea, May 2, 1902

Secretary of State

Sir:-
        I have the honor to inform you that Korea is just now experiencing one of its periodic excitements in which numerous arrests are being made in connection with rumored attempts on the part of the "traitors" in Japan to overturn the Government. As Mr. J. N. Jordan, the British Minister, has received telegraphic enquiries in regard to the matter, from his Government, it may be of interest to you to know the facts to date, though I do not consider the matter of sufficient importance at present, to merit telegraphing.
        The Korean refugees in Japan, who controlled the King, (present Emperor) after the murder of the Queen, in October 1895 and until his escape to the Russian Legation in February 1896, are a constant source of anxiety to Korea's ruler. Evil disposed persons are allways able to alarm him by reports as to the doings of these men who are called traitors in Korea. Many Koreans have secured considerable money from the Emperor on the promise that they will go to Japan and either get or kill these men, one such official messenger did murder the principal refugee, Kim Ok Kiun in the spring of 1894. These political refugees

---

*Handwritten.

moreover cause great trouble to well disposed Korean officials and private citizens, in Korea, by writing to them; soliciting money, and making suggestions as to how Korean public affairs should be conducted.

Moreover, unscrupulous Japanese individuals are constantly plotting with these refugees and bearing messages from them to people in Korea. Sometimes these Japanese let it be known that they have these messages and in that way get paid as informants, or again, they get money from the person to whom the message is addressed, on a threat of making the matter public.

It seems that such a communication, in writing, was received some time ago, by a man named Soh Sang Chip, who has long sustained buisiness relations with the principal American firm at Chemulpo - Townsend & Co. This man Soh, at one took his letter to the local official, who sent it up to the Palace. This letter advised the killing of the Emperor; the Crown Prince; the mother of the baby prince; the Chief eunuch, Kang; and many others. It also advised the formation of a new cabinet to be composed of the best men in Korea, - Pak Chung Yang (First Minister to America and late Prime Minister) Ye Wan Yong (Secretary of Legation and Charge d'Affaires at Washington and later Foreign Minister) Ye Ha Yong (At one yime Charge d'Affaires at Washington and lately Minister to Japan and Special Ambassador on two occasions). Han Qu Sul (Present Minister of Justice - and of the American persuasion), Min Yong Soh (Minister of Education) Sim Sang Hun (Minister of Finance) and General Ye Yun Yong. These are all good men, and the three who are now in the cabinet were placed there during the excitement conected with the receipt of the news of the Anglo-Japanese Alliance. No better cabinet could be made here.

While the letter may have been written, and the writer may have become so enlightened as to wish that good officials should be placed in charge of the Government, his reported proposal to do such wholesale murder, indicates that he cannot have changed much since the autumn of 1895 when several of these above named officials were refugees at this Legation from this very man who tried all he possibly could to get hold of and kill them at that time.

This being the fact and these facts being well known to the Emperor, one would suppose that he would pay no attention to the fact that the names of these men had been mentioned in this reported communication.

That is not the case however. His Majesty is so surrounded by evil, or selfishly disposed courtiers, who will go to any extent to promote their own interests, that we have seen prominent officials done to death on no more serious charge than this.

Being acquainted of the distress in which these men were placed, I decided that I could not let them be arrested and tortured and probably killed without doing something in their behalf. I therefore wrote an informal note to the chief Eunuch for His Majesty to see. My Japanese colleague, to whom I suggested to the Koreans to speak, informed me that he would do the same. Our two letters seem to have called a halt in any proceedings that were contemplated. I was at once assured in the middle of the night, that there was no intention of arresting these men. This seems not to be the real fact however as I was informed that the order had already been previously issued for thier arrest.

Ten arrests of people of whom I do not know much, were made a few days ago, and further daily arrests are being made.

The famine of the past year, which has caused large numbers of people to live on the roots of grasses; the bark of trees, and even to kill and eat their own infants, places the country in a particularly favorable condition for an uprising, since the people have nothing to lose and everything to gain by a disturbance. The arrest and torture of such persons as the seven I have named above, would, in all probability, have caused an uprising in their behalf.

This is probably but the beginning of an excitement of considerable length and possibly of serious consequences.

Japan and England must of course take a deep interest in the matter since the announcement of their Alliance regarding Korea, and especially because of the fact that the present trouble originates with Koreans who are in Japan and under the protection of the Japanese Government.

In this connection I hand you enclosed, a copy of my note to the Eunuch Kang Suk Ho.

Horace N Allen

No. 461   Legation of the United States
                                             Seoul, Korea, May 16, 1902.

Secretary of State

Sir:-
        Continuing the subject of my despatch No. 455, of the 2'nd. instant, on the subject of the reported
conspiracy of the Korean refugees in Japan, I now have the honor to inform you that prompt action seems
to have prevented a dangerous spread of this excitement.
        None of the seven men whose names I mentioned and in whose interest I acted, have been
molested. The man Soh Sang Chip, who received the letter from the refugee You Kill Chun, and two other
prominent officials, were arrested. Twelve lesser personages were arrested on the charge of having been
connected with the former "Independence Party", and Mr. Hayashi, the Japanese Minister, found it necessary
to deport two Japanese citizens, who were living in Seoul, and keeping up communication with the
refugees in Japan.
        It is thought that the imprisoned men will soon be set at liberty and the incident will be closed.

                                             Horace N Allen

No. 627   Legation of the United States
                                             Seoul, Korea, December 4, 1903.

Secretary of State

Sir:-
        I have the honor to hand you enclosed, a clipping from the Japan Daily Mail of November 27,
relative to the assasination at Kure, Japan, of Woo Pom Sun, a former Korean official, who was supposed
to have been implicated in the murder of the Queen of Korea on October 8, 1895. The assasin was also a
former official in Korea and it is generally supposed that he was sent to Japan by secret orders to commit
the deed, as it is known that others have been sent on similar missions continually for a long time, but the
police of Japan have heretofore prevented the accomplishment of the designs of the would biassasins.
        The only other notable success in this line was that of the Spring of 1894, when Kim Ok Kiun
was killed in Shanghai and his Korean assasin was promoted to high rank in the Korean Government.

                                             Horace N Allen

D. Continued Russian Presence

No. 275   Confidential   Legation of the United States
                                                  Seoul, Korea, Aug. 31, 1900.

Secretary of State

Sir:-
        I have the honor to inform you that I was asked to a private audience with His Majesty the
Emperor of Korea, last evening, wich lasted one and a half hours, and on which occasion I was accorded the
unwonted privilege of being seated.
        I will briefly relate the matters of importance that were mentioned during the audience.
        After considerable conversation of an unimportant nature regarding the recent news from China, I
was asked as to the probable fate of Manchuria; whether it would fall into the hands of Russia, and if so,
whether trouble would result between Russia and Japan. I replied that I had no information whatever upon
the subject other than the general public news of the activity of Russian troops in occupying Manchurian
teritory in connection with the protection of their railway lines, and that as the right to build, operate and
maintain these railway lines was supposed to be based upon agreements made between Russia and China, it
was probable that Russia's right to such action would be respected and the territory be regarded as within her
"Sphere of Influence". His Majesty then told me that Mr. Hayashi, the Japanese Minister at Seoul, had

informed him that it was Russia's intention to annex Manchuria and that Japan would resent any such action to the extent of going to war. I replied that if Japan knew of Russia's intentions to this extent, Russia must undoubtedly know of of the manner in which any such intentions would be regarded in Japan, that being the case it was difficult to reconcile with Mr. Hayashi's statement the recent telegraphic information to the effect that Russia had stopped a large detachment of her troops at Odessa from sailing for the Far East because of the lack of necessity for their proceeding now that Pekin had been relieved.

His Majesty was much concerned for the fate of Korea as a result of the trouble in China and its probable settlement. He told me that Mr. Hayashi had sent him word that the Foreign Representatives in Tokio were meeting in council to decide matters relating to the Far Eastern question, and suggested that it would be wise for Korea to send a high official to Tokio as Minister in order that he might take part in these deliberations with a view to securing good treatment for Korea: that Japan and England would take him under their protection if sent, and assist him in securing an international obligation guaranteeing the neutrality and independence of Korea. He said he had accordingly sent Mr. Chyo Pyung Sik (see my despatch No. 272 of Aug. 23), and that he had learned from telegrams from Mr. Chyo, that the Japanese Government was treating him with very unusual consideration. He asked me what I thought of this project. I replied that I did not think the Foreign Representatives in Tokio were meeting for any other purpose than to try to supply the place of their colleagues who were, at the time, shut up in Pekin, and to attempt to advise their respective Governments as to conditions in Asia. I did not think they were empowered to decide questions relating to Eastern matters. As to the question of Korean neutrality and independence, if any such move were contemplated I supposed that Japan and England as proposers of such plan, would be entirely proper. At the same time I reminded him of the fact that America and the European Powers had made treaties with Korea as an independent power and it would be difficult for any one nation to ruthlessly take away this independence. I reminded him of the promise made in these treaties that the treaty powers would assist Korea in time of distress, by their good offices, and recalled to his mind the fact that in 1894, at the time of the Japan-China war, when he had asked the good offices of the United States, he had not asked in vain, for Secretary Gresham had promptly sent a very strong telegram to the Japanese Government in reply to this appeal, which act, I could not but believe, had had much to do with the ultimate course of Japan in respecting and fully establishing Korean independence. To his query as to whether I considered Korean independence in danger, I replied that much depended upon himself and his Government; that corruption and consequent disorder in the country might make the landing of troops necessary for the protection of the growing foreign interests, while a rash promise on the part of Mr. Chyo, or an untimely request for aid from himself, might lay him under unpleasant obligations. He said he would telegraph Mr. Chyo and caution him.

He spoke at length upon the matter of the sudden death of two of the prominent members of the pro-American party, notably of Governor Ye Cha Yun, who was for some years Korean Charge d'Affaires at Washington, and who has been largely responsible for the great advancement of American commercial interests in Korea. The two men died suddenly of a mysterious disease, after attending a gay party a few nights before, and one other very prominent man of the same party is still seriously ill.- I refer to Colonel Min Sang Ho, Head of the Department of Posts, Telegraphs and Communications, who was educated in Washington and was recently delegate to the International Postal Convention at Washington.

His Majesty said he had repeatedly heard of threats that the Japanese party intended to kill off these pro-Americans and he feared these deaths were due to foul means in connection with these threats. I said I could not believe that any such course would be sanctioned by the Japanese who were an enlightened people and not given to such vile acts as assassination, whereupon he reminded me that I had made a similar remark in 1895, when he feared for his personal safety while the Japanese were in power and I had expressed my belief that such fears were groundless so long as regular officers of the Japanese Army were in charge of his surroundings, notwithstanding which he had shortly thereafter seen his Queen murdered by these same people. I could say nothing more.

He told me that the Japanese were very bitter against the Americans for the commercial progress we are now making in Korea and that Mr. Hayashi had sent him word through An Hak Chu, an Imperial Chamberlain and go-between for the Palace and Japanese Legation, that it was a mistake to allow the Americans to have such large interests in Korea, that they would surely rob him and that the Japanese would do the same work much better and cheaper. He cited the proposed 18 mile extension of the Seoul Electric railroad and the erection of the Seoul Electric Lighting plan, now being attended to by the American firm Collbran and Bostwick, as well as the proposal of this firm to loan to Korea Yen 5,000,000 for the establishment of a bank and the construction of water-works. Mr. Hayashi made a strong plea for the divertion of this work to Japanese, notwithstanding the fact that the same is now being carried on by this

American firm. His Majesty says that he somewhat indignantly replied that the matter was settled and the contracts let and he was satisfied. He further said that Mr. Hayashi had sent him word that if he desired a loan, Japan was willing to grant him one to the extent of Yen 10,000,000 to be used for the development of his Army: that it would not be politic for the Japanese Government to make this loan outright, but that a Japanese mercant would come over here and arrange the matter. (I hear that Baron Shibusawa, President of the First Bank of Japan, is expected to arrive in Seoul before before long.) Mr. Hayashi further said that while present engagements with Russia would prevent Japan from loaning Korea the necessary officers for the reorganization of her Army, she would allow a number of her best military officers to come to Korea and become naturalized Korean citizens and be appointed in charge of the army so that they could in this way attend to its reorganization and development. (Such a course was recently followed in the case of Mr. Omiwa who was upon naturalization, appointed adviser to the Korean Government, and he has recently been placed in charge of the ginseng farms,- a charge that was offered to the American firm of Collbran and Bostwick, but which this man Omiwa seems to have gotten away from them.)

My reply to this was, that there were two reputable American firms here, represented my Mr. Leigh Hunt and Mr. H. Collbran, each of whom were willing and anxious to loan to the Korean Government Yen 5,000,000, at very favorable rates and on security that could be easily granted, which would amount to the same sum 10,000,000. I went on to say that our country was now experiencing a period of unwonted prosperity and it was pleasing to me to see that the effects of this prosperity was in a measure, thus extended to His Majesty's Government, with whom my Government had long sustained such peculiarly cordial relations. I explained that these offers were entirely without political significance, being purely business propositions about which my Government had not even been consulted, and if he needed money it would be perfectly safe to accept these offers with no fear of any ulterior political object, while such acceptance would be but a further mark of the cordial relations existing between the two countries.

He seemed greatly pleased at this and said he would instruct the proper officers to confer with the Americans upon the subject.

I regret to see the unfriendly attitude manifested toward us by the Japanese here, and regret that the information I now hand you, comes in such a manner as to be of little use other than as an indication of what we may expect. You will readily see that while all this was told me personally by the Emperor, his advice from Mr. Hayashi came through a third party, and could, and probably would, be promptly denied, though I am perfectly sure it was given as stated only stronger.

While the firm of Collbran and Bostwick actually employ a number of Japanese and buy quite a large amount of supplies from Japan, they have been made to feel all along that they were being watched and hampered in every possible way by underhanded acts of the Japanese, which they claim to have usually been able to trace to the Japanese Legation itself.

The work of this company has been of a good character. They have so far carried out their obligations in a most satisfactory manner and have given the Koreans full value for their money. This is quite the opposite to the Japanese, who make one disgusted with the shoddy character of the plants they palm off upon the Koreans whenever they get the opportunity. This is deeply regretted by the friends of Japan and has been greatly deplored in public by such men as Counts Inouye and Ito who have looked into the matter on the ground. The Japanese who come to Korea seem bent upon ill-treating the Koreans and upon swindling them as much as possible. The result does not diminish the hatred of the Koreans for their old time oppressors.

In connection with the subjects mention in the above cited conversation with His Majesty, I wish to call your attention to the enclosed, excellent editorial, taken from the Kobe Chronicle of August 25, and entitled "Japan in Korea and the Partition of China".

Horace N. Allen.

No. 321

Legation of the United States
Seoul, Korea, March 12, 1901.

Secretary of State

Sir:-

This capital is at present undergoing one of its periodical stages of excitement, due, as usual, to the disclosure of an intrigue. I have the honor to hand you the following brief report upon the subject.

In my Nos. 229 of February 16, and 233 of March 15, 1900, I informed you of the difficulty I was having with a very corrupt and objectionable Korean official, - Kim Yung Chun. At that time, a year ago, my Russian colleague, Mr. Pavlow, saw fit to take up this man privately as a friend. He had him frequently at his house for dinner and appeared desirous of assuring him of Russian sympathy. I won my case and Kim was degraded and banished. He was reinstated in Imperial favor through the influence of Mr. Pavlow, exerted through the two most conspicuous Korean officials who are hangers on of the Russian Legation, Min Kyung Sik and Chu Suk Myun. This influence secured for Kim the apointment of Acting Minister of Justice, in consideration of which, as it now turns out, Kim was to decide in favor of the father of Min Kyung Sik a very important case concerning the illegal sale by the father of a large and important island situated in the harbor of Chemulpo to a Japanese. When Kim was well established in power, however, he refused to do as he is said to have agreed unless he was given a large sum of money. He went even to the opposite extreme and had the father of Min arrested and thrown into prison. This act caused a breach between Kim and the Russian Legation party, which ultimately lead to the disclosures which have caused the present excitement.

From these disclosures it seems that this party was not satisfied with the degree of power they enjoyed, because of the fact that certain Koreans with American and Japanese sympathies were too influential for them. They decided therefore that they must follow the ancient Korean custom and remove this opposition party, chief among which are Prince Min Yong Whan and the Head Eunuch, Kang Suk Ho, (both of the so-called "American Party") and Min Pyung Suk, leader of the co-called "Japanese Party". In order safely to accomplish their design of making away with these men, the party of Kim decided it must have a large Russian guard in Seoul. As a means of inducing the Russian Representative to secure this guard it determined to make a feigned attack upon the Russian Legation, which attack it was arranged should be attributed to hirelings of the opposition party. Meantime Kim and his friends began to send anonymous letters to His Majesty accusing their enemies of various treasonable crimes.

Before the feigned attack could take place, the Kim party broke apart, and I had evidence that Kim was no longer in favor at the Russian Legation, a thing that interested me not a little, considering the manner and time of his being made persona grata there.

As the weeks passed Kim and the Russian party became more and more bitter toward each other, until Min Kyung Sik finally told His Majesty the whole story of the plot, which he attempted to lay entirely to the evil influence of Kim, who thereupon told in turn his version and was able to prove that the anonymous letters were written in the hand of Min. The opposition party was amazed at the disclosures and succeeded in so alarming the Emperor that he caused the arrest of the trio Kim, Min and Chu, upon Sunday, the 3d of March.

It was thought at first that Mr. Pavlow would take up the matter vigorously in the interest of his friends Min and Chu, but while he has made several ineffectual attempts to obtain an audience, he has done nothing more, in fact he is said to have expressed himself as so fearful of affording relief to Kim Yung Chun that he is inclined to do nothing. Meantime the Russian Admiral is expected here shortly with a fleet and and the visit will probably be used to some political advantage.

Another Korean, who with Kim Yung Chun shares a most evil reputation, and whom I have mentioned, notably in my No. 300 of November 22, 1900, namely Ye Yong Ik, is at present a very frequent visitor at the Russian Legation and Mr. Pavlow has expressed himself to me as being in hearty sympathy with some of Ye's schemes. The great hold of the man upon His Majesty is due to the fact that he has secured a large amount of the Emperor's money, which he has in bank in hisown name for His Majesty. With this Mr. Pavlow told me Ye was about to begin a very questionable currency coinage, which must surely cause great distress eventually in the country.

The streets have been placarded against this man Ye, and it was thought the people might perhaps take the administration of justice into their own hands and do him injury. When, to the general surprise, on the 8th instant, the handsome new Mint, which Ye had built at a cost of Yen 300.000 for building (Korean newspaper estimate) and Yen 200.000 for machinery (same estimate), with silver and nickel coin and bullion in stock, was burned and destroyed. The building was of brick, fire proof, with very little wood-work about it, so that the preparation for combustion must have been especially complete.

These disclosures, the resulting arrests and this fire with its great loss and attendant suspicious circumstances, are enough to produce a considerable degree of excitement.

Horace N. Allen.

No. 324   Legation of the United States
                                          Seoul, Korea, March 22, 1901.

Secretary of State

Sir:-

Referring to my despatch No. 321 of March 12, regarding the arrest of Kim Yung Chun and other officials, I now have the honor to inform you that, under torture, Kim confessed to having been connected with a plot to kidnap the Emperor and take him to a detached palace : to kill off a number of the pro-American and pro-Japanese officials : to insure the co-operation of the Russian Legation by a feigned attack upon it, which was to be attributed to members of the opposition Korean parties, and to bring about a re-organization of the Government. He further confessed connection with the anti-foreign secret circular calling for an uprising in December last, as mentioned in my No. 307 of December 14, 1900, and he admitted that he was the author of a threatening letter received by myself and each of the other Foreign Representatives in January last, a copy of which I now enclose. He gave as a reason for his writing this letter, which spoke ill of himself, that he desired to allay suspicion which was beginning to center about him. It was at this time that he secured an interview with me and made most abject apologies for his mis-conduct toward me of a year ago and strove hard to gain my confidence, so much so that I began to think the man in earnest, and I had finally reluctantly agreed to dine with him. His arrest prevented the dinner taking place.

His confession incriminated two Princes and many other conspicuous Koreans, all of whom were arrested. He was hung to death on the evening of the 18th instant, the day his trial ended. Min Kyung Sik and Chu Suk Myun, Korean followers of the Russian Legation, who were arrested with Kim, were banished for life and for fifteen years respectively.

The affair appears to have been purely a Korean one. It is understood that Kim appealed to the Japanese Minister for assistance, but in vain.

                                          Horace N Allen

No. 441   Legation of the United States
                                          Seoul, Korea, February 21st, 1902.

Secretary of State

Sir:-

I have the honor to inform you that I am in receipt of a despatch from Monsieur Alexander Pavlow notifying me that, on February 4th, the Emperor of Russia raised the rank of his Imperial Legation in Korea, and appointed Monsieur Pavlow, formerly Chargé d'Affaires in Korea, His Imperial Russian Majesty's Envoy Extraordinary and Minister Plenipotentiary to His Majesty the Emperor of Korea.

                                          Gordon Paddock

No. 454   Legation of the United States
                                          Seoul, Korea, April 26, 1902.

Secretary of State

Sir:-

During the past winter the Russian Representative in Seoul has made frequent application to the Korean Government for permission to build a telegraph line from Vladivostock down into Korea to connect with the Korean lines running north from Gensan, but the applications were refused on the ground that the conventions between Korea and Japan made at the time of the laying of the cable from Fusan to Japan, prevent any such connection being made. These conventions with Japan have but five years more of life, and I understand the Korean Government feared that by granting the request of the Russians they might have to extend these conventions as an offset to Japan. In February last certain poles were actually erected by a Russian Company upon Korean soil at the North-east border, and the Korean local officials cut them down.

Judging by the accounts published in the local newspapers at the time, the incident caused considerable excitement.

I have the honor to inform you, however, that the matter is now settled, by the Korean Government giving instructions to its Telegraph Administration to connect the Korean lines with the old Chinese lines at Weichu on the North-west border. The Russians having apparantly given up the idea of direct connection with Vladivostock. This old Chinese line has not been in working order for the past two years, having been destroyed by the "Boxers". It is to be presumed that the Russian Authorities in Manchuria intend to rebuild this old Chinese line, and have direct connection with Seoul.

It will afford us two cable outlets instead of one as at present.

Horace N Allen

E. The Masanp'o Issue

No. 235   Legation of the United States
                                                      Seoul Korea, March 19, 1900.

Secretary of State

Sir:-

Referring to my No. 214, Confidential, Nov. 18, and my No 228, Feb. 15, regarding friction between Japan and Russia in Korea, I now have the honor to inform you that the matter of the Masampo purchase is at present under active discussion here.

The case is briefly as follows: - Mr. Pavloff, Russian Charge d'Affaires, in the spring of 1899 selected a site of ground on the fore-shore at the new port, Masampo, on the south coast of Korea. He paid nothing but simply told the local magistrate to reserve this ground for the Russian Government. Sometime afterwards a Japanese purchased this same land of the Korean owner and, whether knowingly or not - for Korean official records are very imperfect - the magistrate issued a deed for the ground to the Japanese purchaser, thus shutting off the Russians from the water. Mr. Pavloff being absent in Russia his relief remonstrated with the Korean Government who referred him to the Japanese. The Government of Japan would not compel the man to surrender the ground and matters were left in this state pending the early arrival of Mr. Pavloff, who says he has only returned to Korea for a very short stay and intimates that he intends to settle this matter in a way satisfactory to his Government.

The harbor of Masampo is pronounced to be a very fine one and probably the best in these waters. Its position, N. 35⁰10' by E 128⁰37', is a most commanding one, being but a few hours from the Shimonoseki fortifications at the western terminus of the Inland Sea of Japan, and at the gateway of the whole Yellow Sea. This harbor possesses an island about 10 miles down the reach from the site of the foreign settlement itself, which island is said to possess a most excellent anchorage for the large ships, and to offer very fine opportunities for the erection of fortificaitons on the island itself.

You will remember that Russia made a determined but fruitless attempt to obtain Deer Island in the harbor of Fusan. See my No's. 8, Oct. 1, 1897; 16, Oct. 8, 1897, and 27, Oct. 25, 1897. This Masampo island is said to be much superior to Deer Island in every way and to occupy a more commanding and easily protected situation.

I am told that Mr. Pavloff has now demanded this Masampo island in settlement of the land question at that port. I am also told that the Japanese strongly object to any such grant, which is contrary to treaty, since 10 li - or 3,1/3 miles, is the extent of the radius from an open port within which foreigners may acquire land, and any grant of this kind to one power of land outside this radius would be unfair to the other treaty powers.

A fleet of three of the largest Russian war vessels arrived at Chemulpo on the 16'th. instant and on the 17'th. the Admiral and a number of his officers, accompanied by a band of forty musicians came to Seoul. The Admiral informed me that he expected to remain in Chemulpo for ten days or more, and it is taken for granted that his visit has to do with the Masampo discussion now in progress.

This visit of the Admiral is having considerable effect upon the timid Koreans who may very probably yield to Russia's demands, regardless of the effect such complaisance may have upon Japan, where I know the war feeling is strong and may not be controllable.

In the meantime the Koreans have what seems to be reliable private information that active war preparations are going on in Japan, with the evident intention of being prepared for the worst should it come. The war office in Tokio is said to be occupied night and day with important conferences while maps and charts of Korea are spread about, and guns; amunition and commissary stores are being hurriedly dispatched to places from which they may be readily embarked. You probably have this information in greater detail however, from our Legation in Tokio.

No one understands Korea better than do the Japanese, who alone possess accurate charts of the coast, while their gendarmery of 20 officers and 200 men stationed in Korea for the past few years for the protection of the Japanese telegraph lines, have really been engaged in the production of accurate maps of the interior.

In this connection I may add that a bonus of Yen 100,000 is said to have been offered to any contractor who will complete the bridge of the Seoul Chemulpo Railway over the Han River, by June next. - The plans of the American contractor for this bridge having been disregarded, two of the piers built by the Japanese have subsided out of line. Also, the survey of the railroad to connect Seoul with Fusan, concession for which was given to the Japanese, is now under way, though the road will be most expensive to construct and cannot be of any real commercial value.

Horace N. Allen.

No. 245

Legation of the United States
Seoul, Korea, April 21, 1900.

Secretary of State

Sir:-

I have the honor to inform you of the final settlement of the question of Russian land at the port of Masampo, which "Masampo question" has been mentioned in the newspapers of nearly every country and was thought for a time might lead to war between Russia and Japan.

In my No. 235 of March 19, 1900, I mentioned the fact that a Japanese subject had slipped in and purchased of the individual owner a strip of land along the foreshore of the new settlement at Masampo, which had been reserved by the Russian Chargé d'Affaires for his government under a liberal interpretation of the clause in the settlement agreement, allowing each Government to reserve from public sale a "consular site". The Japanese Government refused to compel its subject to give up this land and Mr. Pavlow was sent back to Korea, while in Russia on leave, to attend to the matter.

The settlement arrived at is that Russia is granted an exclusive Russian concession for land adjoining the Masampo Foreign Settlement, lying inside the 10 li -- 3 1/3 miles -- limit within which all foreigners may own land adjoining a General Foreign Settlement. This special concession includes the whole coast line of a fine bay, and comprises between 800.000 and 900.000 square metres. Within this area Russian regulations and power will control. There were a few Japanese holdings in the new allotment of ground and the owners were given the option of selling out at an appraisment or remaining subject to Russian regulations. They decided to remain.

The area of this new settlement is more than twice as large as that of the whole Foreign Settlement of Masampo itself. The conceding of such an amount of ground to one power is an injustice to other nations, since their subjects are debarred from enjoying their treaty right to purchase land within the "10 li" radius. This concession will doubtless be followed by demands for similar concessions from other powers.

It was probably with this in view that the Russian Government secured a "non-alienation" clause relating to the island Kojay Do at the mouth of Masampo harbor. See my No. 235 of March 19. Not being able to get this island themselves without causing serious trouble with Japan they in this way prevent its going to anyone else.

I have found it to be a carefully followed policy of Russia in Korea when they fear some important property or right may go into other hands and cause them inconvenience hereafter, to ask for it themselves and get from the Koreans, with the refusal of the request, a promise that they will not grant the same to anyone else. As in the case of the gold mines which were offered to Messrs Hunt and Fassett but which Russia claims by one of their "non-alienation" agreements. In discussing the matter of this island with Mr. Pavlow he very frankly said it prevented unfortunate complications with other powers and left it open for Russia to forcibly "take" the island if it became necessary.

I enclose an extract from the Kobe Chronicle of April 9, 1900, being an extract from the report of Mr. Jordan, H.B.M.'s Chargé d'Affaires, on Masampo harbor which he visited and found to be on the report of his naval people one of the very best harbors in the world. In the same enclosure is an extract from the Kobe Chronicle of April 12, 1900, treating of the subject of the Russian concession at Masampo editorially.

Horace N. Allen

No. 353

Legation of the United States
Seoul, Korea, May 28, 1901.,

Secretary of State

Sir:-

I have the honor to inform you that the Japanese Government has secured a special settlement at the port of Masampo in South Korea.

In my No. 245, of April 21, 1900, I intimated that some such course might be expected as a result of the grant of an allottment of ground at Masampo for a special Russian settlement.

In this case the Japanese have worked very skillfully. Had they secured the allotment outright, other governments might have been compelled to protest, as was the case once before, - see Mr. Sill's No. 111, of May 11, 1895. In this instance private citizens of Japan bought up all the required land, which was later taken over by the Japanese Government and an agreement was made with the Korean Government by which this area is to be used as a special Japanese settlement, and it has now been officially marked out and taken over. Had this land not been bought privately, other Governments might well complain that their treaty rights had been infringed by the grant of a special settlement, for since the land lies within the "ten li radius" it was open to purchase by all until acquired by some individual. As it stands no one has much ground for complaint and it is an offset to the allotment made to Russia last year.

The area of the Japanese allotment is said to be 450 acres. *This is probably an exaggerated estimate.* * In my No. 245, above cited and previous numbers on the same subject, I pointed out the action of Russia in regard to the important island of Kochai Do. at the mouth of the Masampo harbor, which Russia seems to have given up after securing a "non-alienation clause".

Public attention was called to the presence of the Russian fleet near Masampo for some six weeks during the past spring - February and March, and it was apparently believed in Japan that Russia had designs upon Chinhai Bay, lying near their Masampo settlement. The Russian officers report most favorably upon this bay, and the Russian papers published at Port Arthur and Vladivostock have contained statements to the effect that Russia must have a naval base at that point regardless of anything England may do even if the securing of it leads to war.

Masampo is certainly a most valuable point from which to guard the sea between Manchuria and Japan, and the harbor of Chinhai Bay is said to be most admirable for such purposes.

I enclose a tracing of a Japanese chart of the locality, which I have obtained confidentially. I have added in red, the approximate situations of the three settlements, - The General Foreign Settlement, the Japanese Settlement, and that of Russia.

Mr. Pavlow, the Russian Charge d'Affaires, who recently went to Japan to be treated for the bite of a rabid dog, started for Seoul some time ago but has not yet arrived, we now hear that he is at Masampo.

I may tell you confidentially that Mr. Hayashi, the Japanese Minister, informed Mr. Gubbins, the British Chargé d'Affaires, that if Russia insisted upon taking Chinhai Bay, as was feared she would do, the Japanese Government would be unable to avert war with Russia.

Horace N Allen

---

*Handwritten

F. The "Brown Incident," the French Loan, and Ye Yong-Ik

No. 335

Legation of the United States
Seoul, Korea, April 24, 1901.

Secretary of State

Sir:-

Referring to my despatch No. 325 of March 25, regarding the attempted dismissal of Mr. Brown, the Englishman in charge of the Korean Customs, and my No. 329, of April 3, to the effect that Mr. Gubbins, the British Chargé d'Affaires, had reported the matter as satisfactorily arranged, I now have the honor to inform you that Mr. Gubbins' assurance seems to have been premature.

As he supposed, the matter was arranged in audience with the Emperor, who had the Minister of the Household apologize for the intrusion into Mr. Brown's house. The arrangements for turning over the residence of Mr. Brown were, however, left with the Minister for Foreign Affairs.

When Mr. Gubbins met the Minister for Foreign Affairs, to complete these arrangements, the latter presented new and unexpected demands covering the surrender of all the offices and warehouses of the customs headquarters. Mr. Gubbins could not consent to make this transfer on the date named for handing over the house, June 1'st., as such course would leave the customs without any place for transacting business. It became very evident that the demand for the property occupied by Mr. Brown was but a mere pretext to make him trouble and secure his dismissal.

In this connection I may remark that my German colleague, Consul Weipert, told me some time ago, that the Russian Chargé d'Affaires, Mr. Pavlow, had remarked to him that a head office of the customs in Seoul was quite unnecessary, since the commissioner at Chemulpo could well attend to all matters now looked after by the chief officer at Seoul, and I have since heard it reported that a Frenchman has been suggested to the Koreans as a suitable man for the position of "Secretary of Customs to reside at Chemulpo". This bears out the impression that the Brown incident was but a mere pretext to get rid of him entirely. I have tried to avoid discussing this matter with Mr. Pavlow, though he has made the opportunity of expressing himself to me as much opposed to Mr. Brown, and as of the opinion that he is sure to be dismissed. Mr. Pavlow recently remonstrated with His Majesty, in audience, against the employment of foreign assistants, other than Russian, though he seems to have acquiesced in the engagement of a number of Frenchmen. He seems to find much fault with Mr. Brown for his so-called arbitrary manner of employing subordinates without reference to the Korean Government, though that is the only way in which the service can be properly conducted. He also finds much fault with Mr. Brown's strict control of the customs revenues. I know, and it is generally known, that Mr. Brown has an Imperial decree, obtained upon the suggestion of a former Russian Chargé d'Affaires, Mr. C. Waeber, placing him in control of the finances of the Korean Customs and Treasury until such time as the Japanese loan shall have been fully paid. I learn from Mr. Brown that the balance of this loan of three million yen, yet unpaid, is ¥250,000 - not ¥ 50,000 as I stated in my No. 325 of March 25. He also told me that the loan might have been paid off long ago had he not received orders from the Emperor not to pay it.

The Foreign Minister has resigned because of the displeasure of His Majesty on account of the inability of the former to secure the vacation of the customs buildings, and because of the Minister's intentions not to sign certain concessions to France which I will name below.

The Korean Government have acted in a very harsh and rude maner to the British Representative. They have unfairly accused him of discourtesy in the wording of the Chinese translation of of one of his despatches, though the Japanese Minister, to whom Mr. Gubbins submitted the Chinese text, pronounced it to be without fault. The Vice Minister of Foreign Affairs, who is now Acting Minister, informed the British Secretary of his intention to burn this despatch. The Korean Government has also sent Mr. Brown's interpreter, who was formerly the official interpreter of the British Legation and has been the official go-between for the palace and the British Legation, into exile for ten years because of a supposed misinterpretation between His Majesty and Mr Brown. This was really done in order that the blame of the matter might be removed from the Emperor. Mr. Gubbins attempted to prevent this action, but in vain.

On the 10'th., instant, Mr. Gubbins had an audience for the purpose of investing His Majesty with the order of Honorary Knight Grand Commander of the Indian Empire. Some one has persuaded the Koreans that they have been insulted by Great Britain in having an order of this rank conferred in return for the highest order of Korea which was conferred upon Queen Victoria. Mr. Gubbins has told me that the Koreans have asked for the order of the Garter instead of this Asiatic order. I know of the injured feeling the Koreans experience over this matter for they have been to me to discuss the matter. I have declined to discuss the subject on the grounds that, as we have no such system of decorations, I am not qualified to speak. I have added however, that I could not believe that the British Government would care to offend the Emperor of Korea in such a matter, but that I understood the order in question was one of the most gorgeous and striking ones the English have to bestow.

Admiral Bruce with the "Barleur" and the "Bonnaventure" of the British Navy, arrived at Chemulpo on the 18'th. instant, and the Admiral was received in audience on the 22'nd.

It has long been apparent that foreign interference has had much to do with this Brown matter. Such action on the part of the Koreans has hitherto been unknown, and at a recent audience his Majesty assured Mr. Gubbins that he had no complaint to make in regard to the character of Mr. Brown's services. He said this moreover, with the full knowledge that Mr. Gubbins sought the information for his Government. The chief adviser of the Emperor in his course against Mr. Brown, is and has been, Ye Yong Ik, whom I have frequently mentioned as the most corrupt and unscrupulous official, who has of late exerted such a powerful influence with and upon His Majesty. This man (as with Kim Yung Chan, who was recently executed on the charge of treason,) is greatly feared and hated by nearly all classes of Koreans, but he has gotten control of so much of the imperial funds that he seems to have the Emperor entirely in his power. This man Ye is most intimate with Mr. Pavlow, and it is not to be believed that he would adopt any course not approved by the Russian Legation. This man has such a passion for getting control of government funds that it has long been a great disappointment to him that he could not get the customs revenues into his hands.

Recent events force the conclusion that the attempt to dismiss Mr. Brown was a part of a plot to place the customs under French control. And right here I must mention that Russia and France have long seemed to be in such perfect accord in Korea, that the Koreans and others generally, regard a concession to France as a pledge to Russia. In spite of Mr. Pavlow's remonstrances against the employment of foreigners, other than Russian, by the Korean Government, he seems to have readily acquiesced in the engagement of a number of Frenchman. There are now in the employ of the Korean Government, one adviser, two railway engineers, one director of a mining school, two officers in charge of the arsenal, besides school teachers, farmers etc, all from France, while we hear of the engagement of other Frenchmen.

The event which makes it apparent that the attempt to dismiss Mr. Brown was a Russo-French move, is the placing of a large French loan on the security of the customs revenues. A move which has been put through by Ye Yong Ik.

On the 18'th. instant, Ye Yong Ik went before the Council of State with a proposition approved by His Majesty and bearing the seals of the Departments of Foreign Affairs and Finance, attached by minor officials, accepting a French loan of five million yen in gold and silver bullion, at 5% interest, for a period of twenty five years, with 10 percent discount for brokerage. The loan is to be repaid from the customs receipts in annual payments. The bullion will be coined by the Korean mint and be used in exploiting the Pengyang coal mines, which become a further consideration for making the loan. The timid Councillors of State, promptly yielded to the demands of Ye Yong Ik and accepted the proposition, which thus becomes one of the strongest documents hitherto executed between Korea and foreigners. I send a copy.

By this act the Koreans deprive themselves, to a great extent, of the considerable revenues derived from the customs; they give over to France (and Russia) the virtual management of this service, and they rob themselves of the benefits that might be derived from these valuable coal mines.

With the announcement of this successful work of Ye Yong Ik, it is now very clear why this man was so energetic in attempting to secure the dismissal of Mr. Brown, or failing in this to so frighten him as to obtain his acquiescence in the contemplated designs upon the customs, for with the decree the latter still holds, he can refuse to allow the customs revenues to be so used, in case his own government cares to sustain him.

This concession and loan seriously affects American interests. On December 26, 1898, Messrs Collbran and Bostwick, Americans, in contracting for the construction of an electric railway and lighting plant for the city of Seoul, received an agreement covering a water-works plant for the same city. In 1899 I had much difficulty in preventing an Englishman named Chance, from getting this and other American projects into his hands, as I explained in my despatch No. 214, of Nov. 18, 1899. In this instance Mr. Brown worked with the man Chance, but I was able to defeat their object. On July 14, 1900, this agreement was further ratified and put into better shape, but an out and out concession was not entered into (I eroneously called this a concession in my No. 325 of March 25), because of the inability of this firm to definitely agree to raise a loan of five million yen on the security of the customs, for paying for the construction of these water-works and for organizing a Korean bank under foreign auspices. It was desired to delay the matter somewhat until matters in China and the East should become more settled. Engineers have been kept busy making the surveys, during the past winter, and Mr. Collbran is now in America endeavoring to perfect the financial part of the undertaking.

You will see therefore that no definite concession had already been entered into covering a lien on the customs, and could not have been made at once. Collbran and Bostwick have acted in good faith with the Korean Government and expected the same treatment in return. It however, becomes difficult for me to oppose this French project in the absence of any definite prior claim upon the customs revenues.

I have however remonstrated unofficially, through messengers, with His Majesty, but so far without avail. I have shown him also that I have long objected to Collbran and Bostwick allowing the Korean Government to get so deeply into debt with them. But that while they have repeatedly yeilded to His Majesty's urgent requests for temporary assistance in the way of loans and advances on construction work, he has not kept his repeated promises to pay, usually urging the plea that Ye Yong Ik would not let him have the money. I have intimated that if this loan goes through I shall have to call for an immediate and full settlement for Collbran and Bostwick, since their continued stay in Korea was largely in view of the contemplated work on the water supply system.

This has so far had a good effect since His Majesty has now made overtures looking to a better financial arrangement with this firm.

I may add that my British and Japanese colleagues and Mr. Brown, recognize the great necessity for a safe water supply for Seoul, and they regard this as of such a public necessity that it would be a proper work to be undertaken with money from the customs, they fully recongnize the right of Collbran and Bostwick to do the work.

I have asked Mr. Bostwick to cable Mr. Collbran in America and ascertain if he is now able to announce his ability to raise the money for this loan. If he is, I may perhaps be able to come to some arrangement with the Korean Government, or failing in this, I may be able to acomplish some sort of compromise whereby a portion of this French loan shall be devoted to the construction of the water-works by Collbran and Bostwick.

My British and Japanese colleagues were greatly exercised over the news of this French loan matter, which they regard as a Russian attempt to use France in obtaining an undue influence in Korea. They each telegraphed to their governments for permission to formally protest against the allienation of the customs revenues for what is practically a privite enterprise. Mr. Gubbins based his request, as I understand, upon his belief that this is but the culmination of the attack upon Mr. Brown, while Mr. Hayashi informed me that his request was based upon the ground that by treaty with Japan, Korea was compelled to use a large portion of the customs revenues (which are paid chiefly by Japan) for the lighting of the coast: A project that has had the sanction of the Japanese and Russians for a long time, but which has not yet been taken up at all.

I have made off several telegrams to forward you with an account of this matter, but I find it impossible to make myself clear in a short telegram. I have therefore waited to see if the British and Japanese Representatives would be instructed to protest, since that would enable me to telegraph intelligently. I understand that the delay experienced by Mr. Hayashi is caused by the desire of the Japanese Government to have the exact text of the French copy of the agreement. This was sent as soon as obtained, and a reply is shortly expected. Mr. Gubbins is daily expecting a reply to his long telegrams to his Government.

The Yunan Syndicate, for whom the Frenchman Cazalis, obtained this loan concession, is made up of French, Belgian and English shareholders. It may be that the presence of this British interest may complicate the matter for the British Government.

As the matter now stands I hardly see how I can ask to be allowed to protest on the grounds of interference with the loan project of Collbran and Bostwick. I have not neglected the matter, but have repeatedly urged him (Mr. Collbran) to perfect his documents, but he was unable to do so owing to the political situation out here.

The diversion of the revenues of the maritime customs to the use of exploitation of a coal mine for the benefit of private parties might be considered as disadvantageous to the commercial interests of Korea and therefore opposed to American interests. I have intimated as much unofficially, to His Majesty.

If more marked developments take place I shall inform you fully by telegraph.

Horace N Allen

No. 344   Legation of the United States
                                                     Seoul, Korea, May 6, 1901.

Secretary of State

Sir:-

I have the honor to inform you that the British Charge d'Affaires, Mr. Gubbins, called upon me and informed me that he had received advices from his Government, with permission to inform me, that the British Government did not aprove of the French loan to Korea: that they did not approve of the object for which the loan was supposed to be made, and that they did not approve of the pledging of the Korean customs revenues in this private manner, without giving British subjects a chance to compete in the undertaking.

He further explained his annoyance that the French Charge d'Affaires should attempt to put through a measure in which British capital was supposed to be interested, without mentioning the matter to him, or giving him any information on the subject until after the documents were signed, and then only upon request.

Mr. Brown has said that he will not sanction this use of the customs revenues, and as he holds a decree placing him in charge of the same, his objections may have to be considered. He also says that he has the power and now intends to use a considerable portion of the customs revenues for the purpose of establishing lighthouses on the Korean coast. - A thing that is provided for by a treaty provision with Japan.

When I told Mr. Gubbins that I considered the rumor of the probable occupation of Port Hamilton, or adjacent Korean islands, by Great Britain, as of sufficient importance to telegraph to my Government, he told me that, so far as he knew, his Government had no such intention, but that he had refrained from denying the report when asked as to its truth by Mr. Cazalis, the promoter of the French loan, and one or more of his colleagues.

This absence of denial, I may remark, gave color to the report, and the circumstances seemed all to point to the probability of the report being true. Other of the Foreign Representatives, I hear, throught the matter of sufficient importance to justify their cabling it to their Governments.

I have not telegraphed you in regard to the information given me by Mr. Gubbins regarding the attitude of his Government on the subject of the French loan, as I presume you will have received such information from the British Government.

Although the loan was sanctioned by the seals of the Department of Finance and Foreign Affairs, and accepted by the Council of State, the Acting Prime Minister refuses to ratify the action of the Council by attaching his seal and signature. He has memorialized the Throne against the loan and against the Korean promoter, - Ye Yong Ik.

With this Korean opposition and that of the British and Japanese Governments and Mr. Brown, it is thought here that the loan will not be accomplished, unless the French or Russian Governments guarantee its payment.

Horace N Allen

No. 346   Legation of the United States
                                                     Seoul, Korea, May 11, 1901.

Secretary of State

Sir:-

I have the honor to hand you the following in regard to the Brown incident; the French loan and kindred subjects.

The American firm, Collbran and Bostwick, who have an agreement with the Korean Government covering the construction of a water-works plant for the city of Seoul, were recently approached by a representative of an English concern, regarding the raising of a joint British and American loan for that and other purposes. As the matter was laid before me, some days ago I visited Mr. Gubbins, the British Charge d'Affairs, and suggested that he talk with Mr. Brown, the Commissioner of Customs, regarding the possible advisability of using customs funds for the purpose of constructing these water-works. I explained that I had assurances that my people, acting with certain English capitalists, might be able to raise a loan to be secured by the customs revenues, but that I would dislike to see my people make any such attempt at this time, when such active efforts are being put forth to prevent the consummation of this French loan, and that I fancied my Government might not approve of any such attempt as this time. I added that even if the French loan should go through, it was only to be a lien upon the customs in case the annual payments could not be made from other sources, and that any disposition of the customs monies made now, would leave so much less to be used for liquidating the French loan when the annual payments should begin to fall due. He agreed with me that the Korean Government could make such present disposition of the customs revenues and that any such disposition would prevent the further use of this money, but he wished to defer answering my question until he had received expected telegraphic instructions from his Government. On the night of the 8th instant, he wrote me to make an appointment for 10 A.M. the next day for Mr. Brown, and for himself at 11 A.M.

At the appointed time Mr. Brown came and during an hour's conversation he informed me that he was not prepared to exercise the power conferred upon him by Imperial Decree, and use a portion of the customs revenues for public purposes; that the first and most necessary use to which he would apply these funds would be for the erection of lighthouses, buoys and other aids to navigation. He said he had already received an instruction from the Foreign Minister to take up this matter, and he had accordingly set aside ¥250,000 ($125,000) for the purpose, to which fund he would add from time to time. He said that the accumulated tonnage dues now amount to ¥120,000 ($60,000), and the annual receipts from tonnage dues, which must by treaty be used for aiding navigation, now amount to ¥20,000, which would be used for maintenance of a specially built steamer of 500 tons to be used as a lighthouse tender, and for foreign light keepers.

Mr. Brown went on to say that he also considered the furnishing of the city of Seoul with a suitable water-works, a measure of sufficient public importance to sanction the use of customs money for this purpose. He said he was willing to allow something over ¥1,000,000 ($500,000) to be taken from the customs revenues in deferred payments, for this purpose. He admitted that he considered this a small amount for such a work but that it would be enough for a beginning upon which other funds might be raised.

This was quite satisfactory to me. The aids to navigation are greatly needed and are of first importance. The Japanese Russian and British Representatives, have been agitating this question for some time. Of late the Russian has not seemed to be so much interested in it as he was formerly, while the Japanese, whose ships far out-number all those of other nationalities, has been very active in the matter.

As I have before explained, Mr. Brown was placed in charge of the disposal of the customs revenues until the Japanese loan should have been paid. He is therefore still in charge of these funds. The French loan could not become a lien upon the customs without the recall of this decree; the dismissal of Mr. Brown, or the refusal of the British Government to support its subject. The British Government has taken the keenest interest in this matter and thousands of dollars have been spent in telegraphing on the subject. Had the Franco-Russian move against Brown succeeded, it would have been practicable to attempt something of the kind with Sir Robert Hart in Pekin, to whose service, Mr. Brown belongs. I am forced to believe that this attack upon Mr. Brown was originated or sanctioned by Mr. Pavlow, the Russian Charge d'Affaires because of his own utterances to me in regard to Brown and his desire for his dismissal. The above formal statement of Mr. Brown to me indicate that he now has the full support of his Government, and that for the part taken in his support by the Japanese Minister and myself, we are to receive his support in the two public enterprises in which we are respectively, the most interested. I must add that Mr. Gubbins and all concerned, are fully aware that any action I have taken in regard to the matters of Mr. Brown, was taken on my own responsibility and in the interest of American enterprises.

Mr. Gubbins called on me as Mr. Brown was leaving, and, referring to the subjects of my conversation with Mr. Brown, he said he had received the instructions from his Government which he had been awaiting and he was now prepared to support Mr. Brown in his right to control the customs revenues. He said that by instructions from his Government he was also prepared to support the Japanese Minister in his demand for the use of a portion of the customs revenues for the purpose of furnishing aids to navigation, as provided for in the treaty between Japan and Korea, and that he was also prepared to support me in asking for a use of these funds for the purpose of erecting water works for the city of Seoul. He further stated that the Japanese Minister agreed in this water works proposal.

Mr. Gubbins went on to inform me that, under instructions from his Government, he was to see the Frenchman Cazalis, who had negotiated the loan for the Yunan Syndicate, (which I may remind you, is registered in London) and to inform him that the British Government could not sanction this project. Later in the day he told me that he had delivered this message and Mr. Cazalis had seemed to accept it as final and had announced his intention of departing at once for France to lay the matter before the French Government. Mr. Gubbins told me that he had learned that the loan project had been arranged with the French Government by Mr. de Plancy, the French Charge d'Affaires here, before the latters recent return from Paris. He also sated that he had received an intimation, presumably from his Government, that the Russian Government had disclaimed all connection with this loan. This he took to mean that Mr. Pavlow was not fully supported in his recent course in Korea.

I was told by Mr. Gubbins of a very stormy interview he had had on the 8'th. instant with the Acting Minister for Foreign Affairs, who came to him with what he styled the orders of the Emperor, demanding that Mr. Brown should immediately vacate the customs premises, with the exception of the offices, which he might occupy temporarily. Mr. Gubbins said he informed the official that it was not for him to dictate to the British Government in regard to matters already agreed upon and that Mr. Brown would not vacate the premises until a reasonable time had been agreed upon and other suitable quarters had been provided. Mr. Gubbins fears the sudden use of force by the Koreans to eject Mr. Brown, and he has therefore made all arrangements with Admiral Bruce at Chemulpo, for the landing of a very large marine guard on short notice, while the transportation has all been arranged for with the Japanese railway people. He considers the situation to be critical.

It is supposed that the absence of Mr. Pavlow in Japan, tends to restrain the Korean Ye Yong Ik, who is responsible for most of the Korean action in this matter.

Mr. Gubbins then came to the object of his visit. He informed me that, upon instructions from his Government, he had asked for an audience for the purpose of addressing the Emperor upon the subject of the man Ye Yong Ik, Vice Minister for Finance; Director of the Mint; Privy Treasurer of the Emperor, Ginseng Farmer, and General Dictator, of whom I have written you at length during the past few years. He said that the Japanese Minister had similar instructions and had asked for an audience for the same purpose, adding that it was their intention to attempt to secure the removal of this man from his post of influence.

Replying to his queries I told Mr. Gubbins that I considered he was now on the right track and by this action he would strike at the root of the trouble.

He asked me to cooperate with himself and the Japanese Minister in this attempt.

I replied that I could not agree to do so without instructions, and that I doubted my ability to make the matter sufficiently clear by telegraph to obtain such instructions, but that any such course was quite unneccesary since, acting upon my own responsibility and in process of protecting American interests, I had already taken a simlar stand in a letter to His Majesty, wherein I had been forced to decline to accept the latter's word in a matter because of the influence of Ye Yong Ik upon him which had already caused the violation of a solemn written agreement. I went on to say that I was about to follow this up with a stronger note and that this action of mine taken in this independent manner would give them all the support necessary.

In explanation I have to refer you to my despatch No. 339 of April 29, Page 5, wherein I detail the indebtedness of the Korean Emperor to Collbran and Bostwick, amounting to over one and a half million yen ($750,000). In January last His Majesty agreed in writing, over his seal, to pay daily to Collbran and Bostwick from the mint ¥2000, in nickels, toward the liquidation of this debt, and Collbran and Bostwick agreed to accept nickels - which they could use in their further work. Not a nickel was paid on this agreement, though Collbran and Bostwick, with my assistance, have done all they could to secure payment. Messages have come from His Majesty several times to the effect that while he himself was anxious to have the agreement carried out Ye Yong Ik prevented him by one excuse after another,

Some time ago The Emperor commissioned Collbran and Bostwick to purchase for him, from America, ¥350,000 ($125,000) worth of nickel blanks for coining into 5¢ pieces, with the understanding that they should also do the coining, for the alleged reason that His Majesty could not trust Ye Yong Ik. If this were to be done the most natural thing would be for this firm to keep out of a fixed daily amount, to be agreed upon, to be applied toward the liquidation of the debt. I have not given this my official sanction because of the fact that there is so much illicit coining going on with the connivance of the Government, that nickels will soon be practically valueless I fear, and as most of the debt due Collbran and Bostwick is to be paid in Yen, I do not wish to seem to admit that it may be paid in anything else. I was surprised to find that Collbran and Bostwick were willing to accept nickels, but they have large works on hand that require native currency and they considered that they might buy rice or other Korean products with the balance, and they were also anxious to make the payment as easy as possible for the Koreans. The Emperor consulted with the Minister of the Treasury and with other enlightened and impartial officials, who all informed him that the proposed plan seemed to be an excellent one and would enable him to easily pay off the debt and have the electric plants entirely free. He ordered the papers drawn up, when Ye Yong Ik got the news of the proposed plan and was able at once to stop it.

The Emperor then sent Mr. Sands, the American Advisor to the Household Department, to me to explain the matter and to say that he would give me his solemn word that ¥3000 in nickel would be paid daily from now on, to which Ye Yong Ik is said to have agreed with the exception of sundays. I have not been in the habit of communicating with the Emperor through Mr. Sands, as I have not cared to seem to be in any way identified with the advice he might feel called upon to give, but in this case I decided to reply in writing through him. I did so as per enclosed copy, in which I declined to accept the offer of a daily payment from the mint and gave as my reason the previous success of Ye Yong Ik in making His Majesty's orders valueless.

This was justly regarded in the Palace as an attack upon Ye Yong Ik, and the latter is reported to me as having used violent and threatening language against myself and other Americans and to have attempted to secure the dismissal of Mr. Sands.

Therefore, upon hearing of the instructions and intentions of my British and Japanese colleagues, I decided to take an advanced independent step, so that my action against Ye Yong Ik might not seem taken as a joint action with these Representatives. I therefore addressed a private note to Mr. Sands, as per copy, with a careful translation so that it might be shown to His Majesty, in which I announced that I might soon be compelled to take up the case of Ye Yong Ik as I had done that of Kim Yong Chun over a year ago. By reading my No. 233 of March 15, 1900, and references, you will see that the companion of this Ye Yong Ik received his first check by compelling me to move against him. He paid the penalty of his crimes with a miserable death as will be seen by reference to my No. 324 of March 22.

Although this note was purely a personal one and does not commit me to any definite action, I knew it would have all the more effect from being presented in that manner. As a matter of fact, it created a profound impression when presented on the night of the 9'th inst. The Emperor at once announced that the debt to Collbran and Bostwick must be immediately attended to, and he wished to know if that would satisfy me, to which I understand, the Korean who took the note in replied that he thought it improbable.

Messrs Gubbins and Hayashi have not yet been able to secure an audience, but Mr. Gubbins now has a royal letter to deliver, which will compel the grant of an early audience, when he intends to take up the case of Ye Yong Ik. I am sure that my action will greatly strengthen the attack, yet it was entirely independent.

What I have done was of course upon my own responsibility and unofficial. Should it seem necessary to take further action I will ask for instrucitons referring to this letter, unless I see that I can safely do without. I shall be mindful of the aversion of the Department to anything like joint action.

I may add in conclusion that during the past week there has been quite a fleet of warships at Chemulpo. There being as many as twelve at one time, namely: - four Austrians; four British; one Russian, and three Japanese. The French fleet is expected here on or about the 16'th. instant.

Horace N Allen

No. 352   Legation of the United States
                                                Seoul, Korea, May 25, 1901.

Secretary of State

Sir:-

In my despatch No. 349, of May 21, I informed you of the difficulty experienced by the British and the Japanese Representatives, in obtaining an audience with the Emperor, for the purpose of discussing the matters of interest in connection with the Brown Incident and the French loan, and of denouncing the Korean official Ye Yong Ik.

I now have the honor to inform you that the audiences took place on yesterday, Mr. Gubbins, the British Charge d'Affaires, being received at 10-30 A.M.: Mr. Hayashi, the Japanese E.E.&.M.P. was received at 11-30 A.M. and M. de Plancy, French Charge d'Affaires, was received at 2-30 P.M. for the purpose of presenting M. Pichon, the French Minister to China, who arrived at Chemulpo on the French 2'nd. class Cruiser, "Pascal" on the 22'nd. and left Seoul on his way to France, last evening. I do not know that the visit of M. Pichon, had any political significance and I do not know the subjects of the conversation at the audience of M. de Plancy.

Immediately after his audience, Mr. Gubbins came to me and gave me a full account of his interview. He said that at first His Majesty seemed inclined to be disagreeable, but that the audience terminated in a friendly manner. After reviewing the whole of the Brown matter, Mr. Gubbins says he informed His Majesty that his Government had taken a very firm stand; that they would demand a years notice and the selection and provision of a suitable new site and quarters before consenting to Mr. Browns removal from any of the present customs premises; that it now remained for His Majesty to instruct the Minister for Foreign Affairs to consult with Mr. Brown and select a suitable site and provide for the erection of new quarters; that after the site shall have been selected and due official notice given him (Gubbins) of the fact, he would officially notify the Foreign Minister that the period of a years notice would begin from that date. The Emperor is said to have demurred at this but Mr. Gubbins said he informed him that his Government had arrived at this decision after due deliberation and that they would consent to nothing else.

Mr. Gubbins informed me that he then went on to speak of the good record Mr. Brown had made in Korea, and that he called the Emperor's attention to the fact that on May 10 last, in audience, he himself had assured Mr. Gubbins that he had no complaint to make against Mr. Brown. He went on to say that he was now aware that the attack upon Mr. Brown was a part of a great plot in which many persons had taken a part, but that the chief actor in the matter was the Korean official Ye Yong Ik, and - to quote the exact words which I wrote down and submitted to Mr. Gubbins - "it is my duty to advise Your Majesty that the retention of this man (Ye Yong Ik) in any official position, will be detrimental to the relations between our two Governments".

As to the loan, Mr. Gubbins had previously informed His Majesty through the Minister for Foreign Affairs, that his Government did not approve of it, and on this occasion he alluded to the part Ye Yong Ik had taken in this matter, and asked if His Majesty was aware that the Yunan Syndicate Limited, was registered in London. The Emperor asked why, if this was a English Company, the negotiations had been carried on by the French Minister, to which Mr. Gubbins made reply that he wished to know for himself why such had been the case.

I may add that Mr. Gubbins has been most careful in all this matter of the discussion regarding Mr. Brown's dismissal and kindred subjects, to do nothing except upon direct instructions from his Government, and he tells me he has spent many thousands of dollars in telegrams. He says that his Government has realized that this incident actually represents a grave situation and he has allowed me to infer that his Government has been in full and constant communication and accord with the Government of Japan in the matter.

Mr. Gubbins assured me that he and Mr. Hayashi had fully discussed the matter and that their utterances at their respective audiences would be practically the same.

I now hear from the palace that the impression left by these gentlemen was one of indifference so far as the loan was concerned and of only feeble, and chiefly, prospective opposition to Ye Yong Ik. Whether their utterances were couched in language of a too distinctly diplomatic nature, or that the absence of a written memorandum of the remarks made has enabled Ye Yong Ik to minimize the effect of those remarks, I cannot say. I hear now that the loan will be accepted so far as the Koreans are concerned, and a private message from His Majesty makes enquiry of me as to why it is that the British and Japanese Representatives did not object in writing to this project, as I did.

In this connection I wish to state that my letter to the Minister for Foreign Affairs, objecting to the pledging of the Korean Customs for the payment of the French loan, a copy of which I sent you in my No. 350 of May 21, reached the palace on the 22'nd. instant, and on the following day I called upon Mr. de Plancy, the French Charge d'Affaires, and informed him of my action, giving him a verbal account of my letter. I told him that my action was not taken with a view of annoying him, but in the line of my duty as protecting American interests; that if I should let the customs revenues be pledged without comment, I might be made such trouble later on in securing the fulfillment of the water-works agreements. He assured me that he regarded my action as most natural and proper, and that, while he knew of the existence of an agreement with Americans covering the water-works, he was not aware that the customs had been pledged for this purpose, and had been assured by the Koreans and the customs were entirely free, with the exception of the remainder of the Japanese loan yet unpaid. I told him that that was technically correct, since it was only a promise and a mutual understanding that I could urge, since the customs could not be pledged for this purpose until the completion of the survey and the drawing up of the estimates based upon that survey. He said it seemed like an act of bad faith on the part of the Koreans, but as they so seldom knew their own business he thought perhaps the Foreign Office may not actually have known of this promise to Americans. I admitted that this was probably the case and stated that that was another reason why I had wished to record my objections officially, since in so doing I could bring officially before the Foreign Office a matter that had so far been attended to by His Majesty, through the Household Department. Mr. de Plancy seemed very desirous of convincing me that he had not intentionally worked against me, and hinted that as the amount to be drawn from the customs returns for this loan, was really a small affair, there would be ample for both projects.

I am pleased with the effect of my letter to the Foreign Office. It is properly understood as placing me on record in such a manner as to permit my future insistence upon the fulfillment of existing agreements, and it seems not to have caused offence to the French.

In my No. 350 of May 21, wherein I stated that Mr. Hayashi, had informed me that he had protested against the completion of the French loan, and desired me to do something of the kind if possible, I find on further conversation with him that he used the word protest unadvisedly. He says that, under instructions from his Government, he "gave very strong advices" against the measure, basing his objections chiefly on the unfavorable terms of the contract and upon the fact that the pledging of the customs would be contrary to treaty agreements with Japan in regard to the use of such funds for providing aids to navigation. The failure of himself and Mr. Gubbins, to properly present the matter, officially, will perhaps allow the documents to be signed, and thus lay the Koreans open to the payment of a heavy indemnity, for it is not thought that the money will actually be accepted if raised and offered.

In the meantime, M. Tremoulet, the Frenchman mentioned in my No. 314 of February 13, as interested in obtaining a sort of mining monopoly in Korea, has returned from a hasty trip to Paris, and he has taken a stand against this French loan, so that it looks as though the French were not at harmony amongst themselves.

Horace N Allen

No. 356

Legation of the United States
Seoul, Korea, May 31, 1901.

Secretary of State

Sir:-

Continuing the subject of my despatch of the 25'th. instant, No. 352, in regard to the French loan, I now have the honor to inform you that I have received a message from the palace to the effect that the loan was accepted on the 29'th. instant, and Mr. Cazalis, the promoter, was asked to return to France and get the money.

In attempting to ascertain what marked the formal acceptance of the loan, I learned that the project was submitted to the Council of State on April 18, and received a majority vote in favor of its acceptance. The Prime Minister, Chyo Pyung Sik, objected and put in a memorial against the loan. He was compelled to resign. He apparently refused to attach the seal of the Council of State to the documents, and I am now given to understand that his successor has attended to this sealing of the papers. I was told that His Majesty, heeding the objections raised to the loan, endeavored to break the agreement, and actually asked the Japanese Minister to put in formal objections as I had done, but he could not do so. Failing to get foreign backing in his attempts to get out of the matter, His Majesty seems to have accepted the loan and all it includes. As to the latter, I can learn but little except that Mr. Cazalis said to Mr. Gubbins, the British Charge d'Affaires, that the loan itself was a small matter, that he was really after extensive mining franchises, in which the Yunan Syndicate - a British Company - was interested. Mr. Gubbins thinks that these mining privileges were not granted. I cannot feel the same assurance myself. I know that Mr. Cazalis leaves for Europe by tomorrow's steamer, and it is understood that he has succeeded.

Both Mr. Gubbins and the Japanese Minister, announce their belief that that the loan matter has failed. The Foreign Minister informed them yesterday that it had not been passed upon favorably, but the statements of this gentleman have not been found to be entirely reliable of late. Mr. Brown, the Commisioner of Customs, whose consent must be obtained before the customs revenues are pledged, says he has not yet been spoken to upon the subject, and that he will not consent to such pledging for the purpose of this loan. If the British Government sustain him in this position, this may prevent the bankers from advancing the money. In which case Mr. Cazalis may probably get his mining concessions anyway as a sort of indemnity.

My own position is satisfactory. I have lodged my official objections to the pledging of the customs revenues, because such action would interfere with American agreements. I have informed the

French and British Representatives of this action, as well as Mr. Brown. I have arranged with Mr. Brown that at least a portion of the money required for the water-works shall be provided by the customs. What I have done has been fully understood, and has met with no objections from the Koreans or from the French Minister. I am able now to refer to my official objections in the future, if necessary.

Horace N Allen

No. 365   Legation of the United States
                                                          Seoul, Korea, June 12, 1901.

Secretary of State

Sir:-

Continuing the subject of my despatch No, 352 of May 25, relative to the matter of Mr. Brown, the Englishman in charge of the Korean Customs, I have the honor to inform you that while Mr. Gubbins, the British Charge d' Affaires, was entirely pleased with the situation as it was last week, being confident of the satisfactory settlement of pending negotiations for the selection of a new site for Mr. Brown's residence and the offices of the customs, in consideration of which he consented to the departure of Admiral Sir. James Bruce with his flagship the "Barfleur - leaving the "Astrea" at Chemulpo, he now tells me that in an interview with the Minister for Foreign Affairs on the 10'th. instant, the latter unexpectedly showed his former rudeness and he feared no settlement would be arrived at for some time.

Mr. Gubbins tells me that he is infomed, confidentially by Mr. Hayashi, the Japanese Minister, that at an audience with the Emperor on the 8'th. instant, Mr. Pavlow, the Russian Charge d'Affaires, "suggested to the Emperor the dismissal of McLeavy Brown, the appointment of a Russian adviser and the retention of Ye Yong Ik".

Mr. Gubbins thinks this advice is reponsible for the change iof attitude on the part of the Koreans.

You will remember that both Mr. Gubbins and Mr. Hayashi denounced Ye Yong Ik, in audience with His Majesty, and Mr. Gubbins was very strong on the matter, See my No. 352.

Russian influence seems to have been enhanced by the incidents of the attempted dismissal of Mr. Brown and of the French loan, at the expense of the loss of prestige by the Japanese. The latter have worked in close harmony with the English, and Mr. Hayashi has made frequent representations to the Emperor in favor of Mr. Brown and against the French loan, but these have all been unofficial and more or less confidential. When directly asked by the Emperor to officially object to the loan after the manner of my objection to the pledging of the customs, Mr. Hayashi declared he had not instructions to do so and would be unable to take such course. The result is that the Koreans seem to have the idea that Japan is so afraid of Russia that she dare "only whisper secretly in a corner". This has tended to cause the Koreans to listen more carefully even than before, to any remarks of Mr. Pavlow.

As an offset for the recent continued presence of the British ships at Chemulpo, the Russian Government has now sent a man-of-war to remain permanently in Korean waters. Mr. Pavlow brought the Captain around to make official calls on yesterday as though he were to be a permanent attaché of the Russian Legation.

During the recent time of political discussion in Korea, every one of the treaty powers except Italy and the United States have sent ships here and four Admirals have either been here or are on their way. Now I have received a telegram from Captain Sperry at Chemulpo announcing the arrival of the U.S.S. "New Orleans" at Chemulpo, this morning.

Horace N Allen

No. 371   Legation of the United States
                                                   Seoul, Korea, June 27, 1901.

Secretary of State

Sir:-
    Referring to my confidential despatch No. 365, of June 12, and the series referred to therein, I now have the honor to inform you that Mr. Gubbins, the British Chargé d'Affaires, has informed me that, by an exchange of notes, previously arranged for, between the Korean Foreign Office and himself, the matter of the dismissal of Mr. McLeavy Brown, the Englishman in charge of the Korean Customs, and the surrender of the customs residence and office buildings, has been satisfactorily settled.
    Mr. Brown is given a new and suitable site with the funds for erecting proper new buildings: The present buildings, in regard to which there has been so much discussion, will be surrendered within one year from the date of the exchange of these official notes.
    The exchange of notes took place on June 24'th.

                                                   Horace N Allen

No. 541   Legation of the United States
                                                   Seoul, Korea, November 28, 1902.

Secretary of State

Sir:-
    I have the honor to address you in regard to the Korean official Ye Yong Ik, who has usurped the Government here, and of whom I have had to write you so often.
    Mr. Stein, the Russian Chargé d'Affairs, ad interim, today asked me if I would assist him to save the life of this man. I had to reply that it would be impossible for me to interfere in the matter. I understand that Mr. Stein is being assisted by the French Minister, Mr. de Plancy, in his attempts to relieve this man Ye.
    The facts are briefly as follows: - This man, who is of coolie origin, is so detested by the better class of Korean officials, that it is a wonder he has lasted so long. Just now he is engaged in a renewed and very severe attempt to squeeze money from the people. To this end he had himself appointed Chief of the Supreme Court, for the purpose of "trying" the provincial officers for neglecting to send in sufficient funds.
    This trial simply means severe torture, and the aristocracy of the country seem to have arisen with a determination to prevent such a course. The arrest of Ye Yong Ik was ordered some days ago but he remained in the Palace where the warrant could not be executed. It was reported that the order for his arrest had been recalled by the Emperor upon the earnest solicitation of Ye. Now it seems that the warrant has again been issued as the result of a full cabinet meeting held on yesterday, at which a unanimous petition was signed praying for the arrest and trial of Ye Yong Ik. The Palace was consequently closely guarded last night and it was evident that something serious was on hand.
    Mr. Stein informs me that the charge laid against the man is that he made a threatening remark in regard to Lady Om, the chief concubine and mother of the young prince. This woman carried out the plans which resulted in the escape of the King and Crown Prince to the Russian Legation in 1896, and has frequently been proposed as Empress. Recently she was raised to the highest degree of concubine, and the next step will probably give her the coveted Imperial title. Her son is very bright, while the Crown Prince is impotent and can have no children. A measure has been proposed looking to making this boy the successor to the Emperor. Ye Yong Ik has stated, it is said, that for this proposal the boy should be killed. The charge of which Mr. Stein spoke to me however was that Ye Yong Ik had made a reference to a noted Empress of China, comparing Lady Om's fate to hers. It seems that this Empress rose from the common people as did Om, and when she became Empress she ruined the country and suffered death in consequence. This is taken as a threat and is used as a means of inciting Lady Om and the Emperor against Ye.
    Mr. Stein tells me the case is being tried today at the Supreme Court under a judge appointed for the purpose, and that the enemies of Ye have incited the already angered people to be present and murder Ye on his coming out from the Court.

One of the first acts of Ye Yong Ik as Chief Judge of the Supreme Court a few days since, is said to have been the fatal torture of a woman. This it is said, has so angered the people, that they are ready to go to any extent in retaliation.

As I informed you in my despatches No's 533, Nov. 21; 535, November 24, and 540 of today, I made strong representations against this man to His Majesty in my audience of the 17'th. instant; laying upon him the blame of the unfortunate condition into which American matters, especially the affairs of Collbran and Bostwick, had fallen. A number of high officials were present at this interview, and the Crown Prince was particularly pleased with what I had to say of Ye, whom His Highness seems to detest.

I don't think my reference to this man has been the cause of his present predicament, though it doubtless gave his enemies encouragement.

The British Minister, Mr. Gubbins, in 1901, actually demanded the removal of Ye Yong Ik from his post of influence, but his demand went unheeded. See my despatch, No. 346, of May, 11, 1901. Page 5.

The chances are that Ye Yong Ik will escape from his present difficulty as he has in former cases. The Japanese are much connected with him in various ways, and I dont think they would care to see him done to death, while the Russian and French Ministers are doing their best to save him.

Horace N Allen

No. 563   Legation of the United States
                                           Seoul, Korea, January 5, 1903.

Secretary of State

Sir:-

Continuing the subject of my despatch No. 559, of the 29'th. ultimo, regarding the protest of the Japanese Government against the retention in office of Ye Yong Ik, while the latter is under the protection of a foreign power, I now have the honor to inform you that Mr. Hagiwara, the Japanese Chargé d'Affaires ad interum has told me that on the 31'st ultimo, he withdrew this protest in accordance with a joint agreement made by the authority of his Government, between himself; the Korean Minister for Foreign Affairs and the Russian Chargé d'Affaires ad interum, to the effect that "no profit shall accrue to Russia by virtue of the employment of Ye Yong Ik in such office".

Mr. Hagiwara said that he also secured the adjustment of three long pending questions in this connection. These questions were; the removal of further objection on the part of the Korean Government to the issue of notes called "Shibusawa money", by the Japanese branch of the First Bank, in Korea - see my No. 516, Oct. 17; the abolishment of likin on Japanese goods in the interior, which is a case similar to the British one I mentioned in my No. 538, November 25; and the appointment of a Korean minister to Japan. These three questions have been pressed for some time upon the Korean Government, by the Japanese Legation, and their present settlement seems to give the Chargé d'Affairs ad interim considerable satisfaction.

As an instance of the manner in which the Ye Yong Ik incident is viewed in Japan, I enclose a clipping from the Japan Daily Mail of December 22. When I informed you that the Russian Chargé d'Affaires ad interim, Mr. Stein, had placed Ye Yong Ik on a Russian gunboat, see my No. 556, of December 18, I was not aware that Russian marines had been landed for the purpose.

Horace N Allen

THE RUSSO-JAPANESE WAR

The Wrecked Remains of Russian Warships in Ch'emulp'o Harbor

Reprinted from Peter A. Underwood, Samuel H. Moffett, and Normen R. Sibley, eds., *First Encounters: Korea 1880–1910* (Seoul: Dragon's Eye Graphics, 1982), 30.

A. Northern Timber Concessions and Increasing Tensions

No. 604

Legation of the United States
Seoul, Korea, April 24, 1903.

Secretary of State

Sir:-

The Japanese Authorities in Seoul are considerably exercised over the operations of the Russians in connection with a timber concession on the northern border of Korea, I therefore have the honor to hand you the following particulars regarding this concession.

In 1884 Mr. James R. Morse, an American, received a concession for cutting timber on Dagelet Island, of the East Coast of Korea. The island had a heavy growth of great hard wood trees which were much prized in Japan for such uses as temple erections. Soon after this concession had been granted an English company secured one for the same purpose. This resulted in a law suit over timber brought to Japan by the latter and seized by the former. After that time Mr. Morse did nothing more with his concession and private Japanese parties have been doing an extensive illegal business in timber cutting on that island.

In 1896 Mr. C. Waeber, the Russian Representative in Korea, asked me to secure from Mr. Morse the relinquishment of this old timber concession, as a Russian named Bryner desired to obtain a timber concession for the northern boarder of Korea including Dagelet Island. Mr. Waeber had assisted me in obtaining the concession for Mr. James R. Morse, for the Seoul-Chemulpo Railway line just before that time, while the King was living in the Russian Legation. I therefore telegraphed to Mr. Morse who was then in New York, and secured his consent to waive his claim to Dagelet Island in favor of the Russians, who thereupon, August 29, 1896, secured the concession in question. Work was not begun however, and the concession had to be renewed which was done by Mr. Pavlow, the Russian Minister, about eighteen months ago. This concession has now passed into the hands of a Russian company of which Baron de Gunzburg is the local representative.

Baron Gunzburg has sent a considerable staff of workmen to the Yalu River in North-west Korea to begin the cutting and sawing of timber, having also sent a saw mill to that locality. He maintains quite an imposing staff at his office here in Seoul, which office was formally opened yesterday.

The Japanese claim that a large force of cossacks are on the Yalu River or near by, for the protection of this timber cutting expedition, but Baron de Gunzburg assures me there is simply a force of "forest guards".

The situation is somewhat complicated by the fact that Japanese are in the same region cutting timber on some local agreement obtained by certain Chinese. There is a good demand for this timber for use as railway sleepers, hence there is quite a rush to obtain it.

The Russians undoubtedly have the right and they will probably be protected in that right.

I have explained the American connection with this concession to the Secretary of the Japanese Legation who made certain enquiries of me on the subject.

Horace N. Allen.

No. 612

Legation of the United States
Seoul, Korea, May 26, 1903.

Secretary of State

Sir:-

It now seems probable that there may be more or less local friction between the Japanese and Russians over the timber operations of both on the Yalu River.

In my No. 604 of April 24, I explained the nature of the Russian claims for timber rights in this region. They undoubtedly have a legal concession, while the Japanese have none. At the same time the latter have been in that region for some time in considerable numbers, cutting timber on local arrangements such as are not usually not recognized at Seoul. As I indicated in my No. 608 of the 19'th. instant, the Korean Government now seems inclined to try to evade the obligations it is under in connection with this Russian concession.

The Secretary of the Japanese Legation, Mr. Hagiwara, called on me yesterday and informed me that he was starting for the north to look into this timber matter. The Russian Consul at Chemulpo, Mr. Polianovsky, has already gone to that region. Mr. Hagiwara told me that he feared there was some truth to the Korean report that 200 Russians had recently arrived on the Yalu. He said also that if the Russians seized timber already cut by the Japanese, as they have announced their intention of doing, he feared there might possibly be some local trouble over the matter.

As I was dining with Mr. Pavlow, the Russian Minister, last evening, I asked him about the reported arrival of 200 Russians in the Yalu region. He said that the situation was exactly as he had stated it to me before, - see my No. 608, of the 19'th. He however qualified this statement by saying that he had no recent news from that region and was awaiting the arrival of Mr. Polianovsky. The report may therefore be true.

In the meantime, we are indirectly connected with this dispute which has caused much comment in the newspapers published in Japan, as will be seen by an extract from the Japan Daily Mail of the 19'th. instant, which I enclose. It gives an editorial summing up of the case.

Messrs Lee and Moffett of the American Presbyterian Mission of 156 Fifth Avenue, New York City, residing at Pengyang city, have been having much trouble with the Korean Authorities over the seizure of their lumber, which action compelled me to demand and secure the payment of an indemnity to them, see my despatch No. 598, of April 8. Under these circumstances, in order to avoid similar trouble in the future, these missionaries contracted with a Korean to cut and bring them a very large amount of timber from the Yalu River. They did not know of proposed Russian operations in that region. When their timber, amounting to 2800 large logs, was ready for floating down the river, the local Korean Authorities demanded a tax of 360 yen ($180). Instead of paying this tax the matter was referred to me. I found that the tax was considered legal, see my letter to Mr. Lee of today's date, copy enclosed.

At this juncture however the Russians put in a claim for this timber, but considering my original assistance in the matter, as explained in my despatch No. 604 of April 24, Baron de Gunzburg agreed to endeavor to arrange that, while the timber would have to be seized in order not to establish a bad precedent, it would be at once released on a nominal payment for the timber itself, said payment to be practically the same as that proposed to be made to the Americans for the cost of getting out the seized timber. I enclose the confidential letter of Baron de Gunzburg to me on the subject, having retained a press copy. This letter is valuable in showing just what the Russian contentions and intentions are. The latter indend to seize all timber now cut, as it is floated down the river. They also propose to pay back on all such seized timber the actual cost of felling it and getting it out, and then sell it for their own profit.

This will surely anger the Japanese, who have a large amount of cut timber on the upper Yalu ready to be sent down the river. Local disturbance may be expected.

The timber matter can however scarcely precipitate serious difficulties between Japan and Russia, since the latter have a legal concession and the former have none. The case will probably be referred to Tokio and St. Petersburg and result in some international agreement in the nature of a compromise.

I am expecting to leave for Europe and America on the first and would not go if serious disturbances were imminent, but from all the information I can obtain it seems that the matter will hardly be allowed to assume serious proportions.

I have submitted to Messrs Lee and Moffett, the propositions of the Koreans and Russians and have left the decision to them. They have certainly gone into the timber business on a large scale, and they might better have settled the matter locally and secured their timber, rather than report the matter to the central government.

Horace N. Allen.

No. 621
Legation of the United States
Seoul, Korea, November 19th,1903.

Secretary of State

Sir:-
   I have the honor to acknowledge the receipt of your cipher telegrams of the 8th. and the 17th. instant, the reading of which, with that of my cipher replies of the 11th. and 18th. will be found enclosed. Upon receipt of our first telegram I called on the Japanese and the British representatives. I could not, however, reply immediately as it was necessary to await repetition of several of the code words. I found that both Mr. Hayashi, the Japanese Minister, and Mr. Jordan, the British Minister, had entirely given up advocating the opening of Wiju, and are devoting all their efforts to opening Yongampo. They both tell me that they have instructions to "insist" on the opening of the latter place, and Mr. Hayashi said that, if the Korean government fails to act, through Russian opposition, his government will in all probability make it the subject of representations to the Russian government. On receipt of the corrections in transmission of your telegram, I at once wrote to the Korean Foreign Minister, a copy of which letter is enclosed, and on the same day called upon him. After numerous changes during the past six months, due to the demoralized condition of this country, the office of Acting Minister for Foreign Affairs has been given to a Mr. Ye Ha Yung, who accepts it rather under compulsion. Mr. Ye is a man of experience, and friendly to American interests, having been Secretary of Legation at Washington, and being a personal friend of Dr. Allen's. I found that he too is most anxious to open Yongampo, fearing that the present establishment of the Russian timber company at that port is in a line with Russian methods in Manchuria. He has already had several audiences with and has memorialized the Emperor on the subject, but so far without effect. He says he will put the matter through, however, or force His Majesty to accept his resignation. He expressed himself as delighted at the prospect of the support of our government. I enclose his reply to my first letter. I also sent a verbal communication, to the same effect as my letter, to His Majesty through some of the Imperial chamberlains. Upon receipt of your telegram of the 17th. I immediately wrote again to the Foreign Minister. (Copy enclosed.)
   In my former letter, as will be seen, believing from the instruction in your first telegram to "confer with the British and Japanese representatives" that I was to act, so far as possible, in accord with them, and finding that they were concerned only with opening Yongampo, I wrote urging the opening of Wiju, together with Yongampo as a subsidiary port., for reasons mentioned therein. In my second letter, however, since the instructions of your second telegram would seem to cover only the opening of Wiju, I did not further urge opening Yongampo. When Mr. Ye received this letter, he came at once to see me, and begged that I make the letter stronger in support of his efforts by continuing to urge the opening of Yongampo, saying that, if I did so, he believed His Majesty would be induced to order the opening of that port at once. I told him that it was clear from my instructions that my government primarily desired the opening of Wiju; that I would give him such support towards opening the other port as I could, but that I must strongly urge the opening of Wiju, for the reason of it's proximity to Antung, irrespective of Yongampo. He said that if he should now urge on His Majesty the opening of Wiju it would effectually block the opening of the other port, whereas if Yongampo were opened first the opening of Wiju would be comparatively easily arranged. Of this I am not so fully convinced, for the Korean feeling, even when uninfluenced by outside interests, seems to be that they are giving away inherent rights in opening any part of their country. I shall, of course, continue to urge the opening of Wiju, but in such a way as not to interfere with the efforts that are being made to open Yongampo. I told Mr. Ye that I would at once inform you of his desire to open Yongampo, and of the attitude of the Japanese and British representatives.
   The present situation and the conditions that have led to it seem to be as follows: In the early summer the Japanese and British representatives, aroused by Russian activity on the Chinese side of the Yalu, and by the operations of the Russian timber company, which had been begun on the Korean side of the river, (See Mr. Allen's Nos. 612 and 613 of May 26th. and 30th.) proceeded to urge the opening of Wiju upon the Korean government. Mr. Hayashi called on me the end of June to suggest my taking steps in that direction. I told him that I had then no instructions and so could not take any action, but that I believed it to be the policy of my government to favour the opening of such a port. In an interview with the then Foreign Minister on another matter, the subject was informally discussed, and, in reply to his questions, I said that it would seem to be to Korea's advantage to open a port on the Yalu as soon as possible. The Russian Minister, Mr. Pavlow, said at that time that he would not favour the opening of any port on the Yalu until Manchurian matters had been finally settled. Some weeks before this the Russian timber company (See Mr. Allen's No. 612 referred to.) had started an establishment at Yongampo,

ostensibly for the purpose of receiving and shipping the lumber floated down the Yalu. They bought land from the native occupants, without notifying the Korean officals, and to this the Korean government made a vigorous protest on the ground that the place being outside treaty limits the land could not be owned by foreigners. The company claimed that their concession carried with it the right to occupy such land at the mouth of the river as was necessary for their business, but to make their occupation more secure they attempted to get a lease of a considerable tract of land through a subordinate Korean official, who was sent to inspect the premises by the Korean government. This man, named Choh Sung Huip, was taken to the place by arrangement of the company, via Port Arthur, and upon his return to Seoul was appointed "Timber Inspector", an office created for him by the then Foreign Minister. Under this title he signed a lease, which Mr. Pavlow has since been endeavoring to get the Foreign Office to ratify. I enclose a translation of a copy of this lease given me by the present Foreign Minister. Mr. Pavlow has not succeeded in getting the lease ratified, however, although he so assiduously pressed the former Foreign Minister, Mr. Ye Toh Chai, that the latter fled from his office to avoid the responsibility.

Mr. Ye appealed to the Emperor for instructions, but received the evasive reply that it was his duty to settle the matter himself. He attempted to do this by getting the consent of the Foreign Representatives to the opening of Wiju on the condition that the open mart, Pyengyang, should be closed. This of course, failed, and Mr. Ye put in his resignation, which to this time has not been accepted, the present and intervening Ministers having been designated as Acting Foreign Minister. I enclose correspondence which passed between the Foreign Office and myself over the suggestion as to closing Pyengyang. The truth seems to be that His Majesty, apprehensive that his country may be the scene of war, and fearing to antagonize either side, will not order the ratification of the Russian lease, nor, on the other hand, order the opening of a port on the Yalu in the face of Russian opposition. In the mean time the Russians in actual possession at Yongampo have more firmly established themselves, and, perhaps with the idea of making concessions later, if they can obtain such a lease as they wish, they have extended their original reservation about fifty acres, until now the area to which the Timber Company claims exclusive right, I am informed, comprises about one square mile, and includes practically all the land available for a foriegn settlement at that place. This has met with constant opposition on the part of the Koreans, and reports come almost daily of the Koreans having removed the boundary stakes and the Russians replacing them. The Company also attempted, during the summer, to construct a telegraph line from a Korean town, Miruk-Tong, to the Yalu, to connect by cable with Sa-Ha-Cha, on the Chinese Antung side, and erected poles for the purpose, but thus far the Koreans have prevented this, and have, it is understood, removed the poles.

In June last the Chief Commissioner of Korean Customs, Mr. J. McLeavy Brown, (an Englishman,) sent one of his officers to report on the most desirable location on the Yalu for a Korean open port and Customs House. I enclose a copy of this officer's report, together with two very interesting charts made at the time, which give a clear understanding of the situation. These were given me by Mr. Brown. He strongly favours the opening of Yongampo (marked Rongampo on Chart No 1.) as the most suitable place for a foreign settlement, and as the only satifactory location for the Customs, not only because it commands the mouth of the river, but because it seems to be the only spot on the Korean side of the river where there is a channel with sufficient depth of water for steamers, or even deeply laden junks, and where there is something in the nature of a harbour.

Wiju, it seems, is some thirty-six miles (110 li,) by river and thirty miles by road from Yangampo, and it is said to be impossible for even a steam-launch to reach Kurongpo, the landing place for Wiju. Wiju itself is about one and two-thirds miles from the river, and lies in a basin in the hills at some elevation above the river. Baron Gunzburg, the Manager in Korea of the Russian Timber Company, himself told me recently, on his return from a trip to Yongampo, that an English steamer drawing six feet of water had tried to reach Antung, but had to anchor some miles below that place. Wiju is, of course, the largest and best known Korean town in that district. These facts I mention so that you may have what I believe to be accurate information as to the physical conditions of the locality, and in conclusion I must say that I regret extremely that the information contained in some of the enclosures (the Chart No. II, and copy of the lease I have only just now obtained,) should not have been in your hands before, but a rather overwhelming amount of work on local matters, combined with two months of ill-health during the past summer have made it almost impossible for me to do more than keep up the routine work of this office.

Gordon Paddock

No. 636   Legation of the United States
                                            Seoul, Korea, January 2, 1904.

Secretary of State

Sir:-
    I have the honor to hand you enclosed confirmation of my cable message of the 31'st. ultimo.
    In explanation I have to say that the Foreign Minister, Mr. Ye Ha Yong, who was relieved from office on the 19'th. being favorably disposed toward the opening of Wiju, I wrote him on the 17'th. suggesting that he declare the port opened on his own authority; or if he could not do this to secure me an audience for the purpose of explaining further telegraphic instructions I had received from my Government.
    My British and Japanese colleagues each asked for an audience about the same time, for discussing Yongampo matters. Their requests were declined on account of reported illness on the part of the Emperor who was well known to be participating in extreme gaietys connected with the promotion of the mother of his youngest child to the post of "particular consort". My request was not even answered, but on the 25'th. I received an official invitation to attend the ceremonial audience on New Year Day. This I promptly declined on the ground that my request for an audience had not received due attention, see enclosure.
    My British and Japanese colleagues telegraphed to their respective governments for permission to do likewise. The British Government consented and instructed Mr. Jordan to cooperate with his Japanese colleague. The latter however was finally instructed to attend the audience which compelled Mr. Jordan also to accept. Mr. Hayashi told me that his Government had suffered so many indignities at the hands of this Korean Government that it was just as well to let them accumulate for future settlement rather than take issue on a small affair.
    I was finally visited by a delegation from the Foreign Office; the Household Department and the Bureau of Ceremonies, after having received many messages on the subject of the audience. It was explained that a mistake had been made: That the former Foreign Minister had intended to open Wiju on his own responsibility, therefore he had not forwarded my request to the palace so that an audience for me was not thought of. I accepted this explanation and agreed to attend, especially as the U.S. "Vicksburg" had arrived and I wished to take the Captain and officers with me to this audience, which bade fair to be the last under present conditions.
    The audience did not take place, however, as the Empress Dowager began to die with the advent of the new year and completed the process this morning.
    Until within a few days the Emperor has seemed to care nothing whatever for the timely warnings he has had of serious difficulty in store for him. He seems to have put his faith entirely in Russian assurances that there would be no war and they would let no trouble come to him. During the past few days however he has seemed to be quite alarmed and this demise of the Dowager just as the new year came in, has put him into a great state of agitation, as he is morbidly superstitious. I have been approached for some days now on the subject of receiving the Emperor at this Legation as a guest in case of war. I have flatly and unequivocally refused. I have also declined to receive numbers of high officials who have likewise rrqested asylum of me. I shall get a guard for the Legation as soon as the transport "Zaphiro" arrives, and I will then be able to prevent this compound being overrun with refugees.
    It is believed, and I have it on good authority, that the Japanese would be glad to have the Emperor take refuge with the Russian Legation as they would then declare him to have abdicated and take over the administration of the Government.

                                            Horace N Allen

No. 639   Legation of the United States
                                            Seoul, Korea, January 6, 1904.

Secretary of State

Sir:-
    I have the honor to confirm my telegram of today as follows: -
"Twenty five Russian marines marched to Seoul today, failing to secure transportation on the Japanese railroad at Chemulpo".

                                            Horace N. Allen.

No. 640   Legation of the United States
                                                 Seoul, Korea, January 7, 1904.

Secretary of State

Sir:-
        I have the honor to confirm my telegram of today as follows: -
"Yesterday the Japanese landed sixty one packages cases containing four machine guns and ammunition,
from merchant vessel. Customs attempted tp prevent. The Japanese brought them to Seoul where they
have several others. Also they imported fifty thousand bags cavalry barley and we brought guard today one
machine gun concealed among six weeks provisions."

                                                 Horace N Allen

No. 641   Legation of the United States
                                                 Seoul, Korea, January 8, 1904.

Secretary of State,

Sir:-
        I have the honor to confirm my cable message of today as follows:-
"Arrival of the guard having convinced the Emperor the situation may be very serious, (I) we have private
information to the effect that he has ordered opening of Wiju. The British landed twentyone marines for
their Legation this morning".

                                                 Horace N Allen

No. 642   Legation of the United States
                                                 Seoul, Korea, January 9, 1904.

Secretary of State

Sir:-
        I have the honor to confirm my telegram of today as follows:-
"Twenty Italian maries arrived today by railroad. Forty seven more Russians marched to Seoul. Arrived
today. Japanese railroad has refused merchandise for the present because it is engaged in transporting
government supplies".

                                                 Horace N Allen

No. 648   Legation of the United States
                                                 Seoul, Korea, January 19, 1904.

Secretary of State

Sir:-
        I have the honor to confirm my telegram of today as follows: -
"Newspaper reports of guards disorderly conduct unwarranted Guards at the present moment - American
hundred; British forty; Italian twenty; French forty; Japanese and Russian is uncertain, Germans are
expected.
Korean authority Ye Yong Ik, yesterday imported three hundred cases of ammunition for his six, twelve
pound guns from Japan.
Confidential. I have reason to think this man contemplates something like violence to reinstate himself

and defeat his enemies now clammoring for his life; and this would be with the consent of Russian Minister with whom he is constantly in consultation and who controls the situation at the present moment".

Horace N Allen

B. Open Hostilities

No. 658   Legation of the United States
                                                 Seoul, Korea, February 7, 1904.

Secretary of State

Sir:-
    I have the honor to confirm my telegram of today as follows: -
"Government of Korea has received notice of the arrival at Masampo of Japanese naval vessels yesterday afternoon; immediately afterwards telegraphic communication interrupted".

Horace N. Allen

No. 659   Legation of the United States
                                                 Seoul, Korea, February 8, 1904.

Secretary of State

Sir:-
    I have the honor to confirm my telegram of today as follows: -
    "Japanese Minister informed me confidentially, twentyfive hundred Japanese forces are expected to arrive Seoul about tomorrow, and owing to movement of Russian forces to the Yalu the negotiations were suspended and the Japanese Minister has been recalled from Russia. Telegraphic communication with the southern Korean ports is suspended for the present. Munitions of war and a light railway have been landed Kunsan near the terminus of the completed portions of Fusan railway".

Horace N Allen

No. 662   Legation of the United States
                                                 Seoul, Korea, February 9, 1904.

Secretary of State

Sir:-
    I have the honor to confirm my second telegram of today as follows: -
"Running naval engagement took place Chemulpo harbor for forty minutes beginning at noon. Variag and Koreetz again attempted to escape and failed. Former injured. On their return Japanese authority announced officially attack will take place four o'clock P.M. Japanese naval vessels went out of harbor for the attack. At latter hour precisely, Koreetz blew up and sank. She was slow, consequently difficult to save. Japanese naval vessels attacked Variag from outside harbor until sunk".

Horace N Allen

No. 665   Legation of the United States
                                                 Seoul, Korea, February 12, 1904.

Secretary of State

Sir:-
        I have the honor to confirm my telegram of today as follows: -
"Russian Minister with his household; Russian subjects and guard, left here for Chemulpo this morning in
pursuance of an intimation from the Japanese minister: the latter having furnished special train with an
escort. He will embark on the French naval vessel. Russian legation will be under the care of Legation of
France".

                                                 Horace N Allen

No. 668   Legation of the United States
                                                 Seoul, Korea, February 15, 1904.

Secretary of State

Sir:-
        I have the honor to confirm my telegram of today as follows: -
"Russian forces on the French naval vessel will be taken to Saigon tomorrow, where they will be held until
after the close of the war, and those on the British naval vessel will be taken to Hongkong. American ships
will not be needed".

                                                 Horace N Allen

No. 684   Legation of the United States
                                                 Seoul, Korea, February 29, 1904.

Secretary of State

Sir:-
        I have the honor to confirm my telegram of today as follows: -
"Japanese army will land Chinampo about the tenth, when the river opens.
Japanese minister has consented to bring Americans from Pengyang on a returning transport; our's left here
for Philippine Islands.
Russian scouts reached Pengyang yesterday morning. The Japanese chased them".

                                                 Horace N Allen

No. 692   Legation of the United States
                                                 Seoul, Korea, March 7, 1904.

Secretary of State

Sir:-
        I have the honor to confirm my telegram of today as follows: -
"Landing Japanese forces ceased. Pengyang river again frozen. Landing there delayed. Only one division of
Japanese army landed so far. Gensan landing has been abandoned. Cossacks are reported to be committing
depredations north. Japanese pressing them to the frontier. According to latest reports mines unmolested".

                                                 Horace N Allen

No. 695
Legation of the United States
Seoul, Korea, March 9, 1904.

Secretary of State

Sir:-

I have the honor to hand you enclosed, confirmation of my telegram of today, regarding the concentration of Japanese troops at Anju, the chief city in the region of the American mines, and situated about fifty to sixty miles north of Pengyang; and of the concentration of the Russians at Chongju and Kusong, perhaps twenty five to thirty miles to the north of Anju, and lying in an easily defended locality, at which point the Russians are erecting some "minor works" of defense. General Allen had this information from the chief military officer of the Japanese at Seoul - Major General Iditti.

In spite of the current opinion that there are now between 36,000 to 40,000 Japanese troops in Korea with the Twelvth Division, General Allen learns that the actual number including non-combatants, is but 22,000 of which 16,000 are effectives. The fact that it took seventy four transports to bring this number to Chemulpo is explained by the statement that an unusual quantity of supplies had to be brought here while the way was open, and in view of future eventualities that might have made such a heavy landing difficult.

General Allen further learned that the Twelvth Division was mobilized here and some four thousand deficiencies were made up by soldiers already here in civillians garb, as well as by others brought over here with troops.

The twenty five hundred Japanese troops now here and at Chemulpo, belong to the Fourth Division, now being mobilized in Japan. They are therefore about to return and their places will be taken by reservists.

In my No. 685, of February 29, I informed you of the intention of the Japanese to at once construct the Seoul-Wiju railway as a military measure with the intention of making it a permanent road. I now have the honor to inform you that Major General Yamane and three hundred military engineers have arrived from Japn to prosecute this work with all speed possible. I hear they are to employ eight thousand pioneers in the work besides all the Koreans necessary.

The landing of troops at Chenampo was delayed by the closing of the river on the 6'th by ice. Mr. Hayashi informed me however, that one of their transports arrived there yesterday.

As soon as navigation is safe the U.S. Cruiser "Cincinnati" will proceed to Chenampo and take away the American women and children.

On the 2'nd. instant, Koreans made an attempt to destroy the residences of the Minister for Foreign Affairs and his secretary, by the use of dynamite. The attempt was a failure, but Mr. Hayashi informs me that he has reason to believe certain officials in the palace were more or less responsible for the attempted outrage, which was directed against those Foreign Office officials because of their support of the recent Protocol of the 23'rd. instant.

As a result of this Mr. Hayashi has found it necessary to patroll the city with Japanese gendarmes. The ancient Pedlers Guild was also implicated in this dynamite affair and the Japanese Minister has requested that they be disbanded. This is causing considerable disorder of a prospective nature.

I have arranged for the proper protection of American interests here by our own force.

Horace N Allen

No. 701
Legation of the United States
Seoul, Korea, March 17, 1904.

Secretary of State

Sir:-

I have the honor to hand you enclosed a copy of a translation of a telegram received by the Korean Government from its authorities in the North Hamkyung Province, being the reading of a message received from the Russian Authorities on the Tiumen river.

It is a threat of dire vengeance to be visited upon the Koreans if they assist the Japanese.

It is reported that this message has had some effect upon the timid Koreans in that region, so that the Korean Government has been obliged to caution the officials in that region against furnishing aid to the Russians.

Horace N Allen

Copy of a telegram received by the Korean Government, March 12th. From its Magistrate at Kyung Song.

The Russian soldiers are stationed on the other side along the river Tiumen. Yesterday the Russian Officer of the border Komesaly? wrote despatches to the Governor of the North and South Ham Kiung Province, as follows:-

On the 20th, of January 1904. the Russian Government sent to the Powers to inform them of the conditions and the Good Powers know that it was wrong. The Japanese Government sent an announcement of fighting with Russia. Yet the Powers all know that Japan is doing wrong things in Korea.

As Korea is an independent country, Japan and Russia had made contracts in 1895 and in 1902, and the Korean Emperor declared that Korea would do nothing in the matter in case Russia and Japan may fall into a war, and the Government of Russia and Japan said it was right.

However, the Japanese Government ordered its Minister in Seoul, three days before the trouble was broken out, and the latter told His Majesty, the Emperor of Korea, that Korea would thereafter be under the Japanese protection and that if His Majesty may refuse it, he would station the Japanese Army in the Palace.

At this time the Japanese Army came into the city of Seoul without fighting with the Korean Army even for a second and the Minister of the Czar of Russia had to leave the city of Seoul.

His Majesty the Emperor of Korea and the Korean Government is pressed by the Japanese influence, and Japan, therefore, takes away the right of Korean independence, and they recognize and treat the Korean people as their slaves.

Therefore the Russian Government proclaims in all places that she does not recognize at all that Korea has agreed to the demands of Japan, and that Korea is to be notified as to the above facts.

Your excellency must therefore, notify this to all the local officers under you, the officers of all the Militias and even the people.

If the Korean officials, Military Officers and the people assist Japan with all their power and despatch soldiers to the North with the Japanese soldiers and receive orders from the Japanese, when they are fighting with Russia in Manchuria, the Koreans will be considered and treated as enemies the same as Japan and vengeance will be meted out to them without mercy.

No. 707   Legation of the United States
                                                         Seoul, Korea, March 24, 1904.

Secretary of State

Sir:-

I have the honor to confirm my telegram of today as follows: -
"Twenty fourth. Today the announcement is made that Yongampo will be opened.
Thousand Russian forces have advanced to the Anju river. Ice prevents crossing. Skirmishes have taken place. Slight casualties on both sides".

I hand you enclosed a copy of the translation of the letter from the Korean Minister for Foreign Affairs dated today, announcing this proposed opening of Yongampo.

There is little doubt that the successful tactics of Mr. Pavlow, the late Russian Minister, in preventing the opening of this port, had much to do with bringing matters to a crisis between Russia and Japan, as showing what the latter might expect in Korea if Russia shoud be allowed to go on undisturbed.

I find that I am not alone among my colleagues in thinking that had Russia continued to be represented by such a man as Mr. C. Waeber, who was Russian representative here from 1885 to 1897, the present war might have been averted.

Horace N Allen

No. 710

Legation of the United States
Seoul, Korea, March 30, 1904.

Secretary of State

Sir:-
    I have the honor to confirm my telegram of today as follows: -
"Thirtieth. The first land engagement took place twenty eighth. Japanese cavaly regiment attacked six hundred Cossacks at Chongju, losing four killed, twelve wounded. Russians retreated towards Wiju, leaving two killed. Chongju occupied by Japanese".

Horace N Allen

No. 718

Legation of the United States
Seoul, Korea, April 10, 1904.

Secretary of State

Sir:-
    I have the honor to confirm my telegram of today as follows:-
"Japanese forces have occupied Wiju. No Russians in Korea now. Mines not complaining. Only the First Japanese Army landed so far, consisting of three divisions. Second Japanese Army now mobilized, is expected to land shortly in the Yalu region. There was no landing on the East Coast. The Japanese are now erecting three fortifications on the island of Koje, Masampo harbor".

Horace N Allen

No. 739

Legation of the United States
Seoul, Korea, May 12, 1904.

Secretary of State

Sir:-
    I have the honor to hand you confirmation of my telegram of today regarding the incursion of Cossacks into the region south of the Yalu river.
    On the tenth instant I learned that a force of Russians estimated at 200 had reached Anju and were attacking the city, which was held by but seventy Japanes troops. The next day it was reported that reinforcements had arrived from a Japanes post about twenty miles south of Anju, and that the Russians had retreated after having received "about" fifty casualties. (Later reports made the number of Russians 500)
    Now I learn that a Russian force of nearly 3000 were at the American mines on the 8th, and other bands are reported as being in that region and even south towards Pengyang.
    I had not intended to telegraph this Anju skirmish, which seemed to be of no strategic importance, but it now seems to be of a more serious nature as is evidenced by the hasty despatch today of all available Japanese troops from Seoul, to the north.
    From a captured Russian non-commissioned officer, the Japanese report that they learned this Russian force had come from the railway at Liaoyang and by travelling twenty five miles a day, had crossed the Yalu about due north of Anju and had come down through the American mining district.

Horace N Allen

No. 766   Legation of the United States
                                                     Seoul, Korea, Jly 1 (July), 1904.

Secretary of State

Sir:-
            I have the honor to advise you of my telegram of today as follows: -
"First. Yesterday's bombardment Gensan, was by three Russian Naval Vessels, and two torpedo boats, for
about an hour. None killed, four wounded. Steam launch and schooner sunk at anchor. Japanese consulate
and other houses slightly damaged. I had previously removed the American women from there".

                                                     Horace N Allen

No. 798   Legation of the United States
                                                     Seoul, Korea, September 23, 1904.

Secretary of State

Sir:-
            I have the honor to inform you that I am credibly informed that the Japanese are about to begin
construction of a military railway to connect Seoul and the eastern port - Gensan. This will give the
Japanese railway connection between Seoul and Fusan; Seoul and Wiju: Seoul and the western port
Chemulpo, and with the east coast at Gensan, when the lines now under construction are completed.
            Bands of Russian troops have annoyed the Japanese greatly by operating south from Vladivostock
towards Gensan, as I have reported to you from time to time. Railway connection between Seoul and
Gensan will be a necessary thing for strategic puposes if hostilities are to be long continued, and of course
the road will assist in the development of the country.
            Russian troops are again reported south of the Tumen river.

                                                     Horace N Allen

C. U.S. Position vis-à-vis the Combatants

No. 593   Confidential.   Legation of the United States
                                                     Seoul, Korea, March 30, 1903.

Secretary of State

Sir:-
            I have the honor to inform you that I have had a direct, unofficial intimation that the Russian
Authorities at St. Petersburg and Port Arthur, would be glad to see American war vessels at Port Arthur
from time to time.
            This request came to me in the following manner. Baron de Gunsburg, a Russian, stays in Korea
as the agent of General Wogack, who is a "personal representative" of the Czar in Asia. Baron Gunsburg
recently returned from Port Arthur where he had been called by telegram to confer with General Wogack,
who had just returned from St. Petersburg. The Baron brought me this message, saying that it represents
the sentiment of Port Arthur and St. Petersburg. Adding that the British leave Port Arthur very much alone
and that the Japanese are not desirable visitors.
            I do not like to write this to our Admiral, and will not do so, preferring to inform you of the
message in order that you may act upon it or ignore it entirely as you may think best.
            Baron Gunsburg also intimated that Russia would like to see American ships in Korean waters,
but my own feeling in regard to that is that it is not advisable. If our ships are not here too often, their
occasional visits will be more appreciated and may be made of use if occasion requires.

                                                     Horace N. Allen.

No. 629   Legation of the United States
                                    Seoul, Korea, December 9, 1903.

Secretary of State

Sir:-

      I have the honor to confirm my cable message of yesterday, as follows:-

      "In the event of war between Japan and Russia, should we not have a vessel of the United States at hand for the protection of American life and property in Korea? There are ten thousand disorderly Korean forces in the city, scarcely under control. Guards will become necessary".

                                    Horace N. Allen

No. 635   Legation of the United States
                                    Seoul, Korea, December 27, 1903.

Secretary of State

Sir:-

      I have the honor to confirm my telegram of the 23'rd. instant, as follows: -

      "British naval vessel will arrive about tomorrow with a guard to land if necessary. Your attention is called to my telegram of eighth for the protection of American life and property".

      And I acknowledge the receipt of your reply of no date, received today, as follows: -

      "War vessel will be despatched as you suggest".

                                    Horace N Allen

No. 647   Legation of the United States
                                    Seoul, Korea, January 14, 1904.

Secretary of State

Sir:-

      I have the honor to hand you enclosed confirmation of my telegram of today regarding the coming of more guards for this Legation and American property in Seoul.

      In explanation I have the honor to hand you a copy of a letter from Messrs Collbran and Bostwick urging me to afford them protection, which letter is supported by a translation of a leading article in the Korean newspaper of the 12'th. "Che Kuk Sinmun" attributing the present deplorable condition in Korea to the presence of foreigners and inciting the people to arise and do violence to them; attention being particularly called to the American Seoul Electric Company, against whom Ye Yong Ik has been able - as I have fully shown you in many despatches - to stir up unwarranted and unjust opposition which lead to a serious riot on September 30'th last. I also enclose a letter from Rev. Jas. S. Gale, a British subject acting as a missionary of the American Presbyterian Board, to Mr. Morris of the Electric Company, and the answer from Mr. Morris, both of which show the unusual character of stone fights now being indulged in by thousands of Koreans, just in the rear of the Electric Power House.

      The mob of Koreans always gets very much excited during these annual stone fights and it is not safe for foreigners to be near them. The unseasonable time and the close proximity of these fights to the power house, seems to indicate that they and the inflammatory newspaper articles are connected and that Ye Yong Ik must be responsible for them as he was for similar articles and actual violence during the past ten months.

      To support my conclusions I was yesterday informed that the Korean Government had informed Collbran and Bostwick that they would now have to remove the policemen they had stationed for the protection of the Company's property after Japanese policemen had been called in to quell the riot of September 30 over the accidental killing of a boy. Although the Company is exercising the greatest care, similar accidents may occur, and at this time of such suppressed excitement, such an accident may well turn the city over to a mob, and cause the destruction of this vulnerable American property.

In view of all these things I decided to bring up the balance of the guard now at Chemulpo, making the total one hundred men. The coming sixty four will be quartered at the office building of the Electric Company, from whence they may be sent to out to necessary duty.

Horace N Allen

No. 653   Legation of the United States
                                                     Seoul, Korea, January 30, 1904.

Secretary of State

Sir:-
        I have the honor to hand you enclosed, confirmation of my telegram of today regarding Korea's declaration of her neutrality in the event of war.
        You will see from this telegram that the mere acknowledgment, by the Foreign Powers, of the receipt of this announcement, is having an effect that must be quite contrary to that intended by those powers.
        I understand that Russia and Japan have not replied. England replied in the form of a mere acknowledgment, through her minister here. Most of the others have expressed their approval through the Korean ministers abroad.
        There is a rumor today from the palace that you have so replied. I trust it is not correct. It tends to discredit your representative here when you reply direct to messages from the Korean Government, instead of doing so through your representative here.
        I am informed that this message regarding neutrality was forwarded through the French consulate at Chefoo without the knwoledge of the Korean Minister for Foreign Affairs, and with no notification to the foreign representatives.
        The Korean officials responsible for this step had *previously* * been holding constant conferences at the Russian legation.

Horace N Allen

No. 255   Department of State
                                                     Washington, March 4, 1904.

Horace N. Allen

Sir:
        I have to acknowledge the receipt of your despatch No. 653, of the 30th of January last, on the subject of Korea's neutrality in the war between Russia and Japan.
        Respecting your apprehension as to the rumor that this Government had approved Korea's declaration of neutrality, I have to inform you that the declaration, which was communicated to the Department on January 22 by the Korean Minister, was merely acknowledged, with the remark that due note had been taken of the declaration.

John Hay.

---

*Handwritten.

No. 667   Legation of the United States
                                           Seoul, Korea, February 15, 1904.

Secretary of State

Sir:-
          I have the honor to confirm my telegram of today as follows: -
"Have been requested by the Manager of the American mines to send guards to protect the property, located
not far from Yalu. There are sixty Americans there at widely separated mills, with three machine guns and
two hundred rifles, which are sufficient for protection against natives. Russians and Japanese will not
injure American life and property. American syndicate will probably call see you. Preparations are being
made to land Japanese army Chemulpo to march north through that region. Telegraph lines to the north
seized by the Japanese yesterday".

                                           Horace N Allen

No. 673   Legation of the United States
                                           Seoul, Korea, February 21, 1904.

Secretary of State

Sir:-
          I have the honor to confirm my telegram of today as follows: -
"Had an audience with Head of Government of Korea last night. He informed me Japanese Minister
proposed to make an alliance whereby in return for the protection of Korea, Japan will have control over
policy of the Government; the document, promised me, has not arrive. Head of Government of Korea is
very anxious to secure the assistance of the United States: I have pacified him without any promises, and
refused asylum".

                                           Horace N Allen

No. 677   Legation of the United States
                                           Seoul, Korea, February 24, 1904.

Secretary of State

Sir:-
          I have the honor to acknowledge the receipt, after despatching my telegram confirmed in my No/
676 of today, of the following telegram from you: -
"Twenty third not necessary to cable text of Japan Korea agreement. You will observe absolute neutrality".

                                           Horace N Allen

No. 678   Legation of the United States
                                           Seoul, Korea, February 25, 1904.

Secretary of State

Sir:-
          I have the honor to hand you enclosed a copy of a despatch, bearing yesterday's date, sent by me to
the Korean Minister for Foreign Affairs, asking for protection for the American gold mines in accordance
with the mining concession.
          This request was made much against my judgement, and in response to direct telegraphic requests
from the Company's officers in America. I desired an American guard at Seoul to serve as a protection

against the armed Korean coolies dressed up as soldiers; it seems somewhat incongruous to ask that these same disorderly troops be sent to the distant mines, where with arms and the incentive of the local Koreans and the presence of large amounts of gold, they may very likely be a serious danger.

It was very strongly impressed upon me however that this request should be made in order to validate any future claims the Company may be obliged to make in consequence of damage to lives and property during the present warlike operations.

Horace N Allen

No. 688   Legation of the United States
                                             Seoul, Korea, March 2, 1904.

Secretary of State

Sir:-

Referring to the request of the Russian Minister to have the crews of the two wrecked Russian ships at Chemulpo taken away on a vessel of the United States, as I telegraphed you on February 10, see my despatch No. 663, of that date, which telegram was not answered, I now have the honor to inform you of the details of that incident.

On February 10 Mr. Pavlow asked me if I would consent to have such of the Russian crews of the "Variag" and "Koreetz" which were wrecked in the Chemulpo engagement of the day before, as could not be taken by the French cruiser "Pascal" given transportation on the U.S. Transport "Zaphiro" and the Collier "Pompey" then at Chemulpo. He was willing that they should go to Chefoo or the Philippines. I replied that I would have to refer the matter to you and that I could not do even that without ascertaining the view of the Japanese Minister owing to the bearing the action might have upon the question of neutrality. He consented to this reference, and I at once wrote to Mr. Hayashi as per copy enclosed.

Mr. Hayashi replied, as per copy enclosed, that there was no objection whatever to my laying the matter before you by telegraph and he said he would also do the same with his Government.

On the 12'th ultimo Mr. Hayashi informed me, as per copy, of the conditions upon which his Government would consent to the transportation of the Russian refugees.

Captain W. A. Marshall, of the U.S.S. "Vicksburg" has not made me a report on his connection with these refugees, but he told me that he lowered his boats and assisted the Russians to make their escape from the sinking ships. He could not take them upon the "Vicksburg" owing to the lack of space, but he offered them the use of the "Zaphiro". This offer was declined as the transport was not in commission, and might not be regarded as a neutral vessel in the sense of a regularly commission naval vessel of a neutral power.

The men were quartered on the British ship "Talbot", the French ship "Pascal" and the Italian ship "Elba".

Later, the position became somewhat awkward for these vessels and Captain Marshall was called into consultation. He was asked to take the wounded Russians upon the "Zaphiro", but as a red cross hopital had been offered them on shore he very wisely declined to be brought into the difficulty unnecessarily.

As I have already informed you by telegraph, these unwounded Russians have been taken away, those on the "Pascal" to Saigon: Those on the "Talbot" to Ceylon, and those on the "Elba" to Hongkong, whence they will be sent to Italy.

Captain Marshall seems to have done his full duty and at the same time he has skillfully avoided what seems to have been an awkward situation to the others.

Horace N Allen

TELEGRAM. CIPHER

Department of State
Washington, March 2, 1904.

Allen,
Minister, Seoul.

Date. Press reports say Russians have taken possession of American mining district Pyengyang. Presumed you will do all possible for the protection of Americans consistent with absolute neutrality and respecting rights of the belligerents in theatre of actual war.

Hay

No. 689

Legation of the United States
Seoul, Korea, March 3, 1904.

Secretary of State

Sir:-

I have the honor to hand you enclosed, confirmation of your telegram of the second regarding the American mines in northern Korea, as well as my reply of today.

I have done and am doing all in power to protect these people. I have assembled all the American women and children at Pengyang city, which is now occupied by Japanese troops. I will get them away in a few days as the river is about to open. The U.S. Transport "Zaphiro" having been recalled to the Philippines, I saw the Japanese Minister at the suggestion of the Captains of the U.S. Ships "Cincinnati" and "Vicksburg" now at Chemulpo, and secured his consent that the women and children might be brought down to Chemulpo on one of their returning transports, as the Japanese army is about to land at Chinampo, the port of Pengyang, as soon as the ice is out of the river. I did not like this arrangement however and in consultation with Captain Mason of the "Cincinnati" this morning, after receiving your telegram, he agreed to go himself and bring down the women and children.

The manager of the American mines is very desirous of securing a marine guard from one of our ships for the protection of the mines. I stated the circumstances to you in my telegram confirmed in my despatch No. 667, of the 15'th ultimo, after which I was informed that the officers of the mining company had cabled here that after discussing the matter with you it was decided that a guard could not be sent to the mines, and asking me to request protection from the Korean Government. This I did and secured a favorable reply as I informed you in my despatches 678 of February 25 and 682 of February 27.

The Japanese hold all the country south of Pengyang, but between Pengyang and the Yalu river the Russian mounted scouts are present, having come to the gates of Pengyang city on the 28'th ultimo, as I informed in my telegram confirmed in my despatch 684 of the 29'th.

The manager of the mines who is now at Chinampo, urged me in a telegram received last night to send him five marines to act as a guard to a supply train After reading your telegram confirmed in this, I consulted with Captain Mason of the U.S.S. "Cincinnati" who chanced to be with me, as well as with Brigadier General Allen, and we decided that not less than twenty five men and an officer could be sent on such a mission, and that if an armed and uniformed force should be marched through that theatre of actual war it would not be respecting the rights of the beligerents and would subject the force to detention by the Russians, or worse, and might lead to serious consequences. As I was informed by telegrams from the manager of the mines, sent from Chinampo yesterday morning, that all was well at the mines and the mills were working, I informed him I could not send the guard without instructions.

The mines are from thirty to sixty miles from the main road at Anju and there is no reason for them to be mollested, except that they have a large force of Japanese artisans engaged in the mills. Neither the Japanese Minister nor myself can learn why these men were not sent out as we both suggested it. However, the Japanese forces now at Pengyang city and arriving there, will press on to the Anju region and it is expected they will soon hold it, when conditions will be much better than while it is the border land between the two forces.

The landing of troops at Chemulpo has now ceased and all paraphernalia has been taken north, where future landings will be made.

Seoul is now practically deserted by Japanese troops aside from the garrison of a thousand or more troops.

I am of course carefully observing absolute neutrality, but I called your attention in my telegram to the fact that I have not been informed of a neutrality proclamation, as have my colleagues, and have therefore not issued any notice to Americans of the issuance of such an announcement. The British Minister has had his nationals sign a statement that they will observe the rules of neutrality.

Horace N Allen

No. 691   Legation of the United States
                                                      Seoul, Korea, March 7, 1904.

Secretary of State

Sir:-
        I have the honor to acknowledge the receipt on yesterday of your cable message of no date, as follows: -
"Neutrality proclamation dated eleventh ultimo already mailed to you, follows as substitute, our two proclamations, French-Prussian war. See volume sixteen Statutes at Large".
        Volume twenty four, 1885 - 1887, Statutes at Large, is the first of these volumes we have at this office. I was able to find the proclamations in question in Volume VII Messages and Papers of the Presidents, for 1869 - 1881.
        As the present proclamation should soon arrive, I will wait until it comes and will then, probably, have it published and mailed to each American resident in Korea.
        Already I have, on my own responsibility, before knowing anything of your action regarding neutrality, induced an American citizen to decline to act as pilot to Russian war ships.

Horace N Allen

No. 259   Department of State
                                                      Washington, April 14, 1904.

Horace N. Allen

Sir:
        I have to acknowledge the receipt of your telegram of the 20th ultimo, which reads:
        "Your immediate attention is directed my despatch number 587. It is very desirable to arrange pouch service accordingly."
        It appears from correspondence on the Department's files that previous to 1898 it had been the custom to forward official matter for the legation at Seoul in the pouch for the legation at Tokyo, but that such delays occurred in forwarding from there that this practice was discontinued. Consequently on May 5, 1898, in your No. 104, you suggested the advisability of opening negotiations with the Japanese Government looking to the furnishing of a through pouch to your legation. The Postmaster General took the matter up with the Japanese postal authorities with the result that he was informed that the Japanese Government was not able, under the existing circumstances, to enter into an arrangement of the character desired.
        The matter rested until January 19, 1900, when the Korean Government began conveying foreign mails under an agreement with the Japanese post offices in Korea, and since shortly after that date pouches from the Department to your Legation have been despatched to Japan whence they are forwarded without objection by the Japanese office to Korea, and pouches from your Legation are despatched through the Korean post-office to Japan whence they are forwarded to the United States.
        The Department supposed this system was working satisfactorily until the receipt of your No. 587 of March 14, 1903, in which you reported to the contrary and renewed the request of 1898 to arrange for the transmission of your pouches by the Japanese postal service. This despatch, as you have already advised, was communicated to the Postmaster General, who replied as follows:
        "The Minister's despatch is not clearly understood here, but from it it is gathered that there is delay in forwarding from Korea the pouches of the Legation for your Department. If that be the case or if the

fault is with the Japanese service, the remedy should be applied by the Postal Administration of Korea; that Administration being responsible for the prompt despatch of the pouches in question."

You should therefore make proper representations to the Korean Government to the end that the delay of which you complain in the despatch of your pouches may be prevented. In view of the existing situation in Korea, this Department would hesitate to recommend to the Postmaster General to negotiate with a belligerent to convey our correspondence and that of your legation to and from the seat of war.

John Hay

No. 2.

Department of State
Washington, May 1, 1905.

Edwin V. Morgan

Sir:

I have to acknowledge the receipt of Doctor Allen's despatch No. 885, of the 17th ultimo, transmitting copies of the protests of an American missionary and certain Koreans, respectively, against the conduct of Japanese subjects in Korea, and to inform you that his attitude is approved by the Department.

Korea's independence or dependence being virtually one of the causes of the war, our position in that regard should be strictly neutral.

Alvey A. Adee

Ito Hirobumi, Regent General of the Japanese Protectorate over Korea

Reprinted from George Trumbull, *In Korea with Marquis Ita* (New York: Charles Scribner's Sons, 1908), frontispiece.

No. 674   *Confidential* [*]   Legation of the United States
                                             Seoul, Korea, February 22, 1904.

Secretary of State

Sir:-

I have the honor to confirm my telegram of today as follows:-
"Shall I communicate by telegraph the text of the articles of agreement proposed by Japan for the protection of Korea".

I thought that in all probability you might already have been funished with a copy of these articles, though I have had no communication on the subject from my Japanese colleague.

I hand you herewith enclosed a copy of the articles in question, which was furnished me by the Emperor without the knowledge of the Japanese.

I will telegraph the substance if so directed.

                                 Horace N Allen

No. 676   Legation of the United States
                        Seoul, Korea, February 24, 1904.

Secretary of State

Sir:-

I have the honor to confirm my telegram of today as follows: -
"Last night articles of agreement has (have) been signed establishing the Japanese protectorate of Korea. It is very strong. The Japanese agree to maintain the independence and integrity of Korea; in consequence of which Korea is to follow the advice of Japan implicitly in all matters of reform and other political measures. The Japanese also obtain use of territory for military purposes. It is provided against any third foreign power concluding an agreement contrary to the spirit of this agreement.
Ye Yong Ik espoused the Japanese cause after the departure of Russians and is responsible for the agreement. Left here for Japan last night".

                                 Horace N Allen

No. 709   Confidential.   Legation of the United States
                                         Seoul, Korea, March 27, 1904.

Secretary of State

Sir:-

I have the honor to inform you that Marquis Ito left here on his return to Japan, yesterday. He arrived on the 17th on the auxilliary cruiser "Hongkong Maru" formerly of the San Francisco line. The ship remained at Chemulpo for his return. During his stay in Seoul Marquis Ito was give three audiences with the Emperor, who also entertained him at a dinner at which the Emperor and Crown Prince were seated at the table. He was also given a high decoration. The foreign representatives called upon the Marquis on the 19th and he returned the calls the same day. The Japanese Minister entertained the Marquis at dinner with the foreign representatives on the 2ist. On the 23rd I entertained the Marquis and the foreign representatives at luncheon and the British Minister, who is in mourning, entertained the Marquis privately, at luncheon on the 24th. The Marquis gave an evening reception on the 24th.

---

*Handwritten.

125

The visit seems to have been purely one of concilliation. The Korean Court were quite disturbed over the prospect of this visit, but they now seem quite pleased with it.

The Emperor has informed me confidentially of the substance of the chief points discussed in the audiences granted to the Marquis. A synopsis of which is as follows: -

Marquis Ito is reported as having stated that the countries of Asia must stand together as brothers: Otherwise the Western Powers will devour them. He is repotred to have said that the alliance between Japan and Korea may be a good thing. Certainly it is good for Japan. It may prove to be very good for Korea: But good or ill, it had to be. The Korean Government had gotten into such a bad condition that Japan had no other course to follow.

He is reported as advising great deliberation in introducing reforms: That a reasonable number of selected Japanese should be employed as advisers and their advice and that of the Japanese Minister should be carefully followed: That the advice of foreigners, (other than Japanese) should be avoided.

The war that is now begun is a great and serious matter. Although there are now no Russians in Seoul, it must not be supposed that there is no Russia. She is still a great power and will not yield readily, but Japan must eventually prevail. Peace will come in time, and when it comes Korea will find Japan has done well for Korea and she must lean upon Japan alone.

He is also reported as saying that he has seen with regret that foreigners have raised their flag in the centre of Seoul on the most commanding building and over what should be Korean property, - a thing difficult to comprehend. (Referring to the Seoul Electric Company) Refering to the Seoul-Wiju Railway, he is said to have stated that while Japan was obliged to take this as a war measure, the property will be turned back to Korea in time.

If correctly reported this reference to the action Messrs Collbran and Bostwick were obliged to take to protect their interests in the Seoul Electric Company was unkind.

The Japanese seem to feel very sore over their failure to secure this property, though they fully admit that they were given every opportunity to acquire the same and finally announced in December last that they could not purchase it, after which the American firm made other arrangements which they could not break when, after the battle of Chemulpo, the Japanese again tried to open negotiations looking to the purchase of the property.

At present this advice of the Japanese statesman only inclines the Emperor to cling the closer to his interests in the American firm, but it is not improbable that the Japanese will get control of the Emperor's interests in this concern, and probably they may yet acquire the American rights.

It seems to me that if this fiction of Korean independence is maintained with Japanese advice amounting to commands, it will be increasingly difficult to properly protect and advance American interests.

Already we have had an instance of unwarranted interference by the occupation of a part of the American electric railway by the Japanese without permission. I will refer to this later.

If the Japanese succeed in the present war it would seem to be better if diplomatic matters were to be discussed in Tokio with a responsible government, and matters in Korea attended to by an officer of the rank of Consul general and agent.

Horace N Allen

No. 720   Confidential.   Legation of the United States
                                                            Seoul, Korea, April 14, 1904.

Secretary of State

Sir:-

On yesterday I had an audience with the Emperor to express my thanks for the decoration conferred upon me as mentioned in my No. 717 *(not yet received)* * of the 9th, and to explain that I could not accept and wear it until I had obtained permission from my Government.

_____

*Handwritten

Mr. Hayashi, the Japanese Minister had an audience just before me. His Majesty informed me that Mr. Hayashi had urged the signing of a pending concession granting to Japan more extensive fishing rights and one covering "forests; streams, hills and lakes". He told me also that Mr. Hayashi had been making numerous enquiries about the document which had been given to Collbran and Bostwick covering the settlement of the Seoul Electric Company, mentioned in my No 693 of March 8, a copy of which had been furninshed to Mr. Hayashi by the Household Minister. Mr. Hayashi had requested very strongly that as His Majesty had signed that document for the Americans with his own imperial seal, he should sign the documents for the Japanese with the same, To this the Emperor replied that the forests, streams, fisheries, etc, belonged to the people and any document concerning them must bear the seal of the Council of State or the Foreign Office while this electric matter was a personal one in which he had invested his own money.

I do not understand that the Japanese are directly opposing this American enterprise, though the British Minister is and has been doing so. He is reported to me from the Palace as sending in very strong representations against the matter: He loses no opportunity to speak some ill word of the enterprise, and he allowed an English firm to contract to erect a competing plant, shutting the American lights out of the palace and in gross vilotion of the American franchises of which he was well aware. He returned a sarcastic reply to a protest against such action, as I explained in my No. 626 of December 28 last. The British at present in Korea seem to bitterly resent American success and thus injure their own chances by trying to prevent our succeding.

After the China-Japan war, ten years ago, the Japanese failed to secure documents in the shape of concessions covering enterprises they had in contemplation for their people in Korea. The result was that when the Emperor fled to the Russian Legation the Japanese found these matters falling into other hands. The chief undertaking, a railway to connect Seoul and Chemulpo, going to Americans.

The present haste to get these documents signed, covering about everything in Korea, seems to be an attempt to forestall any such fate as that which befel them in 1896.

The Japanese Minister is also showing an inclination to make friends with the so called American party. These men are either of American education; have seen service in Washington, or have come under the influence of Americans. They represent the most enlightened and progressive, as well as the most honest of the Korean official element. Heretofore, the Japanese have taken up with very inferior Koreans and have been discredited in consequence. I have put no obstacles in their way in making up with these people, in fact I think it is the logical and proper course and would not wish to prevent it. During the past two years while the late Russian Minister and his friend Ye Yong Ik have been all powerful, these officials of the so called American party have been out of active office, but now that there is trouble in the country they are being called to the front rank of importance.

The Japanese secured the permission to build the Seoul Wiju railway, as I explained in my No. 685 of February 29, and No. 713 of April 4. The French engineers who had a contract to build this road for the Korean government, were away in France at the opening of hostilities, buying materials. They have now returned to find their occupation gone. I hear they have presented a claim of one million yen.

All these matters, [*diplomatic pressure in regard to various concessions*]* are naturally of serious concern to the Korean Emperor. He falls back in his extemity upon his old friendship with America. It is my endeavor to sooth him all I can at the same time pointing out to him how the course of his Government during the past few years could not well lead to any other result than something like the alliance of February 23rd. I have not encouraged him to send a high offical as Minister to Washington in order to invoke the good offices of the United States as it seems to me that would only be an embarrassment.

At the same time I may as well inform you that the Emperor confidently expects that America will do something for him at the close of this war, or when opportunity offers, to retain for him as much of his independence as is possible. He is inclined to give a very free and favorable translation to Article 1, of our Treaty of Jenchuan of 1882. I trust to be able to prevent a direct invokation of this treaty however though I am obliged to assure His Majesty that the condition of Korea is borne in mind by the United States Government who will use their good offices when occasion occurs.

Horace N Allen

---

*Handwritten.

No. 736

Legation of the United States
Seoul, Korea, May 10, 1904.

Secretary of State

Sir:-

Replying to your despatch No. 258 of April 9, instructing me to transmit, for the use of the Navy Department, two copies of the proclamation of neutrality issued by the Korean Government in connection with the present war between Japan and Russia, I have the honor to inform you that this Government has issued no such proclamation.

About February first or thereabouts, the Emperor of Korea is said to have sent some sort of a notice of neutrality to the treaty powers, without the knowledge of his Minister for Foreign Affairs or the Foreign Representatives. Just what this amounted to I cannot say. But the protocol signed with Japan on February 23rd last, making Korea an ally of Japan, would effectually do away with any such fiction of neutrality.

Horace N Allen

No. 741

Legation of the United States
Seoul, Korea, May 19, 1904.

Secretary of State

Sir:-

I have the honor to confirm my telegram of today as follows: -
"Nineteenth. Imperial edict, last night, annuls all treaties and agreements with the Russian Government, including the Yalu timber concession, and subjects private Russian agreements to a further investigation. Head of the Government of Korea reluctantly complied with Japanese demands in the matter".

I was informed from the Palace last night that this would be done and the Emperor seemed very desirous of finding some way of evading the action, although he had a precedent in a similar course taken towards China after the Japan-China war of 1894.

I enclose a copy of the translation of the above mentioned edict, as it appeared in today's official gazette.

Horace N Allen

No. 751

Legation of the United States
Seoul, Korea, June 6, 1904.

Secretary of State

Sir:-

I have the honor to advise you that I was informed by the Korean Minister for Foreign Affairs on yesterday, that two considerable matters lately under discussion, had been settled in a manner satisfactory to Japan.

The principle one was the grant of fisheries along the coasts of Chung Chong Do; Hwangi Do and Pengyang Do to the Japanese Government for its people. With the already existing rights held by the Japanese, this gives them the whole west and south coast of Korea and quite a portion of the east coast. This industry amounts to millions of money yearly, and is greatly appreciated by the Japanese. In return, the Koreans get certain rights of fishing off the Japanese coast, where they are not likely ever to go. This agreement was confirmed on June 4, I was told.

Mr. Hayashi, the Japanese Minister, who is about to start for Japan for a months absence, has been delaying his departure, I am told for the termination of these negotiations.

The other matter which has been settled, is the payment of an indemnity of Yen 18,000 to a Japanese shop keeper for the wreck of his shop by the Korean mob that attacked the Americans and their electric car, on October 1 last. - See my No. 626 of Novemner 28, Enclosure 14. - One of the Americans,

Mr. Elliott, in order to save his life on that occasion, seized the bicycle of a Japanese postman and rode away. The postman being attacked, took refuge in a small Japanese shop. The mob then destroyed the shop and injured the occupants. Yen 38,000 was demanded as an indemnity, which has been settled by the payment, on June 1, of the above named indemnity of yen 18,000.

Horace N Allen

No. 763
Legation of the United States
Seoul, Korea, June 28, 1904.

Secretary of State

Sir:-

In my No. 720 of April 14 last, I mentioned the attempts of the Japanese to obtain concessions for fisheries, and for "forests hills and streams". In my No. 751 of the 6th instant, I informed you that they had secured the fisheries agreement they desired. I have now the honor to inform you that they are pressing the signing of a concession granting to a Mr. Nangimouri, - said to be a member of the Treasury Department of Japan, - the right to occupy vacant lands in Korea and to utilize water ways. This is known as the concession for "Forests hills and steams". There is a great quantity of vacant land in Korea and if this could be utilized and improved by some system of irrigation, it would support a large population without encroaching upon the rights of the present native farmers. Also, by a simple system of tree planting, the barren hills of Korea could, in twenty years or less, be made to furnish quantities of fuel from trimmings, and the rainfall would be better retained and more beneficial.

When it seemed that the Minister of the Household was apt to grant these "crown lands" to the Japanese, the people were worked up to quite a state of exitement by clever officials who posted a notice pointing out the evils to follow from "Japanese occupation of the soil; the better lot that would await them under Russian rule, and calling upon the people to arise in defence of their country. No one who knows the Koreans would suspect them of getting up any serious revolution, though they could greatly hamper the Japanese at present by a general uprising, and assist the Russians as well. I enclose a translation of the notice with which the country has been pretty freely placarded.

The present Minister for Foreign Affairs, Mr. Ye Ha Yong, who was once Korean Representative in Washington, speaks Japanese fluently and is suspected by the Koreans of being strongly pro-Japanese. He however seems to think the present pressing of this concession, unwise and liable to lead to serious disorder. He was commissioned by the Korean Cabinet to return to the Japanese Chargé d8Affaires, the latter despatch asking for the concession, and he is reported to have done so, at the same time making suitable explanations. The despatch was not received back however. The Foreign Minister is also reported to have said to Mr. Hagiwara, that whereas in February nine men out of ten might have been favorable to Japan, it would now be impossible to find more than one in ten favorable to Japan while the other nine would be found to be praying for the success of Russia.

The Japanese authorities are greatly troubled by a very large disorderly element among the Japanese adventureres who have recently flocked into Korea. Nearly every day the papers of Seoul give an account of some brutal murder of a Korean by these toughs who are abroad in the country. I enclose a translation of an article that appeared in the Che Kook Sinmun of today, relative to two such murders in Seoul itself. I am told by Korean officials that their women, even ladies in closed chairs, cannot pass the works of the Seoul-Wiju Railway in the suburbs of Seoul, without being mollested and that numbers of them have been crimanally assaulted by the coolies working on this railway. Korean men, even gentlemen, are seized in passing these places, I am told, and compelled to do coolie labor while the Japanese coolies rest.

It is these acts that really do inflame the Korean people and if any uprising should occur it would be owing more to despair over such acts than to the matter of concessions.

Horace N Allen

No. 774   Legation of the United States
                                                 Seoul, Korea, July 24, 1904.

Secretary of State

Sir:-

I have the honor to hand you enclosed a copy of a letter I have received from Rev. Dr. S. A. Moffett of the Presbyterian Mission at Pengyang, as well as my reply thereto.

The Korean officials seem to have lost all sense of justice and are taking the property of the natives on all sides, for the Japanese. The latter pay the people for the property, but do so through the officials who neglect to hand it or any portion of the payment, over to the people. I had to interfere to have Koreans released from the imprisonment because of their having sold property to Americans.

I told the Japanese Minister of the condition of affairs as reported in this letter, and he proposes to attempt to take measures to correct the same.

                                                 Horace N Allen

No. 781   Legation of the United States
                                                 Seoul, Korea, August 11, 1904.

Secretary of State

Sir:-

In my Nos. 763, June 28; 771 July 18; 773, July 23; 777, August 2, and 778, of the 3rd instant, I informed you of the growing agitation in Seoul and Korea over the demand of the Japanese for a concession for "forests hills and streams", called also "crown lands" and lately more appropriately styled "waste lands".

This was an attempt on the part of the Japanese Government, acting in the name of an ex offcial of the Japanese Finance Department, to get Korean consent and cooperation in developing the enormous amount of waste or unoccupied lands in Korea, in order to furnish employment for the surplus population of Japan and at the same time increase the supply of bread stuffs in that country, where it is reported some $10,000,000 are spent annually for imported rice, - mostly from Siam and near by countries.

It seems the request, made so comprehensively and in such a bald and objectionable manner, was not at all timely, and it simply stirred up a great and determined opposition to Japan among the Koreans. The latter seemed determined not to grant the request and thus compel Japan, if she insisted upon the acquisition of the lands in question, to take them by force, so that in the event of the holding of an international congress for the settlement of the issues of the present war, such forcible acquisition might result in complete or partial restitution as the result of such congress.

The Minister for Foreign Affairs, Mr. Ye Ha Yong, who has been accused of being too favorable to Japan, in this instance showed marked determination not to grant this concession.

I sent you a translation of a rather impolite letter sent by him to the Japanese Representative, - see my No. 777 above cited. This letter was returned, whereupon Mr. Ye Ha Yong, sent to Mr. Hayashi a long and more dignified letter, a copy of the translation of which I enclose, which letter resulted in a conference in which the question of the waste lands was agreed to be dropped for the time being, and the attention of the Japanese would be given to the reformation of the finances of Korea, which are in a most deplorable condition. For this purpose it seems to have been agreed that Korea should employ certain advisors from Japan, among whom, the Foreign Minister informs me, is to be an American citizen, Mr. D. W. Stevens, now connected with the Japan Legation in Washington, of whom I addressed you in My No. 681 of February 27 last.

During the height of this discussion regarding the Waste Lands matter, the Emperor of Korea telegraphed to the Emperor of Japan asking that Marquis Ito be sent over here as adviser. It is now reported that this request will not be complied with.

The society known as the Poh An Hoi which had charge of the agitation against the grant of the concession in question, sent out circulars to the people and letters to the foreign representatives. I enclose a copy of the translation of the former, enclosure 3/, as well as of the letter sent to me. Enclosure 3.

If the Japanese continue to succeed in the present war, it will probably be impossible for Korea to continue to hold such large quantities of good land unoccupied except for the raising of grass for fuel.

Horace N Allen

No. 783   Legation of the United States
                                                               Seoul, Korea, August 20, 1904.

Secretary of State

Sir:
        I have the honor to advise you of a great improvement now being made by the Japanese, to the harbor facilities of the port of Chemulpo.
        This harbor, the most important one in Korea, is large and safe, but vessels have to land about two miles from the jetty, or further, owing to size, and the lightering in of cargoes is costly and not always safe. The tide rises ordinarily twenty nine feet, and at low water there are vast expanses of mud flats exposed, while the boat channels are so affected by sand bars, that it is almost impossible to reach the shore at low tide even with a ships launch.
        In order to obviate this difficulty in landing military supplies, and materials for the extensive railways now being built in Korea by the Japanese military authorities, the latter have decided upon a bold feat of engineering whereby they are throwing a railway across the upper boat channel by means of tressle work and a bridge, to Rose Island, - a large island consisting of a high hill with a low lying extension to the north east. The railway will skirt the northern side of Rose Island to a wide and high lying mud flat, which is well out of water at low tide, and cross this to Observation Island, which is a small hill on which stands the harbor lighthouse. Off this island at a distance of several hundred yards, is the deep anchorage for sea going vessels. From this island a pier will be built sufficiently far out into the deep water to afford facilities for landing at all stages of the tide.
        I enclose a tracing of the plan of these improvements, and of the harbor of Chemulpo.
        While this work is being prosecuted by the Japanese Military Authorities, it is understood that it will be made a permanent improvement for the use of commerce.
        I am told the cost of this work is to be Yen 450,000 - $225,000. Yen 150,000 for the bridge across the shallow boat channel that opens to the Han River, and Yen 300,000 for the rest of the work.
        The Korean Government seems to have been somewhat perturbed over the beginning of this work without their consent having been first obtained. The fact is that the Korean Government has paid no attention to furnishing harbor facilities, and in this case the matter seems to be covered by the Protocol of February 23rd, which gave Japan the right to the use of land for military purposes.
        Some time ago the Japanese Government asked the Korean Government for the right to establish wireless telegraph stations along the Korean coast. They received a negative reply with the statement that the Korean Government was about to establish wireless telegraph stations itself: This was at a time when wireless telegraphy was so new that it is safe to say the Korean officials had never even heard of it. Recently when the Japanese Government asked for permission to reclaim the waste or unoccupied lands of Korea by the establishment of extensive irrigation systems, in order to provide a food supply for Japan, they received a flat refusal and the announcement that all such lands had just been given to a Korean company for the purpose of reclamation by irrigation and other means - quite unknown to the Koreans. Also, the other day the Japanese asked for an unoccupied hill back of Chemulpo for the purpose of establishing a meteorological observatory. This request was also declined on the grounds that the hill in question had just been granted to the Korean Educational Department for the purpose of establishing such an observatory - a work for which no Koreans are qualified.
        In view of these attempts to secure necessary facilities for carrying on military andkindred opperations with the consent of the Korean Government, it is not strange that in view of the continual failures to obtain any such consent, in the present instance this important harbor work was undertaken without bothering to court a refusal.
        The same seems to be true in Seoul, where land covering a stretch of about two miles, from the city walls to the river Han, has been reserved by the Japanese Military Authorities for military opperations.

Horace N Allen

No. 784   Legation of the United States
                                           Seoul, Korea, August 24, 1904.

Secretary of State

Sir:-

I am informed that on the 19th instant, agreements were signed between the Japanese Legation and the Korean Government regarding the appointment of advisers to the Korean Departments of Finance and Foreign Affairs. The latter, I understand, as I mentioned in my No. 783 of the 17th instant, is to be Mr. D.W. Stevens, the American Counsellor of the Japanese Legation at Washington, while the former is to be a Japanese subject, at present connected with the Finance Department of Japan.

There has been much discussion in regard to these appointments, for the reason that the Japanese Minister insisted that they should be styled "directors". It was finally agreed, I am told, that the recommendation of these assistants should be left to the Japanese Government, and that they shall be given full executive control in their respective departments.

The local newspapers persist in stating that the Japanese Minister has recommended the withdrawal of the useless and expensive Korean missions abroad. I have not yet had official confirmation of this.

                                           Horace N Allen

No. 786   Legation of the United States
                                           Seoul, Korea, August 27, 1904.

Secretary of State

Sir:-

I have the honor to hand you enclosed, a copy of a letter from Rev. Dr. S. A. Moffett, a presbyterian missionary living at Pengyang, dated the 15th instant, relative to the distress caused to the native Koreans by the enforcement of Japanese demands for coolies for use in transporting military supplies in Manchuria. I also enclose an extract from the Korea Daily News, of Seoul, of the 25th instant, upon the same subject.

The Japanese authorities asked the Korean Government to supply them with some eight thousand coolies, and as the natives feared to go, even with the promise of high wages, it became necessary to seize them, with the result of increasing the hatred of the Korean people for the Japanese, and of causing more or less disturbance in the interior.

Mr. Hayashi, the Japanese Minister, told me ot his attempts to have the Korean army disbanded, with the exception of a guard of some fifteen hundred, and he said he had hoped these disbanded soldiers would be willing to go as transport coolies, though he had not attempted to insist upon it. Very few of these soldiers seem to have offered themselves, and apparently the act of disbandment has not really taken place as yet.

                                           Horace N. Allen.

                                    Pyengyang, Korea, August 15th, 1904.

Hon. H. N. Allen:

Several in our community feel that you will be interested in certain aspects of the relation between the Japanese and Koreans in this part of the country, and that we ought to keep you informed. They have suggested that I write you telling you of the situation arising from the impressment of Koreans for work on the Railroad and for labor as coolies with the army in Manchuria. For some days there has been great indignation over the enforced labor on the railroad at wages which in many cases is said to be insufficient to pay for food only, the wages as reported to us ranging from 16 cents Korean to 80 cents Korean a day. Men have been taken in squads 50 or 100 li or more from their houses, compelled to work a few days and then sent back their wages for their work not even paying their board bills not to mention the expence coming and going. This has been done by the Korean officials to the village or township elders or trustees. This is a busy time with the farmers and many have tried to avoid the work so as to care for their crops. The Japanese have resorted to beating them and forcing them to labor. Where the wages earned have not been sufficient to pay for the Board, it is reported that the village or township from which the men come has been levied upon to supply the deficiency. I am told that in and around Pyeng Yang each house has been ordered to furnish one laborer, and that in case of refusal Japanese has entered houses and beaten with sticks the heads of the house until he promised to comply. In one village in Whang Ju some of the Christians refused to work on the railroad and the word was taken to the Japanese that none of the Christians would work. Upon this the Japanese went to the village, beat the leader of the Church and threatened to beat the Evangelist, forcing the two men to sign a paper promising to send 35 men to work on the road.

A number of Christians and other villagers from Chei Chai 25 li from here were taken 50 li to Choong Wha county, among them the leader of the Church. Saturday night this leader asked the interpreter to tell the Japanese in charge that he could not work the next day, Sunday. The interpreter refused. The man then said that unless he would explain the matter the Japanese would think he was running away, but still the interpreter refused, and so when the man went to Church on Sunday instead of working it gave the impression that he was running away from the work.

Along the line of the Railroad there has been a god deal of disturbance, but I have mentioned in detail only these few which have come clearly to our notice.

More serious however has been the agitation caused by the demand for coolies for work in Manchuria. The Japanese Consuls in Chinampo and Pyeng Yang have compelled the Korean prefects to issue orders for as many coolies (one for every 6th, house) to be sent to Manchuria. Some prefects have refused, others have complied. The Governor in Pyeng Yang refused at first but was told that the Japanese would make the Magistrate Paiug Governor in his place unless he issued the order.

This move has caused not only indignation and alarm, but has led to an insurrection in An Ju county, and to such disturbance as to threaten insurrections in Kang Sye, Ryong Kang, Sam Wha, and Chung San counties. While in Anock county an even more serious situation arising. Here the people became alarmed at the threat to send in Japanese soldiers, bind them, and send them bound by ship to Manchuria. Whole villages are reported deserted by all but the old men, the people having fled in consternation.

For a week or more our helpers and leaders have been coming in greatly alarmed over the situation, and the change of the sentiment among the people towards the Japanese. Our people have been, and are strongly Pro-Japanese and wish to remain so, but the mass of the people are becoming outspoken in bitterness against the Japanese, and are openly saying they hope the Russians will come in again.

Just at this time comes the report that the Russians have taken Gensan from which all the people have fled, and that they are now at Cha San, Kang Tong and Sung Chun counties 100 li or more North East of Pyeng Yang. Last Tuesday night Japanese troops went out to this region 1000 of them it is reported.

The country people are getting indignant and excitement and disturbance are growing. While the Japanese are becoming more and more suspicious and overbearing.

Some the Christians and others here have recently organized a debating society here which I understand have aroused the suspicion of the Japanese altho the Society is doing nothing along political lines and its officers assure me they intend to keep it clear of politics.

It looks as though the Japanese were making the mistake of alienating the sympathy of the whole people and of turning them from freinds into enemies by a policy of enforced labor and very unwise administration in matters which affects large number of people. Injustice from their own officials the Korean endures, but from the Japanese they keenly and indignantly resent.

Believing that the Japanese would appiciate it if we reported to the consol here the rumors which were reaching us, Mr. Lee, Mr. Morris, and I called on him and in substance told him what I have written you.

He seemed glad to have us tell him of the situation, and was himself somewhat worried over it. He explained that the people were not to be forced to go to Manchuria but said he thought the Koreans ought to be willing to go and thus to keep safe their country from Russia.

He also explained that work on the Railroad was paid for at the rate of so much per Kan paying for an amount of work which two Japanese would do in a day. If two Koreans did their work in one day they received the same wages Japanese would receive but if it took four Koreans to do this work they each received only half as much. This he said would explain why there was such disparity in wages received and why in many cases it was insufficient. He also said there might be some squeezing, and that the disturbances had been such that he expected soon to put Japanese police along the road whenever work was being carried on. We made one request of him that he arrange with the Japanese supervisors that the Christians at work should be free on Sunday. This he seemed quite willing to do, and I think he appreciated our visit and the spirit in which the information was given, as we assured him that we wished to use our influence to maintain friendly relations between the Japanese and the Koreans.

It is with the same hope in view that we wish to keep you informed as to any movements which seem to threaten trouble.

A good many Koreans come to us to know if they can get any damage for the land which is taken for the Railroad.

I have not as yet been able to learn what the agreement with the Government is. If you can give me any information on this point and through whom the Koreans can secure the price of their land, I shall be greatly obliged.

Mr. Hunt and I have just learned that our claims will be considered at the Railroad Headquarters here.

Samuel A. Moffett.

No. 790   Legation of the United States
                                             Seoul, Korea, September 6, 1904.

Secretary of State

Sir:-

I have the honor to acquaint you with the following notes on the present Japan-Korean relations here.

On August 20th, Mr. Hayashi, the Japanese Minister, was refused an audience with the Emperor of Korea, which audience had been requested for the purpose of delivering some message from the Japanese Government. Failing to secure the interview, Mr. Hayashi went to the palace with his secretary and compelled the guards to admit him. He was accorded an audience and it is now arranged that he may go to the palace when necessary without hindrance. In order to minimize this grant, the other Foreign Representatives have been notified that the may go to the waiting room of the palace, and "sign their names in a book" when they have some congratulations to offer to the Emperor". Although I have been urged to avail myself of this privilege I have not yet done so.

I learn also that a telephone line is being erected to connect the Emperor's palace with the Japanese legation.

Mr. Kato, formerly Japanese Minister to Seoul and lately the adviser to the Agricultural Department, is now transferred to the post of adviser to the Household Department.

The Japanese financial expert who has been engaged to serve with the Korean Department of Finance, is expected to arrive in Seoul within a few days.

Horace N Allen

No. 793   Legation of the United States
                                             Seoul, Korea, September 10, 1904.

Secretary of State

Sir:-

Continuing the subject of my confidential despatch, No. 787 of the 30th ultimo, which need be considered confidential no longer, I now have the honor to hand you enclosed a translation of the Korean - Japanese Protocol of the 22nd August, which appeared in the Korean Official Gazette of yesterday.

This agreement compels Korea to employ a Japanese subject, on the recommendation of the Japanese Government, as an adviser to their Finance Department, whose advice must be taken.

It also provides for the appointment of a foreigner to be recommended by the Japanese Government, to a similar position in relation to the Korean Foreign Office.

The agreement further provides that diplomatic questions and agreements with foreigners must be first submitted to the Japanese Government.

As I have previously informed you, a Japanese official connected with the Finance Department of Japan, is expected here shortly to take up the duties of adviser to the Korean Finance Department, while Mr. D. W. Stevens of Washington, has been named as the adviser to the Foreign Office.

Article three of the enclosed protocol would seem to make the Korean Foreign Office a mere adjunct, for local matters of a trivial nature, of the Japanese Foreign Office.

Horace N. Allen.

OFFICIAL GAZETTE.   SEPTEMBER 9th 1904

KOREAN -JAPANESE PROTOCOL.

1. The Korean Government will employ a Japanese recommended by the Japanese Government, as an adviser to the Finance Department, in order that anything concerning financial matters will be decided by his advice.

2. The Korean Government will employ a foreigner recommended by the Japanese Government, as an adviser to the Foreign Office, in order that any important matters relating to foreign affairs will be decided by his advice.

3. The Korean Government in regard to the making of any treaty; conducting any diplomatic intercourse, or conceding any franchise or contract to a foreigner, must consult the Japanese Government beforehand.

Signed Yun Chi Ho,
Acting Minister for Foreign Affairs.
Kwang Moo, 8th year; 8th moon; 22nd day.

Signed Hayashi, Kenjo.
E.E. & M.P. for Japan.
Maiji, 37th year; 8th month; 22nd day.

August 22nd, 1904.

The first and second Articles of the above protocol were decided upon on the 18th ultimo, by Ye Ha Yong, Minister for Foreign Affairs: Pak Chung Yang, Minister of Finance, and Hayashi, Japanese Minister, and the protocol was signed.
The third article was added and signed on the 22nd ultimo. The former two articles have already been exchanged and recorded

No. 804   Legation of the United States
                                       Seoul, Korea, October 11, 1904.

Secretary of State

Sir:-
I have the honor to inform you that on yesterday a party of six Korean officials and forty six students, started for Japan: The former to look into Japanese methods of government and the students to enter Japanese schools.
Much has been made of this mission by the papers of Japan, as though it indicated a desire on the part of the Government of Korea to come closer to Japan and adopt Japanese methods of Government. Judging from the Korean newspaper reports however, it would seem to be a move owing its initiative to the Japanese authorities entirely, and one moreover that is distasteful to the Koreans. There were daily notices of the attempts to evade the mission by various members appointed, while the students are said to be young men of doubtful character who either wish to get away from home or have little patriotic feeling. They are described as rather a bad lot.
Korean sentiment is not as friendly to Japan as one might suppose from hearing only the Japanese side. The recent protocol, which places the finances and foreign affairs of Korea entirely in Japanese hands, and which is reported in the local Japanese papers as well as in the papers of Japan, as being the forerunner

of the recall of foreign ministers from Korea, seems to the Korean officials to violate the promise of the protocol of February twenty third and presage the lose of independence.

By the attempt to take the waste lands of Korea on which lands the natives raise their fuel; the enforcement of the natives by the thousand, to serve as transportation coolies and other army laborers; the seizure of personal property without adequate satisfaction, due in many cases if not at all, to the fact that the native officials have been allowed to retain such compensation as was made; the failure of the Japanese to listen to Korean complaints of injustice, while if a Korean is found guilty of wrong doing he is promptly imprisoned or shot, all tend to agravate the feeling of distrust on the part of the Koreans toward the Japanese.

As an instance I may mention the shooting under martial law, on the 21st ultimo, of three Koreans who had taken away some railway material in an attempt to get payment for their lands which were ruined and taken away by one of the military railways. Doubtless some such lesson was needed, but the Koreans fail to see why farmers should be brutally killed for attempting to obtain satisfaction for wrongs, while when they complain of soldiers and gendarmes wantonly injuring or killing natives they get no satisfaction.

I hear from our missionaries in the North that the Russian commanders were most strict in punishing their soldiers for any injustice committed against a native, and the Russian officials were reported as being easy of access, while if a Korean went to Japanese headquarters to lodge a complaint, he was "kicked out". The difference in treatment received from these two armies is well known to the Koreans and their is a growing sentiment in favor of the Russians.

I enclose a translation from the Korean Chey Kook Sinmun, a local newspaper, the publication of which has been stopped I hear, in consequence of the publication of this article. The suppression of the paper is reported to have been carried out by Japanese gendarmes.

Horace N. Allen.

No. 805   Legation of the United States
                                                          Seoul, Korea, October 12, 1904.

Secretary of State

Sir:-

I have the honor to inform you of the arrival, on the 29th ultimo, of Mr. Megata, of the Japanese Department of Finance, to serve as financial adviser to the Korean Government, in accordance with the protocol published on the 9th ultimo.

With Mr. Megata came another official, Mr. S. Suzuki, who has on his card "Controller of the Imperial Japanese Customs" but I understand the British Minister has no fear of the Korean customs administration passing from British into Japanese hands.

I was informed last evening by one of the Councillors of State, that the contract of Mr. Megata had been signed yesterday. He is to receive Yen 1,000 ($500.) per month for a period of five years: He is to have access daily to the Emperor: All the revenues of the government must pass through his hands and all orders relating to financial matters must be signed by him. Such was my information.

Ten years ago when there were several American advisers in Seoul, the Japanese on taking charge of the Government, - before their failure due to the murder of the Queen, - caused an edict to be issued fixing the pay of all advisers at the sum of Yen 300 as a maximum. This did not prevent the employment of foreign advisers however. It is interesting in this connection to note that Mr. Megata is to receive Yen 1,000.

Horace N. Allen

No. 808   Legation of the United States
                                           Seoul, Korea, October 17, 1904.

Secretary of State

Sir:-

During the period of Japanese control of Korea ten years ago, following the Japan-China war and prior to the murder of the Queen, one of the most visible reforms insisted upon by the Japanese was that of wearing short hair instead of doing up the hair in the "top knot" so dear to the native. This, apparently trivial, innovation cost so much disturbance that it had to be abandoned. I now have the honor to inform you that the matter is brought forward again and with pretty strong chances of meeting with some success.

In my No. 781 of August 11 and previous despatches cited, I informed you of the disturbance caused by the Japanese opposition to the Poh An Hoi, or Society for the Preservation of Peace. This organization, being unfavorable to the Japanese, was finally suppressed and another was started by a refugee recently returned from Japan, one Song Pyung Chun, under the secret auspices of the Japanese, called the Il Chin Hoi, or Society for United Progress. This society has been under suspicion from the first, but it is succeeding among a certain class who are intelligent enough and bold enough to accept the inevitable and try to make peace with the Japanese. One of the requirements of membership in this society is the cutting of the top knot and the wearing of short hair, which accounts for the greater success of this reform than was met with ten years ago. Certain officials are also required to cut their hair and wear foreign uniforms.

Horace N Allen

No. 823   Legation of the United States
                                           Seoul, Korea, November 11, 1904.

Secretary of State

Sir:-

I have the honor to inform you that the Kanjo Shimpo, a local Japanese newspaper, in its issue of today, states that the Seoul - Fusan Railway was completed yesterday morning by connecting the two ends. Work having proceeded from either end.

I understand that twenty Baldwin locomotives have arrived at Fusan from America for this line, and I am told that dining and sleeping cars will be operated on the line. Also, it is the intention to have fast ferry ships for the crossing of the Korean straits from Fusan to Mogi, and it is stated that in the early part of next year it will be possible to make the journey comfortably from Seoul to Tokio in about fifty four hours. The railway line from Seoul to Fusan being 268 miles in length.

In the meantime the grading is about completed, I am told, on the line from Seoul to Wiju, a distance of over 300 miles. This entire work having been done since April last. Track is down for some distance north from Seoul and trains are running for construction work. Much of the rail and bridge material for this road was brought from America, but as it is imported by the military authorities, statistics are not available.

Survey work is going on rapidly for the military railway to connect Seoul and Gensan, and some earth work is already said to be under construction.

Horace N Allen

No. 824   Legation of the United States
                                           Seoul, Korea, November 18, 1904.

Secretary of State

Sir:-

I have the honor to inform you that I hear from the Korean Palce that the Korean Minister to China has been recalled by telegraph, at the instance of the Japanese Minister, for the reason that the former advised the Russian Minister, at Peking, by formal despatch, of the death of the Korean Crown Princess. It is said that the Japanese Minister, Mr. Hayashi, pointed out that as Korea had abrogated all treaties with Russia and had allied herself with Japan who was now at war with Russia, such communications were out of the question, and that the Minister should return before he makes similar breaks. I am also told that Mr. Hayashi advised the early recall of all the Korean ministers abroad. He is said to have been particularly insistent upon the prompt recall of the Korean Minister to Japan, who seems to have no functions at Tokio.

Japanese advice does not seem to be taken by the Koreans very promptly at present. The Korean Emperor is said to have been assured by his soothsayers that Russia is sure to win in the present war and this seems to have calmed him and made him less amenable to Japanese advice.

One million yen is said to have been appropriated for the funeral of the late Crown Princess without consulting the Japanese financial adviser and in violation of the protocol published on September 9.

                                                            Horace N Allen

No. 840   Legation of the United States
                                                   Seoul, Korea, December 17, 1904.

Secretary of State

Sir:-

In connection with the Japanese-Korean agreements of February 23rd and August 22nd last, considerable Korean property has been taken for military purposes by the Japanese, including land for military railways. It seems that in such cases a more or less fair compensation has been made but it has often happened that this money has not been turned over properly by the native officials to the people who have been deprived of their holdings so that considerable complaint of distress has been heard.

These complaints frequently come to me through some connection of our missionaries with the native complainants. As a rule when I have brought these matters to the attention of the Japanese Legation steps have been taken looking to a redress of the wrong complained of, and my Japanese Colleague, Mr. Hayashi, has asked me to send him copies of all such communications in order that he may be more fully posted as to proceedings in the interior.

I recently received such a complaint of the seizing of a large area of Korean farm land in the province of Whanghai, situated between Seoul and Pengyang, in which six communities of native christians were interested. The letter, bearing date Pengyang, November 24, was from Rev. Graham Lee of the American Presbyterian Mission of 156 Fifth Avenue New York City. I sent a copy of this letter to Mr. Hayashi, in accordance with his request, but did not ask for an explanation or reply and have received none. I enclose a copy of this letter from Rev. Lee. I could not advise him on the subject.

I also enclose a copy of a letter, dated Fusan December 15, from Rev. Walter E. Smith of the same mission, regarding a native church, said to have been taken for military purposes at Masampo.

As treaty provisions were invoked the letter was handed to me by the Consul General, Mr. Paddock, to whom I gave a memorandum on the subject, of which I enclose a copy. I showed that the suposed treaty provisions were non-existent, and that the matter was purely a Korean one in which there was nothing upon which to base a claim for American interference.

While numbers of Koreans have doubtless suffered so far from the military occupation of this country, the general result has been to increase the aggregate prosperity. Work has been plenty at unusually high wages and so much money is being expended in Korea for the construction of railways by the Japanese and for military purposes that the purchasing power of the natives has so increased as to cause a somewhat unlooked for prosperity in general trade.

                                                            Horace N Allen

No. 843

Legation of the United States
Seoul, Korea, December 17, 1904.

Secretary of State

Sir:-

I have the honor to hand you enclosed an extract from the Japan Daily Mail of December 10 relative to the numerous societies that have sprung up in Korea for the agitation of views favorable and unfavorable to the Government. These societies do certainly constitute a menace to the public peace, and it may be that the Japanese authorities will have to take severe measures with them, though it is supposed that at least one of these societies was organized under Japanese auspices in order to counteract the influence of a strong organization that was notoriously hostile to Japan.

Horace N Allen

No. 845

Legation of the United States
Seoul, Korea, December 22, 1904.

Secretary of State

Sir:-

I have the honor to inform you of the arrival in Seoul on yesterday, of Mr. D. W. Stevens of Washington, who comes to Korea under Japanese auspices, to serve as adviser to the Korean Foreign Office.

The Japanese Minister, Mr. Hayashi, informs me that the contract which will be made with Mr. Stevens will be indefinite as to time; that it will probably be for Yen 1000 ($500) per month, with an allowance for house rent, but that the Korean Government wish the monthly salary to be not more than Yen 800. I understand that Mr. Stevens will have access to the Emperor as occasion may require.

The Korean Government now has the following advisers: - Mr. Kato, formerly Japanese Minister to Korea, who is adviser to the Household Department and to the Department of Agriculture, Commerce and Public Works; Mr. T. Megata, Adviser to the Finance Department, Mr. J. McLeavy Brown, Chief Commissioner of Customs, (A British subject), and Mr. Stevens. A Belgian subject, Mr. Delcoigne, who has been holding a nominal position as an adviser to the Korean Government since 1902, is about to take his departure from Korea. A Frenchman, Mr. L. Crémazy, still holds a position as Legal Adviser to the Korean Government.

Horace N. Allen.

No. 848

American Legation. Seoul, Korea,
December 24 1904.

Secretary of State

Sir:-

I have the honor to hand you enclosed, in duplicate, a copy of an article that appeared in the "Anglo-Japanese Gazette' published in London, on October -- 1904, giving a list of the proposed reforms that the Japanese Government are said to contemplate in Korea. The information being from the Tokio correspondent of that journal.

As I had not seen any such complete setting forth of proposed reforms I thought it might be well to send you a copy.

Of these reported reforms the following have been acted upon: -

1. Has been accomplished by the employment of Mr. T. Megata.

3. Mr. Takagi had a scheme to loan Korea Yen 10,000,000, but he has apparently given it up and has left Korea.

4. The mint has been closed but copper coins still circulate.

5. Japanese money circulates freely throughout Korea.

8. Mr. D. W. Stevens has arrived and is employed as Adviser to the Korean Foreign Office.

11. Some few Korean troops have been disbanded. Not many.
13. The soothsayers and necromancers have been banished from the Palace from time to time, but usually turn up there again.
14. The consolidation of the government offices is in progress.
15. A few government offices have been abolished and others will probably follow the same fate, as the country is overburdened with useless offices and officials.

Horace N Allen

FROM THE ANGLO - JAPANESE GAZETTE, LONDON, OCTOBER. 1904.

(From Our Tokyo Correspondent.)

The various reforms which it is the entention of the Japanese Government to introduce into Korea by gradual degrees are set out under twenty-five heads, and are as follows:-
1/   The Korean Financial Department shall engage a Japanese as superintendent of Korean finances in order to carry out fiscal reforms.
2/   In order to enable Korea to effect financial reforms Japan will advance it the necessary funds, ¥3,000,000 being lent as first instalment.
3/   The contract for loan of ¥10,000,000 recently entered into between the Minister of the Imperial Household of Korea and Mr. Bunpei Takagi shall be revoked, as it was made without the sanction of the Japanese Minister at Seoul.
4/   The currency system shall be firmly established by abolishing the present mint and withdrawing the copper coins now in circulation.
5/   A currency union shall be concluded between Japan and Korea and Japanese money shall be circulated among Koreans without hinderance.
6/   A central bank shall be established in Korea for the purpose of facilitating the collection of taxes and the handling of the public money.
7/   As the first step towards the internal reforms in connexion with the management of the local administration and the collection of the local taxes, a model aministrative system shall be adopted in Kyong-kwi Province, and if it proves a success similar systems shall be adopted in other provinces.
8/   In order to improve foreign intercourse, a certain American citizen shall be engaged by the Korean Foreign Department as its adviser.
9/   As soon as the Japanese Government is requested by Korea to take charge of the affairs relating to her foreign intercourse and to give protection to her subjects abroad, the Korea Ministers and Consuls in the foreign countries shall be withdrawn.
10/   Simultaneously with the withdrawal of the Korean Ministers and Consuls from the foreign countries the Foreign Ministers to Korea shall also be withdrawn from Seoul and the Foreign Consuls alone shall remain in their respective posts in Korea.
11/   For financial necessity, the Korean army shall be reduced by decreasing the number of soldiers through the country, at present put at 20,000, to 1,000, and by disbanding all the garrisons in the provinces, keeping only one at Seoul.
12/   A union of military arms shall be effected between Japan and Korea with the object of adjusting the existing military system in the latter country.
13/   In order to uphold the dignity of the Korean Court, the sooth-sayers, fortune-tellers, and other officials whose business is to foster superstition, shall be expelled from the surroundings of the Sovereign.
14/   The abolition and amalgamation of the Government offices shall be carried out.
15/   All unnecessary Government officials shall be discharged.
16/   The appointments to the Government posts shall be made from all classes of the people, without regard to rank and family relations.
17/   The practice of selling Government posts shall be prohibited and the Government officials shall be selected from those who have education and ability.
18/   The salaries of the Ministers of State and other Government officials shall be increased so as to give them a stronger sence of responsibility.
19/   The education policy shall be fixed, and the various foreign language schools now in existence shall be brought under a uniform administration.
20/   The educational system of Universities, middle schoools, and primary schools shall be moddelled after the existing in Japan, in oder to promote education throughout the country.

21/   Technical schools shall be established in order to encourage the industrial prosperity of the country.

22/   A clear distinction shall be made between the court and the Government, and the organisation of each body shall be gradually reformed.

23/   Simultaneously with the abolition and amalagamation of the Government offices, the reduction of the present foreign Advisers shall be effected.

24/   The post of Supreme Adviser to the Korean Government shall remain unfilled for the present.

24/   Agriculture in Korean shall be improved by reclaiming waste lands and developing the natural resources of the soil.

Mr. Stevens, an American, will act as adviser to the Foreign Office, Mr. McLeavy Brown will continue in charge of the Customs, while financial matters will be in the hands of Mr. Megata.

No. 856   American Legation, Seoul, Korea.
                                               January 6, 1905.

Secretary of State

Sir:-

I have the honor to inform you that the local papers of yesterday announce that the Japanese Military Authorities have informed the Korean Government that hereafter the police matters of Seoul will be controlled by the Japanese gendarmerie because of the apparent inability of the Korean police to preserve order.

I also learn that a Japanese police inspector will be placed in each prefecture, and a Japanese adviser, or chief inspector has been sent for to take charge of the Seoul Police Department.

                                               Horace N Allen

No. 859   American Legation, Seoul, Korea.
                                               January 12, 1905.

Secretary of State

Sir:-

I have the honor to inform you that Mr. Hayashi, the Japanese Minister, is reported to have made the following demands at an audience on yesterday with the Emperor: -

1. The reduction of the Army - General Hassegawa, Japanese Commander in Chief, is said to have proposed two battalions of 400 each for an "Imperial Guard".

2. The recall of the Korean legations from abroad.

3. The abolishment of the Korean Department of Posts and Telegraphs (Communications) and the submission of all such matters to the Japanese post and telegraph offices in Korea.

4. A reduction in the long periods of mourning which so burden the Korean people.

5. The appointment of none but Japanese speaking Korean officials to country offices.

6. The payment of a suitable indemnity for each Japanese who has been killed by Koreans during the past ten years. - Just after the murder of the Queen of Korea, on October 8, 1895, over 40 Japanese were killed in the interior by the infuriated Koreans, and quite a number of solitary Japanese have been killed since then. An indemnity waw asked in the case of the deaths following the murder of the Queen, but the demand was not complied with.

                                               Horace N Allen

No. 864   American Legation, Seoul, Korea.
                                                 January 19, 1905.

Secretary of State

Sir:-
        I have the honor to inform you that the local papers announce that on the 17th instant, at a cabinet
meeting in presence of the Emperor of Korea, Mr. Megata, the financial adviser from Japan, proposed the
three following measures: -
1st. That a loan of Yen 10,000,000 be raised in Japan, and used for the establishment of a national bank in
Seoul with branches in each of the thirteen provinces. A period of six months being mentioned for the
execution of this work.
2nd. That the use of counterfeit nickel coins be prohibited in some manner sufficiently drastic to prevent
the circulation of the vast mass of these coins that now flood the country.
3rd. That official salaries be paid in Japanese paper yen.
        It is reported that Mr. Megata intends the substitution of Japanese money for Korean entirely.

                                                 Horace N Allen

No. 885   American Legation, Seoul, Korea.
                                                 March 17, 1905.

Secretary of State

Sir:-
        I have the honor to hand you enclosed copies of two protests against Japanese conduct in Korea.
        One being written by one of our missionaries, Rev. Norman Clark Whittemore, of the
Presbyterian Board, 156 Fifth Avenue New York, on behalf of some of his Korean followers whose village
was burned by Japanese troops near Wiju. This was dated at Syen Chun near Wiju, January 2, and sent to
me to be handed to the Japanese Minister. I spoke to Mr. Hayashi about it and as he signified his
willingness to receive the letter, I have sent it to him unofficially and without comment.
        The other is a circular supposedly sent to each foreign minister with some idea of securing
sympathy and assistance in regard to the maintenance of Korean independence. The paper is signed by
eleven Koreans whose names are quite unfamiliar to me, and are probably assumed. This circular will of
course receive no attention from me.

                                                 Horace N Allen

No. 902   American Legation, Seoul, Korea.
                                                 May 30, 1905.

Secretary of State

Sir:-
        I have the honor to hand you enclosed a copy of the agreement recently concluded between the
Governments of Japan and Korea whereby the former takes over the control and operation of all matters
relating to posts, telegraphs and telephones in Korea.
        In my despatch No. 899 of the 12th instant, I handed you a copy of correspondence between the
Korean Foreign Office, or rather the Japanese Authorities, and myself, relative to the subjection of an
American concession to customs and other taxation, in which correspondence I yielded the point in principle
but objected to the singling out of one American concession alone, meaning that the Japanese and other
concessions should be treated in the same manner.
        In this connection I would call your attention to Article V. of this agreement just concluded, in
which the Japanese Government reserves to this concession the right of free customs entry for all supplies
to be used for the same.

I may add that this will cover a semi-private telephone service in Seoul which violates a telephone concession held by Americans and operated to a small extent, for many years.

Horace N Allen

With compliments of Japanese Minister.

Agreement.

The Imperial Government of Japan and Korea, finding it expedient from the standpoint of the administration and finances of Korea, to rearrange the system of communications in that country and, by amalgamating it with that of Japan, to unite the two systems into one common to the two countries, and, having seen the necessity with that object in view, of transferring the post, telegraph and telephone services of Korea to the control of the Japanese Government, Hayashi Consuke, Envoy Extraordinary and Minister Plenipotentiary of Japan and I-hayeng, Minister of State for Foreign Affairs of Korea, each invested with proper authority have agreed upon and concluded the following Articles:-

Article I. The Imperial Government of Korea shall transfer and assign the control and administation of the post, telegraph and telephone services in Korea (except the telephone service exclusively pertaining to the Department of the Imperial Household) to the Imperial Japanese Government.

Article II. The land, buildings, furnitures, instruments, machines and all other appliances connected with the system of communications already established by the Imperial Government of Korea, shall, by virtue of the present Agreement, be transferred to the control of the Imperial Japanese Government.

The authorities of the two countries acting together shall make an inventory of the land, buildings and all other requisites mentioned in the preceding paragraph wich shall serve as evidence in the future.

Article III. When it is deemed necessary by the Japanese Government to extend the communication system in Korea, they may appropriate land and buildings belonging to the State or to private persons; the former without compensation and the latter with proper indemnification.

Article IV. In respect of the control of the communication service and the custody of the properties in connection therewith, the Japanese Government assume; on their own account the responsibility of good administration.

The expences required for the extension of the communication services shall also be borne by the Imperial Government of Japan.

The Imperial Government of Japan shall officially notify the Imperial Korean Government of the financial condition of the system of communications under their control.

Article V. All appliances and materials which are deemed necessary by the Imperial Government of Japan for the control or extension of the system of communication shall be exempt from all duties and imposts.

Article VI. The Imperial Government of Korea shall be at liberty to maintain the present Board of Communication so far as such retention does not interfere with the control and extension of the services by the Japanese Government.

The Japanese Government, in controlling and extending the services, shall engage as many Korean officials and employees as possible.

Article VII. In respect of the arrangements formerly entered into by the Korean Government with the Government of foreign Powers concerning the post, telegraph and telephone services, the Japanese Government shall in behalf of Korea exercise the rights and perform the obligations pertaining thereto.

Shaould there arise in the future any necessity for concluding any new convention between the Government of Korea and the Governments of foreign Powers concerning the communication services, the Japanese Government shall assume the responsibility of concluding such convention in behalf of the Korean Government.

Article VIII. The various conventions and agreements respecting the communication services hitherto existing between the Governmetns of Japan and Korea are naturally abolished or modified by the present Agreement.

Article IX. When in future as the result of the general development of the communication system in Korea, there is some adequate profit over and above expenditures defrayed by the Japanese Government for the control and maintenance of the old services and for their extensions and inprovements, the Japanese Government shall deliver to the Korean Government a suitable percentage of such profit.

Article X. When in the future an ample surplus exists in the finance of the Korean Government, the control of their communication services may be returned, as the result of the consultation of the two Governments, to the Government of Korea.

No. 11   American Legation, Seoul, Korea.
                                                          August 16, 1905.

Secretary of State

Sir,
      I have the honor to transmit the official text in the Japanese language of the Agreement respecting the Coast Trade of Korea, signed on the 13th instant on behalf of the Imperial Governments of Japan and Korea by Their Excellencies the Japanese Minister, Mr. Hayashi, and the Korean Minister for Foreign Affairs, Mr. Yi Ha Yong, and handed me yesterday by my Japanese colleague. The English translation appended has been prepared by the Legation staff.
      The concessions to Japan embodied in this Agreement were unwelcome to the Korean Cabinet Ministers, who resigned their portfolios in order to indicate their disapproval, and have not resumed them in spite of His Majesty's earnest solicitation. Their objections were twofold. In addition to the belief that the dignity of Korea as an independent Power would be lowered should she grant privileges which Japan would not reciprocate, they were apprehensive that the terms of Article 6, which permit Japanese shipowners to erect wharves and storehouses on the coast and along the interior waters, would enable emigrants to seize land without payment and establish settlements beyond the limits of open ports. Experience in the past gave rise to this foreboding. The railways built during recent years have transported into the interior large numbers of irresponsible coolies between whom and the native farmers armed encounters have not been infrequent. Under the rights of extraterritorality enjoyed by the subjects and citizens of foreign Powers Korean magistrates may not punish Japanese wrong-doers and the consular officials of Japan are as yet too few in number to take cognizance of unlawful acts committed by their nationals outside the immediate neighborhood of the towns in which their consulates are located.
      Japan desired the Agreement to legalize a trade which hitherto has been conducted by subterfuge. Japanese bottoms have carried goods between treaty and non-treaty ports and the letter of the law only has been observed which prohibits foreign ships from engaging in coastwise and riverine trade. Either Japanese vessels have been chartered nominally to Koreans, or transferred to them by paper sales. When registered as Korean owned, though but partly paid for, they have flown the Japanese flag. Under the regulations of the Korean maritime customs they have been authorized to trade by the issue of a "ping piao", a certificate which, if renewed annually, enabled them to touch at certain ports of call on condition that both import and export duty should be paid at an established customs station before proceeding to and upon returning from these ports, en route from or to a foreign country. Since the customs take cognizance only of junks and of ships of foreign style, (under which are included European built steamers and schooners) these vessels must carry a "ping piao" if they desire to trade outside treaty ports.
      It is expected that it will be both impossible and inexpedient to prevent smuggling. The expense of patrolling the coast would not be proportional to the customs duties collected, even were smuggling effectively suppressed. Villages of from twenty to thirty Japanese families have established themselves on the coast facing Japan which conduct a brisk smuggling trade. Should vigorous steps be taken against them a clash between Japanese and Korean authority might occur which would enable Japan to secur still more absolute domain over this portion of Korea.
      Under Article 14 of the Treaty of May 22nd, 1882, between the United States and Korea the privilege obtained by Japanese subjects through this Agreement should be open to the citizens of the United States. The Japanese Minister assures me that this is the understanding of his Government.

                                                          Edwin V. Morgan

No. 14   American Legation, Seoul, Korea.
                                            August 28, 1905.

Secretary of State

Sir:-
     I have the honor to inform you that the Korean Maritime Customs, hitherto a seperate and
independent bureau, will be placed shortly under the Korean Ministry of finance controlled by Mr. Megata, a
Japanese subject, who occupies the position of financial adviser. Mr. McLeavy Brown, a British subject,
the present Chief Commissioner of Customs, has been superceded. The European commissioners of
customs at the Korean ports and the members of the indoor staff, the majority of whom have been detached
from the Chinese Customs Service, will probably resign, although they have been given the option of
remaining, and their places will be filled by Japanese. The transfer of the Customs was arranged yesterday
at an audience accorded by the Emperor to the Japanese Minister and Mr. Megata.
     The Korean Government assured Mr. Brown recently that he should retain his office, and his first
knowledge of his enforced retirement, brought about through an arrangement between the Governments of
Great Britain and Japan, was derived from Mr. Hayashi, the Japanese Minister, who endeavored to pursuade
him to resign. This he refused to do, declining at the same time to accept further remuneration than that to
which he was entitled under the regulations of the Chinese Imperial Customs, in which service he holds the
rank of commissioner.
     Mr. Brown has been the head of the Korean Customs since October, 1893, and has elaborated and
maintained, along the lines of the Chinese service, an organization which is unique among the departments
of the Korean Government for its efficient and honest administration. In addition to superintending the
collection of customs duties at the treaty ports, he has endeavored to correct the abuses arising from the lack
of a national system of finance, as far as the Korean Government would permit him; has supported their
Legations abroad, lighted the Korea coasts, whose dangers have been a menace to mariners for many years,
improved the harbors, supervised the erection of public buildings and constructed roads and bridges in the
capital and its vicinity.
     In 1901 British influence, with the support of the representatives of the United States and Japan,
frustrated an attempt of the Russian and French ministers to dislodge Mr. Brown from his position and to
substitute a Russian in his stead.
     Although urged frequently to pledge the customs revenues for foreign loans and for mining and
other industrial experiments suggested by interested persons, Mr. Brown has combatted intrigue successfully
and has expended the funds committed to his care upon those public improvements only, which committed
themselves to his judgment. He will be able, therefore, upon relinquishing his post, to transfer to the
Finance Department three million Yen, which has been accumulated for the extension of the lighthouse
service and for other specific purposes of unquestioned utility.

                                            Edwin V. Morgan

No. 15   American Legation, Seoul, Korea.
                                            August 30, 1905.

Secretary of State

Sir:-
     I have the honor to confirm below the telegrams which have passed between the Department and
this Legation yesterday and today in regard to the statement made to the Department by the Chargé
d'Affaires of Korea that the Foreign Represetatives at Seoul had agreed, at a conference, to request their
respective Governments to recall them and substitute Chargés d'Affaires in their places.
     Not only has no conference been held but no suggestion has been advanced by any Foreign
Representative that such a meeting should occur. It is true that the Japanese Minister has intimidated that it
is the expectation of his Government that in time the foreign Legations at Seoul will be withdrawn. The
Emperor and his Korean advisers, on the other hand, have expressed their earnest desire that the Legations
should remain as an evidence that Korea is regarded as an independent power. Although this question affects
them nearly the Foreign Representatives have considered the subject to be one upon which their advice
should not be tendered unless requested by their Governments.

I am assured by the Korean Minister for Foreign Affairs, upon whom I called this morning, that the Korean Chargé d'Affaires at Washington was not instructed to make the communication to the Department to which your telegram refers, and that information relating to the avowed conference reached him first from himself.

Telegram Received:

American Minister, Seoul. The Korean Chargé states that he is informed by his Government that a conference of the Foreign Ministers there has agreed they would ask their governments to recall them and substitute Chargé d'Affaires in their places. Is this true. Loomis.

Telegram Sent:

Secstate, Washington. Information mentioned in your cipher telegram yesterday is entirely untrue. Korean Minister for Foreign Affairs denies transmitting the information to the Korean Chargé d'Affaires. Morgan.

Edwin V. Morgan.

No. 16   American Legation, Seoul, Korea.
                                                         September 15, 1905.

Secretary of State

Sir:-
        I have the honor to confirm my telegram in relation to the withdrawal of the Legation Guard sent on the 8th. instant from Chefoo, after consultation with Admiral Train, Commander-in-Chief of our Asiatic Fleet, and to acknowledge the receipt of the Department's telegram in reply which was received on the 15th. instant.
        Admiral Train informs me that he will make provision for the immediate return of the Guard to Cavite.

Telegram sent.

                                                         Chefoo, September 8, 1905.

Secstate, Washington.
        Respectfully reccomend marine guard Seoul be withdrawn. Admiral Train concurs.
                                                         Morgan.

Telegram received.

                                                         Washington.
Amlegation, Seoul.
        The President authorizes withdrawal of marine guard.
                                                         Loomis.

                                                         Edwin V. Morgan.

No. 23   American Legation, Seoul, Korea.
                                                         October 19, 1905.

Secretary of State

Sir:-
        I have the honor to confirm below my cipher telegram of October 14, 1905, reading as follows: -
        Secstate, Washington.

Confidential. The Emperor confides to me that the Japanese representative is pressing him to arrange a protocol by which Japan assumes the complete protection of Korea. Although unwilling to do this he may ultimately be constrained to agree. He desires particularly to maintain the present right of direct relations with the foreign powers through his Ministers abroad and theirs here.

Morgan.

In this connection and in view of the present crisis in the political history of this peninsula, I would submit for your consideration certain facts and conditions existing here at this time.

By virtue of the agreements between Japan and Korea of February 23 and August 22, 1904, the Japanese control the political situation. Their military occupation of the country enables them to quell any disturbance that may arise owing to popular disconect at their assumption of authority. Acting under the former protocol they have condemned tracts of land, particularly at Pyeng Yang and Seoul, for purposes, it is believed, of military colonization, paying only a small portion of the actual value of the land in indemnification for such seizure. Under the latter they supervise Korea's foreign relations, and Mr. Megata the Japanese adviser appointed by the provisions of the same instrument administers the national finances. The Korean Posts and Telegraphs are in Japanese hands and the Customs, the one Department of the Government against which there has been no complaint in the past, is soon to pass under the same direction.

While emigration from Japan to other countries is strictly regulated an exception has been made for Korea. As a result crowds of turbulent Japanese have left home to seek their fortune here. In the cities their authorities even with a well organized police have not dealt successfully with them, while in the rural districts there has as yet been little or no provision for their control. Owing to their extra-territorial privileges the native magistrates have not dared to claim jurisdiction over them, even though they have no right to travel unrestricted in the interior. In consequence of the freedom with which these men have been allowed to colonize, particularly in the vicinity of the railroads, there has been friction with the Koreans in the relations of every day life and especially over questions involving the ownership of land.

It should be kept in mind in this conection that the ill-feeling between the two peoples is not a new or extraordinary phenomenon. On the one hands the Koreans have always entertained a lively hatred for the Japanese, thanks to their relations in the past centuries, and more recently to their fears of Japanese designs on their independence. On the other the Japanese look on the Koreans as a weak and inferior race, incapable of reforming or defending themselves and whose obvious destiny is to pass under the suzerainty of Japan who has fought two great wars to safeguard her sphere of interests on the continent of Asia. It is therefore not surprising if the Japanese immigrants, many of whom are irresponsible characters and no longer feel the firm hand of their own government, readily resort to violence in their treatment of a people whom they respect as little as they fear. This evil has repeatedly been admitted by the Japanese authorities and press and existed in like manner if not to the same extent ten years ago when the Japanese were dominant in this country after their war with China. The well known statesmen Count Inouye adjured his countrymen that "Japanese residents in Korea must be reformed"; and his description of their conduct at that period is equally applicable today when once again they find themselves masters of the situation.

In their various projects for extending their influence the Japanese have associated with themselves natives of doubtful reputation who have taken advantage of their intimacy with their employers to further oppress their own people, and though it is probably true that the generally unsettled state of the country and the lack of cohesion between Japanese civil and military officials have been responsible for many of these excesses, unusually careful attention to their interests now that hostilities have ceased will be necessary to bring complete relief to those who have suffered heavily in the months just past.

The attitude of the greater number of foreigners throughout Korea, particularly of our missionaries who have been brought into direct contact with the rougher elements among the Japanese has changed during the last year from one of sympathetic interest in Japan's cause and a cordial appreciation of her successes to one of distrust of her intentions. This is due mainly to the insolence of the coolie class, the overbearing actions of the military authorities and the fact that in cases before the Japanese consular courts where Koreans are concerned there has been little evidence of an attempt to remedy or check abuses. While making allowances for the complexity of the problem which the Japanese officials have been called upon to face and the difficulties of a transition period, there is still a want of confidence in the future impartiality of their courts and the justice of their administration.

At the present time both the Japanese press and public advocate a strong and active policy toward Korea. Although the Government and a certain section of the educated class desire to treat her leniently, the mass of opinion regards the exploitation of this country as a practical means by which Japan may reimburse herself for the losses of the war. To the same feeling is due the Government's anxiety to prevent the reappearance of Russia as a political factor, since the re-establishment of a Russian Legation here would encourage the Koreans to begin anew the intrigues which were partially responsible for the late war. Even though a freshly accredited Russian Minister were to observe scrupulously that article of the treaty of peace which recognizes Japan's supremacy, the fact of his presence here would tend to encourage an agitation that would be anti-Japanese in character. The Japanese newspapers accordingly have entered upon an active campaign in favor of the abolition of the right of Korea to communicate directly with foreign powers and have persistently cited the departure on leave of the Italian Minister and the imminent return of the English representative to Europe as evidence that Italy and Great Britain have decided to recall their missions. It has been rumored, moreover, in the same connection that the United States may agree to abolish her Legation. As stated in my dispatch No. 15 of August 30th last, Mr. Hayashi, the Japanese Minister, some time ago intimated that it was the expectation of his Government that the foreign legations here would be withdrawn in the not distant future.

The Koreans on their part dread an extension of Japanese power and are endeavoring by every means to awaken foreign sympathy with their plight. The Emperor fears the declaration of a protectorate and clings to the fiction of his independence, regarding the privelege of direct diplomatic representation as a right, the waiving of which will portend the final absorption of his country by Japan and whose continued recognition will insure the preservation of her individuality and autonomy. To maintain his representatives abroad and the foreign ministers here is the plan which he considers best calculated to enable him, not to reform his administration, but to retain his position as an independent sovereign by resuming his former tactics of playing one dangerous neighbor against another. Intercourse with the other rulers of the world on equal terms is a privelege which not only appeals to the vanity of an eastern monarch and which the present Emperor has shown on many occasions during his reign that he prizes highly, but it is also the outward evidence of the right of this nation to shape it's own destinies as it claims to have done for three thousand years. Emperor and people are in entire accord on this point and are seeking anxiously foreign support since they are too weak to help themselves.

Because of our treaty relations with Korea and the part taken by our missionaries in her development the United States has seemed the power most likely to afford assistance in this crisis, and through certain minor officials the Emperor has not infrequently called the attention of this Legation to the second clause of Article I of the treaty of 1882, but ivariably in such a manner that I have not considered myself justified in transmitting such representations to you.

The Koreans were anxious to make political capital of the visit of Miss Roosevelt and her party. In this they were discouraged. Availing themselves, however, of the presence of members of both the Upper and Lower Houses of Congress certain high Korean officials besought their aid claiming that this country was "oppressively and unjustly" dealt with and that the United States is bound by treaty to use her "good offices to bring about an amicable arrangement". They were thereupon informed that should they desire to present a petition to the American Government they should carefully specify in their statement the abuses of which they complained and should furnish proofs that their grievances were just and authentic. They were also advised the a document of this character should be prepared by an expert and that only when Korea was ready to make a direct and dignified appeal could her plea be given serious consideration.

As for this Legation it has throughout maintained the attitude that unless otherwise instructed it has no direct concern in the relations between Japan and Korea and between their respective citizens. It has made no comment on the complaints brought by the Koreans and held out no hope of intervention of any kind. At the same time I have not felt that I should be justified in refusing to transmit to the Department an appeal presented by the recognized government here should such a one be made in proper form. With regard to the Japanese representatives at Seoul my intercourse with whom is characterized by the most cordial relations, I have confined myself to impressing upon them that where they assume authority they must also assume responsibility, and I have endeavored to keep vigilant watch in order that no missionary or other American citizen may be imposed upon or interfered with in the enjoyment of his legitimate rights.

Edwin V. Morgan

No. 29   American Legation, Seoul, Korea.
                                                          November 10, 1905.

Secretary of State

Sir:-

    I have the honor to report that Marquis Ito, Special Ambassador of the Emperor of Japan, who arrived in Seoul yesterday, was received in audience by the Emperor of Korea today.

    The visit of this distinguished Japanese statesman which will last the better part of a month though announced as one of ceremony only has undoubtedly a deeper significance, and after a portion of it has been passed in a study of the political, economic and social conditions which prevail here, it is not unlikely that terms will be formulated under which Japan will assume the protectorate of this Empire, a step which was foreshowed in the Treaty of Peace with Russia and the expanded alliance with Great Britian. The Koreans are aware of this and although they show outward signs of satisfaction that the Marquis is their guest and bestow honors upon him which they have reserved hitherto for princes of royal blood, there is an understanding on the part both of Emperor and people that the independence of their country may terminate within a few weeks, a fact which though clear to the world for some time past they could or would not comprehend before.

    Marquis Ito has visited Korea on two previous occasions. He was last here in March, 1904, a month after the Protocol of February 23rd was signed which placed the two Empires in their present political relation. His influence is considerable with His Majesty, whom he is likely to assure during the frequent conversations which he will have with him that under the new arrangements his personal safety will be guaranteed and that he will retain a portion at least of his privileges as a sovereign.

    It is not known what form the protectorate will assume and especially to what extent if any the interests of foreign residents in this country will be affected. The application to the intricate Korean problem of the experienced statesmanship of Marquis Ito should go far to solve it, but if there is not a radical change in the general attitude of Japanese toward Koreans and an indication that justice will be meted out by Japanese consuls, magistrates and police to Japanese offenders against the persons and property of Koreans, then no amount of revision of Protocols or administrative reforms will reconcile foreigners to a Japanese protectorate over this country, weak and ineffective though its present Government may be.

    I enclose the views of the Japanese press on the visit of Marquis Ito as reproduced in translation by the Japan Chronicle of Kobe, and an editorial on the same subject in the Japan Weekly Mail of Tokyo.

Edwin V. Morgan.

No. 34   American Legation, Seoul, Korea.
                                                          November 20, 1905.

Secretary of State

Sir:-

    Continuing the subject of my No. 29 of November 10th concerning the mission of Marquis Ito, I have the honor to report that on the 15th instant after several days delay caused by His Majesty's suspicion that his next conversation with the Japanese Ambassador would relate to matters of a painful nature, the Emperor of Korea received the Marquis in a strictly private audience lasting more than three hours during which the terms of a new political agreement between Korea and Japan were proposed and explained.

    Although he pressed him to accept these terms without hesitation Marquis Ito succeeded only in persuading His Majesty to refer them for discussion to his Minister for Foreign Affairs, Mr. Pak Che Soon and to Mr. Hayashi, the Japanese Minister, who conferred together at the same hour that the other members conferred with Marquis Ito. These conferences occupied the whole of the 16th and the morning of the 17th and it was not until mid-afternoon of that day that the Cabinet repaired to the Palace with the Japanese Minister to announce to His Majesty that they had accepted the terms in principle and awaited his instructions to sign the document which gave their formal sanction to the signature of the instrument of Agreement by the Minister for Foreign Affairs.

    It is impossible to acertain with exactitude the character of the arguments or the nature of the pressure brought to bear upon the Cabinet either before or after they entered the Palace. In the early evening General Hassegawa, Commander-in-chief of the Japanese forces, and Marquis Ito joined Mr. Hayashi and his staff. The building in which the negotiations were conducted and which immediately adjoins that occupied by His Majesty is not seventyfive feet from this Legation from which it is separated only by a low wall. The weather was clear and the moon high. Japanese gendarmes and police could be seen posted both on the verandah of the conference chamber and in the lane which leads to the only exit at the rear of the Palace. No one could enter or leave without passing these sentries, who though ostensibly stationed to guarantee the safety of the Japanese plenipotentiaries, served also to impress upon His Majesty the inexpediency of resisting their demands. The bodies of Japanese infantry and cavalry which had made a conspicuous display in the streets of Seoul during the two preceding days had brought the same idea home to the minds of the people, and though it appears improbable that physical force was employed the members of the Cabinet cannot be considered to have acted entirely as free agents when, with the Emperor's sanction, they authorized the Minister for Foreign Affairs in the early morning of the 18th to sign the Agreement which relegated Korean to the position of a protected state.

The Prime Minister Mr. Han Kiu Sul steadfastly refused to consent and the next day was deprived of his office and banished from the capital. It is characteristic of the insensibility of the Korean court to the significance of the night's events that Mr. Han was punished not because he refused to obey His Majesty's instructions or declined to sanction the Agreement but because he committed a breach of etiquette by entering a private room unannounced while on his way to beseach His Majesty not to yield.

During a visit paid him the next morning the Japanese Minister informed me that that instructions from his Government prevented him from communicating to myself and his other colleagues the official text of the Agreement which would be furnished Foreign Powers by the Japanese Foreign Office and not through the Foreign Legations here.

He has handed me since then, however, an English version of the text marked "Unofficial and Confidential" which I have the honor to enclose with this dispatch together with a copy, in translation, of the Letter of Credence of Marquis Ito as Special Ambassador of the Emperor of Japan and an extract, also in translation, from a native newspaper the "Hwang Sung Sin Mun", describing the events herein recorded and for the publication of which the journal was suspended by Japanese gendarmes.

Edwin V. Morgan.

No. 35   American Legation, Seoul, Korea.
                                                          November 20, 1905.

Secretary of State

Sir:-

In a series of dispatches beginning with No. 808 of October 17, 1904, my predecessor reported the foundation and leading characteristics of the IL CHIN HOI, "The Band for Mutual Progress", which was established in Seoul in the summer of that year to strengthen among the Koreans the political influence of Japan. Since his report was sent you the membership of the society in the capital alone has increased several thousand while in the provincial cities and throughout the rural districts many thousand more have been enrolled. Precise information regarding its numbers, tenets, and organization is difficult to obtain but it is safe to state that the band is encouraged if not indirectly supported by the Japanese authorities who are not unwilling to utilize its services to secure an appearance of popular support for the program which is embodied in the new agreement between the two Empires signed on the 17th instant which I have reported in my No. 34 of today's date.

Shortly before the arrival of Marquise Ito a fortnight ago to arrange with the Korean court the terms of his agreement a circular was distributed through the country by the IL CHIN HOI counselling the Koreans to accept a protectorate. In an official proclamation the Minister for the Home Department urged the people to pay no heed to this document. Japanese police and gendarmes tore down copies where-ever they were posted at the city gates or in other public places and arrested the men responsible for a similar protest issued in the name of the people of the thirteen Korean provinces and distributed both by hand and post to native and foreign residents.

Although of interest chiefly from an historical standpoint, since the Koreans are likely to accept the new political conditions without serious protest after their first discontent has passed, I have the honor to transmit for your information copies, in translation, of the documents referred to above, which comprise a circular from the IL CHIN HOI advising Korea to accept a protectorate, a proclamation by the Home

Minister denouncing those responsible therefor, a reply to the IL CHIN HOI from representatives of the thirteen Korean provinces, and a further circular from that society.

Edwin V. Morgan.

No. 36　　　　　　　　　　　　　　　　　American Legation, Seoul, Korea.
　　　　　　　　　　　　　　　　　　　　　November 22, 1905.

Secretary of State

Sir:-
　　　In the course of a private interview accorded me yesterday Marquis Ito, Special Ambassador of the Emperor of Japan to the Court of Korea, expressed certain personal opinions regarding the relation of his Government to the Korean problem which I have the honor to report to you.
　　　The conversation opened with a reference to the character of the administration which Japan would inaugurate under the terms of the Agreement recently concluded between the two Empires. The Marquis stated his belief that the new regimé would recognize, as a fundamental principle, the personal rights and liberties of the Korean people who at present were discontented on account of their inability to obtain justice in cases tried before Japanese Consular Courts, and because of the inadequate compensation received for houses and fields, covered not infrequently with growing corps, which were condemned to facilitate the construction of railways and to provide sites for military camps.
　　　The presence of a strong Japanese military force while it insured the preservation of public order had alienated the sympathies of the peasants who looked to Japan to free them from the oppression and injustice which they endured under their own officials by substituting honestly administered civil laws for the tyrannical and whimsical jurisdiction of magistrates who were obliged to regain by "squeeze" the sums originally expended in securing their positions. The appointment of a civilian and not a military official as Resident General would do much to restore the people's faith in Japan's justice which had existed before the war but which the soldier's habit of justifying his acts after and not before their commission had somewhat shaken. In more than one case relating to the condemnation of property for railway and military purposes he admitted that considerable difficulty had been experienced in securing just compensation, the military authorities being inclined to pay only for the land actually taken for cuttings, roadbed and tunnels, and not easily persuaded to reimburse the owners for the damage which they suffered through the presence of a railway line and the nuisance created by the passage of trains.
　　　His Excellency assured me that he had already called the attention both of the military and civil authorities to the harsh treatment to which Koreans were subjected by Japanese and that in accordance with his recommendation the Japanese Minister had instructed the consuls under his control to announce that since Japanese were inclined to maltreat Koreans the latter must be assured that offenders of both nationalities would be duly punished by their respective authorities without favor, and that law-abiding Japanese residents should not fail to report their own countrymen on finding them guilty of improper conduct.

Edwin V. Morgan.

No. 50　　　　　　　　　　　　　　　　　American Consulate General
　　　　　　　　　　　　　　　　　　　　　Seoul, Korea, February 26, 1906

Assistant Secretary of State

Sir:
　　　I have the honor to confirm my telegram of the 3rd instant, reading as follows: -
Secstate, Washington.
"I have received this afternoon official anouncement General Hasegawa has assumed the duty of Acting Resident General. Paddock".
　　　I sent the above telegram on receipt of a note announcing the opening of the Japanese Residency General at Seoul and Residencies at the various ports on the 1st instant. This note, a copy of which I

enclose, is addressed to me by Baron General Hasegawa, Commander in Chief of the Japanese military forces in Korea, who assumes charge as Acting Resident General pending the arrival of Marquis Hirobumi Ito, and I thought the information worthy a telegram for the reason that all of my colleagues, with the exception of the Chinese acting Consul General, had previously told me that they were in receipt of telegraphic instructions from their respective governments to communicate with the Japanese Resident General after the date of the 1st instant.

As a matter of record I will give the dates of withdrawal of the various Legations at Seoul, as follows:

The Italian Minister Resident and Consul General announced his departure from Korea on leave on October 15, 1905. The Italian Legation has since been charge of a care-taker, and Italian interests in care of the British Representative.

On December 4, 1905, the German Minister Resident and Consul General announced the transfer of diplomatic matters to the German Legation at Tokyo, the office here being left in charge of the German vice Consul.

On January 6, 1906, the Minister of France, who was also Consul General, announced that, having been permitted to return to France, he handed over charge of the service here to the French Vice Consul, who would act as Consul General.

On the 12th instant the British Chargé d' Affaires announced that he ceased to exercise the function of Chargé d'Affaires while continuing to act as Consul General.

On the 14th instant, the Chinese acting Consul General, (the Chinese Envoy Extraordinary and Minister Plenipotentiary being on leave,) announced the withdrawal of the Chinese Legation and his having taken over charge of Chinese affairs in Korea.

The Belgian Representative here has always been Consul General, so his office has continued as before.

Gordon Paddock

THE UNITED STATES IN KOREA

Horace N. Allen, U.S. Envoy Extraordinary and Minister Plenipotentiary

A. Korean-American Relations

No. 132

Department of State
Washington, January 11, 1896

John M. B. Sill

Sir:

I have received your Nos. 175 and 177, of the 2nd and 3rd ultimo, respectively, reporting on events at Seoul.

With your No. 175, you enclose a memorandum of the conversation between the King and the members of the diplomatic corps during the audience granted November 26th for the purpose of His Majesty informing them of the revocation of a former decree of October 8th, by which the Queen had been degraded, and of her restoration to her previous rank. In the memorandum you state that you expressed to the King your satisfaction with this action, and you added that you had intended to ask him whether the previous decree had been his own action, and that you wished also to say for yourself that you had never recognized the decree of the 6th October as from His Majesty.

It was quite within the line of your duty to report to the Department that, in your belief, the decree of October 8th last had been issued by the King of Korea under compulsion, but it was neither a matter for you to discuss in your intercourse with the officials of the country, nor one in regard to which this Government could have any concern or express any opinion.

The Department has to express its astonishment and thorough disapproval of your conduct in this matter. It is incomprehensible, in view of the cablegrams sent you on November 11th and 20th (the receipt of which you duly acknowledged) by which you were instructed to confine yourself exclusively to such questions as involved the direct interests of American citizens, and to refrain from mixing yourself in any way with the internal affairs of Korea, that you should, as late as November 26th and 28th, without directions from the Department, have acted and spoken as the despatches under acknowledgement state you did. In view of these actions and utterances I sent you, under yesterday's date, the following cablegram instruction:

"Your despatches No. 175 and 176 [177] received. Your course in continued intermeddling with Korean political affairs in violation of repeated instructions noted with astonishment and emphatic disapproval. Cable briefly any explanation you have to make - also answer whether you intend to comply with instructions given."

In your No. 177 you state that the Americans now resident in Seoul are exposed to much danger, apparently by reason of the anti-Japanese opinions to which they have openly given voice and their indiscreet expressions of sympathy for the party opposed to Japanese influence. You should, on receipt of the present instructions, inform all Americans resident in Korea that they shoud strictly refrain from any expression of opinion or from giving advice concerning the internal management of the country, or in any intermeddling in political questions; that if they do so, it is at their own risk and peril; that neither you nor the government of the United States can approve of such action on their part or perhaps be able to adequately protect them should they disregard this advice. They should strictly confine themselves to the missionary work, whether it be teaching in schools, preaching the gospel, or attending to the sick, for which they went to the country. Use such other arguments as you properly can to discourage and stop, if possible, the habit which has steadily increased since the arrival of American citizens in Korea, of irresponsible persons advising and attempting to control, through irregular channels, the Government of the country.

Richard Olney

No. 238   Legation of the United States
                                                     Seoul Korea Oct. 13. 1896

Secretary of State:

Sir:-

I have the honor to hand you under separate cover a book in Chinese. called "The Warp and Woof of Confucian Scholarship," edited by Mr Sin Key Sun, at the time Korean Minister of Education. and published at the press of the Department of Education for use in the Korean Schools.

This work comments most ungraciously upon foreigners; their religion and customs. I hand you translations of two passages in the book.

It was thought that the use of this work in the schools of Korea might cause trouble in time. while the comments upon Westerners were not such as the Representatives of these powers could allow to pass unnoticed. The Representatives of Western Powers at this Court, therefore decided to hand the Minister of Foreign Affairs identical notes protesting against the publication and circulation of this work. I hand you a copy of my letter to the Foreign Minister as well as a copy of his answer to my letter.

While it is stated in the letter from the Foreign Minister, that this book was not published at the expense of the Government. we know that the Department of Education furnished the paper, press and labor.

This Minister has been one of the most objectionable of the ultra conservatives. He has opposed the teaching of Western languages and science in the schools and has done all he could to force the schools back into the exclusive study of Chinese and the Confucian Classics. The publication of this book, since it has forced his resignation has therefore been a good thing for progress in Korea.

H. N. Allen

1/

North America is situated on the West and South of Europe and North of Equator. It is in the opposite direction from Asia and its area is the same as Africa but less than Asia.

The Northern parts are controlled by England.

The East and South of North America was inhabited by barbarians in former times - these barbarians differ from the barbarians of Europe - . Later the English conquered these barbarians. More than one hundred years ago a man named Washington threw off the English rule and founded an Independence and united 30 or more nations into one country which is called the United States. This Washington was the same spawn as the English. A head man is selected every four years by the people.

The Machinery, Education and business are about the same as those of Europe but the Agriculture and other resources are better. Russia is said to be the largest, England the strongest and America the richest of these Countries. The area and climate are about the same as of China.

2/

According to the views of recent generations what westerners call the Christian religion is vulgar, shallow and erroneous, and is an instance of the vileness of barbarian customs. which is not worthy of serious consideration.

The terms used by Christians in speaking of Heaven, Happiness and Misery are similar to those employed by the Buddhists.

They worship the heavenly spirits but do not sacrifice to parents, insult heaven in every way, and overturn the social relations.

This is truly a type of barbarian vileness and is not worthy of treatment in our review of foreign customs, especially as at the present time the religion is somewhat on the wane.

Europeans have planted their spawn in every country of the globe with the exception of China. All of them honor this religion but we are surprised to find that the Chinese scholars and people have not escaped contamination.

No. 244   Legation of the United States
                                               Seoul Korea Nov. 4. 1896

Secretary of State

Sir:-
     I have the honor to inform you that arrangements have been made for the sending of the Second
Prince - Son of His Majesty the King of Korea - to America for his education.
     It is likely that this bright young man, now about 20 years of age, may succeed to the throne of
Korea, as his brother - the Crown Prince - is in a feeble condition.
     This Prince - Wui Wha, has been at school in Japan for some months. but he has long been
desirous of going to America. Rev Henry Loomis. of the American Bible Society at Yokahama, became
interested in the case and came to Seoul, where he obtained written permission. by order of the King. to
send Prince Wui Wha to the United States. in care of Rev S. A. Moffett. a returning American missionary
who has lived several years in Korea. Mr Moffett in conjunction with the Presbyterian Board of Foreign
Missions - his employers - will place the young Prince in a good school. and the Finance Department of
this Government will remit. through this Board of Foreign Missions. $100. gold per month to defray the
expenses of the Prince.
     This Legation has not been instrumental in bringing about this arrangement. Rev. Mr. Loomis
was able to attend to the matter through Mr. Brown; the English Commissioner of Customs and actual
controller of the Korean Financial Department. The matter met with the approval and support of the
Russian Minister, and gives satisfaction to this Legation and the American residents in Korea.

                                               H. N. Allen.

No. 3   Legation of the United States
                                               Seoul Korea, September 17, 1897.

Secretary of State

Sir;-
     In conformity with the spirit of my instructions I have the honor to wait upon you with a short
account of affairs as I find them upon taking charge of American interests in Korea.
     We have 140 Americans-men, women and children, residing in Korea, which is a much larger
number (not counting soldiers) than those of any other western country.
     Most of our citizens are connected with one or other of the Missionary Society's, and they have the
reputation of being an unusually select and high class of missionaries. Owing to certain indiscretions of
one or two in the recent past, some considerable unfavorable comment was made in the Asiatic press in
regard to American missionaries in Korea, but I do not think there will be cause for complaint in the future,
and I doubt if the charges made against them were warranted by the facts.
     We have two American publications here; a monthy magazine, and a tri-weekly news-paper,
besides three papers published in Korean. A news-paper may always be expected to give offence to some
one, and these publications constitute an element of future contention, though the editors seem desirous of
giving no offence.
     The chief financial undertakings now on foot in Korea are the result of American enterprise. I refer
chiefly to the Gold Mines and the Seoul-Chemulpo Railway, the concessions for which I was able to obtain
for America while Secretary of Legation, as the result of years of consistent effort, and against much
opposition from the Representatives of some other Powers. It is a source of gratification to me to be able
to state that the Railway, which bids fair to be a profitable enterprise, is being rapidly built with American
capital in a satisfactory manner. The Mining Company is investing a great deal of money in its work, but
as yet the mines have not been sufficiently exploited to determine just what may be expected, though the
prospects are reported as being very favorable.
     We have here one merchant firm of importance doing an extensive commission business and
conducting a large and profitable rice mill enterprise. They are agents also for the Standard Oil Company,
which supplies Korea almost all its kerosene.
     We have several Americans holding offices of trust and importance in the Korean Government, and
a few individuals engaged in private enterprises.

It is always commented upon favorably by American travellers, that in this country they find the only Asiatic community of foreigners, where American influence predominates, and an American press helps to mould public sentiment.

Japanese subjects constitute the largest number of foreigners in Korea. They are largely merchants and artisans; no Japanese being now employed by the Government. The travelling Japanese merchants are to be found all through Korea, and many have settled down in various parts of the interior in spite of the absence of treaty provision for such residence. They afford a ready means for the distribution of foreign goods throughout the country, but being exempt from Korean laws and taxes, they are not well liked by the natives who suffer from this protected competition.

Japanese influence has been on the wane for some time and has now largely given place to the overpowering influence of Russia.

There is much friction between these two powers over Korea and this is bound to increase.

Russian interference in Korea now extends to the most intimate matters connected with military and political affairs. Owing largely to Japanese objection and the unlooked for firmness of then Korean Minister for Foreign Affairs, the Russian Legation failed to put through an arrangement, last spring, for the employment of 160 Russian officers to drill and officer the Korean troops. 21 of this number were brought out however, to reinforce the 15 now employed, but as yet the contracts for the employment of this new contingent have not been made, though in attempting to obtain these contracts, the Russian Legation is credited with the dismissal of one Minister for Foreign Affairs; one Minister of War, and the Acting Minister of War has presented his resignation rather then sign the contracts.

I am privately informed from the Palace, that Mr. de Speyer, the new Russian Chargé d'Affaires, has informed the King very plainly and forcibly, that he must take Russian advice upon all matters and advise only with Russia: that Russia will see that he is not troubled, and that he will have ample funds for his enjoyment.

This greatly alarms the King as he takes it to mean that he is desired to act as a mere figure head while allowing the control of the country to pass to Russia, - a thing that he would not for one moment consent to.

It has been quite evident for some time that this was Russia's desire. The retiring Russian Representative, would never admit a fault on the part of the King, who was his guest for over a year, and he allowed many grave abuses to pass rather than speak a word of rebuke to His Majesty, when it seemed to be his duty to do so. For a time it seemed that he might wish matters to come to such a pass that Russia might have excuse for intervening to save the country, it seems now that it is Russia's intention to make much of the King and through him find an easy means of controlling the country without prejudicing its independence or being compelled to absorb it.

Korea independent with Russian influence paramount is vastly more valuable to the latter than it would be as an out and out dependency of the Czar, with its tremendous coast line contiguous to Japan. In view of this, it is not likely that Russia will be seriously inclined to interfere with American interests in Korea, or do anything to openly act against Korean independence.

The French are chiefly interested in Korea through their Missions. They have about 30 priests here, with a Bishop and a Cathedral. They have a very extensive following; own fast tracts of land in the interior, upon which they have christian colonies, and they exert a very great influence in Korea. They always have the firm and prompt support of their Representative.

The French have a concession for a Railway from Seoul to Weiju, on the northern border - a road that could not possible pay unless it were to connect with lines in Manchuria. Mr. de Speyer informed me recently that the Manchurian lines would be built, and gave me to understand that this Korean road would also be built to connect with them and that Russia would be interested in, if not the actual builder of it.

German interests in Korea are chiefly commercial.

China now has no treaty relations with Korea, but a Commercial Treaty is being talked of. There are hundreds of Chinese residing in Korea, mostly employed as merchants and laborers.

England seems to take a keen interest in Korea, more so since Russia has taken such an active part in Korean politics. The finances of Korea are at present controlled by the British Commissioner of Korean Customs, - J. Mc'Leavy Brown, who has done a most remarkable work in so conserving revenues as to enable Korea to pay off one third of its indebtedness of three million to Japan within a year from the date of his taking charge, while the balance is now on hand for payment and over a million dollars will be left in the treasury. He has done all this while the most unprecedented expenditure for the building of palaces, temples, cemeteries and roads has been going on. He has shown Korea to possess ample revenues if controlled with even approximate honesty, for he has been consistently hampered by more or less successful efforts to divert the revenues into other channels before they could reach him. His integrity has made him obnoxious to the majority of the officials and it is supposed that Russia does not want him retained, as a man of financial training is about to arrive from Russia to act as an adviser to the Korean Government, and the Koreans report that he is to have the place of this Mr. Brown.

The condition of the native people is very distressing. The system of "squeezes" is again in vogue and so many new methods are devised for extorting money, that the people may be led to rebel again; threats of this have already been made.

The Government is controlled almost entirely by the Household Department, - or in fact the King. The council of State that superseded the Cabinet, has practically nothing to do with controlling affairs.

His Majesty is listening to the advice of courtiers who to gain favor, are continually urging him to assume the title of Emperor. The funeral of the late Queen has been postponed form time to time in order, it is said, that His Majesty may be an Emperor and the Queen an Empress at the time of the funeral and have their titles as such inscribed upon the funeral tablets.

Wise officials advise against this from time to time, but it is feared that the advice of the ignorant and selfish ones may prevail.

Two extensive cemeteries have been prepared for the Queen's remains at a cost of $100.000 each, and if she is given the post-humous title of Empress, a new and still greater one must be prepared. This involves, in each case, the use of about 1000 acres of land, which the farmers near Seoul can ill afford to spare.

Even those Representatives of Western Powers, who do not favor Russian Supremacy in Korea, yet confess that if Russia will use her influence firmly here, it cannot but result in good for the people of Korea.

The situation may be summed up as follows: Korean politics have not been in a worse condition for many years; Russian influence is paramount, and upon Russia devolves the duty of bringing order out of this chaos. Japan had the opportunity of doing this, and had the good wishes of a number of Western Powers, but she failed and is now watching and endeavoring to check Russian progress, but her influence now is small. England is on the alert in regard to Russian designs upon Korea, and she may be driven to act with Japan, though I am informed that no such formal agreement is known to exist at the British Consulate General here.

Both Japan and Russia maintain considerable bodies of troops in Korea, ostensibly for the protection of their Legations and Consulates. England has a small Legation guard stationed at Seoul, with a sargeant engaged in drilling the students of the "Royal English School", - a school taught by two Englishmen.

American influence is as great as it could be, unbacked by any show of force. It is probably as great as we have any desire it should be, and aside from the protection of our new considerable interests, it tends only to the furtherance of friendly relations and the encouragement of educational and similar work.

From the very disinterestedness of our position, America is often turned to for advice.

Horace N. Allen.

No. 14

Legation of the United States
Seoul Korea, October 5, 1897.

Secretary of State

Sir:-

Referring to my No. 3, Sept. 17, Page 6, in which I mentioned the agitation of the subject of conferring the title of Emperor upon the King of Korea, I now have the honor to inform you that this has gone on until, as announced formally in the Official Gazette of today, the King decided to take this new title and named the 12'th day of October as the the day for the ceremony connected therewith.

Formerly the Japanese advocated this step, but I believe they have opposed it of late. The Russians were formerly opposed to it, but they must have removed their objections. The German and English Representatives do not like it.

The foremost official in proposing this course has been Mr. Chyo Pyung Sik, the new Minister of Justice (of whom I wrote you in my No. 10, Oct, 2. and who, I neglected to inform you, is more fully and graphically described in Mr. Sill's No. 264 March 22.)

Horace N Allen

No. 24   Legation of the United States
                                          Seoul Korea, October 20, 1897.

Secretary of State

Sir:-
        I have the honor to hand you enclosed a copy, with translation, of a letter sent me from the
Foreign Office while I was absent in Chemulpo on Consular business, informing me that the name of this
country had been changed from "Chosen" to "Tai Han", as well as an extract from the Seoul "Independent"
containing a translation of the edict ordering this change of name, and giving the reasons for the change.
        I also send a copy of the Ministers personal note to me, asking me to change my title in
conformity with this change of names.
        I informed the Minister that I would communicate the intelligence of this change to you, but that I
could not change my title until I heard from you.
        I told him personally that I would continue to write Korea as heretofore, but that in the Chinese
translations of our despatches, the interpreters might write "Tai Han" instead of "Chosen," just as they have
always translated "Korea" as "Chosen".

                                          Horace N. Allen

No. 23   Confidential   Department of State
                                          Washington, November 19, 1897

Horace N. Allen

Sir:
        I have to acknowledge the receipt of several despatches from you bearing in different ways upon the
course of the Russian representative at Seoul, the policy of the Russian Government with respect to Korean
matters, the course of Russia in obtaining a part of the reservation at Foosan for use as a coaling station,
notwithstanding that the land in question had been reserved for the general foreign settlement of Foosan
under the stipulations of treaties and surveys heretofore made.
        This latter question is presented in your No. 8 of the Diplomatic Series dated October 1st. Your
representations to the Minister for Foreign Affairs on September 14th as therein recited by you, would seem
to have been discreet and proper, and your independent action appears to have been followed by the
coincident action of the British Japanese and German representatives in the same sense. The assurance,
however, which you then reported; that nothing would be done in the matter without first consulting the
foreign representatives, does not appear to have ended the question, as your No. 16, of October 8
communicates the apparently oral statement of Mr de Speyer to the German Consul that the matter of the
coaling station had been settled by purchase of the land from the owners, he claiming that, even if the treaty
site had been duly selected, his Government could buy land therein just as any individual could buy it.
        It may not be necessary to my present purpose to consider in detail your other despatches, Nos. 9,
12 and 17 of October 1 - 5 and 9. The Department would be glad to believe that you have been
scrupulously careful not to give to your intervention in the matter of the Foosan coaling station, or to any
other matter in which Russian policy or conduct may be involved any appearance of a desire merely to
thwart the purposes of Russia. It is incompatible with your representative mission to appear in opposition
to any course of action on the part of a foreign power, unless some vested rights of citizens of the United
States should be concerned, and then even only in the most cautious manner, and if possible after full
representaion to the Department, and instruction in the premises. You have been appointed to this
interesting mission at a time when there is reason to believe that rival purposes and interests in the east
may find in Korea a convenient ground of contention, and it behooves the United States and their
representatives, as absolutely neutral parties, to say, or do nothing that can in any way be construed as
taking sides with or against any of the interested powers. Any such partiality would not only be in itself
improper, but might have the undesirable and unfortunate effect of leading the Koreans themselves to regard
the United States as their natural and only ally for any and all such purposes of domestic policy as Korea's
rulers may adopt. This government is in no sense the counsellor of Korea as to its internal destinies,
neither is it bound to Korea by any protective alliance. The only contingency in which the amicable
mediation of the United States in any matter between Korea and other powers may be extended is defined in

Article 1 of the treaty of 1882 and is reciprocally limited, in the case of unjust or oppressive dealings of other powers with either the United States or Korea, to the exercise of the good offices of the other to bring about an amicable arrangement. It is hardly necessary to observe that good offices in the proper sense of the term can only be used with the assent of both the parties with whom the offering government seeks to mediate.

I mark this despatch confidential in view of the frankness with which it deals with the question, and the earnestness with which it expresses the hope of this Department, that you will not only hold the influences of the Legation strictly aloof from any question whatsoever concerning the internal government of Korea, or the relations of Korea to other powers, but that you will exert all possible control upon American citizens residing in Korea to constrain them to observe alike conduct of absolute neutrality.

John Sherman

No. 25

Department of State
Washington, November 30, 1897

Horace N. Allen

Sir:

I have to acknowledge the receipt of your No. 18, Diplomatic Series, of the 14th ultimo, in relation to the ceremony attending the assumption by the King of Korea of the title of Emperor.

The Department commends your prudence in dealing with His Majesty's assumption of the Imperial title and understands, as you do, that is not a change of Government, but merely a change of style on the part of "The Chief Ruler of the Country", and as such needs no formal entrance upon new relations, as in the case of a revolutionary Government assuming power, or a dynastic or constitutional change in the organization and function of a state.

Should any other Governments take official cognizance of the change in His Majesty's title, and re-accredit their envoys accordingly, you will at once report the fact to the Department and await further instructions.

John Sherman

No. 52

Legation of the United States
Seoul Korea, December 30, 1897.

Secretary of State

Sir:-

I have the honor to acknowledge the receipt on yesterday, of your despatches, No. 20, Nov. 17: No's. 21, 22, and 23, of Nov. 19.

I have carefully read despatches 22 & 23, and am very glad to be able to inform you that the instructions therein contained are exactly in line with the course I have been pursuing. Having been especially careful to avoid even the appearance of interference in questions here, the Department cannot but approve of my conduct.

After reading over my despatches to the Department, it has occured to me that I may have given too much prominence to the fact that I receive early advice of a private character from the Palace. I therefore wish to say that while the Koreans are particularly fond of these confidential communications, I have discouraged them and have not shown undue anxiety to keep posted on the doings at the Palace. I do not claim to be especially favored over others in this matter of information, though long years of friendly acquaintance with His Majesty gives me opportunities which others might wish to enjoy.

I have from time to time, given what I deemed to be necessary advice to our own people as to caution, and this advice was in every case taken in good spirit. Our missionaries are conducting themselves so discreetly that no complaint has been heard regarding them of late.

It seems to be my duty to send promt advice to the Department of any occurrence of importance here, but I trust you will be assured that in obtaining such information I do not adopt any course that could meet with your disapproval.

I shall not give advice however much it may be asked, and any opinions it may seem incumbent upon me to express, I will express to the Department.

In regard to the Fusan Coaling Station, asked for by Russia: Nothing that I did in this connection was ever objected to by any one here, and had I let the matter pass without comment, it would have seemed so strange as to excite remark, whereas some remonstrance seemed naturally to be expected, to the giving up of what may well be called, American rights.

By reference to my No. 27, Oct. 25, Page 3, and my No. 48, Dec. 20, you will see that the matter of this Coaling Station has been settled, and that I refrained from further action when I saw that such action might cause me to appear to be working with another power.

I am very glad to have these clear and concise instructions. I will do my very best to carry them out in a satisfactory manner.

Horace N. Allen.

No. 60.   Legation of the United States
                                                                     Seoul Korea, January 10, 1898.

Secretary of State,

Sir:-

I have the honor to append confirmation of my telegram of last evening informing you of the death of the mother of His Majesty, and suggesting the advisability of sending a telegram of condolence in reply to one which I understand His Majesty sent to The President upon the death of the latter's mother.

I did not send this telegram until after due deliberation. My reasons for sending it were, that I am, owing to the war excitement, constantly being asked for advice and assistance by these people, all of which requests I decline to accede to; His Majesty seems to *feel* hurt at my persistent refusal to offer him assylum at this Legation, to which he wishes to come in case of trouble between the Japanese and Russians, as it is the only strictly neutral place in Seoul. He knows now that this is impossible, and regrets it, so that the opportunity to show him a little kind personal attention, such as would be the sending of a telegram of condolence, seems to be very timely. We now have very considerable commercial interests to protect here, and I need the good will of His Majesty. I hope the telegram will be sent.

I may add that the deceased, being the wife of the Tai Won Kuhn, the Kings father and worst enemy, the son has not seen his mother much of late, but that does not prevent the display of due fillial piety in mourning.

Horace N Allen

Tlegram to the Secretary of State, from Mr. Allen,
        U.S. Legation, Seoul Korea, January 9, 1898.

"His Majesty's mother died last night. Understanding His Majesty telegraphed condolence on the death of the President's mother, it is very advisable to reply".

No. 75   Legation of the United States
                                                                     Seoul, Korea, February 24, 1898.

Secretary of State

Sir:

I have the honor to confim my telegram of yesterday as follows: "Emperor's father died today."

The deceased, who has been very frequently mentioned in this series since the opening of this Legation, under his title of Tai Won Khun, was one of the most remarkable characters in modern Korean History. He secured the crown for his infant son, and acted as Regent till the son became of age. He quarreled with the Queen and her family, the Mins, many of whom, with thousands of others, he killed. Though he was cruel and uncompromising, he was inclined to mete out justice and was always true to his country. Until his union with the Japanese in killing the Queen, he was greatly beloved by the people, the majority of whom would have welcomed him back to power.

The recent death of his consort hastend his own end, it is supposed.

The flag of this, and the other Legations, is at half mast for three days in honour of the deceased, and I promply made a call of condolence at the Foreign Office.

Horace N. Allen.

No. 82   Legation of the United States
Seoul Korea, March 8, 1898.

Secretary of State

Sir,

I have the honour to hand you enclosed an extract from the Seoul "Independent" of today, being an interview with myself in regard to a telegram from Seoul dated January 26, to the New York "Herald", to the effect that His Majesty had asked me for protection and that Captain Wildes of the U.S.S. "Boston", had refused to furnish the necessary guard.

I see this telegram obtained some credence in Washington and is being copied by the news-papers of the Far East.

It is very annoying to be dragged thus into unpleasant prominence in connection with these Seoul intrigues, when this Legation is known here to be entirely free from such connection.

About the date of the above-cited telegram, some one, not His Majesty, did start a rumour that His Majesty was about to take refuge at this Legation, but as I had made it perfectly plain to him, - see my No. 51, Dec. 27, - that I could not allow such a course, I paid little attention to it.

The last time I was asked for a guard was in connection with the funeral of the Empress, - see my No. 39, Nov. 27, - I declined at once, and have never asked our Naval people for a guard.

I do not approve of Legation guards.

As a possible explanation of the above-cited rumor and telegram, I may state that since the attempt upon the life of the Interpreter of the Russian Legation - see my No. 76, Febr. 24, - I have been several times informed that Mr. de Speyer is strongly urging His Majesty to return to the Russian Legation, urging as a pretext that the British Representative is preparing to take him to his place, which adjoins the palace. Mr. Kato, the Japanese Minister, informed me that Mr. de Speyer had made this statement to him personally. Mr. Jordan, British Consul-General, was highly incensed at this report, and called to inform me of it, and to say that it had not the least foundation; that he could not even contemplate such a course, and should His Majesty come to his place, he would have to send him away at once.

This reply is substantially the same as I made, as cited in my No. 51, Dec. 27.

I trust that the Department will feel assured that I do not intend to convert this Legation into an asylum for Korean refugees.

Horace N. Allen.

No. 69   Department of State
Washington, April 19, 1898

Horace N. Allen

Sir:

I have to acknowledge the recept of your despatch No. 82, of the 8th ultimo, in relation to the rumor, that the Emperor of Korea is to take refuge at your Legation, and expressing your annoyance thereat.

In reply, I have to inform you, that this Department commends the prudence shown by you in this delicate matter.

John Sherman

No. 168   Legation of the United States
                                                Seoul Korea, Dec. 23, 1898.

Secretary of State

Sir:-

I have the honor to acknowledge the receipt, day before yesterday, of your despatch No. 108 of Nov. 14, replying to my No. 150 of Oct. 7, relating to my action in protesting against the reintroduction of torture in Korean prisons.

I note with care your unfavorable comment upon my use of the word protest and shall be careful in this regard hereafter. I had not properly appreciated the full sense in which this term is held in diplomatic usage.

My notes to the Korean Government have to be translated into Chinese and I endeavor to make the English as plain as possible, so that it may at times seem a little bald.

As a matter of fact, the term used in the Chinese translation of my note in question means literally "regret very much". "Protest" has a stronger expression. I send you a copy of the Chinese translation of my despatch with the characters used designated by pencil mark, while the proper characters for protest are given on the margin. I will see that my English is more guarded hereafter.

I thought that a remonstrance against the reintroduction of torture was allowable and proper in the interests of humanity, and am glad to see that I was not mistaken in that regard. I was particularly careful not to join with my colleagues in asking for the dismissal of the Minister of Justice, as being an interference in Korean matters, and the note I did send was distinctly an independent one and inteded to be so regarded.

In my No. 161, nov. 14, I explained wherein I again had occasion to protest, or more properly object, verbally, to bloodshed in dispersing the peoples meeting. This action seemed to me to be necessary in the interest of American lives and property. I trust I may not meet with the Departments disapproval in this regard.

It would be a matter of great regret to me if the Department should get the idea that I am inclined to interfere in Korean matters where American interests are not directly involved. I have constantly in mind former admonitions to my predecessors and myself in this regard as well as in the matter of joint action with the representatives of other powers.

I have the reputation of being particularly well posted as to Korean customs and politics, and my advice is often sought. It would be a most easy thing for me to take a prominent part in Korea affairs. I carefully abstain from any such interference or from giving advice. No Foreign Representative in Seoul is more free from any implication of such interference in Korean matters than myself. Yet the condition of affairs is so corrupt, and the country is in such a state of misrule or disrule, that it seems necessary at times for me to speak of practices which will, if unchecked, become beyond control to the severe detriment of interests purely American, which must be my excuse for the action I took as reported in my above cited No. 161.

                                                Horace N. Allen.

No. 184   Legation of the United States
                                                Seoul, Korea, March 22, 1899.

Secretary of State

Sir,

In connection with the discussion of the question of the residence of foreigners in Seoul, which occupied a prominent place in the correspondence I have recently held with the Korean Foreign Minister, regarding the opening of new ports. (See Enclosure in my No. 112, June 3, 1898,) I now have the honour to hand you enclosed a copy of a letter I recently addressed to the Foreign Office regarding the subject of title deeds for property in Seoul. In this letter I explain the unsatisfactory condition of real estate records in Seoul, and allude to certain difficulties that have already arisen in consequence.

In complete disregard of treaty provisions, the Korean Government has firmly refused to issue deeds to foreigners for ground in Seoul upon which there is no house. Personally, I have avoided difficulty by having our people see that any such purchase is provided with some hut or other and have therefore been able to secure a deed in every case where I have applied, while others of my colleagues have been unsuccessful in this regard for over a year past.

The real cause of this refusal to issue dees is the fact the thousands of Japanese and Chinese in Seoul, are, by foreclosing mortgages, obtaining possession of much of the property of the Korean residents in Seoul.

I was assured that the subject of my letter and of similar letters sent to the Foreign Office at the same time by the other Foreign Representatives at Seoul, has been favorably considered, but the dismissal of the Cabinet mentioned in my No. 182 of today's date will probably cause this matter to be indefinitely postponed, and I send you a copy of my letter on this subject now as I am leaving for my vacation and visit to the United States in a few days.

Horace N Allen

No. 185   Legation of the United States
                                                   Seoul, Korea, March 23, 1899.

Secretary of State

Sir,
        I have the honour to hand you enclosed copies of a correspondence between myself and the Korean Foreign Office which has resulted in settling a vexed question by the announcement of a date for the formal opening of the new ports declared open by Imperial Decree in May last, See my No. 112, Dipl., June 3, 1898, and my No. 13, Cons., of the same date.

Probably one of the most successful mission stations in Asia is that of the American Presbyterian Church at Peng Yang, Korea. Our missionaries have been living there for eight or nine years on passports, occupying houses owned by Koreans, and conforming with the treaty regulations. During the past few years their success has been so great as to cause comment by writers of books on Korea. This success has made necessary the erection of suitable buildings for the reception of the increased staff of workers, and when the city of Peng Yang was announced as one of the new ports to be opened, it seems that our people openly acquired certain building sites, - without mentioning the fact to this Legation, however - seeming to consider themselves well within their rights. They were probably warrented in this belief by the fact that many Japanese merchants had acquired property at Peng-Yang and were openly engaged in trade there.

Being in urgent need of roofing tiles for repairing the old houses they were then occupying, as well as for covering the new ones they proposed to build, and being unable to purchase them because of the monopoly of the tile manufacture by one of the vexatious guilds that are such a curse to this country, they appealed to me and I forwarded a request for permission for an American to make the tiles necessary for their personal use, so that the local regulations should not be infringed.

In reply, I received permission for such manufacture at the port of Chenampo, a day's journey down the Ta Tong river from Peng Yang, and was informed that Americans were not allowed to build houses at Peng Yang.

To this letter I replied as per Enclosure 1, taking the ground that the status of Peng Yang and the other ports declared open by the above decree, was the same as that of Seoul, Fusan, and Gensan, - declared open in 1883, but never regularly furnished with settlement limits and regulations. Incidentally, a timely discussion of the question of residence in Seoul took place. The Koreans are trying to forbid the further purchase of land by foreigners in Seoul, and every Foreign Representative here has had more or less trouble with the question of title deeds, which may have to be referred to the various Treaty Powers.

To the last named despatch the Foreign Minister replied as per Enclosure 2, taking a very advanced position in claiming that these new ports are "interior places", and not yet open, and asking me to instruct our people that they must not buy land at these ports, under pain of punishment for so doing.

At Kunsan, another of the new ports in question, Japanese merchants do a regular shipping business, it being a port of call for Japanese and Korean ships. There are Americans residing there also.

Fortunately, the Foreign Minister forwarded a despatch of similar tenor to each of my colleagues, and when I explained, at our weekly meeting, the cause of the correspondence, they each decided to ask for an early announcement of the date for the formal taking effect of the Settlement Regulations, at the new ports.

I replied to this last despatch with care, See Enclosure 3, endeavoring to cover the whole case, and going into the question of residence in Seoul, as fully as the circumstances seemed to warrent. The result was that the day after its receipt the Foreign Minister gave instructions to the Commissioner of Customs to send officers at once to lay settlement limits at these ports. The men were sent the next day for this purpose, and I was promptly informed, verbally, by the Foreign Minister, that while April 1 was too soon for the accomplishment of the necessary preparations attending the laying out of the settlement limits, that they will be ready by May 1, and on that day the new settlements will be formally opened, under the same set of regulations now in use at Chenampo and Mokpo. See Consular Reports, Vol. LVI, page 228.

I have since received an official despatch to the same effect (Enclosure 4,) - to which I have replied, reverting to my original request for permission for the Americans to make tiles, which small request will doubtless now be granted since it has served to clear away the objections to residence of Americans at Peng Yang.

I may add that the real reason for the declaration of these places as open ports, a year ago was the alarming alienation of Chinese territory and the fear that this movement might extend to Korea. The Koreans were, supposedly, the chief beneficiaries by the action.

Horace N. Allen.

No. 213   Legation of the United States
                                                       Seoul Korea, Nov. 17, 1899.

Secretary of State

Sir:-

Referring to Mr. Adee's despatch No. 136, Sept. 12, relative to the opening of the port of Peng Yang to foreign trade, I have the honor to inform you that the Korean Government has failed to carry out its written agreement to fulfil that undertaking, and, having exhausted all reasonable measures in attempting to bring this matter to a satisfactory conclusion, the Foreign Representatives, at a recent meeting, decided to wait upon the Foreign Minister in a body and once more attempt to come to some amicable and satisfactory agreement, failing in which we were to declare our intention of regarding the whole city of Peng Yang as open to foreign trade and residence, and to inform His Excellency that we would protect our people in their right to enjoy these privileges in pursuance of the Imperial Decree opening the place to trade.

We waited upon the Foreign Minister on the 4'th. instant, but got absolutely no satisfaction whatever, even upon our announcement of the alternative to which we would be driven.

We therefore each addressed a note to the Foreign Minister in the same sense, citing the whole circumstances of the case, and announcing our intention, in the absence of any suitable provision for a Foreign Settlement, of regarding the city of Peng Yang in the position as is Seoul, and of protecting our people in their right to reside and carry on trade at that place.

I have the honor to hand you enclosed, a copy of my note of the 16'th. instant, to that effect.

Horace N. Allen.

No. 229   Legation of the United States
                                                       Seoul Korea, February 16, 1900.

Secretary of State

Sir:-

In my No. 214, Nov. 18, I had the honor to inform you of the corrupt condition of this Government at present; of the fact that public interests are almost entirely in the hands of a few of the most unprincipled of the Korean officials, and that an anonymous memorial had been presented accusing some 33 of the better class of officials of conspiring with me to overturn this Government and establish a republic instead.

I paid no attention to this annonymous slander at the time but I was most credibly informed that the report had again been sent in to His Majesty on the night of Jan. 18, by Kim Yung Chun, Commissioner of Police and Acting Minister of War, and that he was pressing the matter in such a manner as to do great injury to the friendly Korean officials through whom I must work in gurading the now considerable American interests in Korea.

This man Kim is most repulsive, and cruel beyond description. During the past winter he has caused the death of several supposedly innocent Koreans of wealth whom he had imprisoned and tortured on a trumped up charge for the purpose of extortion. He has made himself very rich of late and has at the same time brought very large revenues to the Imperial Privy Purse. He is violently hated by the people but has been so surrounded by police and soldiers as to be safe from assault.

Feeling that the matter had gone as far as I dared allow it to go and that further silence would be injurious to the good standing of Americans here as well as harmful to our Korean friends, and knowing that with this man in power no Korean would dare testify against him, I decided to take the matter direct to His Majesty, to whom the charge was made, and either get from him a denial that he had received the report, thus insuring its suppression, or have the man punished and so prevent a repetition of the offense.

I therefore wrote a note to the Household Department, - enclosure 1, suggesting that if the report had been made I be received in audience.

The audience was granted but the night before it came off, His Majesty sent me word that he would dismiss Kim if I would withdraw my complaint. This message came too late for me to act upon it, but it was evidence of the fact that the report had been received.

At the audience I confined myself to reading my carefully prepared remarks, see enclosure 2, His Majesty was very evasive in his replies and had evidently been persuaded by Kim and his friends that he would "lose face" if he did not support Kim. He sent the Acting Minister for Foreign Affairs, - a friend of Kim, who had been appointed in order that he might attend to this matter, - we had several interviews at my house in which it was claimed that the report had not been made and that I had been deceived, which was a clever ruse to get my friends into trouble. I maintained that the fact of the report's having been made was admitted by the act of granting me an audience upon the conditions I named, and as the matter had been made public it was too late for me to withdraw. Also I had frequent messages from the Palace to the effect that the Emperor was inclined to support me but the Japanese Minister kept urging him not to drop Kim, who has sustained more or less intimate relations with that Legation.

I finally received a written statement from the Foreign Office that the Council of State had found that the report I complained of had never been made. As Kim was one of that Council I could not accept its verdict and replied in the same sense as my verbal replies. Enclosure 4. *I sent one other letter. Enclosure 4A/* *

After three weeks discussion in which the city and much of the whole country took the deepest interest, the man was compelled to resign all his offices in the Government after several days refusal to do so.

I was duly notified of this fact and asked to accept it. Enclosure 5. I did accept. Enclosure 6.

Nothing has been done here for a long time that has so added to American influence. Kim will doubtless be reappointed again as he is of great pecuniary value to the throne, but such men will have learned that it is not polite or politic to frivolously attack a foreign representative. This man was the most powerful and cruel man Korea has had in office for many years.

I enclose copy of another letter 7. that I had to send to the Foreign Office regarding a man who made pretenses that he could settle this matter with me if appointed to office. He was also dismissed. I also send enclosure 8. from a local newspaper showing that this man received similar treatment from my British Colleague, with whom I had had no communication.

Horace N. Allen.

No. 313   <u>Confidential.</u>   Legation of the United States
Seoul, Korea, January 24, 1901.

Secretary of State

Sir:-

His Majesty the Emperor of Korea has of late been giving a series of audiences, followed by dinners accompanied by music and professional dancing, and presided over by one of the Princes.

I was somewhat surprised after having attended with my wife one such dinner, given to the members of the Corps Diplomatique, to be invited to another of a private nature with my wife, the Secretary of Legation and a few Americans connected with the Government, upon the evening of the 22d. After the formal reception and dinner I was asked into a private room with His Majesty and the Crown Prince where, being seated, we had a conference lasting over two hours.

---

*Handwritten.

The chief point of this interview seemed to be His Majesty's desire to have the rank of the United States Representative to Korea raised to its former grade of Envoy Extraordinary and Minister Plenipotentiary, -- a desire of which he has frequently spoken before but which he appears to be especially determined upon just now owing to the fact that it is reported that the French Representative has been raised to the rank of Envoy Extraordinary and Minister Plenipotentiary. His Majesty is about to despatch a Representative of this grade to Washington in the hope that he may through this means succeed in gaining the object he has in view. I endeavored to show him that his action was useless, that the United States, as I put it, could not well do this for Korea without raising the rank of its representative at several other Courts, which might not be expedient at present. I presume he will send his Minister nevertheless.

I have the honor to acquaint you with one important bit of information gleaned at this interview. His Majesty informed me that on the previous evening the Japanese Chargé d'Affaires ad interim, Mr. E. Yamaza, had had a formal audience at which he had requested permission to speak privately to His Majesty. The latter sent away his attendants and Mr. Yamaza informed him for his Government that it had proof that the local officials, presumably the Governor, of Manchuria had entered into a formal compact with the chief officials at Port Arthur handing over Manchuria to Russian protection, and that France was aware of this compact. Lunching with Mr. Yamaza yesterday I took occasion to inquire if he considered the newspaper report of a secret agreement between Russia and China as true or not. He replied that he felt convinced that a local agreement existed which had not yet been ratified and might not be for the present, as it would make possible the denial of the existence of any such agreement by Russia.

Horace N Allen

No. 174   Department of State
                                                Washington, July 5, 1901

Horace N. Allen

Sir

Referring to your despatches Nos. 335, 339 and 346, dated respectively, April 24 April 29 and May 11 last, in which you describe the personal relations you have sustained to the Brown incident, the French loan and the removal of Ye-Yong-Ik, I have to say that while the Department recognizes the possible necessity of a certain personal influence at the Korean court, having in view the interests of American citizens as affected by collateral incidents, it should not be overlooked that interference even though non official, in the affairs of other nations in their relations with Korea involves a certain departure from our traditional methods of diplomacy and from our present policy among foreign peoples.

The attempt to secure the removal of an official of the Korean Government because of his attitude to the representatives of other powers, or in combination with the diplomatice representatives of other powers, would hardly seem to be justified on the part of of the United States.

Without a more complete knowledge of the circumstances of the case, the Department is not disposed to censure your conduct in stating in a private note that circumstances compel you "to take action looking to the final and complete removal from public life" of a Korean official.

Still, with the Department's present knowledge it seems prudent to suggest that caution should be employed in assuming an attitude which though intended, perhaps, to be purely personal may involve the risk of drawing your government into an embarrassing situation. While intimating the desirability of exercising great prudence in matters of this kind, the Department realizes that the circumstances of the case necessarily involve a wide use of your personal discretion, in which it reposes confidence.

David J. Hill

No. 378   Legation of the United States
                                           Seoul, Korea, July 19, 1901.

Secretary of State

Sir:-

I have the honor to inform you that September 7'th. next, is the fiftieth birthday anniversary of His Majesty the Emperor of Korea.

Very great preparations are being made to make this a memorable occasion. Poor as the country is, large sums of money are being expended in erecting special new buildings for the proper celebration of the event, and corps of dancers and musicians are being trained and provided with costly wardrobes. The officials are preparing extensive and expensive gifts for their Sovereign, to be presented on that day, and I am inclined to think that some of the Representatives, especially those of Russia and Japan, may make similar gifts on behalf of themselves or their Governments.

I think it would be a good thing for American interests here, as well as highly appreciated by His Majesty if the President should send a telegram of congratulations to the Emperor on the occasion in question.

I do not know that others will follow this course, as I prefer not to indicate what my own views are on the question.

Horace N Allen

No. 422   Legation of the United States
                                           Seoul, Korea, November 1st, 1901.

Secretary of State

Sir:-

I have the honor to inform you that the Governor of Seoul, Um Choon Won, resigned his office on the 24th. October, and that a young man, named Ye Han Yung, was appointed to the office on October 28th.

This would seem to be a favorable change for Americans resident in Seoul, and others, for the former Governor was so incompetent that the affairs of the office were given over to the Vice Governor, a man most difficult to deal with, and apparently unfriendly to Americans.

The newly appointed Governor called on me today to pay his respects, and assures me that he will manage his own office, and that his feelings are most friendly.

Gordon Paddock

No. 463   Legation of the United States
                                           Seoul, Korea, May 22, 1901.*

Secretary of State

Sir:-

I have received your despatch No. 190 of April 8, handing me copies of a correspondence you have had with Mr. W. G. M. Thomas regarding the title to certain property at Songdo Korea, upon which his brother-in-law, Rev. Chas. G. Hounshell of the Methodist Episcopal Church, South, is about to erect buildings.

I am instructed to report to the Department whether any greater privilege respecting the title to such property than that accorded by Article VI of the treaty between the United States and Korea, is claimable as of right, under the most favored nation clause.

In reply I have the honor to inform you that as the British treaty with Korea is more favorable than that between the United States and Korea, I have usually followed its provisions in availing ourselves of the privileges granted by the most favored nation clause. I hand you enclosed, a copy, in duplicate, of Article

---

*This despatch was incorrectly dated. The correct date is May 22, 1902.

IV of the British treaty, with a note as to the bearing of the French treaty on the subject. This completes the treaty provisions covering the subject in question. From this it will be seen that the residence of foreigners in Korea is restricted to the open ports except when travelling on passport.

In spite of treaty restricitons, in the absence of any system of rentals or of suitable places of entertainment, our people have, in endeavoring to secure stopping places in the country, purchased suitable sites and have remodeled or erected houses for their more or less permanent occupation. This course was not approved of by this Legation from the outset, but as people of other nationalities were stopping in the interior, our people could not well be forbidden to do the same. They purchased the property in each case, in the name of a Korean - usually a helper, and they were well aware of the risk they were taking, since the documents could not be registered in the U.S. Consulate. Where disputes have arisen however, the Korean local authorities have always put themselves so much in the wrong by violent acts contrary to express provisions of the treaties that it has been an easy matter, comparatively, to adjust the dispute to the satisfaction of the American, so that they have come to regard the above mentioned risk as merely nominal.

There are large numbers of Japanese living throughout the interior of Korea, and the reported colonization plans of the Japanese Government in connection with the building of their railway of 280 miles connecting Seoul and Fusan, will, if carried out, do much to settle this question of foreign residence in the interior. In times of disturbance a number of these Japanese in the interior have been killed. This was notably the case after the murder of the Queen of Korea in October 1895 and the disordered condition that ensued in Korea.

In every instance of the purchase of property in the interior by Americans in the name of a Korean, the matter has been brought to this Legation by the resulting opposition of the local officials.

In my despatch No. 318 of March 5, 1901, I explained in detail the trouble that the American Presbyterian Missionaries were experiencing at Taikoo, wherein, owing to the fact that the Governor had grossly violated the treaty in four of its distinct provisions, I was successful in securing a settlement that allowed these people to occupy the property in question.

You replied to this despatch at length in yours of April 18. 1901, No. 166, and I suggest a reference to this exhaustive reply written in regard to a case similar to that now referred to me.

In my No. 359 of June 7, 1901, I referred to similar difficulties our people had experienced at Sunchin, and in my No. 410 of October 14 1901, I detailed like troubles that I had just succeeded in adjusting at Soowon. The Soowon matter was gone into at some length by Mr. Hill in his reply of November 19, 1901, which I have quoted extensively in a despatch I was again obliged to write in regard to this matter, on May 14 last. I enclose a copy of this despatch of mine with the quotations above cited. I also enclose a copy of the reply of the Minister for Foreign Affairs, dated the 19'th. instant, in which he cites the usual objections to the residence of foreigners in the interior and declares that he is now investigating the matter and is about to call upon the representatives to withdraw their people from the interior. I may add that this is the common reply received in such cases, but no determined attempt has yet been made by the Korean Government to carry these announced intentions into execution.

In this connection I would like to state that it seems to me to be a mistake for our missionaries to take their women and children into the interior away from any means of protection. Sooner or later disaster will result from this course. It would apparently be much better if missionary residence were restricted to the treaty ports, where theological, medical and kindred schools could be maintained in safety for the education of a native force who could well and safely proselyte in the interior under the supervision of itinerating male missionaries travelling on passport.

Even if treaties should eventually be concluded, granting rights of residence in the interior similar to those enjoyed by foreigners in China, the danger to women and children would be just as great in the absence of any means of protection, while the question as to the propriety of foreigners residing so far away from the jurisdiction of their consuls in a land where they enjoy extrateritorial rights and are not amenable to the native courts, would be just as pertinent.

In conclusion I regret to say that there is no treaty provision whereby foreigners may secure title to property in Korea outside of the limits of the treaty ports, of which there are eight, situated on various parts of the coast so as to reach all portions of the country, in addition to the city of Seoul (Hanyang).

Horace N Allen

No. 470   <u>Confidential</u>   Legation of the United States
                                                Seoul, Korea, May 31, 1902.

Secretary of State

Sir:-
    I have the honor to address you briefly upon the condition of Korean affairs at present.
    The promotion of myself and some of my colleagues is now shown to have been not altogether a good thing as it has seemed to give the Emperor an undue estimate of his importance.
    The recent alliances between England and Japan and between France and Russia, caused some degree of alarm to this Emperor at first, and induced him to begin to institute certain needed reforms. His alarm has now subsided and things are worse than ever, while the Emperor seems to feel greatly elated over his seeming importance, as indicated by these alliances with Korea as one of the important objects. He seems to think that he now has the long desired guarantee of neutrality, and that he can go ahead with an utter disregard for consequences.
    Mr. Pavlow, the Russian Minister, said to me that he regarded the announcement of the Franco-Russian alliance at this juncture, a mistake since it increases the Emperor's mistaken sense of security.
    There is practically no Government in Seoul. No minister or head of a bureau can do anything but upon the order of the Emperor.
    The Minister for Foreign Affairs recently resigned in consequence of difficulties he was having with the Russian Minister over the establishment of a telegraph line to the Russian frontier. Another man was appinted Acting Minister, but he soon obtained "sick leave" though he attends functions at the Palace. A young man who has recently served as an interpreter, was made Acting Minister ad interim, but he has no semblance of power and no business can be done with the Foreign Office direct though despatches are sent in as usual to be forwarded to the Palace.
    Even if the Emperor had the ability and inclination, it would be impossible for him to attend to all the details of the business of the country.
    What is true of the Foreign Office is even more true of the Governor's Yamen, which is supposed to attend to matters of a consular nature. The Governor is a mere figurehead and a recent incumbent who received his appointment through a court lady, could not even read or write. The Vice Governor is a very rude and disagreeable person. He recently returned a despatch from Mr. Paddock because it was not signed by myself, though the Foreign Office had been duly notified of Mr. Paddock's consular functions and of my promotion and had agreed to everything. Exequaturs proper are not issued in Korea. I had to take this and some very vexing property matters to His Majesty. When a thing is taken to the Emperor however, it is but just begun, since he forgets and has to be constantly reminded. It is not always convenient to secure the ear of the Emperor moreover.
    I was quite discouraged with the state of affairs on my recent return from America until I found that my colleagues were each experiencing quite as much difficulty as myself.
    Although thousands of people are on the verge of starvation and hundreds have died owing to the famine resulting from the short crops of last year, the Emperor is going on with the most lavish and useless expenditure of money. At the same time he is trying on all sides to secure a foreign loan.
    He is now building on ground adjoining this Legation, two large European houses for the reception of the foreign ambassadors he has invited, through his ministers abroad, to the fortieth anniversary of the commencement of his reign, in October next. He has been assured that no such ambassadors will be sent, but he seems to think that he can circumvent the local representatives by sending these invitations through his own ministers abroad.
    He is also building a very extensive ceremonial hall for this coming celebration. This is estimated to cost Yen 500,000. He is building a very extensive foreign style house for his residence next to this Legation, and he is now trying to include the most important streets of this locality in his palace enclosure, with absolute disregard for foreign property rights, or the convenience of the foreign representatives who mostly live in or near this quarter of town.
    The British Minister has recently made a careful computation of the cost of the foreign employees in Seoul, very few of whom are doing anything to earn their salaries. He finds that Yen 200,000 ($100,000) are spent annually for this purpose. We have the smallest proportion I am glad to say, having only three Americans in the employ of the Korean Government- : Mr. Sands, connected with the Household Department; Mr. Hulbert, a teacher in the school of English, and Mr. Krumm employed in a survey bureau which seems to have no real function.

There are eighty Korean dancing girls constantly employed in the Palace. They receive Yen 10 and a roll of silk daily. Recently it was arranged to secure a French ballet troupe at an initial cost of Yen 100,000. This was prevented at the last moment.

The people have been on the point of revolt for some time, and local outbreaks are of frequent occurrence, but there is no concerted action that would lead to a rebellion. All that is necessary however is that a leader should appear.

Our missionaries report the most awful oppression of the people by their officials. I quote from one letter just received from the South. "They come down (officials) with no thought of ruling the people in justice and judgement. They buy the office as a speculation. It becomes their private franchise, and they have no other purpose than to work it for all it is worth to fill their own pockets. They seize men without even any pretext save the demand for money. I am compelled to keep my mouth shut even with my own people, and teach them to honor and obey those set in authority over them, but in my heart I pray that the swift judgement of the Lord of the poor and oppressed my come upon them."

The sale of offices has become such a curse that it is surprising purchasers are still to be found at steadily increasing rates, knowing as they must, that they will soon be changed in order to make a new sale.

The Emperor is alone responsible for all this. It is hard to attend to many affairs where there is great corruption displayed, because when the truth is finally learned, the matter has usually been traced to His Majesty or his immediate courtiers.

After the Japan-China war in 1894, the Japanese Government induced the Korean Emperor to swear to a solemn oath before the tablets of his ancestors, that he would faithfully carry out certain needed reforms according to a plan drawn up by a great council of state after months of deliberation. This oath is now entirely disregarded.

One of the provisions of this oath was the abolition of the torture of witnesses in Korean courts, and during the life of Mr. Greathouse, the American Adviser to the courts, this provision was carried out. It is now entirely disregarded, and the papers of the past few days have had accounts of torture so severe as to cause the breaking of bones, practiced upon witnesses arrested as mentioned in my despatch of May 16, No. 461.

Some of the foreign representatives as well as some Korean officials of intelligence, have expressed themselves to me as believing that nothing better may be expected so long as Japan remains so inactive, and they have usually seemed to be of the opinion that Japan may not be averse to allowing things to get into a pretty bad state in the peninsula.

Influence seems to be about equally divided between Russia and Japan in Korea. The Emperor has the faculty of playing off one against the other, though the Russian Minister being a much more able and energetic man than his Japanese colleague, and being farther removed from his own government, seems able to make more of an impresion upon the Korean mind than does the latter.

American interests are represented by the extensive gold mines, which give very little trouble just now: By the import of Kerosene and other supplies which is growing and requires little attention from the Legation: By the American firm controlling the extensive electric plant and who are soon to erect water-works, if His Majesty will carry out his agreement. Over Yen 1,500,000 is due this company already and this business is a constant source of difficulty. Then we have our very large force of missionaries scattered all through the country and always coming in contact with the prejudices of the people and the bitter animosity of the officials. No day passes that some missionary trouble or complaint or request for assistance does not have to receive attention, and with the Central Government radically opposed to the missionary propaganda and the country officials fierce at the missionaries because they do more or less interfere with the extortions these same officials wish to practice upon the Christian converts, it can be readily seen how difficult it is to attend to these cases. So far there has been no dissatisfaction but quite the reverse, which is probably due to the fact that the Koreans have in most every case put themselves in the wrong.

With no government enpowered to act in regard to matters, and with the Emperor at times absolutely inaccessible, it is very difficult to attend to matters in an emergency.

For nearly five years the Koreans have had no overlord; a condition that has not happened before, for China, Japan or Russia has at various times succeeded each other in controlling Korean affairs, until the final withdrawal of Russia in the spring of 1898, and the Russo-Japanese agreements of that time check further interference of eith nation in Korean affairs. This attempt at self-government has shown that the Koreans are very far from ready for it as yet, and the present chaotic state will sooner or later end in interference from the outside, which will probably give to Korea the guiding hand she so greatly needs.

Horace N Allen

No. 471

Legation of the United States
Seoul, Korea, June 3, 1902.

Secretary of State

Sir:-

Replying to your despatch No. 191, of May 1, in regard to the sending of special envoys to the Korean Court on the occasion of the celebration, in October next, of the fortieth anniversary of the accession to the throne by the Emperor of Korea, I have the honor to refer you to my despatch No. 459 of May 10 continuing the subject of Mr. Paddock's despatch No. 444 of March 15 last.

In this despatch I announced the decision that had been reached by the Foreign Representatives which was to the effect that we be empowered to present written felicitations on that occasion. I will quote the minutes of that meeting relating to that particular subject, as follows: - "It was unanimously agreed to submit the following resolution to the home governments: 'that the Representatives of the Treaty Powers in Seoul be charged by their respective Governments to present such felicitations as may be deemed appropriate, to His Majesty on such occasion; that these felicitations should take the form of Letters from the Sovereigns or Heads of States of the various countries'".

Perhaps I should add for your information, that, while the Emperor celebrated his fiftieth birthday last September, he will celebrate his sixtieth anniversary in October next at the time of celebrating the fortieth anniversary of his accession to the throne.

It is needless to go into this matter of the juglery with dates, except to say that as old age is the most honorable of attributes in Korea, and as the Emperor wishes to be an old man while still young, he has availed himself of the Imperial perogative by deciding to celebrate this sixtieth anniversary at the end of the first year of the sixth decade. By actual statistics, he was born September 8, 1852: He was crowned King in March - 1863, his father ruling the country as Regent for nine years thereafter: He assumed actual control of his kingly office in 1873, and was crowned Emperor on October 12, 1897. His country covers an area of some 100,000 square miles, and has a population of about eight to ten millions. The country is rich agriculturally and in minerals; the people are docile and easy to govern. They are exclusively an agricultural people. With a depleted treasury and official salaries unpaid, really vast sums are being expended on these unnecessary ceremonies, which seem to occupy the official Korean mind to the exclusion of matters of importance. The newspapers estimate that upwards of Yen 6,000,000 ($3,000,000) will be expended in connection with this celebration. This money is wrung from the miserable and destitute people. The idea of asking for foreign envoys seems to have been purely a Korean one, probably proposed by some courtier who wished especially to please his sovereign.

The United States Government was the first among Western Nations to make a treaty with Korea and we are largely responsible for introducing the country into the brotherhood of nations.

From the above brief facts a suitable letter may probably be prepared.

Horace N Allen

No. 501

Legation of the United States
Seoul, Korea, September 2, 1903.

Secretary of State

Sir:-

I have the honor to acknowledge the receipt on the 30'th. ultimo, of Mr. Adee's telegram of the 29'th. in regard to representation by the United States on the occasion of the anniversary coronation exercises to be held at the Court in October next. A reading of this telegram is appended.

I note that I am instructed to inform the Korean Government that I myself am to represent the President on that occasion for the delivery of his letter.

I have so informed the Acting Minister for Foreign Affairs, verbally. I did not care, at this juncture, to embody this information in an official despatch, lest such formal notice might have to do with a later discussion regarding precedence.

I may add that I now understand that Mr. Hayashi, the Japanese Minister, will also represent the Emperor of Japan on that occasion, but that a Japanese Prince will also be present in some special capacity.

Horace N Allen

Reading of telegram from Mr. Adee, dated August 29, 1902 "Do not wish supercede you. Notify Government of the Korea that you represent President for delivery of his letter."

No. 517   Legation of the United States
                                             Seoul, Korea, October 20, 1902.

Secretary of State

Sir:-
        Referring to my despatch No. 509 of September 23, announcing the postponement of the coronation services to next year, I now have the honor to hand you enclosed a translation of a note I have received from the Korean Minister for Foreign Affairs, informing me that the fortieth anniversary of the accession to the throne, of the Emperor of Korea, will be held in this city on April 30 next, and I am instructed to inform you of this fact so that you may send a representative here in time to be present on that occasion.
        If it is decided to have me present a letter of felicitation from the President in accordance with previous arrangements, I suggest that a new letter be sent to me in accordance with suggestions contained in my despatch No. 509 of September 23. If this is not thought to be advisable, and I am to hand in the original letter, it should be returned to me with some sort of a letter of credence, naming me as the President's representative for the occasion.
        I venture to suggest also that a little more display in getting up the letter's enclosing envelope would be a good thing. I saw the letter presented by the Russian Representative and found it was enclosed in an envelope of gold cloth, with tassels adorning it.

Horace N Allen

No. 518   Legation of the United States
                                             Seoul, Korea, October 20, 1902.

Secretary of State

Sir:-
        I have the honor to inform you that on the 18'th. instant, on the occasion of the anniversary of the founding of the present dynasty and the fortieth anniversary of the crowning of the present ruler, an audience was given to the Foreign Representatives, which was followed by a luncheon, with the usual music and dancing. The great celebration of this event, for which extensive preparations were made, was abandoned on account of the presence of cholera in Seoul, as I informed you in my despatch No. 509 of September 25.
        Mr. C. Waeber, the Russian Special Representative to the proposed coronation event, having gotten so far on his journey to Seoul as to make it inexpedient to turn back, came to Korea, arriving at Chemulpo on the 16'th. instant on board the "Admiral Nakimoff". He was met by Korean officials and brought to Seoul on a special train. Grand Duke, Prince Cyril, who is second in command of the "Admiral Nakimoff" came to Seoul at the same time and remained one day. He was accorded the full honors of a prince except that the Emperor excused himself from sitting at table with him, on the plea of illness. As the Foreign Representatives had suggested that His Majesty seat himself at table with us on this state occasion, in accordance with our representations noticed in my despatch No. 509 of Sept. 23, it is thought that the Imperial reluctance to comply with this request made it impracticable for the Emperor to honor Prince Cyril in this manner.
        The Foreign Representatives called upon Prince Cyril in full uniform. He received us at the Russian Legation.
        Mr. Waeber presented his letter of felicitations and credence to the Emperor in a special audience held on the 18'th. instant just prior to the audience granted to the Foreign Representatives.

No other letters were presented. Those Representatives who did not return their letters of felicitation to their Governments are holding them for presentation when the coronation ceremonies take place next year.

I may add that it is generally supposed that the real reason for the postponement of these coronation festivities was due to the fact that the Koreans had not realized the magnitude of the undertaking and could not complete the buildings and other preparations in time.

Also, the money for the purpose was not forthcoming.

In further celebration of the above mentioned aniversary, an evening party was given at the Foreign Office on the 18'th. to which the Foreign Representatives were invited. This seemed to be unnecessary in view of the postponement of the celebration, and we, the Foreign Representatives asked to be excused from attending the party, as a mark of respect to the memory of our late colleague, Count Francesetti di Malgra, Italian Consul, whose death I mentioned in my despatch No. 515, October 14.

The Russian Envoy, Mr. Waeber, acted with us in this matter.

Horace N Allen

No. 201   Department of State
                                           Washington, July 16, 1902

Horace N. Allen

Sir:
I have to acknowledge the receipt of your despatch No. 463 of the 22nd of May last answering the Department's inquiry as to whether any greater privilege respecting the title to certain buildings that the Reverend Charles G. Hounshell contemplates erecting at Songdo; Korea, than that accorded by Article VI of the treaty between the United States and Korea, is claimable as of right under the most favored nation clause of the treaty, because granted by Korea, by treaty, to other foreigners.

You make it clear the Mr. Hounshell cannot under the provisions of any of the existing treaties with Korea, obtain title deeds himself for his property at Songdo. His native "helper" can however, you say, obtain such deeds, which will, under ordinary conditions, be sufficient security for Mr. Hounshell; that as these deeds will stand in the name of a Korean, they cannot, of course, be registered in the Legation, and that the missionaries are usually satisfied with deeds of this character.

I enclose herewith for your information a copy of a letter from Mr. W. G. M. Thomas, suggesting that the time is opportune for negotiating a treaty with Korea that will eliminate the inequality in the treatment of American citizens in Korea and of Koreans in the United States set out in Article VI of the present treaty.

I also enclose herewith a copy of a petition of the same tenor, from the Right Reverend. A. W. Wilson and nine other bishops of the Methodist Episcopal Church. South.

You will bring the matter to the attention of the Korean Government, and invite a revision of the treaty between the United States and Korea with a view of securing ampler privileges, in the line of the advance of Oriental sentiment during the elapsed twenty years, and the larger recognition of private foreign rights in China and Japan. Korea should give to the United States no less privileges in this regard than her neighbors have done, or than she may accord to the subjects of any other power.

John Hay

No. 529   Legation of the United States
                                           Seoul, Korea, November 19, 1902.

Secretary of State

Sir:-
In reply to your despatch No. 201 of July 16, I regret to inform you that I have not met with success in carrying out your instructions therein contained to invite a revision of the treaty between the United States and Korea, with a view to securing ampler privileges, in the line of the advance of Oriental

sentiment during the elapsed twenty years, and the larger recognition of private foreign rights in China and Japan.

I promptly addressed myself to the Acting Minister for Foreign Affairs, at whose request I embodied my invitation in writing as per enclosed copy of my letter of September 1.

This letter having been laid before the Emperor, the Minister for Foreign Affairs visted me and we had a long discussion of the matter.

The gist of the conversation was that it was impossible to grant my request, not from any hostility to Americans, and the missionary character of these our people was not objected to. The real objection was very frankly stated was that thousands of Japanese were coming into the country and settling in every town, where they control the trade and make difficulties for the Korean Government and people while constituting a dire menace in a political sense. At present this course on the part of the Japanese was without right whatever and the Korean Government would not like to grant to one power privileges that would accrue to Japan and thus sanction this custom against which the Korean Government is continually protesting.

I asked that an answer be delayed until the Council of State could deliberate upon the question and until I might present a proposition that might be free from the objections urged. This was agreed to, but the Council of State has not had the matter under discussion.

After frequent conversations on the subject, I laid before the Foreign Minister on October 15, a plan embodied in a verbal note, a copy of which I enclose.

I had discussed the matter fully with Mr. Hayashi, the Japanese Minister and I had his consent to refer to the practices of his people as I did in this note. I may add that all the foreign representatives here have been deeply interested apparently, in this matter, for in the case of each new treaty anything like a grant of greater liberties of residence in the interior has been firmly refused by the Korean Government, and I think I had the good wishes of my colleagues in this matter.

In this note I requested permission for our missionaries to own and occupy property and buildings in the interior for their use as dwelling houses and churches, which would exclude merchants and agriculturalists from interfering with the people in the interior.

The Minister for Foreign Affairs seemed not to disapprove of this plan but assured me he could do nothing in the matter and I was obliged to ask for an audience with the Emperor, which was not granted until November 17'th.

At this audience I secured a reading of a translation of this verbal note, by the Emperor, and we discussed the matter. I was referred back to the Minister for Foreign Affairs, and in spite of my urgent request that the matter be discussed by the Council of State, I saw that the Emperor had made up his mind to have no treaty revision and that it was useless to further urge the matter. All I could get was His Majesty's assurance that he would have the Minister for Foreign Affairs reply to me in the most satisfactory way possible.

As my reply has been so long delayed, I have decided to write you without waiting further.

I wish to remark that I did not favor this proposition myself, though that has in no way influenced my action. Had I been at liberty to do so I would have advised against it, but I saw the instruction was mandatory and I did my best to carry it out.

There is no opposition to our missionaries here on the grounds of their missionary character. It is as foreigners that they meet with difficulties because of the apparent absorption of the country and its interests by foreigners.

Missionaries enjoy more privileges here than they do in Japan or China and they are never treated here as they are in China. As I showed you in my despatch No. 463 of May 22, they can get along with their property matters with a little trouble which falls chiefly upon this office and has never been a cause for objection.

It is certainly very questionable whether or not it is proper for our people to reside hundreds of miles in the interior in a land where they have extrateritorial rights and thus are exempt from the action of the native law while far removed from the exercise of the laws of their own land. Some of them too are of the avowed belief that, being"viceroys of Christ" they are "subject only to a higher law" than that which this office is called upon to interpret and enforce.

I have discussed this matter fully with Bishop Galloway, one of the signers of the petition you forwarded to me. Bishop Galloway visited Seoul after I had begun the discussion of this treaty matter. He had just visited Japan where he had been interested in the settlement of the land troubles of the missionaries there. He promptly took in the situation here in a broad minded manner and expressed himself as very sorry that he and his colleagues had joined in that petition to you, since the position of the missionaries here was much better than it was in China or Japan and it was liable to be injured by an attempt to better it.

Rev. Chas. G. Hounshell, whose letter to Mr. W. G. M. Thomas of Chattanooga, seems to have originated this attempt to secure greater missionary rights, did not see me or discuss the matter with this Legation before writing it as his belief "that our Government can now accomplish much toward opening up the interior and benefitting the natives by offering to them the christian religion and schools of education".

Numberous testimonials from missionary societies show the approval of these bodies of the support this Legation has given their people, I do not understand that it is the duty of this office to do more than afford all possible protection when necessary.

Mr. Hounshell wrote the letter above cited after but a few months residence in the country when his enthusiasm must have been very great. It is a mistake to take too seriously the utterances of new missionaries who have not yet succeeded in getting their halos adjusted so that they will not obstruct their vision.

I regret to have to announce this my failure to succeed in carrying out your instructions.

Horace N Allen

No. 534   Confidential.   Legation of the United States
                                                    Seoul, Korea, November 21, 1902.

Secretary of State

Sir:-

From a perusal of my despatches Numbers 529, 530, and 531, of November 19, 532 of November 20, and particularly my report of the Collbran and Bostwick claims No. 533 of today, you will see how difficult it is becoming for me to secure a proper settlement of matters under discussion with the Korean Government.

There is really no government here in fact. The Emperor insists upon attending to everything himself, and he has become so absorbed with vanity and conceit that he will only attend to matters that minister to his personal pleasure or pride.

The Minister for Foreign Affairs is a mere figurehead. He cannot even obtain access to the Emperor. He tries to do his duty and duly forwards copies of despatches to the palace where they are laid aside, for it is notorious that His Majesty will not read long despatches. For that reason, and at the suggestion of the Foreign Minister, I always send in a Chinese synopsis of important despatches, to be forwarded to the palace.

You will see that with a Foreign Office without power, and without access to the ruler, I am unable to even secure consideration for matters however important they may be.

It is somewhat different with others. Japan and England, since the recent alliance was announced, are in a much better position in Korea than is the United States. The Representatives of these two Powers can secure the ear of the Emperor and accomplish results. The same is true of Russia and to a certain extent of France. I refer you for further details under this head to my confidential despatch, No. 470, of May 31, last.

Formerly, by my personal influence with His Majesty, I was able to accomplish even greater results than the others, but with the rise of this man Yi Yong Ik, of whom I have been obliged to write you in so many despatches, this influence is rendered of little use.

This man who cannot read or write, is corrupt and stupidly brutal beyond description. He was opposed in his rise - which was due to his ability to squeeze money from the people, by the better element among Korean officials, who chanced to be freindly to America and personal friends of mine. He succeeded in removing or frightening off the most of these men, in which he was aided by untimely and not altogether unsuspicious deaths, and he is now supreme in authority next to the Emperor. He is chief or director in almost every department or bureau of importance, and he is greatly feared by even the highest officials, who chiefly try to make peace with him. He has the idea that whatever is done to the Americans will not be resented and his advice always opposes us on all sides so that even the most trivial matters of routine cannot be put through. His numerous followers think to give him pleasure by following his lead in regard to matters wherein the interests of Americans are concerned.

This man had one serious set back a year and a half ago, when the better element seemed about to prevail against him. At this time he made a deal with the Russian Minister, Mr. Pavlow, which I chanced to learn from Russian sources amounted to practically selling himself and his influence for Russian protection. Since then he has become more powerful than ever. When it seems however that his actions bid fair to bring matters to an issue with Japan, he promptly grants some concession to them that averts complaint. Just at present I learn that he is not giving to his Russian protectors the satisfaction they might expect. They are trying to obtain an extensive mining concession in the province of Hamkyung, on the North-eastern border of Korea, with non-allienation rights covering that whole large province. They seem to intend to interest American capital in the actual working of these mines, but Ye Yong Ik is said not to know of this, which is problematical at any rate, since Americans may not care to invest. In this matter Ye is either unable or unwilling to expedite matters and but for the sudden accession of support brought him by the Special Envoy from Russia, Mr. C. Waeber, he might find that his Russian support was weakening.

It seems as though the Koreans deserve a lesson that will show them the fallacy of following the lead of such a man in his contemptuous treatment of the interests of the people who have done most for their land.

During the visit of Rear Admiral Rogers U.S. Navy, in September, he told me that the Navy Department were desirous of obtaining a naval station on the Southern Coast of Korea, and that he had made somewhat extensive surveys of various harbors. He said he had found that Sylvia Bay, near to Masampo, was entirely satisfactory and he had or was to make, a report to the Navy Department favorable to it, with the view of securing it upon a long lease.

I refer you to my despatch No. 525 of November 6 last, in regard to Russian movements in that region.

If anything of this kind is contemplated I am quite sure the Korean Government will not agree to lease the harbor even on most liberal terms.

If the place is seriously desired there is the precedent of England's taking Port Hamilton near by, and of her maintaining more or less of a claim to it ever since even though she gave it back - to China. This makes it possible for her ships to rendezvous there whenever there is disturbance in these waters. See Mr. Foulk's despatches 223, September 1, 1885; 189, June 29 1885; 173, May 19, 1885 and previous ones therein cited.

If it should by any chance become necessary to bring pressure to bear upon these people in the settlement of pending claims, the occupation by our naval forces of this harbor would promptly bring them to terms. At the same time such action would, as matters go in this part of the world, give to the United States an interest in this particular part of Korea that would prevent Sylvia Bay from going to anyone else and when Korea has finally brought upon herself the crash that seems inevitable, this harbor would probably fall to us. It is also possible, that, once having occupied the port a lease might perhaps be negotiated on amicable terms.

As to the Collbran and Bostwick claims, Mr. Brown has ample funds in the customs surplus to pay the whole amount but he has told me he will not pay a cent on these accounts. He frankly admitted that it was because he was desired to make payment that he was given charge of the audit and settlement of the matter. His conduct in the matter was doubtless influenced by this reluctance to let go of the money in his hands and we know full well from the experience of others that he will not pay this money of the Koreans even upon the order of the Emperor, unless he personally approves of it. A course in which he seems to be sustained by the British Government. Mr. Brown claims that the whole trouble was caused by Ye Yong Ik, in which I agree with him. He insists that as Ye Yong Ik is Minister of Finance and Director of the Mint and has been ordered long since to make daily payments, he must now clear off the whole debt. The latter went so far as to declare Mr. Brown's report on the Collbran and Bostwick claims, as unreliable and Mr. Brown an "irresponsible person". He therefore gave to Mr. Krumm, of whom I wrote you in my despatch No. 462 of May 30, an order on Mr. Brown for the Collbran and Bostwick accounts which this man was asked to examine, apparently for no other reason than that he was an avowed and bitter enemy of this firm and a great annoyance to me.

This constitutes a deadlock that I doubt if even a resort to arbitration will break, in which case some such course as that I have mentioned above would bring prompt satisfaction, or the precedent of England and European countries in South America might be followed and the customs revenues be attached.

Horace N Allen

No. 237   Department of State
                                                  Washington, June 23, 1903.

Gordon Paddock

Sir:

Referring to Mr. Allen's No. 534, of November 21 last, relating to the desirability of securing Sylvia Bay, Korea, for a United States Naval station, I have to inform you that the Secretary of the Navy, under date of the 19th instant, informs this Department that the General Board of the Navy. Department to whom the matter was referred, does not recommend the acquisition of Sylvia Bay, or any other site in Korea for the purpose mentioned.

                                                  John Hay.

No. 542   Legation of the United States
                                                  Seoul, Korea, November 28, 1902.

Secretary of State

Sir:-

I have the honor to inform you that on yesterday the corner stone was laid for a modern hospital building for the city of Seoul, on an elevated site just outside the South Gate of the City.

The funds for this purpose to the extent of $15,000 were given by Mr. Louis H. Severance of Cleveland Ohio, and the institution is to be known as the "Severance Memorial Hospital".

It will be under the auspices of the Presbyterian Board of Foreign Missions of 156, Fifth Avenue, N.Y., from which society it will draw its support.

The ceremony of laying the corner stone on Thanksgiving day, was attended by the Foreign Representatives and some of the higher Korean officals, besides the foreign community generally and many natives.

I had the honor of laying the corner stone, having had something to do with medical work here in the early days. I enclose a copy of the remarks I made on the occasion.

                                                  Horace N Allen

No. 546   Legation of the United States
                                                  Seoul, Korea, December 4, 1902.

Secretary of State

Sir:-

I have the honor to inform you that on yesterday the Koreans began the native part of the celebration of the foriteth anniversary of the coronation of the present ruler, which was postponed from October 18'th. on account of the prevalence of cholera. The Foreign part of the celebration will take place, as I have informed you, on April 30'th. next. Foreigners are in no way concerned with this present celebration.

It seems unfortunate that so poor a government should spend so much money upon these constantly recurring celebrations, while neglecting to meet their just financial obligations. Since having been left to themselves by the withdrawal of Russia from her large undertakings in Korea, in the spring of 1898, however, there has been one continuation of these celebrations, to the detriment of the country and the stoppage of regular business. At present urgent communications to the Korean Foreign Office are not even answered, this too happens in the case of joint notes from the Foreign Representatives.

The matter of Ye Yong Ik, referred to in my No. 544 of the 2'nd. instant, will rest in abeyance until the present celebrations are over, when the Korean Cabinet officials will again renew their petitions.

                                                  Horace N. Allen.

No. 552   Legation of the United States
                                                            Seoul, Korea, December 10, 1902.

Secretary of State

Sir:-

I have the honor to hand you enclosed four copies of an edict issued by the Emperor of Korea on November 16 and published in the Official Gazette on November 20'th. regulating the emigration of Koreans to foreign countries.

There are quite a number of Koreans now residing in the United States, whither they have gone chiefly in quest of an education, the desire for which is so strong that genteel Koreans have taken up menial callings to that end. Other Koreans wish to get to the United States but it is not always easy for them to leave their country, since if they steal away without proper papers they are liable to suspicion on the charge of treason, which would make it dangerous for them to return. Passports have not been easy to obtain, chiefly since a native having sufficient funds on which to emigrate would be liable to such a system of "squeezing" that before he could obtain the necessary documents providing for his departure he would probably have exhausted his small capital.

Lately Koreans have become interested in the Hawaiian Islands where large numbers of Chinese and Japanese reside, and considerable numbers have desired to go to the islands with the hope of bettering their condition and escaping the persistent oppression of their tax collectors. The idea of obtaining an education for their children seems to be an incentive as well.

The severe famine of last winter seems to have brought this matter to a head, while the difficulty of feeding the large numbers of famished people probably induced the Government to look favorably upon the project. At any rate there has been talk of organizing an emigration bureau, ever since last winter. The Emperor seems to feel considerable pride in the fact that while Chinese may not enter the United States, Koreans will be allowed to do so.

On my return from the United States last Spring I was visited by an official from the Emperor to ask if it were true that Chinese could not enter the United States while Koreans might do so. In replying in the affirmative I took occasion to explain the nature of our laws regarding immigration; Chinese exclusion and contract laborers, so that intending emigrants might not get into difficulties. I understand that the recently issued regulations were modeled after the emigration laws of Japan.

I hear that a number of Koreans have banded themselves together with the intention of going to Honolulu during the coming winter. Some of them will take their families it is said. If they make a favorable report on conditions in Hawaii it is quite probable a considerable number of Koreans may follow them or goto the Philippines. Though the number can never be very great I fancy since the Korean Government would probably take alarm at anything like a great exodus and withhold the necessary passports, for it seems that the population of Korea has been greatly exaggerated and it is not supposed now to be over eight millions so that the one hundred *(thousand (100,000)* * square miles of territory cannot be said to be overcrowded except that much of it is mountainous and unfit for agriculture.

The Korean people are a docile, good-natured, patient and hard working race. They differ from the Chinese in being able to take on our ways rather easily. Koreans have become naturalized American citizens and are a credit to us. There are quite a number of Koreans here in office and in public life who have been educated in the United States and who are conducting themselves excellently. One being a practicing physician.

Ages of subjection to their superiors make them law abiding and easy to govern, at the same time they seem able to absorb ideas of liberty and equality very redily.

It would seem that if these people actually go to our islands and make a report that will lead others to follow; and if the Korean Government allows them to go, they may help to solve the labor question in these islands.

I am satisfied that the Korean Government is not engaged in assisting these people to emigrate by advancing them funds. Rather do they probably hope to gain from them on their return. Most of these people will undoubtedly be too poor to be able to raise the necessary funds for emigrating to any distance,

---

*Handwritten.

especially with their families, unless their neighbors and friends contribute to assist them with the hope of being able to follow later on with funds sent by these pioneers.

I close a copy of a letter I am sending to Governor Dole of Hawaii on the subject.

Horace N Allen

No. 574

Legation of the United States
Seoul, Korea, February 7, 1903.

Secretary of State

Sir:-

I regret to have to inform you of an unfortunate shooting affair at a "stone fight" near Seoul, on the 5'th. instant, in which an American wounded a Korean.

These fights are common at this season. They are supposed to promote a courageous spirit and are therefore allowed to take place annually. In them, rival villages assemble their best men in line and stone the opposing line of villagers. If damage is done by the stones the men rush at each other and fight with clubs. Severe injuries are always received on either side and there are usually several deaths each year. Thousands of spectators cover the adjoining hills and when a rush takes place the whole crowd surges back to avoid the flying stones. Foreigners are usually careful to keep well out of reach of stones when visiting the scene of one of these fights.

On the 5'th. instant, a young man recently employed in the American gold mines in North Korea, Clare W. Hess by name, of Columbia City Indiana, went to take pictures of one of these fights. For some strange reason he took with him a very large and powerful revolver, loaded. It seems that while he was on the outskirts of the crowd one of the surges above described took place, and the young man says he fired his revolver in the air to scare the people away. These people on such an occasion are in no mood to be trifled with, and they apparently ran at the young man, though it seems inconceivable that he was even then in danger of his life. He then shot again, and a third time, hitting one man in the leg. the crowd then became very ugly on seeing a Korean shot, and they chased the American.

It chanced that just at this time I was taking an evening walk with Mr. C. de Waeber, the Russian Special Envoy, and we witnessed the last shot and the flight of the man. When I found on his approach that it was an American, I was horrified, and at once removed the revolver from the young man, against his will, and am sure he would have fatally shot some one had I not done so. I enclose a copy of a sworn statement of Mr. de Waeber and myself.

The man reached the Legation with much difficulty, and I found a large and angry crowd there on my arrival. In fact my companion and myself were in no little danger from the angry crowd. Later the wounded man was brought to the Legation; his wounds were dressed and he was sent to hospital. He is not dangerously wounded.

Hess was not intoxicated, nor is he insane, which makes the shooting seem all the more incredible. It is a disgraceful thing for Americans.

The man Hess is now in the U.S. Consular Jail, and the case is in the hands of the Consul General, who will report the final settlement.

Horace N. Allen.

No. 606

Legation of the United States
May 8, 1903.

Secretary of State

Sir:-

I have the honor to acquaint you with recent diplomatic changes in Seoul.

The German Government has raised the rank of its representative from consul with diplomatic powers, to minister resident with consular functions. Mr. C. von Saldern, lately German minister resident in Siam, took charge in the above capacity in Seoul on the 6'th inst. relieving Dr. H. Weipert.

The Italian Government has also raised the rank of its representative here from consul to Minister resident and consul general. Mr. Attilio Monaco, took charge of Italian interests in Korea, in the above capacity, on the 6th. instant, relieving Lieut. Carlo Rossetti.

The foreign representatives in Seoul are all now of ministerial rank except the Belgian who is still consul general with diplomatic functions.

Japan; America; China; Russia and France have ministers plenipotentiary here, while England; Germany, and Italy have ministers resident.

Horace N. Allen.

No. 609   Legation of the United States
                                                          Seoul, Korea, May 19, 1903.

Secretary of State

Sir:-

I have the honor to inform you that I called upon the Korean Minister for Foreign Affairs, on the 16'th. instant to complain of notices appearing in a Korean newspaper published in Seoul under official patronage, to the effect that Korean emigrants to the Hawaiian Islands were being sold into slavery.

I explained the nature of our immigration laws and how manifestly absurd and unjust such notices were.

I showed that the favor was to the Korean Government rather than to the United States and that the latter was not interested in having these people go to the islands, intimating that if these people were found to be undesirable as immigrants or given to attempts to violate our immigration laws, the Government of the United States might probably feel bound to prevent the coming of any large numbers.

I suggested the appointment of a Korean consul to reside in Hawaii and report on conditions there affecting Korean immigrants.

I understand that about one thousand Koreans have gone to Hawaii, and the Minister for Foreign Affairs frankly told me that the real objection to the movement was that it removed these people from the operations of the Korean tax collectors, in other words they were supposed to be leaving in order to avoid the "squeeze" and official oppression generally.

I hear from reports from Hawaii that the Koreans find ready employment as farmers, and that they are considered a desirable set of workers, being patient and docile, and a good offset to the Japanese and Chinese.

The Minister endeavored to assure me that the damaging reports did not emanate from his office, but they seem to be in accordance with a general attempt on the part of Korean officials headed by the notorious Ye Yong Ik, to do everything possible to annoy Americans.

While the newspaper reports have not been corrected, no similar ones have appeared, and I am informed by some of our missionaries that the people generally do not credit the reports.

Horace N. Allen.

No. 614   Legation of the United States
                                                          Seoul, Korea, May 30, 1903.

Secretary of State

Sir:-

I have the honor to hand you enclosed a copy of a translation of a remarkable petition signed, in the original, by fourteen hundred Koreans living in and about the city of Pengyang, which with its port, Ching nampo, or Chenampo, is the place of entry for the supplies for the extensive American gold mines in that northern region.

The petition was presented to the American Methodist Mission of 150 Fifth Avenue, New York City, and prays for the establishment of a school of manual training, in order that the Koreans may learn to compete with foreigners.

I also enclose a copy of the letter from Rev. W. A. Noble, Ph.D. Presiding Elder of that Mission, explaining the petition, and making some valuable suggestions as to the establishment of an American consulate in that region.

Horace N Allen

Petition from the citizens of Pengyang Porvince requesting the establishment of a school of technology in the city of Pengyang.

To the Annual Meeting oftthe Methodist Episcopal Church

We the undersigned respectfully petition your honorable body clemency, while we presume to speak a few words for the material welfare of Korea.
The time has come when we must defend ourselves agains the foreign industrial invasion. Our shops and our markets are crowded with foreign goods. Foreigners exploit our mines and deplete our waters of fish. We are helpless to defend ourselves against the Japanese, Chinese, Europeans and Americans because of our lack of industrial training.
Even the land itself groans aloud for the development of its own people. Foreigners erect magnificent houseswhile our own hovels fall into decay. Even the building sites dumbly plead for us. The seas and rivers beg for Korea, they would pour into her lap her wealth, but she is ignorant of how to use these gifts. Foreign ships alone plow the face of the deep. Is not our ocean a sea of tears? The fish of the deep long for the nets of our own people but the Japanese waste the riches of our fisheries, till even the fish leaping in the net sobs for the Korean fishermen.
The highway seeks to bless our people, but we are ignorant of the science of building highways and can not even develop a single foot of the way. But, on the other hand, we hear the echo of the locomotive with its thundering train and the whirl of the electric car built entirely by foreigners
The mountains groan to place their wealth at the feet of their own children but it is given to other nationals till our gold becomes a curse and a shame to us while it enriches others.
To whom should we turn in our helplessness if it not be to the generous, the rich and the strong? Who are the people thus rightly named if it not be Americans?.
We offer no apology for asking for aid of the strong. The American revolutionists did not refuse the aid of France. During the late Chino-Japanese war distressd China did not hesitate to ask help of foreign powers. We do not ask as the beggar, who by receiving is impoverished, but we ask that we may be freed from the thraldom of ignorance that we may fight our own battles. Give us knowledge and we will do the rest.
Therefore we, your humble petitioners, beg your honorable body to erect at as early date as possible a school of technology in the city of Pengyang where we may send our sons and begin in earnest the fight for Koreas industrial liberties.

TELEGRAM CIPHER.   Department of State,
                                                 Washington, November 7, 1903-

American Charge d' Affaires,
Seoul.

Confer with British and Japanese representatives concerning opening to international trade of Wiju on same conditions as other treaty ports. With opening of Antung on the other side of Yalu, this Government particularly anxious Wiju also be opened. Urge at once this step in writing to Minister of Foreign Affairs of Korea and support by oral representations.

Hay.

No. 238   Department of State
                                                 Washington, July 1, 1903.

Gordon Paddock

Sir:

I have to acknowledge the receipt of Mr. Allen's No. 610, of May 20 last, relative to Korean students being sent to various foreign countries for education.

The Department would be interested to learn why Korea does not send some students to this country.

                                                 Francis B. Loomis

No. 623   Legation of the United States
                                                 Seoul, Korea, November 25, 1903

Secretary of State

Sir:-

I have the honor to acknowledge the receipt of your despatch No. 238, of July 1, last, addressed to Mr. Paddock, relative to Korean students being sent to various foreign countries for education, in which the query is made as to why Korea does not send some students to the United States.

In reply I have to state that the United States has all along been the favorite place for Korean students. Korean students have been at school in the United States constantly for the past eighteen years, and there are some sixteen there now, including the second prince, Eui Wha, who is at school at Delaware Ohio where he attends the Ohio Wesleyan University, - incognito.

This young man should some day be the ruler of this country, and his presence at an American school is as much of an honor as could be paid our country in the matter of the education of Korean youths.

It would seem to me to be quite inadvisable for the Korean Government to officially send a company of its young men to school in America, for the reason
that I have found it to be the experience heretofore that remittances for the support of such students sent abroad, usually fail after the first one and the boys become more or less of a public charge.

                                                 Horace N Allen

*   Department of State
                                                 Washington, November 12, 1903.

Gordon Paddock

Sir:

The treaty signed between the United States and China on the 8th of last October provides, among other things, for the opening of Antung on the bank of the Yalu River to international trade, on the same conditions as at the other open ports in the Chinese Empire, on and after the exchange of ratifications of said treaty. The town of Wiju, which faces Antung on the Korean side of the Yalu River and which has for a long time been an important center of Korean trade with China through the latter locality, now becomes of importance to the commercial interests of the United States.

The Department has been advised that for some time past the British and Japanese Governments, through their representatives at Seoul, have been urging upon the Korean Government the opening of Wiju on the same footing as other localities now opened in Korea to international trade.

The bulk of the trade at both Antung and Wiju would unquestionably be very considerably increased, if both of these localities, were made treaty ports, and it is for this reason that this Government is now most desirous that the latter place should also be made open as soon as Antung.

---

*Unnumbered

You are therefore instructed to confer fully with the British and Japanese representatives, and bearing always in mind the purely commercial nature of the interests of the United States in this matter, to urge on the Korean government the early opening of Wiju to international trade as of equal advantage to Korean trade and to that of the world.

I confirm on the overleaf my cabled instruction to you of the 7th instant, on this subject.

Copies of this instruction have been sent to the United States Ministers at Peking and Tokyo for their information.

John Hay.

No. 244

Department of State
Washington, November 19, 1903.

Gordon Paddock

Sir:

The Department learns for the first time, officially, from your telegram of the 11th instant, that the British and Japanese representatives were urging on the Korean Government the opening of the port of Yongampho, near the mouth of the Yalu River. This, however, in no way lessens the desire of this Government to see the town of Wiju palced on the footing of the other localities in Korea opened to international trade.

The opening of Yongampho, which faces on the Korean side of the mouth of the Yalu River the Chinese town of Tatungkou, which under the Japanese treaty recently signed with China is also to be opened at an early date to international trade, will probably be of as much benefit to the latter port as the opening of Wiju will prove to be to Antung, which is similarly situated facing Wiju. However, in view of the strong opposition which you report against the opening of Yongampho, on the part of the Russian representative in Seoul, and in view of the policy of this Government not to take, in the furthering of its commercial interests, any step which might be construed as joint action for the advancement of the political purposes of any Power or group of Powers, we can only, at this time, express the pleasure which we would have in seeing Yongampho opened to foreign trade; but the representations of this Government must be confined to securing from the Korean Government the opening of Wiju.

I confirm on the overleaf the telegraphic instruction sent to you on the 16th instant, and your telegram in reply dated the 18th.

John Hay.

TELEGRAM. CIPHER.

Department of State,
Washington, December 11, 1903.

Allen,
Minister, Seoul.

Continue to press for opening Wiju. We do not ask Yongampho also, nor, if Korea is willing to open both ports, do we oppose. You need not seek concurrence of Russian Legation. To do so is virtual invitation of Russian objection.

Hay

No. 634   Legation of the United States
                                             Seoul, Korea, December 23, 1903.

Secretary of State

Sir:-

    I have the honor to acknowledge the receipt of your despatches number 734 of November 12 and 244 of November 19, relating to the opening of the port of Wiju, and to confirm my telegram on the subject of the 9'th. instant, and your reply of the 12'th. Enclosure 1.

    I also hand you readings of my telegram to Mr. Conger, dated December 9 and his reply dated the 12'th instant.

    I will simply say now that I am doing all in my power both privately and officially, to carry out the instructions contained in your telegrams and letters regarding the opening of Wiju. The Minister for Foreign Affairs is willing and anxious to open both Wiju and Yongampo, but he can get no authority so to do.

    I enclose a copy of my last letter to the Foriegn Office on the subject, as well as a copy of a similar letter sent by Mr. J. N. Jordan, my British colleague, who of course directs his efforts entirely toward the opening of Yongampo, as does our Japanese colleague, who also has a request at the Foteign Office for an audience with the Emperor. The latter declines to see us however as he is said to be suffering from a cold.

    I shall hope to be able to communicate with you on this subject, shortly, by telegraph.

                                             Horace N Allen

No. 638   Legation of the United States
                                             Seoul, Korea, January 5, 1904.

Secretary of State

Sir:-

    I have the honor to hand you enclosed, confirmation of my cable message of today relative to the landing of a guard of marines for this Legation.

    It was not my intention to land the guard until the situation became more critical. All is quiet here in Seoul, though the situation is grave, as I am informed by my Japanese colleague, while Mr. Griscom, our minister in Tokio, telegraphed me confidentially, on the 1'st. that an ultimatum would be delivered to Russia by Japan on yesterday.

    The U.S.S. "Vicksburg" has too small a force to land much of a party, and one hundred marines arrived at Chemulpo on the 2'nd. on board the transport "Zaphiro".

    It is bitterly cold weather here and the "Zaphioro" has no heating arrangements. She will probably have to go to Japan to be fitted for this cold weather. For this reason and the fact that a guard is liable to become very necessary here at any moment, and in such emergency the transportation facilities may not be available, I decided to bring up as many men as I could accomodate at the Lagation at once. Thirty six men came to the Legation today therefore. If it becomes necessary to reinforce this guard, all arrangements have been made for quartering them comfortably at the modern office building of the American, Seoul Electric Company, not far distant, as I have already informed you.

    Out of courtesy and as a usual method of prodedure, I duly informed the Korean Foreign Office of my intention to get up a guard, having ample assurance from numerous officials that such a course would be not only agreeable but pleasing to the Korean Government. See enclosure 2.

    To my surprise I was interogated on yesterday as to my reasons for this action, by an official from the Foreign Office. I hand you enclosed a copy of these questions and my answers, delivered in writing.

    Last night about ten oclock I received a despatch from the Minister for Foreign Affairs, denying the fact that any guard is necessary here and asking me not to get up one now or ever.

    It was too late to stop the landing of the guard as the telegraph lines were closed for the night. I did not care to court Korean opposition further by submitting to this strange request to the extent of reembarking the men once they were landed, so I let them come. There was no opposition to their entrance to the city.

I had previously informed my Russian, British and Japanese colleagues of my intention. To the Japanese Minister I submitted the question as to whether he felt that it might be inexpedient for foreign guards to land now, as such action might excite the now quiet populace. He expressed himself as entirely in favor of my landing my guard.

Guards are, and have long been, maintained at the Japanese and Russian Legations, and the Japanese are just now completing a very substantial brick baracks for one thousand men, near their Legation.

In view of all the circumstances, the letter of the Foreign Minister to me was decidedly impertinant.

I must explain again that the Emperor, who is weak beyond explanation, is completely in the hands of the man Ye Yong Ik, of whom I have written you so often. This man would be but a coolie, as he was formerly, were it not for the support of the Russian Legation.

It seems to be the policy of the Russian Authorities here to persuade the Emperor that there is no likelihood of anything like war or serious trouble occuring to harm him or his country. In this they are ably seconded by the French. This man Ye Yong Ik who is the spokesman in the palace for the Russian Legation, has therefore calmed the Emperor's fears, and kept him close under the guidance of the Russians, as is well seen by his preventing any action in regard to Wiju. When my despatch went to the Foreign Office, a copy of which I enlcose, it was sent at once to the palace, and from reports given me, and the fact that the Russian and French Ministers were closeted with Ye Yong Ik soon after my despatch reached the palace, as I saw myself on going to dine with Mr. Pavlow, I am convinced me that this impertinent letter from the Foreign Office was dictated by Ye Yong Ik, very likely at the suggestion of Mr. Pavlow, which impression is confirmed by Koreans.

I enclose a copy of my reply to this letter of the Foreign Minister's.

My British colleague congratulated me on getting my guard as he thought their presence would make for the peace of the city. He had hoped to get his guard, now at Chemulpo, at the same time that I got mine, but he has telegraphed to his Government for permission and has not yet received a reply. He said that owing to the British alliance with Japan, his Government might prefer to wait and trust to Japanese protection in an emergency.

This Legation, like that of Great Britian, adjoins and is largely surrounded by the palace enclosure, where there are now thousands of Korean soldiers posted all around the outside of the wall owing to the death of the Dowager Empress. I will now be able to prevent this compound from being overrun by refugees in case of trouble.

Horace N. Allen.

Despatch No. 2.   Foreign Office, January 4, 1904.

H. N. Allen

Your Excellency:-

In reply to your latter received on the 3rd. instant in which you informed me that in view of the warlike reports now circulated and the probability of disorder arising in Seoul owing to the number of undisciplined soldiers here, you were about to bring a guard for the protection of your Legation and other American property, I have the honor to inform you that as Korea is friendly with all Foreign Power, there is no chance of having a war; that I really cannot well understand what you said in your letter about war. As to the soldiers in Seoul, they are always strictly ordered and restrained and there will not be any disorders arising.

However, in case of any accident happening or being caused, the Korean Government will take responsibility in protecting the native and foreign lives and property.

I, therefore, beg to ask you not to bring in any guard at all forever.

(Signed) Ye Che Yong
Acting Minister for Foreign Affairs

No. 245   Department of State
                                                     Washington, January 9, 1904.

Horace N. Allen

Sir:
        I have to acknowledge the receipt of Mr. Paddock's despatch No. 621 of November 19 last, reporting the situation respecting the desired opening of Wiju to international trade.
        The Department feels great regret that anything should have prevented Mr. Paddock from reporting to the Department, at once, the conversation which he had had in June last with the Japanese Minister

concerning the opening of a port on the Yalu River. Neither the "overwhelming amount of work on local matters", nor the "two months of ill health" should have made him defer for an instant doing so.

                                                     Alvey A. Adee

No. 680   Legation of the United States
                                                     Seoul, Korea, February 26, 1904.

Secretary of State

Sir:-
        I have the honor to hand you enclosed a reading of my telegram of today announcing the opening of Wiju, as well as a translation of the official despatch from the Korean Foreign Office announcing the fact.
        I had understood that, in response to former requests from the British and Japanese Ministers, the port of Yong Am Po would also be opened at the same time, but nothing is said of this.

                                                     Horace N Allen

No. 682   Legation of the United States
                                                     Seoul, Korea, February 27, 1904.

Secretary of State

Sir:-
        In my No. 678, of the 25'th. I handed you a copy of a despatch I had sent to the Korean Foreign Office asking for protection for the property of the American Mining Company in Northwestern Korea, near the scene of present activity between the Japanese and Russian forces.
        I now have the honor to hand you a copy of a very satisfactory reply I received on yesterday.
        I have been quite astonished at the punctuality and civility of the Korean Foreign Office during the past few days, since the departure for Japan of the notorious Ye Yong Ik. Matters long unheeded are now being attended to by the Foreign Office in a spirit similar to that I was accustomed to before this man began dictating the despatches from the Foreign Office to this Legation.

                                                     Horace N Allen

No. 799   Confidential.   Legation of the United States
                                                      Seoul, Korea, September 30, 1904.

Secretary of State

Sir:-
    I have the honor to hand you enclosed a copy of the translation of a despatch written at the order of the Emperor of Korea, by Chyo Min Hui, lately Korean Minister at Washington, to Charles W. Needham, Counseller of the Korean Legation at Washington.
    I secured this copy through being asked to put the original into English.
    On his recent return to Korea, after a few months spent in Japan as Korean Minister, Mr. Chyo related to me a conversation he claimed to have had with you just prior to his departure from Washington, in which conversation he claimed that you had kindly agreed to assist Korea in her troubles caused by the difficulties exisiting between Russia and Japan, adding that you would do this in the interest of American commerce with Korea.
    Mr. Chyo told me that the Emperor was greatly delighted with this information and desired to send him, or someone else, to Washington as minister to confer with you further, but that the Japanese did not favor the sending of new Korean Minsiters abroad (see my No. 787 of August 30) and it would be difficult to act contrary to this suggestion.
    I have recently had occasion to speak in high terms of Mr. Charles W. Needham, in conection with my efforts to collect back salary due to him. This may have given the Emperor the idea of availing himself of Mr. Needham's services in the manner indicated by the enclosed copy of a letter to him.
    In this letter Mr. Needham is informed of the conversation Mr. Chyo claims to have had with you and he is asked to see you and explain the dire straits in which Korea finds herself and to ask you to assist her, since Japan is claimed to be usurping public functions without awaiting a settlement of the present war.
    The facts regarding the situation are briefly that there is no government in Korea, properly so called. The Emperor continues to control everything himself and his ministers are mere figureheads. He is moreover most easily influenced by his favorites and he seems to have the faculty of choosing about the worst counsellors, one after another, that are to be found. Just at present it is a lamentable fact that the person credited with having the most influence with the Emperor is a notorious female, the concubine of a man generally accredited as being about as common and despisable an official as is to be found in this country. This man, <u>Hyun Yang Woon</u>, has risen to very high rank through the influence of this woman, he being now a general and a cabinet minister.
    This pair are reported to have been used by the Japanese authorities to influence the Emperor favorably to the objects - the woman having recently been sent to Japan by the Emperor to consult with Marquis Ito, with whom she claims to have made friends during the recent visit of the Marquis to Korea.
    I have no doubt that the recent agreements entered into between the Emperor and the Japanese Government, culminating in the Protocol published on the 9th instant and reported in my No. 793 of September 10th, were entered into freely and more or less voluntarily by the Emperor, at the instigaiton of his favorites, and that the Japanese could well deny any show of "force" whatever.
    I therefore pointed out to the Emperor's messenger, that this request was not a thing that could be entertained privately or acted upon secretly, as seems to be the desire of the Emperor in all such matters, but that it would probably have to be made more or less public and in that event it might act somewhat in the nature of a boomerang and come back to make trouble, since upon learning that such a request had been preferred the Japanese might well inquire why it had been made without first consulting them, since the Emperor had apparently freely entered into the agreements regarding the control of Korea's domestic and foreign relations, of which control he now seems to complain.
    The difficulty seems to be that the Emperor will never assert himself openly and express the real convictions he may hold. He will not accept responsibility, but having embarked upon a course which he may have been persuaded to believe was proper, upon being persuaded by someone else that such course will result in disaster, he will invariably shift the responsibility upon someone else. In this case he might well place the blame of any trouble arrising from the presentation of this request for assistance, upon the shoulders of the inoffensive ex minister Chyo. He seems further, to always desire secrecy in all such dealings, failing to realize that the very act of compliance with his request must of necessity destroy any such secrecy.
    I therefore deemed it my duty to retain a copy of this letter to Mr. Needham for immediate reference to you with the necessary brief explanations of the situation.

It is possible, though not altogether probable, that my message of caution may result in saving you the preferment of this request, which it seems to me might possible, be awkward for you to either decline or comply with.

Horace N Allen

Translation of a letter from Chyo Min Hui, lately Korean Minister to Washington, to Dr. Chas. W. Needham, the Counsellor of the Korean Legation Washington.

Seoul Korea, September 30, 1904.

Dear Sir:-

When I was in Washington I had the honor of an interview with His Excellency, Mr. Hay, the Secretary of State. I explained to him the dangerous position in which Korea is now placed. He considered the friendhsip existing between the two nations and said it was his intention to help my country when the opportunity offers. I thanked him warmly and when our Emperor came to know of the message of the Secretary he also thanked him deeply.

Now the war between Russia and Japan has not yet been settled still the Japanese stretch their hands by force upon Korea and it will result in the domestic affairs and the foreign relations of Korea passing entirely into the hands of Japan, and the independence of Korea will be lost.

Is it not regrettable?

I know your good reputation and your willingness to help the weak. You have remained several years in the service of my Legation and have always endeavored to assist us.

His Majesty our Emperor believes in your ability as he has heard of you through Dr. Allen.

At this critical time of danger we need your kind assistance therefore I beg to ask that you will take the opportunity to describe the condition of Korea to the President and to the Secretary of State, and help to maintain the independence and integrity of the imperial household of Korea.

No. 863   Confidential.   American Legation, Seoul, Korea.
                                                           January 19, 1905.

Secretary of State

Sir:-

I have the honor to inform you that I have had a very confidential communication from the Emperor of Korea, through one of his high officials, in which the Emperor is reported as soliciting asylum in this Legation. I have endeavored heretofore to head off any such request, and to that end I have made various excuses of late when it has been suggested to me that I ask for an audience, knowing that something of the kind would be put to me by the Emperor. I have taken every opportunity to show how utterly impossible any such course would be, and when the matter was finally brought to me this morning I made this impossibility so clear that I think the request will not be heard of again.

Certain officials fared so well after assisting the Emperor to take refuge in the Russian Legation in February 1896, that it is but natural to suppose that others would wish to profit by some such coup at this time of trouble. I shall not allow anything of the kind to take place in connection with this Legation, and should the Emperor scale the wall into this compound, I would have to ask him to withdraw and the Japanese would probably, in that event, take him to one of the distant palaces. All of which I fully explained to the messenger of the Emperor today.

Horace N Allen

No. 869   American Legation, Seoul, Korea.
                                                 January 28, 1905.

Secretary of State

Sir:-
    I have the honor to confirm my telegram of today as follows: -
"It is reported Korean have been sent to Washington to secure your assistance regarding terms of peace
relating to Korea. Exact nature of his mission uncertain. The matter was concealed from me fearing
disapproval. Messenger has left ninth. He informed me he was going to Japan. He was educated Virginia".
    The name of this official is Suhr Pyung Kiu, he styles himself in English, Q. B. Suhr. It is
supposed he worked up the scheme for his own advantage.
    It is possible he may be indefinitely delayed in Japan in case his mission became known before
sailing from Yokohama.

                                                 Horace N. Allen

TELEGRAM   Seoul, Korea
                                                 March 25, 1905

President Roosevelt
Washington

    Am greatly grieved to learn that Minister Allen will be superseded. Our friendship is of long
standing and my confidence in him complete. His long experience and ablility make him most desirable
representative for your government. Will be much gratified if he be retained.

                                                 Hiung Emperor of Korea

No. 7   American Legation, Seoul, Korea.
                                                 July 20th., 1905.

Secretary of State

Sir:-
    During a visit recently paid me by a confidential chamberlain of the Emperor's, I was asked in his
name, whether an attempt on the part of Korea to gain admittance to the peace negotiations at Washington
would receive the support of the United States and failing this, whether she would use her good offices to
obtain favorable terms for Korea.
    I have the honor to report that in my reply I stated that although I was wholly without instructions
which would guide my opinion it was my personal belief that as negotiations were to be conducted by the
two belligerents alone, the presence of a third power, which had not participated in the war, might be
unwelcome. Although the United States had been instrumental in bringing Japan and Russia together she
was no more able than other neutral Powers to intimate her preferences in regard to articles of peace. In the
same unofficial manner I expressed my hope that Korea would await calmly the result of the negotiations,
assuring my visitor that the peculiarities of her international relations were well known abroad and that
special representatives could increase but slightly the information of foreign chanceries which were
watching her interests with sympathetic and intelligent insight.
    Inquiries similar in nature to those made me were addressed to other Legations and, in general, the
same answer was returned. An incentive for them may be found in the note transmitted by China to Russia
and Japan and communicated to the Korean Foreign Office, in which China stated her unwillingness to
accept arrangements affecting her interests, concluded during the negotiations unless she should be consulted
regarding them. Although the political connection between Korea and China has been broken for ten years,
Korea is sensitive still to the diplomatic procedure of her neighbor.

A considerable sum of money has been obtained from the Emperor by two minor officials who desire to visit America for the avowed purpose of enlisting public sympathy in Korea's behalf. These men, however, may not be permitted to enter upon their mission. The powerful influence of the Japanese Minister is against them, and their undertaking is regarded, in general, as unwise, since they command confidence neither at home nor abroad.

Edwin V. Morgan

No. 24   American Legation, Seoul, Korea.
                                                  October 19, 1905.

Secretary of State

Sir:-

I have the honor to inform you that Mr. Homer B. Hulbert, an American citizen who has been employed continuously by the Korean Government since 1886 as a teacher of English in the middle and normal schools in Seoul will proceed to Washington, probably at once, in order to lay before the President, certain statements which he believes should prove that Korea is being dealt with "unjustly and oppressively" by Japan and that in conformity with the second clause of Article I of the Korean American Treaty of 1882 this Government is entitled to call upon the United States to exert her "good offices", on being informed of the case, to bring about an amicable arrangement", with the power against whose aggressions the Korean Government may lodge a protest.

I do not know with what credentials Mr. Hulbert is furnished nor with what authority he speaks but it is not unlikely that the Emperor is acquainted with his mission and has supplied him with money with which to defray his travelling expenses. A certain portion of the foreign community supports his views and will follow his course with sympathetic interest.

Although of good intelligence and energetic character Mr. Hulbert's judgement is not infrequently colored by prejudice and his statements should be tested before being accepted as facts. As the Editor and leader writer of "The Korean Review" a monthly periodical which has been published for several years and which is quoted frequently by the principal foreign newspapers of Japan and China, Mr. Hulbert is recognized as the spokesman of the local critics of Japanese administration in Korea.

Edwin V. Morgan.

Department of State
Washington, December 19, 1905.

Min Yeung-Tchan

Sir:

Referring to your visit to this Department on the 11th instant, when, after having first stated that you had no credentials to the Government of the United States and could make no official communicantion, you stated to me in effect that the treaty of November 17, 1905, under which the direction of the external relations of Korea is to be conducted through the Department of Foreign Affairs in Tokyo, was procured from the Emperor of Korea by duress and should therefore be ignored, I beg to inform you that this Government has considered whether it could receive this statement as calling for or justifying any action by the Government of the United States, either upon the general ground of friendship which this Government has long felt for the Emperor and people of Korea, or upon the specific ground in the first article of the treaty between the United States and Korea of May 19, 1883, as follows:

"If other powers deal unjustly or oppressively with either Government, the other will exert their good offices, on being informed of the case, to bring about an amicable arrangement, thus showing their friendly feeling."

Since your visit we have received the following communication from Mr. Kim, the regularly accredited Charge d' Affaires of Korea in Washington.

"I have the honor to acknowledge the receipt of your note of the 24th ultimo, informing me that by agreement signed on November 17th, by the Plenipotentiaries of Japan and Korea, by which Japan becomes the medium for conducting the foreign relations of Korea, you had under date of the 24th ultimo telegraphed the American Minister to withdraw from Korea.

"I have further to inform you that I have this day received instructions from Mr. Yi Wan Yong, the acting Minister of Foreign Affairs of Korea, to transfer to the Japanese Legation the archives and other property in my charge.

Mr. Secretary, in taking leave of my diplomatic relations with your Department, I beg you to accept my thanks and the assurances of my high appreciation for past courtesies shown me."

In view of this official communication, it is difficult to see how the Government of the United States can proceed in any manner upon the entirely different view of the facts which you tell us personally you have been led to take by the information which you have received. It is to be observed, moreover, that the official communications from the Japanese Government agree with the official communications from the Korean Government, and are quite inconsistent with your information.

If, however, the difficulty of complying with your wishes were surmounted, we should be met by the fact that, on February 23, 1904, and on August 22, 1904, the Korean Government concluded with the Japanese Government treaties which are not now in any respect impeached or questioned, by which Korea gave to Japan such extensive control over her affairs and put herself so completely under the protection of the Government of Japan as to render completely impossible the application of the provisions of the treaty with the United States above quoted. The above mentioned treaties between Japan and Korea appear to be of such a character as practically to give Japan control over the foreign relations of Korea, and to make the latest treaty of November 17, 1905, which is now called in question, but a slight advance upon the relations of control previously existing. Those previous relations of control amount to acomplete bar to any interference by the United States under the treaty of 1883.

Under all these circumstances, I feel bound to advise you that the Government of the United States does not consider that any good purpose would be subserved by taking notice of your statements.

Elihu Root

B. American Missionaries

No. 172   Department of State
                                                 Washington, January 5, 1897

John M. B. Sill,

Sir.
        I enclose herewith copy of a despatch from Mr. McIvor, Consul General of the United States at Kanagawa, Japan, reporting an interview he had with two missionaries from Korea who called upon him to secure his assistance in prevailing upon the son of the King of Korea to go to the United States, and in securing for him a guard from his residence in Tokyo to the steamer.
        Your attention is called to Mr. McIvor's statement to them concerning the attitude which this Department expects American missionaries to maintain regarding political matters in the country where they reside as set forth in its instruction to you No. 132 of January 11, 1896.
        As that instruction directed you to make known its substance to American residents in Korea, the Department is surprised that the two missionaries in question should have no knowledge of it, as they stated to Mr. McIvor.
        The Department will be pleased to receive a copy of the notice which you issued in compliance with the instruction referred to.

                                                 Richard Olney

No. 179   Department of State
                                                 Washington, March 30, 1897

John M. B. Sill

Sir
        Your despatch No. 259, of the 24th ultimo, has been received. You therein review at some length the circumstances and considerations which led you to refrain from advising American missionaries (or other citizens of the United States) in Korea of the attitude which this Government expects them to maintain regarding political matters in the country where they reside, as set forth in the Department's instruction to you, No. 132 of January 11, 1896.
        The Department thus learns, after the lapse of more than a year, for the first time, and in response to the categorical inquiry made of you in its instruction No. 172 of 5th January last, that its contemplated course in this regard has not been followed by you as its responsible agent.
        Briefly stated, your reasons for non-compliance appear to be - that you regarded the instruction of January 11, 1896, as merely an advisory suggestion; that you deemed its terms ambiguous in that it applied in one part to all Americans resident in Korea, and in another referred to their "missionary" work, whereas some few are not missionaries; that you thought its tenor harsh and offensive to the persons it was designed to reach; that you considered it based on erroneous premises not deducible from your despatches; and that, had you understood, as you suppose you are to understand now, that you were imperatively directed to issue at once this instruction to all your "nationals" in Korea, you certainly would have preferred recall to compliance, which latter view you appear to have since modified. You say, in conclusion, that, although you now know that the Department intended to make execution of its instruction mandatory, circumstances have so radically changed during the year and more that has since elapsed that you deem it your duty to await further directions before sending it out as a circular notice.
        All of these considerations, as well as the other pertinent views of your present despatch, would have been entirely proper subjects to lay before this Department at once upon receiving the instruction in question: that is, assuming that the tenor thereof left doubt as to the Department's intention that the defined notification was to be made on receipt of its instructions, - a point as to which your view is not shared here. In ignoring that instruction until expressly recalled to your attention a year later, you adopted a course which the Department cannot commend.
        Although circumstances may have gratifyingly changed in some respects during the past year, past occurrences in Korea, and a due regard for the contingencies of the future do not justify withholding from

any of our citizens in that country knowledge of the view of this Government touching the neutral obligations incumbent upon loyal citizens of the United States in any foreign country whatsoever. Such knowledge appears to be generally possessed and acted upon by our citizens abroad, and the announcement of that view need imply no accusation of any man who may be exceptionaly ignorant of his duty or unconscious of violating his international obligation. On receipt of this instruction you will communicate a copy of the following Circular to each and every citizen of the United States whom you may know or ascertain to be sojourning in Korea.

Legation of the United States
Seoul, Korea 1897

Sir:

By direction of the Secretary of State I am required to make publicly known to each and every citizen of the United States sojourning or being temporarily or permanently in Korea, the repeatedly expressed view of the Government of the United States that it behooves loyal citizens of the United States in any foreign country whatsoever to observe the same scrupulous abstention from participating in the domestic concerns thereof which is internationally incumbent upon his government. They should strictly refrain from any expression of opinion or from giving advice concerning the internal management of the country, or from any intermeddling in its political questions. If they do so, it is at their own risk and peril. Neither the representative of this government in the country of their sojourn, nor the Government of the United States itself, can approve of any such action on their part, and should they disregard this advice it may perhaps not be found practicable to adequately protect them from their own consequences. Good American citizens, quitting their own land and resorting to another, can best display their devotion to the country of their allegiance, and best justify a claim to its continueed and efficient protection while in foreign parts, by confining themselves to their legitimate avoctaions, whether missionary work, or teaching in schools, or attending the sick, or other calling or business for which they resort to a foreign country.

(Minister's Signature and title)

I will thank you to report compliance with this instruction.

John Sherman

No. 9

Legation of the United States
Seoul Korea, October 1, 1897.

Secretary of State

Sir;-

I have the honor to report a somewhat important conversation I had on yesterday, with Mr. A. de Speyer, Russian Chargé d'Affaires at Seoul.

It had been reported to me several times, that Mr. de Speyer had spoken in a very heated manner against American Missionaries, Americans in general and the American publications in Korea, (see my No. 3, Sept. 17, page 1), saying he would drive them out of Korea. Later it was told me by Korean friends of mine that he had assured them that no Korean with sentiments friendly to Americans would be allowed to remain in office.

This seemed to demand some notice, and thinking that in all probability there might be some mistake in interpretation, I called upon Mr. de Speyer and after a friendly talk with him on other matters of interest, he voluntarily introduced the subject by obtaining my permission to speak frankly and then detailing his grievance against our missionaries.

I think I was able to show him that his impressions were obtained while in Japan from reading the often unjust criticisms of the Japanese press: that the unfortunate impression had gone out that these people were misconducting themselves, chiefly because of the misguided zeal of one silly woman, who to herald the fact that her husband had gone to the Palace as interpreter to the Russian and American Ministers, had rushed into print in a manner most regretted by the whole American Community, (see Mr. Sill's No. 177 Dec. 3, 1895): that as a rule our people were very much given to minding their own affairs.

He then assured me that he was the direct cause through Mr. Dun, lately U.S. Minister to Japan, of the issuance of the circular from the Department of State, last Spring, in regard to missionaries, and that now that I was provided with these definite instructions for regulating these people, he would feel it his duty to call my attention to any violation of these public printed instructions. I told him it would be unnecessary for him to trouble himself as I felt quite capable of carring out the instructions of my government, and he was quick to assure me that he felt sure he would have no cause to complain.

I then told him that as he had been frank, I wished also to frankly tell him that I had heard it reported that he had at various times spoken in a manner very uncomlimentary towards America and Americans, and that he had stated to certain Koreans that "no Korean entertaining friendly sentiments toward America should have a place in the Government".

He replied with some agitation, that he believed in but one party in Korea and that should be the party of the King: That he had said to some Koreans that their should be no American party in Korea, that America was the place for that: that the King had asked for Russian advice and he intended to advise him: that conflicting advice could only produce disorder: that if a Korean official gave good advice he would be allright, if he gave bad advice he would have to go, whether he might be friendly to England, America, Japan or Russia.

While this answer was rather general, I though it best not to press matters further than to say, that I wished to assure him that my Government would tolerate no meddling on the part of our missionaries with Korean politics, and while I understood my duty in preventing such interference, I was also well aware that my government would most faithfully support and protect its own interests, and I could not let pass unnoticed the dismissal of an official at the request of another power for the simply reason that he was friendly to the United States.

Whereupon we had much friendly talk upon the close and amicable relations that our two countries have so long sustained toward each other, but I fear all that is said of him is true and that he is a rash man who will make trouble. He has many enemies here among his own people, who resent his persistent efforts to have Mr. Waeber recalled, and they are doing what they can to prepare the way for the latter's return. From what I have heard these people say, I infer that they expect Mr. de Speyer's vigorous measures to get him into serious trouble by so complicating the situation as to demand his being relieved.

Horace N. Allen.

No. 57   Legation of the United States
                                                Seoul Korea, January 7, 1898.

Secretary of State

Sir:-

In my No. 52, Dec. 30, replying to your earnest admonitions as to my conduct in these times of international controversy in Korea, and the necessity of caution upon the part of our people here, I took occassion to remark that my admonitions had been kindly received by our people, who were conducting themselves well.

I am sorry now to have to inform you that the editors of the "Repository" have erred and done just what they agreed not to do. This "Repository" is a monthly magazine, published in English at Seoul, by two clerical missionaries of the American Methodist Mission. It has no connection whatever with the Mission proper, and is supposed to be a literary journal and repository of facts. As such it is esteemed by all. Of late however, it has shown a marked tendency to dabble in politics and act as a censor upon the doings of the nations represented in Korea. Owing to some ill-timed remarks published about the time of the arrival in Seoul of the present Russian Representative, Mr. de Speyer spoke to me of this journal and I assured him that we did not favor utterances such as he complained of, and that I would speak to the editors upon the subject. I did so, and they cheerfully agreed to confine themselves to a mere chronicling of facts of a political nature, without comment.

In the December number of the magazine, issued Jan. 4, I was amazed to see that the editors had gathered up most of the adverse criticism of Russian acts in Korea, published in the English papers of Japan, and had so quoted these as to give one the impression that they represent the views of this journal, and therefore of the large body of American Missionaries in Korea.

I saw the Superintendent of the Methodist Mission, who fully agreed with me that the publication of this magazine was not the proper work of missionaries; that such publications as the one I cited could only work injury to all Americans in Korea, and he further stated that he had many times urged the suppression of this puplication entirely. I then saw the editor in chief Rev. H. G. Appenzeller, who, after some discussion as to the question of propriety and right in the matter of such quotations, and after I had told him what I might of my recent instructions, was convinced that he had erred, and after some deliberation he gave me a written statment, agreeing to observe the strictest care in regard to such publications in the future. I hand you enclosed a copy of his letter.

I also enclose a marked copy of the number of the "Repository" in question, and send you under separate cover, two extra copies, which you may wish to use.

I can do no more in these matters than I have done. I feel sure that the Mission Boards who support these people will be only too glad to heed the admonitions of, and cooperate with, the Department in compelling caution on the part of their workers here. A few of these people have the unfortunate, and at present, most pernicious habit, of corresponding with the papers in China and Japan, upon the Korean political situation. All this comes back to us here and places us in a most unfavorable light.

I respectfully suggest, therefore, that the Department correspond with these societies, with the view of getting them to issue strict instructions to their employees in Korea, to abstain from all such writing. I feel sure that this, with what I may be able to do here, will finally settle this vexed question of missionary intermeddling with Korean political affairs.

While the complaints I make do not particularly apply to each of the Missions, I hand you the addresses of all the American Mission Societies opperating in Korea, in order that you may impartially address them all alike, if such course is thought to be wise.

The addresses of these Mission Boards are as follows: -

The Presbyterian Board of Foreign Missions,
    53, Fifth Avenue, New York City.
The Methodist Episcopal Board of Foreign Missions,
    150 Fifth Avenue, New York City.
Board of Missions of the Methodist Church South,
    Nashville Tenn.
Board of Missions of the Presbyterian Church South,
    P.O. Box, 457, Nashville Tenn.
The "Ella Thing Memorial Mission" of the Baptist Church,
    P.O. Box, 3423, Boston, Mass.

Horace N. Allen.

No. 281

Legation of the United States
Seoul, Korea, September 15, 1900.

Secretary of State

Sir:-

I have the honor to hand you a short report upon Missionaries and the Far Eastern Question, being a brief reply to many inquiries I have received for such information, prepared for publication should the Department consider it desirable to publish it.

In case the report is published I would like to have fifty copies for distribution among our missionaries in Korea.

Horace N Allen

MISSIONARIES AND THE FAR EASTERN QUESTION

I have received a number of letters of inquiry as to the situation in Korea with relation to the Chinese Question, as well as several somewhat flattering requests for articles upon the same subject for publication. I have heeded the Departments instructions relative to writing for publication and have declined to comply with these requests. I submit the following to the Department however, touching upon the main points covered by these requests.

Our interests in Korea are cheifly commercial and philanthropic or missionary.

We have about 250 Americans resident in Korea, over 150 of whom are connected with missionary work.

American commercial interests are chiefly represented by gold mining operations and such construction work as the building of railroads; electric plants and similar improvements. When the present American electric plant is completed, giving to Seoul an overhead trolley railroad some 27 miles in length with a complete system of electric lighting, Korea will have the largest electric plant in Asia.

It was feared that when the gold mines should actually be developed and operated by foreigners, much opposition would be met with on the part of the natives. These fears have not been realized. Some opposition did appear at first on the part of petty officials who had profited by handling the proceeds of the work of the native miners, but the people themselves finding that they would be given employment at good and sure wages, with no danger of "squeeze" soon learned to appreciate their improved opportunties, and the mining district is now said to be the most prosperous of the surounding regions. The American mining company gives employment to some 3000 natives and employs 60 or more foreigners in its works. Money has become comparitively plenty in their district and supplies are furnished by the company at such reasonable rates that the standard of living is materially improved.

It was feared that the railways would also meet with much opposition. The street railway did experience some trouble at the outset from the annimosity of the carriers, but that has practically passes away.

During the early part of the troubles in China it was feared that the disturbances might spread across the northern border into Korea, for the Koreans are really Chinese in their sympathies and there is no doubt that they sympathize with their "Elder Brothers" in the recent uprisings. The Government of Korea however, took great pains to demonstrate the fact that it was not in sympathy with the "Boxers", and if a knowledge of the results of the Chinese uprisings is well disseminated among the Korean people, no further fears need probably be entertained of similar occurrences in Korea.

As a rule our American Missionaries in Korea are of a particularly high class, and their intelligence is well shown in the fact that they carefully abstain from supporting their followers in their contentions with the local magistrates. The native Christians in Korea have oftentimes a very hard lot, for the very fact that adherence to the instruction of their teachers induces more or less temporal prosperity, makes them a target for designing officials who would like to get control of their little accumulations. The constant listening to these heartrending tales of persecution has often caused the missionary, especially if she be a lady, to break down from pure sympathy and overstrained compassion. Yet the general policy is a wise one and the converts obtained under such conditions are a hardy set, capable of becoming martyrs.

The conditions of mission work in Korea and China are much the same. In each country our people enjoy extrateritorial rights and are chargeable only before their own Consuls. In China it is even more favorable for the missionary, for by virtue of the French agreements with China, the Priest has more or less judicial powers and can greatly influence the local magistrate in favoring a Christian client or petitioner. Although our people could claim the same privileges by virtue of the "most favored nation clause" I understand they do not avail themselves of their full right, and in many instances actually refuse to accept a convert who has on hand a "case at court". At the same time a great deal of protection must incidentally come to even the protestant converts, and in spite of the fact that the missionary body includes such a high class of men, there are unfortunately too many who are not able to wisely enjoy the wonderfully broad priviledges they have in being amenable to no law but that dispensed by a Consul who may be hundreds of miles distant. Even if the individual missionary may not desire to influence justice in favor of his follower, the banding together of so many natives as Christians, and the knowledge that through their foreign leader these people may go over the head of the local magistrate and reach the ear of the high authority at Pekin, cannot but influence the local judge in his verdicts lest he lose his expensively purchased position. In this way actual injustice may be done and a bitter spirit of opposition may be engendered among the natives less favored, or who feel, justly or otherwise, that they have not been treated with fairness.

It has long been a question as to whether or not it was wise to allow the foreign missionary to reside so far from the jurisdiction of his authorities, and whether it would not have been better to restrict missionary residence to the open ports, where by the maintenance of schools, seminaries and hospitals for the education of native teachers, preachers and doctors, a body of native missionaries could be raised up who could be sent into the interior to gather together companies of believers who might be further instructed from time to time, by the itinerant missionary travelling on a passport.

In Korea, foreign residence, except in the case of distant mines covered by special concession, is restricted to the open ports and a defined radius therefrom. Yet some of our people, following the example of persons of other nationalities, have gone into the interior upon passport and have acquired a permanent residence far from the localities defined by treaty. In these cases they have avoided violating the strict letter of the law by buying the property in the name of a native helper, who has then given a private document covering the transaction so as to safeguard the foreign interest. The Legation has had nothing to do with furthering these transactions yet it has had to seem to support them in one or two instances, in protecting American interests in view of what is allowed to people of other nationalities.

While there is not in Korea anything like the opposition to Christianity that exists in China, the elements for inciting such opposition are present, and when the work has reached something approaching the magnitude of its scope in China, we may expect similar results. Certainly the Chinese have some reason for the opposition they have so unwisely shown. A distasteful religion is more or less forced upon them to the temporal detriment of those who refuse to accept it, and when the masses rise in opposition to it, the foreign nations exact such severe indemnities that the natives are compelled to witness the loss of portions of their territory or the collection of increased dues to cover resulting money indemnities. As an Italian Priest has well said; the mission work of his church was far better off when they had not the violent protection that is witnessed of late, when they took their lives in their hands and were willing to become martyrs for the cause if necessary, then, he says, the people realized the disinterestedness of their motives as they cannot now realize it.

There seems to be quite a controversy going on at home as to whether or not the missionary work is responsible for the present troubles in China. The representatives of the work seem generally to hold that the work of the missionary is not responsible. The controversy seems to be an idle one. There can be no question as to the facts. The mission work supported as it now is and used as it too often is as a means of agression, must necessarily be held so responsible. Would it not be better to frankly accept the situation and the responsibility and then put the querry: - Does it pay?

Apparently no well posted person would question the fact of the great service to Christian Civilization, commerce and general enlightenment that has been done by the faithful spread of mission work in all its branches. The details of the execution of this work may perhaps be called in question in some instances, but that would only result in a better understanding and a change to methods that would be quite as beneficial and free from the danger of inducing future trouble.

A more careful selection and training of the mission worker would certianly be in order: Fewer acts in gross violation of native customs and traditions, such as the promiscuous mixing of the sexes in country travelling, would stop much of the cavilling: More restriction upon persons exercising the great priviledges that one who is only amenable to a jurisdiction far removed, must exercise - consciously or otherwise, - would certainly be proper. Frankly, restrict residence to the districts within the immediate jurisdiction of the Consular official before whom alone the foreigner may be charged. And the policy of our missionaries in Korea in refusing to interfere in the contentions of their followers with the local authorities, and their practice of teaching their people to "be subject to the powers that be" is worthy of adoption.

A years service as a medical missionary in the interior of China: Three years similar service in opening Korea to mission work, followed by three years service in the Korean Government and ten years in the Diplomatic Service of the United States in Korea, enables me to see this question from both sides; that of the missionary and that of the official who must stand between the missionary and the local Government in the constantly occuring cases. Perhaps therefore, the above statements and suggestions may be of some service.

Horace N Allen

Legation of the United States,
　　Seoul Korea, September 14, 1900.

No. 300

Legation of the United States
Seoul, Korea, November 22, 1900.

Secretary of State

Sir:-

Continuing the subject of my despatch No. 299 of the 20th instant, regarding an anti-foreign uprising in Korea set for December 6th, I have now the honor to inform you that I have other reports to the same effect from different parts of the country. I enclose a copy of some information given me by the Reverend C. H. Jones regarding the connection of Confucianists with this proposed uprising. I have shown a copy of this informaiton to some of my colleagues and to the Korean Government. I now learn from the

Foreign Minister and from His Majesty that it is true that a secret circular letter has been sent broadcast through the mails to all officers in the country calling for a general uprising on the 15th of the 10th Moon -- December 6th -- for the purpose of killing off the foreigners and the native Christians, and that the author of this circular states that he has the Emperor's secret instructions to issue it. The signature is a fictitious one, and the Government has known of the existence of the circular for some days. None of my colleagues knew of it, however, until I brought it to their attention. The Foreign Minister and His Majesty assure me that they are doing all they can to discover the author of the circular, and upon my urgent presentation of the case and my argument that even though the circular be a fictitious one the uprising might well occur if active measures were not immediately taken to prevent it, very strong telegrams were at once sent all over the country commanding the utmost diligence on the part of the civil and military authorities in preventing any thing tending toward such an uprising. I now hear by telegraph from Dr. Underwood at Hai Chu that "the orders have been countermanded from Seoul". I think therefore that the Government is doing actually all in its power to prevent any trouble of the kind.

I am sure the case is one that called for the most prompt action and I think the steps I took were timely. My Russian colleague has called to thank me for my prompt action and to say that in his opinion the uprising would probably have taken place in a greater or less degree but for this action; while my Japanese colleague has expressed himself in much the same manner in a note of which I sent you a copy.

It is very probable that some innocent persons may be persecuted for the authorship of this circular. Already the two most corrupt officials in the Government service -- Messrs Ye Yong Ik and Kim Yung Chun, of whom I have frequently written, especially in my No. 229 of February 16, 1900 -- are mentioned as the authors of the circular. This mention of these men displeases Mr. Pavlow, as they chance to be friendly to Russia at present.

I have seen it stated in newspapers published in China that the "Boxer" movement was actually set for the 10th Moon, but that it came off prematurely. If this is true I am inclined to believe that concerted action was arranged and the Chinese expected to be supported by the Koreans in their uprising.

I am convinced that His Majesty had no guilty knowledge of this circular. He has taken steps all along to show his disapproval of the troubles in China and his sympathy with the foreigners. Some of his actions in fact -- such as sending supplies to the allied troups -- indicated an almost unaccountable desire to prove his friendly feeling toward foreigners. It is possible he may have feared his inability to fully control the sympathies of his people in the matter.

While I think that the steps already taken will prevent any general uprising, still I have considered it advisable to send a circular letter of caution against exposure by travelling to the heads of the American Missions in Korea: for already, as pointed out in my despatch of the 20th instant, acts of violence have occured, and with the disquiet induced by the circulation of this call for an uprising, I think it best to caution our people. I enclose a copy of this circular.

Horace N Allen

Confidential Circular to American Missionaries.
LEGATION OF THE UNITED STATES,
Seoul Korea, Nov. 22, 1900.
In view of the disturbed condition of the country, and beause of the rumors of a possible anti-foreign and anti-christian movement, designed to take place during the tenth moon, I suggest that you expose yourselves as little as possible during December, by travelling, and especially that the ladies of your missions do not travel, during that month, in the interior of Korea. While I think there will not be any serious trouble, owing to knowledge of the proposed movement having leaked out, yet I think it best to give you the above caution.

Horace N Allen
Sent to the heads of the various American Mission stations in Korea.[*]

H.I.J.M's Legation
Seoul, Korea.
Nov. 20, 1900.

---

*Handwritten

Dear Dr. Allen:-

Thanks for your note. I think the steps taken by the Korean Government are entirely owing to your prompt action. I hope they will stop any real rising. If I have any fresh news I will let you know at once.

(signed) G. Hayashi.

No. 307

Legation of the United States
Seoul, Korea, December 14, 1900.

Secretary of State

Sir:-

Reffering to my despatches Nos. 299 of November 20 and 300 of November 22 last, regarding an anti-foreign uprising that was reported as expected to occur on or about December 6 to 11, I have now the honor to inform you that aside from the decidedly anti-American acts of the Governor of Kyung-Sang province in forcibly entering the quarters of Americans at Taikoo, of which I wrote you in my despatch of yesterday's date, No. 306, and a robbery and attempted murder committed by a Korean in the house of a Japanese merchant in the General Foreign Settlement at Chemulpo, on the night of December 7, there has been no excitement. Frequent robberies have been committed indeed and the country seems to be terrorized by lawless bands of natives, but there has been no general anti-foreign movement.

I feel sure that something of the kind might have been expected had not prompt and vigorous methods been adopted at once upon learning of the existence of the secret circulars mentioned in my despatches above cited.

I have seen one original copy of this circular, a translation of which I now enclose. It bears the seals of the two very corrupt and objectionable Koreans who at present appear to be all powerful in this Government. I refer to Messrs Ye Yong Ik and Kim Yung Chun who have been mentioned frequently in my despatches of late, especially in Nos. 290 of October 20 and 292 of October 29.

I send you also a translation of another one of these circulars which was received by the Governor of Chinampo, Mr. Yun Che Ho, who was educated in the United States. The translation is his own. He had to give up the original.

I enclose a report of the substance of yet another of the circulars, which report was made to me by the Reverend Dr. Underwood.

I hand you a copy of an Imperial Decree, issued on November 23 in response to my representations and widly circulated. Like all such documents it is vague. In fact it is so vague that some of my colleagues thought the Foreign Representatives should complain that the Government was not acting with sufficient vigor. I was able however to prove that this was not the case as I had received from the Reverend S. A. Moffett of Pyeng-Yang a copy of a telegram sent to the Governor of Pyeng-Yang, which I am assured is the same that was sent to the other Governors. I enclose a translation of this telegram which indicates that the Central Government was actually in earnest in its attempts to prevent disorder.

It is believed generally that the seals used upon these circulars were false ones. Messrs Ye Yong Ik and Kim Yong Chun are so universally hated by the natives that it is not improbable that some of their enemies took this means of attempting to get them into trouble. At the same time had not the authenticity of these circulars been denied, it is more than probable that the existence of the circulars merely, knowledge of which was spreading rapidly, would have caused a serious uprising against foreigners. I do not regret the action I took even in telegraphing you on the subject.

Kim Yong Chun published promptly an announcement in a local newspaper pronouncing the impression of his seal attached to this circular a forgery. I send you a translation of this notice from the "Hwang Sung Sin Mun" of November 23.

Our missionaries are refraining from travelling in the country just at present. In addition to the danger from the effects of the secret circular the Government is about to collect increased taxes, the land tax having been raised from six to ten dollars per measure of land. This increase is though by many Koreans to be a very dangerous one and may very well cause disorder, which, if it occurs, will be apt to endanger foreigners.

At my suggestion the American Mining Company is importing three Colt automatic guns and fifty Mauser rifles with an ample store of ammunition with which to protect their issolated mining camps, where any disorder would be likely to become acute.

Horace N Allen

Copy of a translation of an original of a secret circular which came into the possession of the Japanese Minister.

Secret Circular.

Our Eastern Land was founded by Kui Cha. It progressed until the dynasty of Chosun, the rites and ceremonies were modeled upon those of China and the rays of the sun gave light to our country. But the unrighteous religious faiths of Japan and the Western nations have taken hold of our people. Trators murdered the Mother of the Nation (the late Queen) against whom the feeling is so strong that we can not permit the sun to shine both upon them and us. One or two of these trators have been killed but the Queen's murder has not been avenged adequately. The Emperor fears his neighbors, who are Japan and the Western nations, and has given us a secret order, which we hereupon promulgate, that throughout korea all people who entertain the same opinion of foreigners that we do shall meet upon the middle of the 10th moon to destroy the interlopers. They shall first burn the houses of the foreigners at the open ports and then kill their inhabitants, who are as beasts and can not live side by side with the Koreans. Should this order be disobeyed the disobedient shall be considered as trators and shall be treated accordingly.

((signed))

Kim Yung Chun.	seal
Ye Yong Ik	seal

No. 318

Legation of the United States
Seoul, Korea, March 5, 1901.

Secretary of State

Sir:-

I have the honor to hand you a statement in regard to the ill treatment of two American missionaries at Taiku, the capital of the province of North Kyung Sang, to which I alluded in my No. 306 of December 14th, 1900.

The facts are briefly as follows: -

Messrs Adams and Johnson, American missionaries residing under passport at Taiku, had some trouble over a contract for tiles to cover a house they were preparing for themselves at that place in the name of a Korean. The matter was brought to the attention of the local Governor, who is reported as being a man of conservative and rather independent ideas. Upon the order of this Governor the Korean writer employed by the Americans, who had written the contract with the tile-burner, was arrested, the police forcibly entering the domicile of the Americans to make the arrest. The man was taken before the Governor and most inhumanely beaten. When the Americans went to the Governor's Yamen to inquire into the case, the Governor refused to see them, pronounced their official Korean passports valueless and treated them with great indignity, compelling them to stand in the court-yard with the rabble, and refusing to hear their explanations though they were the principal parties to the transaction under discussion.

Mr. Adams telegraphed me upon December 5th and I sent him immediately a long telegram en claire in which I stated that the Governor was at fault and that I would take up the matter with the Korean Government. I saw the Foreign Minister as soon as possible and obtained from him an order for the release of the Korean writer Kim, which however did not reach Taiku for some days owing to a sudden break in the telegraph lines. The Governor had in the meantime presumably read while in transmission my telegram to Mr. Adams for he at once announced that his mother had died and left his post to go into mourning. Upon December 17th I formally addressed the Foreign Minister as per enclosure No. 1, detailing the case upon information received from the Reverend Mr. Adams by letter and contending that the Treaty had been violated in four particulars. I saw the Foreign Minister several times and insisted on his replying to my letter. Upon January 25th he replied by quoting from a report of the Acting Governor, who was one of the chief culprits. This reply was not satisfactory and was almost if not quite discourteous. The principal points in this reply are included in a letter which I prepared on February 1st.

In 1890 a French priest was very badly treated at this same city of Taiku, his property was stolen and he himself was imprisoned. This incident formed the subject of despatch, No. 141 of April 2, 1891, from Mr. Heard, to which Mr. Adee replied in No. 95 of May 19, 1891, instructing him to demand equal rights and privileges for Americans. No such demand has had to demand equal rights and privileges for Americans. No such demand has had to be made, as our people have kept "within the letter" of the Treaties, but I thought I might well use these instructions in this case. I wrote therefore another letter, referred to above as having been prepared upon February 1st, replying to the chief points of the letter of the acting Governor of Taiku and enclosing a memorandum of the French case of 1890-1891. In this communication I informed the Foreign Minister that I was compelled reluctantly to fall back upon instructions my predecessor had received in connection with the above cited French case, and that in view of the fact that the action of his Government had rendered practically inoperative the treaty provisions restricting the residence of foreigners to the open ports, I should inform my people that they were at liberty to live anywhere in the interior where foreigners of other nationalities were sojourning. This I knew would be a most distasteful measure, for Japanese are living everywhere throughout the interior and the Government greatly desires to induce them to leave. If I should adopt such a course it could not be otherwise than very agreeable to the Japanese.

My object in writing this letter was that I might lay the whole matter before His Majesty and have the position of the Americans at Taiku made more comfortable. His Majesty has requested me to consult with him personally before taking any decisive action with the Foreign Office. I wrote this letter therefore with the intention of sending it informally to the Emperor to read before delivering it. I felt certain that His Majesty would not permit it to go officially to the Foreign Office, a surmise in which I proved to be correct when the translation of the letter was returned me with the request that I retain it for a few days while His Majesty had the Foreign Minister adjust the matter to my satisfaction.

The Foreign Minister called upon me twice and arranged with me that he should write a careful instruction to the Governor of North Kyung Sang Do, who had meantime succeeded the former one, and that he should send me a polite and satisfactory letter on the subject. He offered to punish or dismiss the chief culprit, Noh Chusa, but in discussing the matter he begged that I would allow the new Governor to examine first the said Noh. This suggestion met with my approval, as I did not desire the man to be punished without a hearing. I agreed to send the Foreign Minister an unofficial copy of my withheld letter of February 1st, that he might give it to the new Governor for his guidance.

Upon February 26th the Foreign Minister sent me therefore a letter, a translation of which I enclose, It proved to be unsatisfactory as it did not include a copy of the instruction of the Foreign Minister to the newly appointed Governor of North Kyung Sang Province, and said nothing in regard to the examination and punishment of Noh Chusa. I had my interpreter return it in person with a verbal statement as to the ommissions, and upon the same day I received a satisfactory reply, a translation of which I enclose, handing me a copy of the Foreign Minister's instructions to the Governor, a translation of which instructions I enclose also.

I consider this settlement of the case to be satisfactory. The actual money loss was made good finally by the local officials at Taiku. The Americans themselves ware not harmed, and for the violation of their treaty rights, their presence at Taiku is now officially recognized and sanctioned. I think they will experience no further difficulty.

In the discussion of this case I have had to allude to the robbery by highwaymen of the Americans near Taiku, which occurred upon October 14th last, and which I have referred to in my No. 301 of November 25th. This case is also now in process of settlement. I have received one note from the Foreign Minister upon the subject and I think he will do all he can to secure justice. I do not consider it necessary to ask for instructions in regard to the matter and I will report upon it at length when I have brought it to a settlement, or if I fail to obtain satisfaction.

Horace N Allen

No. 410   Legation of the United States
                                             Seoul, Korea, October 14, 1901.

Secretary of State

Sir:-

I have the honor to call your attention to the enclosed correspondence relating to the satisfactory settlement of troubles between the American Missionaries of the Methodist Church, and the Governor of Soowon, -- the large provincial capital some 20 miles Southwest of Seoul.

It seems that the Rev. Wilbur C. Swearer, who itinerates in that region, furnished money to his Korean Employee, Kim Tong Hiun, with which to purchase a couple of small houses in Soowon for a native helper to reside in, one of which was to be kept in order for the use of the Missionary on his country trips. When the news of this purchase came to the ears of the Governor, he had the employee of the American arrested and demanded from him the return of the deeds on the alleged ground that he had bought property in the interior for a foreigner, in violation of treaty stipulations. As a matter of fact the deeds were in the name of two native christians, and the treaty provisions had not been violated. Further a large French Catholic establishment is openly maintained at Soowon, while an Englishman and a number of Japanese have houses there.

Bearing in mind the endorsement of the Department contained in your despatch No. 166 of April 18, replying to my No. 318 of March 5, relative to the matter of the violation of the domicile of American Missionaries at Taiku, Korea; and believing this action of the Governor of Soowon to be unjust, and contrary to the provision of Art. IV Sec. 6 of the British Treaty granting permission for travel in the interior on passport, as well as of Art. IX Sec. 1, of the same treaty, which by "the most favored nation clause" provides that Americans "in Korea shall be allowed to employ" Korean subjects as teachers, interpreters, servants, or in any other lawful capacity, without any restriction on the part of the Korean authorities", I at once saw the Minister for Foreign Affairs, on September 28, and requested the immediate release of Mr. Swearer's helper. The Minister saw the justice of my request and sent orders to the Governor of Soowon for the release of the man. The Governor, instead of complying with these instructions, placed the man in the felons' quarters of the jail, and wrote a reply to the Minister for Foreign Affairs saying that the property was bought for the foreigners, who intended to build a church thereon, and as the land was near to an ancient Korean temple, he, the Governor, would not release the man until he secured the return of the deeds.

Hearing of the man's increased punishment, I again saw the Foreign Minister and told him, among other things, that our people had no intentions of erecting a foreign building on the site in question. As a result of our conversation, the Minister asked me to put my statements in the form of a despatch, and he would see that the man was released.

I did so as per copy of my despatch, dated October 4. When the Governor received a copy of this despatch from the Minister for Foreign Affairs, he was said to have placed Kim in the stocks with his limbs so stretched as to cause him much agony, - further the Governor was reported as having threatened the man with death if he did not promptly turn over the deeds.

At this stage, I sent the matter direct to the Emperor, detailing the whole case. His Majesty at once issued an order over the seal of the Home (Interior) Department for the immediate release of the man.

I sent Rev. Geo. H. Jones, the Superintendent of the Mission, - a man of good tact and bearing, together with Mr. Swearer, and one of my Legation runners, with my card to the Governor of Soowon, to see that these orders were carried out, and with the view of clearing up the whole matter.

They reached Soowon on the 10th. instant and were received by the Governor, who pretended to be unaware of the extreme measures said to have been adopted, and explained that the site in question was exceedingly objectionable owing to its close proximity to the sacred temple before mentioned. The Governor gave our people full permission to secure other property in Soowon; released the man Kim, as well as some other christians, who had been arrested in his district for other reasons, and our people are eminently satisfied with the result, agreeing to hand back the deeds for the property in question on receipt of the money paid, and to secure other property in Soowon.

I believe the man Kim was not as badly treated as his friends reported.

I enclose a report from Mr. Swearer in regard to the settlement of the case, and I think our people will have no further trouble at Soowon.

                                             Horace N Allen

No. 185

Department of State
Washington, November 19, 1901

Gordon Paddock

Sir:

I have to acknowledge the receipt of Mr. Allen's despatch No. 410, of the 14th ultimo, reporting that the Governor of Soowon imprisoned a Korean employee of the Reverend N. C. Swearer, an American missionary of the Methodist Episcopal Church, on the alleged ground that he had bought property in the interior for a foreigner in violation of treaty stipulations.

The Department is gratified to learn from Mr. Allen's despatch that the matter has been satisfactorily settled.

The reported transaction having taken place in the interior, outside of the treaty ports, and having been effected in the name of a native Korean, did not fall within the purview of Article VI of the treaty of 1882.

It was simply a question of comity, as to whether the American missionary, who furnished the money to the native for the purchase, under a contract of occupancy by the lender, should enjoy the indirect privileges which appear to be enjoyed by citizens of other nationalities. The local authorities appear to have acquiesced in his claim, the only question being as to the proximity of the foreign leased premises to a sacred temple. Under the circumstances the latter point may be deemed to have been well taken. Our treaty with Korea is silent in this regard, but the principle laid down in the treaty of 1858 with China as to foreign rental and occupancy of houses and sites in the open ports of China may be an appropriate criterion with regard to such rental or occupancy in the non-treaty towns of Korea. It is therin stipulated, that on the one hand the local authorities shall not interfere "unless there be objections offered on the part of the inhabitants respecting the place" and on the other hand that "The citizens of the United States shall not unreasonably insist on particular spots, but each party shall conduct with justice and moderation" These provisions replace the older provisions of Article XVII of the treaty of 1844 with China, preserving the spirit of the stipulation that in selecting sites for foreign occupancy, due regard shall be had "to the feelings of the people in the location thereof."

David J. Hill

No. 493

Legation of the United States
Seoul, Korea, August 19, 1902.

Secretary of State

Sir:-

Continuing the subject of my despatch of today, No. 491 regarding the difficulty experienced in transacting business with the Korean Government, I now have the honor to acquaint you with another case, in which I was obliged to threaten to telegraph the facts to my Government.

This was made necessary by the arrest and reported torture of a teacher of an American missionary for aiding in purchasing certain property in the city of Seoul.

The facts are briefly, that while the American missionaries settled around their Legation in Seoul, the building of the present palace in that locality compelled them to move out. The place was no longer suitable for their work, and they did not wish to displease the authorities by refusing to sell.

They went to a distant part of the city where there can be no valid objection to their residing, and began to purchase property. Some little difficulty having been experienced I saw the Emperor and informed him of the circumstances. The difficulty was stopped for the time and His Majesty assured me there could be no objection to purchase of land by our people, in that region. Such assurances are of litte value however, for some petty offical who may have some ulterior design of his own, may easily get an order to make difficulty by urging some imaginary wrong.

Recently these missionaries completed their purchase and sent in their deeds for registration. Almost immediately their employees were arrested, and I wrote to the Foreign Minister on July 16, as per enclosed copy, citing the treaty and noting the violation that had been made.

Learning on the 19'th. that my letter had had no effect and being assured by Dr. Vinton, the missionary whose teacher had been locked up, that the latter was being brutally tortured, and that his family had witnessed a part of the torture, I wrote a second letter as per copy enclosed, demanding the release of the man and announcing that if he was not released by the 21'st. I would telegraph my Government. He was released on the night of the 21'st.

I received a reply from the Foreign Minister dated July 23'rd. denying that the teacher had been tortured, which I found to be chiefly correct, since the man had greatly misrepresented his sufferings, and had imposed upon his employer and myself thereby. See copy.

The Foreign Minister urged a feeble complaint made by the Governor, to the effect that the property in question could not be registered because it lay too near to an unused palace. I offered to take part in a joint investigation of this subject but my offer has not been accepted and probably will not be, for the reason that the excuse urged for the refusal to register the deeds, will probably be found to be a very weak one.

I presume I will have to follow the example of other of my colleagues and simply have these Americans occupy this property upon the quit claim deed of the former owner, pending some proper arrangement for the regular issuance of deeds.

I brought the subject before the last meeting of the Foreign Representatives, with the result that we are now preparing a scheme to submit to the Korean Government whereby they may make certain reservations of land within the walls of Seoul, such land not being purchaseable by foreigners, but other sites are to be open to purchase and prompt attention must be given to the issuance of deeds. Present ownership is to be recognized.

Something of the kind must be acted upon, as the present condition is so bad that the very fact that a foreigner has purchased ground is sufficient to cause Korean authorities to try to make the purchaser trouble.

                                                                    Horace N Allen

No. 700   Legation of the United States
                                                           Seoul, Korea, March 16, 1904.

Secretary of State

Sir:-

I have the honor to acknowledge the receipt on yesterday of your despatch No. 252 of February 10, handing me copies of correspondence from Reverend Arthur Judson Brown, relative to the safety of the Presbyterian missionaries in Korea.

I also confirm my telegram of today regarding my efforts to bring the women and children to a place of safetly.

The missionaries at Pengyang city sent me frequent messages by wire and mail, asking for the presence of a ship in the near by waters; for a marine guard to be stationed near them; and generally intimating that they considered their situation serious.

Desiring to do all in my power to assist them and the Pengyang inlet being fully closed by ice at the time, I informed them that at the first opportunity I would send a ship up there to take off the women and children. I at the same time, requested those in the far north to come to Pengyang. All the latter did so with the exception of one family, which were reported to me as detained by sickness. I now learn that the man, a physician, regarded it as his duty to remain with the Koreans and his wife refused to leave him. Being on friendly terms with the Russian troops whom he is said to have assisted in some manner - presumably medically, it was though he would not be disturbed.

The example of this family seems to have had the effect upon the Pengyang people of inducing them to remain, though while not ordering them to send their women and children away, I stated plainly that I could not send a ship a second time.

Only one family came from Pengyang on the "Cincinnatti" and they were leaving for America anyway and found this a convenient means of starting.

From the American mines and the far north, twenty four came altogether by the cruiser "Cincinnatti" arriving in Chemulpo yesterday. They were mostly women and children.

If the Japanese continue to prosper in the war, there is little danger of trouble at Pengyang, in which case the Americans there will be same enough.

                                                                    Horace N Allen

No. 828

Legation of the United States
Seoul, Korea, November 21, 1904.

Secretary of State

Sir:-

In my No. 542 of November 28, 1902, I advised you of the laying of the corner stone of the Severance Memorial Hospital in Seoul, - a charitable institution provided for by Mr. L. H. Severance of Cleveland Ohio. I have now to inform you that this institution has been completed and is in active operation, a formal opening having been held in the building on the 16th instant. This opening was attended by most of the foreign ministers resident in Seoul as well as by quite a representative gathering of foreigners and Korean officials.

This institution is under the control of the Presbyterian Mission Board of 156 Fifth Avenue, New York City.

A Japanese official sent to Seoul to report upon the sanitary conditions here, is reported as having stated that while Japan has larger hospitals, they have none so complete and up to date as this one.

I have the honor to hand you enclosed a short report upon the institution and its scope and the intentions of its managers and supporters.

This is practically the only general hospital for this city with its three hundred thousand population. It is a fine testimonial to the charitable intentions of Americans toward this people.

Horace N Allen

No. 853

American Legation, Seoul, Korea.
December 29, 1904.

Secretary of State

Sir:-

In my No. 834, of the 3rd instant, I handed you copies of a correspondence I had had with the Korean Minister for Foreign Affairs, resulting in the punishment of a minor Korean official at Pengyang, for injustice to American missionaries of the Presbyterian Board, No. 156, Fifth Avenue, New York.

I now have the honor to hand you enclosed copies of a letter from Dr. S. A. Moffett showing that the effect of this action has been to bring about a much more friendly attitude on the part of the Pengyang officials to our people, even to the extent of inducing them to go to Church - an effect not exactly contemplated in the attempt to secure redress of wrongs and a better future treatment.

Horace N. Allen.

C. American Advisors

No. 95

Department of State
Washington, September 20, 1898,

Horace N. Allen

Sir:

The Department has received your despatch No. 132, of the 8th ultimo, in regard to the claims of General W. M. Dye against the Government of Korea.

Your report that General Dye was one of three military officers selected by General Sheridan, at the request of the Korean Government, through the State Department, as instructors for said Government; that General Dye arrived in Korea in the spring of 1888, and contracted to serve as military instructor for a period of two years at the rate of five thousand dollars silver per annum; that this contract was renewed from time to time at six thousand, sixty-eight hundred, and eight thousand dollars per annum, the last sum being for the period of two years on the contract made in 1894; that during these eight years of service, his salary was frequently in arrears, and the Legation used its good offices in getting for him at least a portion of his dues; that about 1896, he was mentioned as manager of the Government Farm, which service he accepted, but performed no work in that connection, and months afterwards endeavored to put through a scheme of his own for a farm, ignoring his connection with the Government Farm; that General Dye, in the summer of 1897, requested your predecessor to demand salary from the Korean Government for services in connection with this farm; that after your appointment as Minister you presented the matter unofficially to the Minister of the Household, and got the promise of settlement, resulting in the payment to General Dye of three thousand dollars, which was paid to him on April 30, last.

You state that on April 19 last, General Dye handed to you a further claim of $4,209.86, alleged to be due him, covering a period of ten years, on a bill of items of interest for deferred payments, for medical bills, house repairs, horse keep, money advanced for purchases, and traveling expenses; that when you began negotiating for the collection of the three thousand dollars above mentioned, you supposed that this was a final settlement, and that you should have been so informed at the time if such was not the case; and stating that you hesitate to undertake the matter of the collection of this claim without instructions, and that you asked General Dye to furnish you with the orders upon which he made the expenditures.

Your refer to his complaints against your conduct and to the extent of the assistance rendered him.

You further report that in 1895 General Dye went to America for his son, upon a supposed request from His Majesty, but that you could get no admission that such request was made and that no recognition has been made of the claim on behalf of the son by the Korean Government; that this claim and that of the father amount to nearly nine thousand dollars. You refer to Mr. Uhl's instruction No. 4, May 31, 1894, to Mr. Sill, that "Americans are aware of what they are exposing themselves to in entering the Korean service", and you state, that no one knew of this condition of things better than General Dye; and that his troubles have arisen from his own careless business methods, and from his neglecting the admonitions of the Legation, and that you do not think the favorable disposition of the Korean Government towards American citizens should be made use of to enforce questionable personal claims.

The Department concurs in the views expressed by you on the facts stated, and approves your action in the premises. If, on a full and careful consideration of the matter, you feel that you ought not further to extend your good offices in the collection of these claims, and that to do so would have the appearance of bad faith and injustice towards the Korean Government, you are authorized to decline to take any further action, and you are at liberty to inform General Dye of the tenor of this instruction, and the decision of the Department.

Alvey A. Adee

No. 101

Legation of the United States
Seoul, Korea, April 27, 1898.

Secretary of State

Sir,

I have the honor to inform you that the Korean Government has dispensed with the services of one of its American Advisers, Dr. Philip Jaesohn, paying him the full amount due him on the unexpired term of his contract, which was made in 1895 for a period of ten years. The amount paid him was 28,800 yen, ($14,400 gold).

Dr. Jaisohn is a Korean by birth, but naturalized in America. This naturalization seems to me to be in violation of the. Revised Statutes as quoted in Diplomatic Instructions, Par. 140, but as he brought Passport No. 5031, issued Nov. 8, 1895 by Secretary Olney, he was accepted as an American citizen by my predecessor and I did not raise the question when his case demanded consideration.

As an impetuous young student of military science in Japan, Dr. Jaisohn, whose Korean name was Soh Jai Pill, became involved in the bloody emeute of 1884, in Seoul, and had to flee from the country. He went to America; educated himself; secured a good position in our civil service; graduated in medicine; married an estimable young American lady, and practiced his profession in Washington, until the Autumn of 1895, when he left for Korea at the urgent request of the then Korean Cabinet. He was made Advisor to the Government, and later began the publication of a news-paper in English and Korean, in the interest of the Korean Government. This paper, the "Independent" is generally conceded as having been one of the greatest instruments of enlightenment and progress Korea has ever had. It was the first paper to be published in these languages in Korea. The editor, by attacking corruption in high places won the bitter emnity of an official who afterwards became for a short time Minister for Foreign Affairs, and while in that position secured the dismissal of Dr. Jaisohn. I enclose copy of a letter to me on the subject from this Minister, Mr. Chyo Pyengchik, as well as my reply to the same.

While this correspondence took place in December last, a settlement was not reached till a few days ago, because of the fact that the three gentlemen who have held the Foreign Office Portfollio since then, as well as almost all the people, did not wish him to leave.

The Russian Legation, under Mr. Waeber, had much to do with starting the "Independent" and encouraging the Independence Club of which Dr. Jaisohn was the leader. Mr. Waeber's successor, Mr. de Speyer, did not approve of Dr. Jaisohn, his paper or his Club, and he is largely responsible for Dr. Jaisohn's dismissal. The present Russian Representative, Mr. Matunine, has expressed to me his regret that Dr. Jaisohn is to leave and does not wish the paper discontinued. Dr. Jaisohn leaves for Washington in a few days, although strong efforts are being made by many high officials to have him retained.

He thinks it would be an act of bad faith to listen to these overtures after having been paid off and dismissed.

Horace N. Allen.

No. 50,

Korean Minister for Foreign Affairs, to the Minister Resident and Consul General of the United States.

Seoul, December 13, 1897.

Sir:-

In continuation of our conversation of yesterday, regarding the dismissal of the American Adviser Jaisohn, I find that he was not employed by our Government upon the recommendation of Your Excellency's Government, but by the recommendation of some private individual at the time.

It is ijconvenient for us to wait for the fulfillment of his contract, and we wish to terminate it and dismiss him now.

I now request therefore that you will have him return his unexpired contract.

Signed - Chyo Pyung Sik
Minister for Foreign Affairs

No. 22, F. G.   Legation of the United States
                                                     Seoul Korea, December 14, 1897.

Chyo Pyung Sik
Minister for Foreign Affairs

Sir:-

I have Your Excellency's letter of yesterdays date, continuing the subject of our conversation of yesterday in regard to the American adviser to the Korean Gov'mt, Dr. Philip Jaisohn.

You state that you wish to terminate his contract and give as the reason, "that he was not employed by our Government upon the recommendation of Your Excellency's Government".

I am surprised to hear of this objection, which was not mentioned yesterday, and must inform Your Excellency that it is not the policy of the Government of the United States to recommend Foreign Governments to give employment to its citizens, and the Diplomatic Agents of the United States carefully refrain from recommending any person at home or abroad for any employment of trust or profit under the Governments to which they are accredited. I have personally, on several occasions, declined to accede to requests from the Korean Gov'mt to recommend Americans for positions of trust and profit in the Korean Departments, and none of the Americans now drawing salaries from your Government were recommended for these positions by or through this Legation. So that the objection that Dr. Jaisohn was not so recommended does not influence me.

Dr. Jaisohn was given a contract as adviser, by the reactionary Cabinet in power after the death of the Queen. His contract was recognized and sanctioned by the present Government, which came into power when His Majesty was relieved from restraint. The present Gov'mt has seen fit to give him increased duties and responsibilities, and I know of no instance in which he is charged with any fault in the excecution of the duties imposed upon him. On the contrary, I have heard him universally spoken of in terms of praise for the work he has done.

Nothing in our conversation of yesterday, or in Your letter, to which this is meant as a respectful reply, convinces me of any guilt or misbehavior on the part of this American citizen in connection with the discharge of the duties which he contracted to discharge, and I see no valid reason for breaking his contract.

Neither Dr. Jaisohn or myself however, wish to inconvenience the Korean Government, or force upon it the services of an American where they seem not to be desired. I have consulted with Dr. Jaisohn, and he therefore authorizes me to say that he is willing to surrender his contract upon receiving payment in full for the unexpired term still remaining.

Horace N. Allen

No. 466   <u>Confidential</u>   Legation of the United States
                                                                   Seoul, Korea, May 26, 1903.[*]

Secretary of State

Sir:-

I have the honor to hand you copies of a correspondence I have had with the Korean Foreign Office, relative to the employment of an American as adviser to that office.

In an audience with the Emperor on the eve of my departure for America last autumn, he personally requested me to secure a good man for that position. He was quite insistent though I did what I could to discourage him. On my return I announced that I had been unable to learn of a suitable man. For the past two months I have received renewed and repeated requests that I get an American for this position, and finally His Majesty sent me word that he wished me to ask my Government to assist him in the matter.

My reply was to the effect that I could not address my Government upon the subject unless it should be made official and the terms etc. stated in a despatch from the Foreign Office, since otherwise, if the man should come here without any such official arrangement, there might be changes in the Government that would cause much delay and difficulty in arranging his contract.

The Emperor was reluctant to have a letter sent me from the Foreign Office with nothing to precede it, lest he be accused of showing undue preference for Americans,

At his request therefore, I agreed to write to the Foreign Minister and cite a previous correspondence on the subject, stating the terms upon which I would proceed in the matter. This was highly acceptable and I was promised a prompt and satisfactory reply. When the reply came however, it was equivocal and undecided and altogether unsatisfactory.

Evidently some one had induced the Emperor to change his mind and he ordered the writing of a reply that might be taken as an acceptance or a refusal. The local news-papers announced that an American adviser had been asked for.

I replied to this letter, declining to act upon it, or to listen to further suggestions in regard to the employement of an American for the post in question.

American interests have never been enhanced by any of the American advisers Korea has employed in the past, They have usually been men who have been in the U.S. Service and they have been inclined to wish to control this Legation and failing in this they have in some noted cases taken what little influence they had to the legation of some other nationality. No advisor has been able to accomplish much however for the reason that the Koreans have not acted upon any such advice unless it conformed with their own desires and intentions. They have sometimes used the Adviser as a buffer in some of their foreign complications and for that reason I felt reluctant to assist in calling a man here who might lead us into some of the severe complications this unhappy country seems plunging into.

I could not flatly refuse to listen to the Emperor's request, but I am glad the matter has turned out thus.

---

*This document was dated incorrectly. The correct date is May 26, 1902.

I enclose copy of my letter to the Foreign Office of 1899, and the reply thereto: My letter of May 13 and the reply of the Foreign Minister, and my final answer.

Horace N Allen

No. 601   Legation of the United States
                                                               Seoul, Korea, April 23, 1903.

Secretary of State

Sir:-
        I have the honor to inform you that on the 14'th. instant I received a despatch from the Korean Minister for Foreign Affairs, as per copy enclosed, informing me that the Korean Government intends to dispense with the services of Mr. R. Krumm, an American employed as Engineer in the Survey Bureau, and asking me to notify Mr. Krumm that his contract will not be renewed upon its expiration on August 31'st. next. I enclose a copy of my reply complying with this request, and of Mr. Paddock's letter to Mr. Krumm conveying the information to him. I also enclose a copy of Mr. Krumm's reply with its attached enclosures, as well as a copy of his contract.
        As the case of this man has formed the subject of some correspondence with the Department, my last communication on the subject being my despatch No. 545, of December 2, I think it but fair to the Legation to state that this action on the part of the Korean Government was a complete surprise to us. Neither the Secretary nor myself have made any suggestions that would lead the Korean Government to take this action.

Horace N Allen

D. American Business Interests

No. 266   Legation of the United States
                                                 Seoul Korea. April. 12. 1897.

Secretary of State

Sir,-

   I have the honor to inform you that work on the Seoul Chemulpo-Railroad has been begun and is progressing favorably.

   You will remember that the concession for this road was granted to James R. Morse, an American, on March 29. 1896. By the terms of the concession work had to be begun within one year from the date of the concession, and it is a matter for congratulation to all Americans here, that, in spite of difficulties, this stipulation was fully complied with.

                                                 John M. B. Sill

No. 277   Legation of the United States
                                                 Seoul Korea, July 13, 1897.

Secretary of State

Sir;-

   I have the honor to inform you that the question of opening the ports of Chenampo and Mokpo has at last been happily settled. I enclose herewith a letter from Min Chong Mook, Acting Minister for Foreign Affairs, announcing the opening of these ports on October 1. 1897, and with this, a copy of the resolution of the Council of State approved by His Majesty decreeing said opening and setting forth the reasons for this action.

   Chenampo is the sea-port of Peng-yang, the most important city in Northern Korea. It is on the right bank of the Ta Tong river, about twenty-five miles from and below the above city. It is a sea-port of large importance from which the distribution of imports to all upper Korea are sure to be made. Heretofore goods intended for this region, except those smuggled into landings near the mouth of the river, have largely been entered at Wonsan, on the Eastern shore, and carried upon coolies or ponies by roads almost impassable, across the peninsula to Peng-yang City, which has been the convenient Northern distributing point.

   The opening of Chenampo is of course likely to lessen the importance of Wonsan as a port of entry and is certain to add very largely to the customs revenues of the Korean Gov'mt.

   Mokpo is a sea-port on the West coast near the Southern point of the Korean Peninsula. It is in South Chulla Province, at the mouth of the Yong San river. It will doubtless become in time an important point for the export of rice, which is raised in great abundance in the southern part of the peninsula.

   There is a matter connected with the opening of these ports which is, in my judgement, of vital importance to American interests here, and I desire to put a statement of it on record for the information of the Department, and as a fact concerning which the archives of this Legation should afford a full account.

   In February 1896, the Legation was coming to an agreement with the Korean Government concerning the contract with James R. MOrse for the construction and operation of a Railway between Seoul and Chemulpo. In order that there should be no possible cause for any ill-feeling on the part of the Japanese Authorities, I conferred on February 17, fully with Mr. Komura, the Japanese Minister here in reference to our proposed arrangement. He expressed much satisfaction at the prospect of the construction of the road by an American, said he knew of no objection on the part of Japan: he would telegraph his Government and inform me at an early date if they saw any reason against completing the proposed contract. I replied that we would not hasten the transaction but should, after reasonable time, conclude it, in case no valid objection should be made.

   Mr. Komura never made further communication with me on the subjects.

   The contract was signed on March 29, 1896, forty days after the communication with Mr. Komura.

On April 17, Mr. Komura wrote the Foreign Office complaining that he had now heard that a contract for the construction of a railroad between Seoul and Chemulpo had been made with a a foreign Commercial Company; that he finds that such railroad has been described in a temporary agreement between the Korean and the Japanese Governments, said agreement having been made in August 1894. He added " Ibeg leave to state That if Your Excellencys Government have any disagreement with the said agreement, Your Government should first obtain my Governments consent before entering upon any such transaction".

This was the first knowledge we had of any such temporary agreement. It is now known that Mr. Otori, then Japanese Envoy Extraordinary and Minister Plenipotentiary here, secured the signature of Kim Yun Sik, then Korean Minister of Foreign Affairs, to such a secret memorandum, (see enclosure) on August 20, 1894, less than a month after the violent taking of the palace by Mr. Otori's order, and the dispersion and disarmament of the Korean royal guard. His Majesty was at this time a close prisoner under charge of a Japanese guard, detested but greatly feared by the King and his government and the text of the agreement reveals the fact that the ultimate removal of the guard was conditioned upon the signing of said agreement.

Mr. Komuras letter noted above was the beginning of a series of vain attempts on the part of the Japanese authorites to secure from the Korean Government something in the way of Korean recognition of this temporary agreement which had been secured by threats and coercion of the King in 1894.

Mr. Komura made strenuous efforts to secure an apology from Korea to Japan for giving this concession to Americans. He failed in this attempt and was withdrawn, and Mr. Hara replaced him at this Capital. Mr. Hara, as vice Minister of Foreign Affairs had in March 1896, informed Mr. Morse's friends that Japan would be glad to see him receive the railway concession, (see my No. 211 April 16 1896). He was probably ignorant of the existence of such an agreement when he made this statement, and, certainly, Mr. Komura must have shared this ignorance when he gave me the assurance noted above. Mr. Hara vigorously pursued Mr. Komura's scheme of securing an apology for the Morse contract and, this failing, he brought certain Japanese railroad men and, in their behalf urgently pressed their proposition to build and equip the Seoul-Fusan line, basing his urgency upon the force of the "temporary agreement". But the Korean Minister of Foreign Affairs, Ye Wan Yong, stood out firmly against anything that would give the least color of authenticity to an incomplete memorandum procured by coercion from his predecessor.

Mr. Hara, failing in the object for which he was sent to Seoul, was also withdrawn, and Mr. Kato was made Minister to Seoul in his place. Mr. Kato has also pressed the Seoul-Fusan Railway scheme for the same purpose, but without success.

The copy of the agreement, see enclosure, also mentions the opening of Mokpo, one of the ports herein described. Mr. Kato, who is a quiet but most persistent diplomat, has made every possible effort to have Mokpo opened by special treaty with Japan, in consideration of the alleged promise in the "agreement". This again would give Korean recognition to said agreement and offer standing ground for Japanese interference with the Morse concession. I considered the scheme very dangerous to American interests here, and I would have opposed it vigorously if there had been any occasion to do so. But it failed and I think the failure largely due to Mr. J. Mc'Leavy Brown, Chief Commisioner of Korean Customs and Financial Controller and Adviser of the Korean Government, who clearly saw its injustice and the danger to Korean interests in it.

I believe the Japanese Authorities will not abandon their plan to get recognition for this agreement. The matter will bear close watching, since Japanese success in securing such recognition would mean danger to American interests, which are now considerable in Korea.

John M. B. Sill

No. 73   Legation of the United States
                                               Seoul, Korea, Feb. 15, 1898.

Secretary of State

Sir:-

It is very gratifying to me to be able to inform you that an American, Mr. H. Collbran, has received a contract from the Seoul Electric Company, for the construction of a street railroad through the main thoroughfares of the city of Seoul.

While it was known that a Korean company for this purpose was being organized, no one seemed to take the matter seriously, and nothing was known in regard to it until Mr. Collbran had received $100 000 with his contract for the construction and equipment.

I then informed Mr. de Speyer, the Russian Representative, who was much surprised but professed to be entirely pleased that Americans should be in charge of this new enterprise.

I may add confidently, that the money paid down, ($100 000), while ostensibly coming from a wealthy Korean, is really from His Majesty's private purse, though it is desired that this should not become publicly known.

His Majesty has long desired to see his capital supplied with such a railroad, and has of late been especially anxious to have a convenient means of visiting the tomb of his late consort. The idea of the street railroad seems to have originated with him.

I have done nothing in furthering this matter that the Department could possibly object to, and have not evinced undue anxiety in regard to it. It is very evident that no one of any other nationality than American could have obtained the contract for this work, and in the general strife for Korean interests, we alone are in position to profit by such opportunities as this.

As the matter can be the cause of no complications, I trust that the Department may be pleased that we have obtained this contract.

I have written a consular despatch that may be published.

Horace N. Allen.

No. 108   Legation of the United States
                                            Seoul, Korea, May 23, 1898.

Secretary of State

Sir,

        I have the honour to inform you that I am in receipt of definite advices from Mr. James R. Morse, the Concessionaire of the Seoul-Chemulpo Railway, to the effect that he has arranged to transfer that railroad, upon completion to a syndicate of Japanese capitalists of which he is a member.

He expects to be left in control of the road. His explanation for this course is that political complications in Korea during 1897 frightened the American capitalists who were backing him, and they withdrew, so that he was compelled to accept Japanese capital on a mortgage loan. Later, Russian and French syndicates endeavored to purchase the property, but the negotiations ceased when Russia suddenly withdrew from Korea. Mr. Morse then made the present arrangement with the Japanese.

Horace N Allen

No. 197   Legation of the United States
                                            Seoul, Korea, June 5, 1899.

Secretary of State.

Sir,

        I have the honour to report to you certain troubles which have arisen in Seoul, in connection with the new electric street railway built here recently by Mr. Collbran, an American.

He has been most successful in running his cars through these crowded streets without accident, until a few days since, when a young child was killed, quite without the fault of the motorman. It was an unavoidable accident. The father, showing the horridly mangled body to the people, aroused a mob which burned one car and wrecked another, happily without serious damage to the foreigners in charge, who were able to fight their way through the crowd to a place of safety.

The rioting was stopped before the mob could destroy the powerhouse and plant, as was their intention.

I considered that the Korean Government was, in a degree responsible for the danger to the lives of these foreigners, as the police and soldiers are not permitted to interfere in disturbances of this kind without special orders from the Palace. As the trouble occurred in the early morning, and His Majesty does not rise until the afternoon, protection from the local police was impossible.

I have therefore insisted that this absurd rule be changed, and that as long as Americans are connected with the company, the police and military be given the strictest orders to protect their persons and property at all risks to themselves.

The matter is not yet settled, for several of the Ministers of State, belonging to the Conservative party, are making it an indirect excuse for abolishing everything modern, and, incidentally, "western" from Korea.

In this connection, I have the honour to report that the revival of an old law was discussed in the Council of State, a few days ago, by these same Ministers, by which, for certain crimes, not only the criminal himself is punished, but all his family and relatives. This measure is being strongly opposed by the Foreign Representatives in Korea.

William Franklin Sands.

No. 242

Legation of the United States
Seoul, Korea, April, 18, 1900.

Secretary of State

Sir:-

Continuing the subject of my last dispatch No. 241, of April 14, regarding Japanese interference with the Seoul Electric Railway which is held by Americans as mortgagees, I have the honor to inform you that on the 15th instant I received a dispatch from Mr. Hayashi, the Japanese Minister, replying to mine of the 9th, a copy of which I enclosed in my No. 241. In this dispatch Mr. Hayashi disclaims any intention of demanding a removal of the railway in question. See Enclosure No. 1.

I am fully aware that he did all he could to secure this removal, his railway people said to the Governor of Seoul that he must not heed the Americans as they amounted to nothing. I was assured that so much pressure was being brought to bear upon the Koreans that but for the fact that Americans were objecting to any such move they would have been compelled to yield. On the night of the 14th instant I was informed that the Cabinet had definitely refused Mr. Hayashi's request for the removal of the railway and the allotment of the ground in question. I received his letter next day informing me that he had no intention of demanding the removal of the road.

He further informed me in the dispatch that he reserved the prior right of the crossing mentioned to the Seoul-Chemulpo Railway. That same day, the 15th, the official Japanese newspaper published in Seoul contained a notice to the effect that the rails laid down by the Americans at this crossing would be removed in the presence of the Japanese Minister. See Enclosure No. 2. I therefore called on Mr. Hayashi on the 16th and explained that after seeing the official plan of his engineers and their proposed changes to this American road I had felt it my duty to distinctly acquaint him with the conditions of our ownership and to assert out right to a crossing by allowing my people to lay down rails in advance of the Japanese railroad people: that I did not wish to appear to be obstructive or to cause trouble to much needed industries: that if it were a mere matter of the cost of maintenance of the crossing and if there would be no question as to the right of the electric road to cross the steam road, I felt quite sure we could arrive at a satisfactory arrangement. He agreed that there should be no question of the right to the crossing and that he was aiming at compelling the electric road to share the cost of maintenace. I assured him they would do so and that we might leave the matter in the hands of the managers of the two roads, Messrs Collbran & Bostwick had given me assurances to this effect as they desired no trouble over the matter.

Being aware of all the representations that were made to the Koreans in this matter, and having seen plans and documents in support of the same, I am entirely confident that prompt and firm action alone prevented grave annoyance and loss to the American firm who hold the Seoul Electric Railway, as well as an unfortunate blow to the prestige of Americans in Korea by the Japanese who do not seem to take kindly to the fact that Americans are so influential here in commercial matters.

My relations with the Japanese Minster, while they have been entirely cordial all along, are apparently much improved by the above incident.

Horace N. Allen.

No. 256   <u>Confidential</u>   Legation of the United States
Seoul, Korea, June 6, 1900.

Secretary of State

Sir:-

I have the honor to acquaint you with the facts regarding recent American concessions either granted or under negotiation by this Government.

In my No. 214, of November 18, 1899, I explained the proposition made to Messrs Leigh S. J. Hunt and J. Sloat Fassett, the operators of the present American gold mines in Korea, for a loan of Yen 5.000.000 to be made to the Korean Government on the security of all the mines of the Household Department. I explained the unfavorable and underhanded action of certain Englishmen in that connnection, and the real barrrier that existed by virture of a foolish "non-alienation" promise made by the Korean Foreign Office to a Russian covering these mines. I also explained that it seemed very probable that Mr. Hunt could arrange for the setting aside of this promise and that he had gone to St. Petersburg for that purpose. In my No. 228, of February 15, 1900, I informed you that Mr. Hunt's negotiations with Russia had been broken off and that he was not receiving fair treatment. In my No. 239, of April 5 last, I explained that I had received a document over the seal of the Household Department that would at least prevent others from obtaining any of these properties while the matter is under negotiation. I now hand you a copy of a letter I am sending to the Korean Foreign Office on this subject in order to keep the matter fresh and to prevent grants to others pending a settlement of negotiations with the Americans.

I must call your attention to the objection to this proposition made by my British colleague, Mr. J. N. Jordan, who persistently claims that what we propose will amount to a monopoly and that his Government will not sanction it.

The "Household Mines" consist of some forty three more or less developed mining districts. It is true that this list comprises practically all the known mines of Korea, but it is believed that the unknown properties are quite as good as these. Already a British subject, Pritchard-Morgan, has obtained one of these Household Mines. See my No. 234, of March 17, 1900. Mr. Jordan has asked for other mines for other Englishmen. As I told him, he has demanded enough to absorb the whole territory in grants to individuals, which would be quite as much of a monopoly as though the whole list of mines went to one concern. I make this full explanation in view of the fact that the charge of a monopoly may be mentioned to you.

Mr. Hunt arrived in Korea soon after the first of April, and as he had received certain assurances from Russian friends he felt inclined to await Russian action in regard to greater matters in Korea, with the reasonable hope, based upon said assurances, that he would then be able to complete his negotiations satisfactorily.

He earnestly desired, however, that the concession under which he is now operating should be extended and formally ratified by the Korean Foreign Office. At that time this concession had twenty four years to run, and was based entirely upon the seal of the Household Department and many despatches from the Foreign Office. I agreed that in case of this country falling into the hands of another Power it would be much better that this document should be authorized by the Foreign Office. After a month of very difficult negotiations, made difficult by the suspicions of the Koreans and the energy of rival interests, the matter was most happily consummated, and a thirty year extension granted, instead of the one for twenty five years as originally proposed, and the entire file of documents connected with the whole transaction was formally ratified over the seal of the Foreign Office and the signature of the Foreign Minister. I have marked this despatch "Confidential" because of the earnest desire of the Korean Foreign Minister that the fact of this extension should not be made public at present, lest others demand the same. He stood out, indeed, very firmly for a fortnight after the document had been sanctioned by His Majesty and the Household Department because of his fear of this renewed application on the aprt of other concessionaires. It is undoubtedly true that Americans have been the pioneers in Korea in the matter of concessions, and that as soon as we obtain one the other nations demand the same notwithstanding that they may have done all in their power to prevent our succeeding in opening the way.

We are to the fore in other matters as well. I have in previous despatches and consular reports called attention to the steam and electric railroads, electric lighting plants and water-works for which agreements have been entered into with the firm of Collbran & Bostwick. This firm, moreover, is the confidential banker of His Majesty, and it never fails to profit in a legitimate business manner from any excitement or threats of disturbance caused by such action on the part of a foreign power as the Russian action regarding Masampo, or the recent difficulty over the killing of the refugees returned from Japan. His

Majesty then turns to the Americans and is apt to give them what they want rather than have it go to his enemies.

Of course this is unpleasant for other nations to witness. It seems especially to anger the Japanese. Yet there is really no cause for their anger. We do not interfere with them so long as they do not disturb vested American rights. If the Koreans turn to us in their troubles and give us opportunities for useful and profitable development it is not a thing for which we should be blamed. Americans treat the Koreans kindly and justly. We are not feared for any land grabbing tendencies. We are spending large sums here in development and our business man are of such an enterprising nature that they are always ready to listen to any reasonable propositions involving the expenditure of money. Our missionaries mind their own business and do not interfere with or brow-beat the local officials as do the French, who are vigorously supported by their Legation. It is not unnatural therefore that we should find success less difficult than it is to those of different tendencies.

I must add that there is considerable difficulty at times in dealing with the Korean Foreign Office. Not because the Koreans are opposed to Americans but because they seem to have learned that any favor granted to an American will lead to similar demands from others. It has therefore become their settled policy to oppose anything we ask for on general principles and even the execution of rights granted by concession is sometimes fraught with vexatious delay and arrogance.

Horace N Allen

No. 358

Legation of the United States
Seoul, Korea, June 6, 1901.

Secretary of State

Sir:-

Referring to my despatch No. 350 of May 21, handing you a copy of my note to the Korean Foreign Office objecting to the pledging of the customs revenues for a foreign loan, on the ground that such act would interfere with existing agreements with Americans covering the erection of water-works for the city of Seoul, I now have the honor to inform you that I have received a reply to that note, though I expected no reply. I had simply intended to file my objections for future use. My action moreover, was so satisfactory to the Emperor that he asked Mr. Hayashi, the Japanese Minster, in audience, to do likewise, and the latter said he replied that he would gladly do so had he possessed so good a reason for so doing as I had.

In his reply, of which I enclose a translation, the Minister for Foreign Affairs attempts to cite an old decree to the effect that contracts with foreigners must bear the seal of the Foreign Office.

This decree was issued on August 3, 1885 and was referred to the Department by Mr. Foulk in his No. 212 of Aug. 6, 1885. It has been apparently forgotten by the Korean Government and is constantly violated in practise. Many of the important foreign contracts bear only the seal of the Household Department, as in the case of the concession for the Japanese mines. I have however appreciated this decree as one issued at a time when such decrees were less numerous than at present, and apparently issued in good faith, it moreover seemed to fix a status of legality for foreign documents; moreover it was referred to our Government and apparently accepted. I have therefore followed the practice of having all American contracts formally ratified by the seal of the Foreign Office when practicable and in the spring of 1900 I devoted much time and energy to securing the formal ratification by the Foreign Office of the concession and documents covering the operations of the American Mining Company, as mentioned in my No. 256 of June 6, 1900. These mines, being the personal property of the Emperor, were granted over the seal of the Household Department and it was insisted upon by the Korean Government that such sanction was entirely sufficient.

The contracts covering the work for the Seoul Electric Company, which include the water-works, were however made by His Majesty over his personal seal and later ratified by the Minister of the Household. This course was made necessary by the fact that the "Seoul Electric Company" is in reality the Emperor himself. While the water-works agreement was included in these documents it has been my intention to have it formally ratified by the Foreign Office when the special document shall be drawn up.

Since the agreement for a water-works was given to the Americans in December 1898, there have been serious attempts to get it away from us. I cited the attempt of the Englishman Chance, in my No.

234 of March 17, 1900. I was also told by the Russian Chargé d'Affaires that he intended to secure it for a Frenchman. In all this discussion of the question of water-works it has always been understood that the work would be paid for by funds drawn from the Customs which are the only available revenues for such purpose. Had I possessed no documents therefore, pledging the Customs revenues, I would have been still been authorized in objecting to pledging revenues that would have necessarily to be used for the execution of this water-works contract. On April 4, 1900, however, I received a document mentioned in my No. 239 of April 5 1900, pledging the customs and mines for a loan to be raised in America. I was safe therefore in filing my objections to the pledging of the customs for another purpose. I would have been remiss in the discharge of my duties had I not done so. I promptly informed Mr. de Plancy, the French Minister, of my action, as cited in my No. 352 of May 25, page 4, and he had nothing to say against my action. In the course of our converation, the subject of the decree in regard to foreign contracts bearing the seal of the Foreign Office, was discussed.

When I received this reply from the Minister for Foreign Affairs to my letter objecting to the pledging of the customs revenues, I decided that I must not let it pass, as otherwise it might affect the validity of existing agreements, and I felt strongly inclined to believe that the letter had been inspired by my French colleague, - it seemed to be connected in some way with our conversation.

I therefore immediately addressed a note to the Minister for Foreign Affairs, asking for an audience with the Emperor, since it was upon the latter's order that the contracts in question had been made, and stating that I could not conceive that His Majesty would be found at fault in the matter. I enclose a copy of this note.

This letter had the effect of bringing the Foreign Minister to me promptly on Monday the 3'rd. instant. At his request I showed him the water-works contract, which he found correct except that it had not the seal of his office and did not definitely specify the pledging of the customs, whereupon I showed him the other document of April 3, 1900, wherein the customs are definitely mentioned. This also was without the seal of the Foreign Office. I met this objection with the statement that it was not for me to advise His Majesty as to the validity or otherwise of his actions: if he chose to voluntarily enter into agreements with Americans without consulting me, and to seal these documents with his own seal or with that of his Department of the Household, I could not believe that he would do so knowing that this was an irregular or illegal course: that if the seal of the Household Department was of no value, the personal seal of His Majesty would make him personally responsible.

In the course of a long conversation the Minister for Foreign Affairs took my view of the matter entirely and he told me that he had not wished or intended to reply to my letter, but he had been told he must do so or the Americans would claim the customs. Without mentioning names, he gave me plainly to understand that my French Colleague, through his henchman - Ye Yong Ik, was responsible for the letter.

The implication that His Majesty might be found at fault in this matter was most objectionable to the Koreans as I knew it would be. The Minister said he would have to resign if my note went on file, since it was a letter of his that had called forth my reply containing the implication.

We arranged the matter by the exchange of notes, the Foreign Minister took back his letter of May 31, and I took back my reply of June 1, asking for an audience. My letter of objections of May 21 remains on file at the Foreign Office in full force, and it seemed that I had accomplished what I set out to do.

While writing this letter however, I was surprised at receiving another letter from the Minister for Foreign Affairs, of much the same tenor as the one he took back but omitting the most objectionable expressions. I enclose a copy of this letter to which I have replied as per enclosed copy, maintaining my objections although the Minister denies knowledge of the documents in question.

I fully recognize that I am not dealing with Koreans in this matter. The Foreign Minister has no power or influence. He simply does as he is told. At present the man Ye Yong Ik is all powerful with the Emperor, and Ye is strongly backed by the Russian and French Representatives, with whom he passes much of his time. It was a matter of comment that while the Representatives, generally could not learn when Mr. Pavlow, the Russian Charge d'Affaires, was due from his recent leave of absence, this man Ye was awaiting him on the dock at Chemulpo when he did return.

Mr. Pavlow's absence seems to have had some relation to this French loan matter. He left for Japan for medical treatment, for the bite of a mad-dog, though he himself was not bitten, but had merely handled the dog, while two of his attendants had recieved bites. He said he would be gone for a fortnight only. His departure, which I mentioned in my No. 337, April 26, was just after the loan matter was made public and the reason for the attack upon Mr. Brown was made apparent. He was away for more than a month and stayed for some time at Masampo on his way to Chemulpo via Port Arthur. His return on June 1, was coincident with the departure of Mr. Cazalis with the loan documents. Ye Yong Ik would hardly have been so energetic in pressing this matter had he not felt sure of the support of Mr. Pavlow, to which his present influence is attributed. It is quite probable that Mr. Pavlow may not have cared to appear openly in the matter, in which case his absence was opportune.

Horace N Allen

No. 368

Legation of the United States
Seoul, Korea, June 19, 1901.

Secretary of State

Sir:-

I have the honor to acquaint you with the following in regard to the satisfactory settlement of a case of interference with American interests in Korea.

The Standard Oil Company of New York, maintains an extensive warehouse at Chemulpo for storing their product, and last year they obtained, with my assistance, and the consent of the Foreign Office, a plot of land on Deer Island at Fusan. There was some trouble in securing this land, as I had to show that it did not interfere with the limits of the proposed General Foreign Settlement proposed to be made on that island. Also, there was trouble in regard to the purchase owing to a squabble between the petty local officials and the owner, which resulted in the latter being thrown into prison on what was pronounced by the Commissioner of Customs at the port - a French subject - to be an attempt at extortion. The matter was finally arranged by me through the Foreign Office and the deeds were at last issued in due form. The Agent of the Standard Oil Company began the erection of extensive buildings on the land purchased, and as they were nearing completion this Spring, the seller of the land was again arrested and thrown into prison, where he was severely beaten for "selling Government land to a foreigner". I was informed of this on the 27'th. ultimo, and at once saw the Foreign Minister, to whom I recited the previous transactions, shoed the deeds and referred him to our former concersations and correspondence. I took the opportunity of explaining to him the extent of the Company's business in Korea and that this was an interference that could not be tolerated, since the place was an open port where foreigners were allowed by treaty to purchase land, and the owner had shown that he actually was in legal possession of the land by submitting his deeds. I demanded that he be released at once and stated that I would regard further persecution of the man for the reason given, namely selling this land to the Americans - as intimidating the natives and preventing them from having dealings with Americans as provided for by treaty.

The Minister for Foreign Affaires agreed with me that the treatment of the man as reported was wrong and that the purchase of the land was regular and entirely proper. He also agreed to send telegraphic instructions to release the man and not to molest him further.

That there might be no mistake in regard to the release of the man, I had the son of the local Governor telegraph fully to his father in regard to the matter.

I heard by telegraph that the man was soon released, and I am now advised by letter that the release was prompt; that the persecution of the man seems to have ceased, and that the incident seems now to be satisfactorily closed.

Horace N Allen

No. 484

Legation of the United States
Seoul, Korea, August 1, 1902.

Secretary of State

Sir:-

In his despatch <u>No. 448</u>, of March 28, Mr. Paddock, Chargé d'Affaires, ad interim, handed you a copy of a joint note sent to the Korean Foreign Office, by the Foreign Representatives in Seoul, making certain suggestions in regard to the coinage of nickel coins, which had then become a serious menace to trade because of the illicit coinage of great numbers of these coins, which coinage was believed to be with the connivance of the officials.

No reply was made to this joint note until July 8, last, when we received a ridiculous reply, a copy of which I enclose, to the effect that the Government had decided to do about as was suggested, before receiving the joint note.

At a meeting of the Foreign Representatives held on the 29'th. ultimo, it was decided to drop the matter.

The joint note did have the effect of stopping the heedless coinage of these depreciated coins, and of causing more or less active measures to be taken for the suppression of the illicit coinage.

It is recognized that, while the Korean Government did heed the remonstrance of the Foreign Representatives, they attempted to "save their faces" by the reply of which I have the honor to hand you a copy.

Horace N Allen

No. 500   Legation of the United States
                                           Seoul, Korea, August 29, 1902.

Secretary of State

Sir:-

I have the honor to hand you the following details in regard to a claim upon the Korean Government, of a million and a half yen ($750,000), which I am attempting to bring to a settlement, in favor of an American firm, Messrs Collbran and Bostwick.

On February 1, 1898, Mr. H. Collbran, contractor for the construction of the Seoul-Chemulpo Railway, received a contract, enclosure 1, for the construction of an electric street railway for the city of Seoul. This contract was made with the "Seoul Electric Co". which was in reality the Emperor himself. An advance payment was made at the date of signing the contract. which money was furnished from the Emperor's own purse. A regular charter was issued to this company as per copy enclosed. The contract carried with it such other rights as the construction of telephone lines.

When the road was first operated in April 1899, a mob did some damage to the cars and it was seen that it would be necessary to replace the Japanese employees with Americans, with the idea of training up natives to serve as car men. This has been successfully done.

With this end in view, Mr. Collbran took over the operating of the property upon a contract, dated April 29, 1899. See enclosure 3. The operation has been attended with a loss to the Company, attributed to two causes. First; the retention of the costly staff of American employees long after their presence was a necessity, for the reason that the Emperor insisted upon retaining them that they might act as a sort of personal guard whenever he should leave his palace. Second; because of the great depreciation of the native currency, which fell to a discount of from 160 to 200% thus cutting the returns almost in half.

On August 15, Mr. Collbran received another contract calling for the erection of a lighting plant for Seoul to be run by electricity generated by the same power plant which ran the railway. See enclosure 4.

This necessitated the increase of the plant, and this agreement was amplified and Mr. H. R. Bostwick was taken into partnership with Mr. Collbran by an agreement dated August 15, 1900. See enclosure 5.

On April 28, 1900, Collbran and Bostwick contracted to build an extension of the electric street railway to a point in the country, at the head of river navigation, thirteen miles east of Seoul. The power from the one plant being sufficient for this purpose, and an increased earning power for the road being assured. See enclosure 6. By request of the Emperor, a delay of one year was agreed upon in building this extension, owing to a change of counsellors and an apparent cooling off of imperial interest in the matter. This delay came after all contracts for materials had been placed, and as the staff of people had to be kept on hand, it was agreed that 10% on the cost of the extension should be paid to cover cost of delay. This delay proved to be a permanent one. The extension was never built, though the extra cars, were gotten out and in fact all the necessary material except rails and wire, which were held back by telegram, at considerable cost. Collbran and Bostwick now claim the whole cost of the building of this extension, which they agree to turn over completed.

On April 15, 1900, Collbran and Bostwick entered into a new agreement extending the operating contract mentioned as enclosure 3. See enclosure 7.

During all this time, Collbran and Bostwick regarded the properties they had erected as security for their cost, and it will be seen that such an understanding was incorporated into each document. Enclosure 8, is a file of the mortgage documents running from a to g. Exhibit F. being the final and complete mortage, which came due on August 15, last and which seems to place Collbran and Bostwick in possession of the properties. I may add that this firm does not wish to keep and operate this property. They wish to receive their pay, or be allowed to sell the properties.

In addition to these purely electrical matters, Collbran and Bostwick received a contract, which they did not care to accept, for the construction of an imperial highway from Seoul to the site of the Imperial Cemetery, some thirteen miles east of the city. They could not well refuse this work and as their extension of the electric railway was to be laid down on this road when completed, they took up the matter. This work had to be pushed very rapidly and they were ordered to complete it regardless of expense, as an imperial procession was to pass over the road within a month or two from the date of the commencement of work. The contract was dated April 28, 1900, and the document was completed by an Imperial order of February 6, 1901. Enclosure 9.

Mr. Collbran also received an agreement covering the construction of a system of water-works for Seoul, dated December 26, 1898. See enclosure 10-A. This was amplified and confirmed in the name of Collbran and Bostwick July 14, 1900, (10-B). For the execution of this agreement, the Emperor issued an order on October 22, 1901, to the Commissioner of Customs to set aside Yen 200,000 a year for eight years, which would practically provide for the complete payment, (10-C).

This project was postponed until Collbran and Bostwick could wait no longer and on the maturity of their mortage, August 15, they gave up the water-works matter and now demand 25% of the estimated cost in order to compensate them for the expense of maintaining a large staff of engineers here in getting up surverys and the other necessary expenses, as well as compensation to them for their loss of profits. I think that this claim will be recognized, though not to the full amount of 25%.

On December 17, 1900, Collbran and Bostwick agreed to purchase for the Emperor, enough nickel blanks to coin 2,000,000 dollars, Korean, See enclosure 11-A. And on May 20, 1901, they received an agreement for the daily payment of a considerable sum in nickel, which they could use at the time. This last agreement, enclosure 11-B, was not fulfilled. I regretted to see this firm enter into this nickel agreement, for nickel coins had become a great source of difficulty in Korea. Mr. Collbran hesitated himself at accepting the contract, but as it was a personal request of the Emperor, who seemed to have some private coinage scheme of his own, the contract apparently had to be accepted. The nickels proved to be better and cheaper than others obtained elsewhere, but by the time they had arrived, the Emperor had changed his mind in regard to coinage, and their acceptance was refused for some time, necessitating a reference to the Department of State, by Mr. Paddock.

Collbran and Bostwick also recieved other agreements of more or less value, including a bank charter, a telephone right, and an agreement covering the construction of a railway connecting Songdo with the river. 12.

I enclose a statement of the Emperor's account with Collbran and Bostwick, showing him to be in their debt for actual completed contracts, to the amount of Yen 438,849,53.

While for other obligations including the whole amount of the cost of the completed extension of the railway, which was not completed, and 25% on the water-works estimate, he is further indebted to them in the amount of ¥ 1,258,124,90, making a total of ¥ 1,696,974.

Of course if the extension of the railway is not to be completed there will be a reduction from the amount of the claim of ¥ 700.000 for this. I understand it will take ¥ 300,000 to complete the work.

It is probable that the claim for compensation on the water-works will be modified in case a proper disposition is shown on the part of the Koreans, Certainly Collbran and Bostwick have been shamefully treated in regard to this matter.

In April 1900 Collbran and Bostwick agreed to hold certain funds of the Emperor in trust, to keep them out of other hands. These funds amounted to over ¥ 1,000,000 and were only to be drawn upon by the Emperor's own order. The presence of these funds, which Collbran and Bostwick could not but regard as something of a security for the Emperor's debts, induced them to accept obligations that they might otherwise have rejected. But so many drafts were made upon this deposit, that it was reduced to about ¥200,000. The nickels were made a charge upon this account, owing to failure to pay for them as agreed. See statement, enclosure 14.

On June 30'th. last, I had an interview with the Emperor and explained the whole situation to him. I further explained that I was most enthusiastic about the water-works matter, which I regarded as one of the most necessary and useful things for the people of Seoul. But that I had not particularly favored the electric development, for the reason that it seemed rather premature, and a horse railway would have served the purpose at less expense, owing the small number of cars that would necessarily be run. I told him that it was owing to my own admonition that Mr. Collbran had hesitated at the beginning and had only signed the contract after ¥100,000 had been paid down in advance, which, with the property, would probably have secured him against loss.

The later development had been the Emperor's doing, persuaded by councillors who desired something of the kind, and now that the day of settlement was at hand I could not do other than enforce a just settlement, no matter how much I might wish to assist him. I stated that if the order for the commencement of work on the water-works was issued before August 1, Collbran and Bostwick would enter into new arrangements for the extension of the time of settlement and would continue to conduct the property while constructing the water-works.

His Majesty said the matter should be attended to at once.

As I expected, nothing came of this interview, and on August 1, I sent in an official notice to the Foreign Minister, announcing foreclosure proceedings, for the 15'th. I showed this despatch to Mr. Collbran before sending it, and it had his entire aproval. Enclosure 15.

In a country without courts, - properly so speaking, - proceedure of this kind is very uncertain. I have tried to avoid legal terms or any attempt at legal usage, knowing that tact and common sense will be of most avail.

On August 7 I received a reply to this despatch, as per copy enclosed. This letter was drafted by Mr. J. McLeavy Brown, Chief Commissioner of Customs, who has seemed to be friendly to the water-works scheme, and who was appointed to settle the matter of the claim of Collbran and Bostwick. In this letter Mr. Brown separated the electric railway and lighting matter from the other claims, even leaving out the Tokso extension, which came in after the mortgage was issued. It seemed to me that these matters were, by subsequent documents, placed under the scope of the mortgage, and I replied in this sense in my letter of August 8, as per copy enclosed.

I also asked in this letter for the appointment of Mr. Townsend, one of our most influential citizens, as a joint auditor with Mr. Brown, of these accounts.

Hearing nothing from this letter I spoke to Mr. Brown about it and he wrote me a letter of which I enclose a copy, informing me that he had been appointed Acting President of the Seoul Electric Company. I replied to this, as per enclosed copy, showing him that there was very little for such an officer to do.

On August 13, I received another letter from the Foreign Minister accepting my nomination of Mr. Townsend as an auditor, and explaining that Mr. Brown was chiefly to manage the affairs of the Company. See enclosure 20.

On the 14'th. I replied to this after first discussing the matter with Mr. Brown and finding that he had no intention of trying to use his official connection with the Company as a means of interfering with the conduct of the properties. In this letter I claimed that Collbran and Bostwick were mortgagees in possession. See copy.

On August 15, I sent in a formal notice that Collbran and Bostwick were in possession owing to default in payment, and I named October first as the last date for final settlement, reserving the right to sell. This delay being necessary for the full examination of the accounts, and the discussion of the claims in connection with the failure to build the water-works and the Tokso extension. Also, Mr. Collbran was obliged to go Port Arthur, and is expected back daily. Mr. Bostwick being now in America. I enclose a copy of this letter. Mr. Brown had agreed to this date, and I sent him a copy of my despatch, as the Minister for Foreign Affairs had died and the Foreign Office was even more disorganized than usual.

To this I received a reply as per enclosure 23, accepting October 1, as the date when all the claims of Collbran and Bostwick must be settled. I also had a reply from Mr. Brown, enclosure 24, which is important since he tells me he drafts all the letters on this subject for the Foreign Minister.

I understand that the audit of the accounts of the Seoul Electric Company, pure and simple, have been completed and everything was found in good order. Mr. Brown said to me that he did not see that Collbran and Bostwick had been making excessive profits out of this matter, that is the operation of the Companys properties.

It is the desire of certain Japanese parties to obtain this electric plant, and Collbran and Bostwick thought they would also be glad to secure their documents covering water-works; Tokso extention; telephones; Songdo railway and a bank charter. They hoped to sell the whole thing to them and thus leave the completed properties in good hands, where they would be successfully operated, and be able to realize well on the charters and agreements. Mr. Brown expressed himself as favorable to this transfer also, as it would place the property in competent hands and relieve the Koreans of the payment of such a heavy debt. I also let Mr. Pavlow, the Russian Minister, know of this at once, so that there might be no misunderstanding as to Americans selling out to the Japanese. He telegraphed to his Government about it, thinking some Russian might wish to bid on the property. I also informed his Korean Majesty, at my audience on June 30'th, and I had several talks with the Japanese Minister on the subject, so that there could be no misunderstanding. Mr. Hayashi took a great interest in the matter, seeming to prize the documents more highly, if anything, than the electric plant. He had his secretary go over the documents carefully and he then sent him to Tokio to explain the whole thing. I have not heard what the decision was in regard to the matter in Tokio.

A very strong aversion to such a sale has sprung up among the Koreans. They fear it would admit the Japanese into the palace in connection with the electric lights, and that the policing of the railway would give them practical control of the city. They have caused Mr. Brown to change face in regard to the sale, and it now seems to be their intention to pay off the actual debt secured by the mortgage itself, which would set free the electric railway and lighting plant, if the mortgage is held to include only so much, and Collbran and Bostwick would have no means of reimbursing themselves for the other claims, especially the heavy ones connected with the water-works and the Tokso extention of the railway, amounting together to more than ¥1,100,000.

I can do nothing more in the matter until the return of Mr. Collbran from Port Arthur.

Horace N Allen

No. 533

Legation of the United States
Seoul, Korea, November 21, 1902.

Secretary of State

Sir:-

Continuing the subject of my despatch No. 500 of August 29, last, relative to the settlement of the claims of Messrs Collbran and Bostwick upon the Korean Government, I now regret to have to inform you that the Government has not carried out the official promises made in that connection and the matter has assumed an acute aspect which may require somewhat extensive telegraphing. I hope to place this report before you prior to telegraphing extensively.

In my despatch of August 29 above cited, I informed you that the audit of the accounts was entrusted to Mr. J. McLeavy Brown, the Englishman in charge of Korean Customs, who was to be assisted by Mr. W. D. Townsend, an American business man. I will omit further particular mention of Mr. Townsend in this connection as he was unable to do much for the reason that Mr. Brown kept the matter quite in his own hands.

October 1 was selected by Mr. Brown and agreed upon by myself with the Foreign Office, as the date for the final settlement of these claims. It was understood that Mr. Brown's report would be made long before that date in order that disputed items might be discussed.

I had frequent interviews with Mr. Brown in the interest of expedition, and I offered him all assistance in my power. He began by an endeavor in a letter he drew up for the Foreign Minister on August 7, (see enclosure 17 in my despatch No. 500), to exclude from this examination the larger matters known as the "Tokso extension" of the street railway, and the water-works. In my letter to Mr. Brown of August 13, (enclosure 19, despatch No. 500) and in my despatch to the Foreign Minister, August 15, (enclosure 22, despatch No. 500), I protested against this exclusion and on August 20, the Minister for Foreign Affairs wrote me officially, the letter being drafted by Mr. Brown as he told me, that these matters would be taken up and examined at the same time and settled upon the same date. (See encl. 23, despatch No. 500)

On September 29, the Acting Minister for Foreign Affairs sent me a letter drafted by Mr. Brown, Enclosure 1. asking for an extension of the time allowed for settlement to October 15. I had agreed to this in conversation with Mr. Brown and I did so officially in my letter of October 1, to the Foreign Office. Enclosure 2.

Finding that Mr. Brown would not make the complete examination promised me, and that he had not even gone into the matters of the "Tokso extension" and water-works and that it was doubtful if he would have even his partial report ready by the last date set for settlement, which would preclude any possibility of discussion or arrangement for settlement, and having exhausted all my powers in endeavoring to secure his earlier action, I prepared a despatch which I forwarded to the Minister for Foreign Affairs at noon on October 15, no response having been at that time received from Mr. Brown or the Foreign Office. See enclosure 3/

In this despatch I recited what had taken place and called the Ministers attention to the fact that no settlement had been arranged for or porposed and that the time set by himself for such settlement having expired, I was compelled to give Messrs Collbran and Bostwick instructions to make such disposition of the property as to them might seem best.

To this I received no reply, but on November 1'st. I received from the Foreign Minister a copy of Mr. Brown's report, in Chinese, with the intimation that the Korean Government would not consent to the sale of the property. In this report of his examination of the Collbran and Bostwick accounts, Mr. Brown admits that the "Tokso extention" is a part of the property of the Seoul Electric Company, and as such is included in the mortgage on those properties in favor of Collbran and Bostwick, wich matured on August 15'th. last. Nevertheless he failed to examine the accounts connected with this large item. He also admitted that compensation should be allowed in connection with the water works matter but he failed to go into these accounts as well.

Of the actual matters which he took up he found that ¥510,000 was undisputedly due to Collbran and Bostwick at once and he seems to have recommeded the immediate payment of this amount and the further investigation of disputed claims. No such payment has been made nor has there been the offer of any payment.

I enclose a copy of this report of Mr. Brown, made from the English copy he kinly furnished me and compared with the Chinese text. Enclosure 4.

I also hand you a copy of a reply to this report sent me by Mr. Collbran, which I commend to your perusal. 5.

In this reply Mr. Collbran allows me the privilege of proposing arbitration, of which I shall make mention later on. I could not make such offer at the time.

I replied to this report of Mr. Brown's on November 12. Enclosure 6. I showed that the incomplete character of the report made it of little practical use, even had it been presented in time. I tried to show the fallacy of Mr. Brown's argument against the existence of a contract for water works, and I informed the Foreign Minister that active negotiations looking to the sale of the property covered by the mortgage, were then in progress.

I may explain that representatives of two responsible - would be purchasers - had come from Japan and made very favorable reports of their examination of the properties. Also the Japanese Minister, Mr. Hayashi, had sent his secretary to examine all the documents and he was then sent to Tokio to report on the same. I am told his report was favorable to the purchase of the property by Japanese. At the time of writing my despatch, a Japanese banker, highly recommended by Mr. Hayashi, was on his way to Korea to make an offer for the property.

It was with great reluctance that we came to the point of making a transfer of these properties to outsiders, especially as the Koreans seemed to be very much averse to having them go to the Japanese, but it seemed to be impossible to arrive at a settlement otherwise. The Emperor refused to carry out his agreements regarding the extension of the street railway and the building of the water works, and Collbran and Bostwick were remaining here at a loss. They had large sums of money tied up in these properties and it seemed to be my duty to assist them in getting in out by permitting this sale of property which was theirs by foreclosure of motgage.

At this time Mr. Collbran was unfortunately in a most destracted mental state because of serious illness in his family, a daughter dying while a son was dangerously ill. He was moreover needed in Port Arthur, where he was bidding on large contracts for construction work.

While in this condition and without consulting me, in an attempt to hasten a settlement, he allowed Mr. Sands, the American advisor to the Household Department, to lay his matters before the Emperor, giving him access to all documents of mine in his possession, so that he was able to say about all that I could say, and did say things that I would prefer not to have said at that juncture.

As I feared, this brought about a determined effort on the part of the Koreans assisted by Mr. Brown, to forestall my efforts and prevent a transfer of the property. Mr. Brown and Mr. Hayashi were called to the palace in audience, and on the 17'th. a letter, drafted by Mr. Brown as he admitted to me, was sent me by the Minister for Foreign Affairs. Enclosure 7.

In this letter it is claimed that the delay in settlement was entirely due to the fact that Collbran and Bostwick had not presented original vouchers supporting their accounts, and I am possitively informed that the transfer of the properties will not be allowed. I am further informed that the Foreign Representatives have been advised that they must not allow their nationals to negotiate for the purchase of these properties.

To this I replied on the 19'th. instant, as per copy enclosed. I endeavored to show that the only accounts disputed by Mr. Brown in his report were those relating to the expenses of operating the electric plant, amounting to Yen 80,000 in all and that he had suggested the preliminary settlement of these disputed items by the payment of Yen 50,000 pending further presentation of vouchers, which proposal had not been rejected. Thus for the matter of Yen 30,000, an offer for settlement of which had been made and not rejected, claims amounting in the aggregate to over a million and a half yen were rejected, since no settlement was offered and this ¥30,000 was urged as the reason, while no transfer of the property whereby the creditors could recover the debt, was allowed.

On the 17'th. however, prior to receipt of the last letter above cited, I had my long deferred audience, which I had applied for on October 16'th. Before going to the palace I had a visit from Mr. Hayashi, who told me that at his audience the day before he had been obliged to assure His Majesty that he would not agree to the purchase of this property by a Japanese without the consent of the Korean Government. He said however that he thought a contract might be made with Japanese to operate the property for the Koreans.

Mr. Hayashi seemed to appreciate the gravity of the situation and that the Koreans were placing themselves in a false position by refusing what seemed to be the legal right of Collbran and Bostwick to make this sale.

He suggested that it might be well to move the Koreans to ask for the appointment by the Government of the United States, of an impartial American arbitrator from abroad, say from China or Japan, whose award would be accepted as final by both parties.

I assented to this in principle and had the permission of Mr. Collbran to do so, embodied in his letter, enclosure 5. I therefore told Mr, Hayashi that I would suggest to His Majesty, if it became necessary, that he send for Mr. Hayashi and ask him for some suggestion in regard to a settlement.

At my audience I was assisted by Rev. Geo. H. Jones, of the Methodist Missionary Society, 150 Fifth Avenue, New York City, who is one of the best speakers of the language among resident Americans. I desired his presence as a witness of what took place and also that he might say things that a Korean might hesitate to utter.

I was met at once in discussing these claims by the statement that Collbran and Bostwick had not presented proper accounts and vouchers, which I fully refuted. I was then referred bak to Mr. Brown but I declined to reopen the matter, stating that Mr. Brown had had sixty days to do a job that could well have been done in six days and that it would require years to complete the work with him. I fully explained Mr. Brown's course in refusing to take up matters he had officially agreed to examine and report upon for settlement.

I could make no headway however and when I announced that parties had arrived to purchase the property, His Majesty informed me that he had the assurance of Mr. Hayashi that he would personally prevent the sale of the same to a Japanese without the consent of the Korean Government, and he further informed me that he had caused his Foreign Office to inform all the Foreign Representatives that they must not allow their people to negotiate for the purchase of the property.

I pointed out the gravity of the situation this was bringing upon Korea in refusing to Americans the enjoyment of their legal rights; that he had gone into this development work of his own accord and that I had not urged it; that there would now be little or no debt if Ye Yong Ik had allowed the payment daily from the Mint under his control, of nickel payments according to Imperial orders, and that the whole situation seemed to have been caused by this man who seemed determined to oppose any and everything American.

I finally requested that His Majesty should advise with the Japanese Minister, who was a mutual friend, and see if he could not suggest some way out of the difficulty. He agreed to do so at once, and I left with the consciousness that the palace officials were much pleased with themselves for their seeming frustration of my plans.

On the 19'th. instant, Mr. Hayashi called upon me to say that the Emperor had indeed sent an official to see him after my audience to ask him if he were still sure that he could prevent the sale of the property to a Japanese. The man was not empowered to say or discuss anything more, which confirms me in my belief that numerous rumors from the palace are true, to the effect that the Emperor cares nothing about a settlement so long as he is assured that the property cannot be sold.

In explanation to Mr. Hayashi of the Korean statement to him that the trouble was caused by the failure of Collbran and Bostwick to present true accounts and vouchers, I read him a copy of my letter to the Foreign Office, enclosure 8. He seemed to be entirely satisfied and admitted the impossibility of continuing negotiations with Mr. Brown, who he said had seemed to give the Koreans wrong advice in the matter.

He agreed to ask for an early audience for the purpose of proposing to His Majesty the suggestion of an arbitration in accordance with our conversation of the 17'th instant. Page 6.

I shall not hold this report for this reason, especially since Mr. Hayashi informed me on yesterday that there was considerable discussion going on as to what he wished to propose at his audience, and although he had explained the matter, he had not yet been told when he would be received. On yesterday he brought with him Mr. Yasuda, a banker who came here to purchase this property and who is going about the negotiations in a business like manner as though he had the full approval of his Minister. Mr. Hayashi further told me that Baron Komura, Japanese Minister for Foreign Affairs, had telegraphed him to know if I would sanction a transfer of this property as legal. I replied that I had already done so.

If Mr. Hayashi's suggestion is made and followed and an arbitrator is appointed it will bring matters to a crisis though not necessarily to a settlement, for heretofore the Korean Government has regarded very lightly the awards of regularly appointed arbitrators. In a recent case the streets leading to a French property were arbitrarily closed and the property rendered worthless thereby. The matter was submitted to local arbitrators, whose award was not pleasing to the Government, and was therefore refused payment. The matter is still under discussion, being somewhat trivial in amount.

If no satisfactory proposal regarding arbitration is made, or if an award is secured and payment is not forthcoming, it will be necessary to bring some pressure to bear upon these people otherwise American interests will suffer, not only in this particular case but generally.

Should you be asked to select an arbitrator, I think it would be well to send someone from Japan, since the Japanese Minister has offered his kind mediation in the matter. I can suggest the names of Messrs McIvor, Dun and Scidmore. Mr. N. W. McIvor was formerly our Consul General at Yokohama and is now practicing law in Japan I believe. Mr. Edwin Dun, formerly our minister at Tokio, would be acceptable I am sure, but he is engaged in active business, as is Mr. Scidmore, our Deputy Consul General, at Yokohama.

Horace N Allen

No. 544   Legation of the United States
                                                 Seoul, Korea, December 2, 1902.

Secretary of State

Sir:-

Continuing the subject of my despatch No. 541 of the 28'th. ultimo, regarding Ye Yong Ik and the Collbran and Bostwick claims, I now have the honor to hand you enclosed a translation from the Official Gazette of the 28'th. ultimo, being a copy of a petition sent to His Majesty by the Cabinet Officials praying for the trial and punishment of Ye Yong Ik. To secure the acceptance of this petition, which was forwarded a second time, on being answered in an unsatisfactory way, these high officials knelt on the ground in front of the Palace gate during the day and night of November 28 and 29.

When it seemed that Ye Yong Ik was about to be given over for trial, he persuaded the Emperor to grant him four days in which to adjust his finances so that His Majesty would not lose all his private funds which were in this mans hands. This time was of course granted, and to prevent a breach of the Palace by the incensed populace we were duly informed that a heavy guard would be placed around the Palace during the night of the 29'th. This was done and promptly thereafter His Majesty had the police drive away the kneeling ministers on the grounds of their creating a traitorous disturbance. Korean officials are very much averse to being styled traitors. They therefore reparied to a near by house, where they remained until Ye made his escape to the Russian Legation on the 30'th., which was as follows, as described to me by Mr. Stein, Russian Chargé d'Affaires ad interim.

Mr. Stein told me that while he was at luncheon on the 30'th. with the French Minister, Mr. de Plancy, and the Italian Consul, Mr. Rosetti, as guests, he was informed that Ye Yong Ik would be obliged to follow His Majesty through the streets to a near by temple where the Emperor had to make sacrifices, and that the occasion would probably be seized by the people for doing injury to Ye. Mr. Stein says that he therefore went with his guests and a few cossacks and as Ye came out from the small gate at the rear of the Palace, just next to the gate of this Legation, he Mr. Stein, after saluting the Emperor, advanced and shook hands with Ye, whom he then took with him to the Russian Legation where he has since remained.

The Official Gazette of yesterday announces that Ye Yong Ik is dismissed from all his offices prepartory to an investigation. This is taken to mean that he will be banished, - a punishment that may be made very light, especially if he passes his perod of banishment at the Russian Legation.

Mr. Stein called upon me on the 29'th. to ask if he might not speak to His Majesty at an audience he was to have the next day, about the question of arbitration in the Collbran and Bostwick matters, since he feared the Koreans did not realize the false position they were placing themselves in by refusing my request to submit the matter to arbitration. I said I would be glad to have him do so. He said he would say. "I understand the American Minister has proposed to submit the matter in dispute to arbitration which I hear has been refused. I wish to say that I consider such a proposal most excellent and fair, and in refusing it you are laying yourself liable to serious difficulty". He said he would also intimate personally to the Emperor that as Mr. Yamada was actively engaged in negotiating for the purchase of the electric property there could be no doubt but that the Japanese intended to obtain control of it in some manner, and it might be their desire to have the United States obliged to bring pressure to bear upon Korea so that the transfer would be made to a Japanese. I said I could not control his personal remarks, but I would be glad to have him explain the advantage of arbitration.

Mr. Stein called upon me again on the 1'st. to say that he had been unable to discuss the matter of arbitration with the Emperor owing to the press of other matters. He said he had seen in the Palace, a note from Mr. Hayashi, the Japanese Minister, in which the latter had stated that it would be useless to attempt to do more in the Collbran and Bostwick matter through Mr. Brown as the latter was so procrastinating that he would never get the matter finished and he had had time enough as it was.

This was most grateful news to me as indicating that the Japanese were not supporting the English in backing up Mr. Brown in this matter.

Mr. Stein related a long and serious conversation he had had with Ye Yong Ik relative to his unwise action in trying to defeat all American business, which seems according to this conversation to have been actuated somewhat by antagonism between Ye Yong Ik and Mr. Sands, the American Advisor to the Household Department. Mr. Stein said that Ye became quite reasonable; expressed his regret at his "stupid" course and wished to make friends with me. I agreed to receive him but when Mr. Stein asked me to come to lunch with him and meet Ye while he is stopping at the Russian Legation, I had to decline, as such a course would be quite misunderstood. I asked him to postpone anything of that kind until after I had secured a settlement of the matters in hand, and until I had seen some evidence of a change on the part of Ye.

Mr. Stein took occasion to inform me in this connection that his Government had intimated their pleasure at seeing the advance of American commercial interests in Korea, and would now even be pleased to see Korea secure an American loan when such a thing becomes necessary. He further told me that he believed, and he thought his Government also believed, that the reported new agreement between England and Japan regarding the controll of Korean affairs, was true. I reported this in my No. 476, of June 20, last. He said his latest reason for believing this report was that Mr. Hayashi had recently written a personal or semi-official note to the Minister for Foreign Affairs, objecting to Korea's making a reported loan from Russia, on the grounds that she had already agreed only to loan money of Japan.

Mr. Stein said Mr. Hayashi had denied having officially addressed the Foreign Office in this manner, but on further questioning he admitted that some such arrangement had been verbally agreed upon between himself and Pak Chai Soon, the Minister for Foreign Affairs recently removed from the office at the request of Mr. Pavlow on account of troubles over the erection of a telegraph line; Ye Yong Ik and another Official. Although Mr. Jordan denied having anything to do with advice such as that mentioned in the agreement between England and Japan reported above, there are many happenings here that point to the existence of agreements not included in the published text of the Anglo-Japanese Alliance. I refer you for instance, to the statement made to me by Mr. Jordan, the British Minister, in regard to the right of Great Britain to exercise some control over the customs revenues of Korea. See my despatch No. 535, of November 24, page 2.

Horace N Allen

No. 553

Legation of the United States
Seoul, Korea, December 15, 1902.

Secretary of State

Sir:-

Continuing the subject of the claims of Collbran and Bostwick, I now have the honor to hand you enclosed a copy of a letter I have received from the Minister for Foreign Affairs, written as I am satisfied, by Mr. Brown, as well as a copy of my reply thereto.

I learn from friends in the Palace that Mr. Brown had telegrams sent to the Korean Minister in Washington instructing him to get you to order me to reopen this case, though I had assured His Majesty that it would be useless to refer the matter back to Mr. Brown, who would not finish it "in five years". Mr. Hayashi told me he also sent word to His Majesty that Mr. Brown had been so very dilatory that it would be useless to try to deal through him any further. After demanding a reply from the Korean Minister at Washington, one came a few days ago to the effect that he had seen you and you had said the matter must be settled here; that you would not interfere.

This seems to have alarmed the Koreans though Mr. Brown is said to have quieted them with the assurance that he would settle the matter without trouble to them. A further disturbing factor is that a Japanese Banker, Mr. Yasuda, has left for Tokio with a most favorable report on the properties and intends to telegraph a proposal to purchase, within a few days.

Mr. Brown spoke to me personally about the absence of vouchers relating to a few minor accounts, during the summer, though he added that he could not see that the firm had been making excessive charges. He admitted to me personally that he feared the firm had been paying commissions to certain Koreans and he wished to find out about this with a view to ventilating the matter.

Collbran and Bostwick declare that most of these current vouchers were destroyed in the burning of the building last January, and they will not have Mr. Brown, with his known animosity to them, go over their personal books, though they are entirely willing to allow an impartial examiner to do so.

It therefore seems to be that Mr. Brown is making the trouble and he has put the Koreans at fault. I do not care to reopen the matter for him to trifle with it further, not do I care to weaken the position taken on the mortgage by so doing. If Mr. Brown was not afraid of being obliged to use Customs Funds for paying this claim he would long ago have proposed a lump sum in settlement. No such offer has been made and I wish to wait to see if the Japanese make a satisfactory offer.

Also, as I have reported the whole case to you I would rather not reopen the matter until you have had time to make an expression thereon in case you may wish to do so. I have therefore in response to this request for the "original vouchers" replied in a non-committal sense, rehearsing what has gone before.

I have yet to see the first indication of a real intention to make a payment on the claims, and as the only available funds are those in Mr. Brown's custody, and as he has flatly refused to "use one cent" for the payment, I see no other way than to sell the property to the Japanese, who by the way are the only ones that can manage it cheaply and profitably. It will be a ruin to the whole plant within one year if the Koreans get possession of it.

Horace N Allen

No. 558　　　　　　　　　　　　　　　Legation of the United States
　　　　　　　　　　　　　　　　　　　Seoul, Korea, December 24, 1902.

Secretary of State

Sir:-

In my despatch No. 555 of the 18'th. instant I informed you of a conversation I had had with Mr. Hayashi the Japanese Minister, in regard to the reference of the Collbran and Bostwick claims to an English Judge, Mr. Wilkinson of Shanghia, for arbitration. I declined this suggestion and in doing so quoted remarks of Mr. Jordan, the British Minister to me, to the effect that the British Government would not consent to the use of customs funds for the settlement of these claims - the right of his Government to take such a position being questioned by me at the time.

This conversation of mine with Mr. Hayashi seems to have been reported to Mr. Jordan who came to me this morning to assure me that he was in no way opposing the settlement of these claims; that he had made no utterances against the matter or connected his Government with it in any way, and that he very much regretted that Mr. Brown was mixed up in the matter. I cited what he had said to me in an interview which I showed him was of his own seeking, and of which I could not very well be mistaken since I had written it down after he left. He however insisted that it was merely a casual conversation and that what he had said about the use of customs funds was purely a personal statement and not made with the authority of his Government. He reiterated that fact that he would "deplore" the use of such funds for the settlement of this debt.

I simply cannot be mistaken in this matter as I reported the conversation to you immediately after Mr. Jordan left. See my No. 535 of November 24, page 2. At the same time I assured Mr. Jordan I was willing to accept his statement that he was speaking personally and not for his Government.

We had some talk about Mr. Brown's action in which the statements of Mr. Brown to Mr. Jordan that he could not get from Collbran and Bostwick the necessary accounts for examination conflicted with my statements to the effect that Collbran and Bostwick urged the accounts upon Brown but he would not take them up. We therefore went to see Mr. Brown together and meeting Mr. Collbran on the way, took him with us. Mr. Brown insisted that he examined everything that was given him. Mr. Collbran showed that he, (Brown) through his deputy had refused to go into anything but the accounts of the electric company as represented by the original account. I showed that Mr. Brown had promised officially over the seal of the Foreign Office to take up all the matters; that I had been to him repeatedly and urged him with all my power to attend to the matters; that I had proposed to have the larger accounts sent to his office but that he had said "no I will go down one of these days", and that he had not done so. Each side refused to be convinced.

Mr. Brown seems to have taken exception to my prompt action in closing the matter at noon on October 15. I showed him I had no other course if I wished to preserve the mortgage in force, since he had not handed me his report or made any offer of settlement.

Mr. Brown has acted very wrongly in the whole matter and wishes now to excuse himself. Mr. Jordan does not wish to be drawn into the discussion.

Horace N. Allen.

No. 567

Legation of the United States
Seoul, Korea, January 22, 1903.

Secretary of State

Sir:-

Continuing the subject of the claims of Collbran and Bostwick, last mentioned in my No. 558, of December 24, I now have the honor to hand you enclosed a copy of a letter from the Japanese Chargé d'Affaires, ad interim, Mr. S. Hagiwara, handing Mr. Collbran telegraphic information from the Japanese banker, Mr. Yasuda, who has been actively negotiating for the purchase of the electric properties from Collbran and Bostwick, in which Mr. Yasuda announces that the will have to abandon further negotiations owing to the fear of difficulties from the Koreans in regard to the transfer of the property. - A contingency that Mr. Yasuda fully understood while here, and which he seemed to accept.

This information constitutes a distinct surprise as well as disappoinment, to Mr. Collbran, though I do not feel greatly surprised myself. It has certainly seemed that Mr. Yasuda was sincere in his negotiations and Mr. Hayashi informed me that Baron Komura, Minister for Foreign Affairs, had telegraphed him on the subject, see my No. 533, November 21, page 8. At the same time I could not believe that these Japanese would actually work counter to the interests of their British allies.

From reading my No. 558 of December 24, you will have seen the interest taken in the matter by the British Minister, whose chief business here seems to be to protect Mr. McLeavy Brown in his position as Chief Commissioner of Customs, etc. etc.

At first, Mr. Brown was decidedly in favor of letting this electric property go over to the Japanese on sale. Later however, as I stated in my No. 500 of August 29 last, pages 8 & 9, he changed his opinion in this regard after having been induced to assure His Majesty that he would settle the whole matter and save the property for him - a promise that now seems to disagree with the interests of the Japanese. By his culpable delay in attending to the audit of the accounts, he allowed the foreclosure to go by default and if the property should now go to the Japanese in consequence of his failure to do his duty, he would lose prestige at a time when such loss would work an injury to both Japan and England owing to apparent Russian designs which I will briefly allude to.

Ye Yong Ik, of whom I last wrote you in my No. 563 of January 5, returned to Korea from Port Arthur on a Russian gunboat, reaching Chemulpo on Russian New Year day, Janauary 14. He was met by a guard of honor (or protection) and together with the Captain of the vessel and the Russian Chargé d'Affaires, ad interim, was given a "welcome home" dinner at the Palace. Mr. Waeber, the Russian Special Envoy, has been reported as having urged the Emperor to fully reinstate Ye Yong Ik in office, a thing that seems to be so agreeable to His Majesty that he at once set about complying with this request. Ye is shortly to be gazetted at Minister of Finance and will attempt further control of Korea's finances than he had before his downfall. In this work he will need good advice, and following an old plan, the Russians are now persistently reported as urging the appointment of Mr. Kir Alexeieff as financial adviser again. He held this post in 1897-8 - see my despatches No. 29 of Nov. 7, 1897 and No. 36 of November 19, 1897. He left when the Russians withdrew from Korea to attend to the Liautung Peninsula, see my No. 90, of March 22, 1898. My No. 29, fully explains the designs of which Russia is now accredited. I enclose an extract from the Kobe Chronicle of January 10, giving a copy of a telegram from London in regard to rumored Russian intentions herewith.

Since 1898 Mr. Alexeieff has been in Japan as "Russian Financial Agent" and the Japanese papers have had frequent notices regarding him and his intentions toward Korea.

At the time of the withdrawal of Russia from Korea, this Government agreed not to employ other advisers, but this agreement was broken by the employment, with Russian assent, of M. Kato, formerly Japanese Minister to Korea, as Adviser to the Department of Agriculture, Commerce and Public Works, see my despatch No. 485 of August 1 last.

It is also persistently rumored that a Belgian syndicate is about to loan to Korea a sum of ¥10,000,000 ($5,000,000) and in return the syndicate is to organize a Korean bank and collect all the revenues of Korea. (This is the old Russian scheme mentioned in my No. 29) I think from private advices from the Palace that there is something in this loan proposition and I know that this Belgian syndicate, which is supposed to be a mere Russian agency, has been trying to get an option from Mr. Collbran on his electric and kindred properties, but was unable to do so at the time, owing to Mr. Collbran's agreements with the Japanese negotiators.

If this loan project goes through and the syndicate is entrusted with the collection of the Korean revenues the presence of Ye Yong Ik at the head of the Finance Department with a Russian adviser, will be quite in order, and it may further be necessary to secure the removal of Mr. Brown from his post of Commissioner of Customs, as was formerly attempted, see my No. 29. This being the case it would be unwise for the Japanese to discountenance him by buying this electric property and causing him to fail in carrying out his agreement thereupon, with the Emperor.

I have had reports from the Palace to the effect that Mr. Brown will shortly "pay up" to Collbran and Bostwick, and secure the return of the property. I do not place much confidence in these reports for Mr. Brown is not the kind of man to bring anything to completion.

It is quite likely however, that the Japanese will loan the money for buying back this property and then take an operating contract, as mentioned on page 1 of my despatch No. 535, of November 24, last. In this way Mr. Brown would "save his face" and the Japanese would make a good bargain, while the property would eventually go to them just the same.

In the meantime the property is steadily improving in its capacity as an investment and Collbran and Bostwick will have to continue to operate it until the Belgians buy it or the Japanese get it outright or through a loan to the Koreans.

The Japanese have expressed themselves as fully of the opinion that the property is forfeit to Collbran and Bostwick, and Mr. Collbran secured a legal opinion to the same effect from Mr. N. W. McIvor, of Japan, formerly our Consul General at Yokohama, which I enclose. I may add that had I known Mr. Collbran intended addressing Mr. McIvor on this subject I would have asked him not to do so since I suggested him as a possible arbitrator, see my despatch No. 533, November 21 p. 9.

Horace N Allen

No. 611   Legation of the United States
                                               Seoul, Korea, May 25, 1903.

Secretary of State

Sir:-

Since my despatch No. 567 of January 22 last, was sent you, the Japanese have renewed and continued active negotiations looking to the purchase of the mortgaged properties of the Seoul Electric Company, held by Collbran and Bostwick.

Some time ago Mr. Collbran received a verbal offer for his rights in these properties, from the Secretary of the Japanese Legation, Mr. Hagiwara, amounting to one million yen, exclusive of water-works.

This being satisfactory, Mr. Collbran went to Japan to complete negotiations. He telegraphed to Seoul however, on the 22'nd. instant, that there was some delay on account of the political situation in the

East and that he was therefore returning to Seoul, but that he was confident of an early and satisfactory conclusion of the proposed transaction.

I will briefly bring the matter down to date.

After a long period of silence, the Koreans again took up the discussion, and on April 6 last, I was surprised at the receipt of the despatch of which the enclosed is a copy, informing me of the appointment of a committee of five ignorant Koreans to audit the accounts of Collbran and Bostwick.

When I received your telegraphic instructions of February 28 as follows: - "Refusal of Korean Government to allow sale of mortgaged property to pay any sums actually secured by mortgage is a denial of Justice. If Government refuses prompt adjustment of accounts and to permit sale for sums covered by mortgage, you will request international arbitration of whole controversy. Submit arbitration agreement to the Department before signature". - I was acitvely engaged in a renewed attempt to secure arbitration which I had tried in vain to arrange for earlier, see my No. 540 of Nov. 28. Owing to my renewed representations His Majesty sent me a request that I should submit the whole controversy to Mr. C. de Waeber, Russian Special Envoy, for settlement. I assented to this. See Mr. Collbran's note to me on the subject, of April 19 last, copy enclosed.

Ye Yong Ik, who had deserted the Russians by that time, was able to prevent Mr. Waeber from doing anything in the matter and the latter was placed in the humiliating position of being unable to obtain an audience with the Emperor or of even getting his messages conveyed to the latter.

Nothing came of this new attempt therefore, and on April 3'rd. when I had a three hours interview with Ye Yong Ik on the subject, he flatly refused to listen to proposals for arbitration claiming that this was a Korean matter that must be settled by Koreans.

After preventing Mr. Waeber from doing anything in the matter, Ye Yong Ik attempted to persuade the Japanese that he would arrange for their purchase of the property, but they soon found he was simply triffling with them.

He then went to the French Minister, Mr. de Plancy, and asked him to arrange for him an interview with me. In telling me of this Mr. de Plancy added that he would advise me not to place any dependence upon Ye as he was convinced the man had no desire to bring the matter to a settlement that would be acceptable to the Americans.

Ye's next move was to approach me through an old friend of mine, a Korean official. I consented to see Ye and he came on the 3'rd. of April. I talked with him for three hours and found him absolutely unreasonable. For instantace, when I asked him why he had not acted upon Mr. Brown's report or let the matter go to Mr de Waeber, he said they were both foreigners and Mr. Collbran was a foreigner while this matter would have to be settled by Koreans. He said that all the books and documents of Collbran and Bostwick must be turned over to him and he would say what was necessary to be paid, if anything. As he cannot read his own language much less English, this attempt was very plainly a mere scheme to get possession of and destroy the Imperial orders upon which this claim is based.

He has made serveral foolish attempts to induce me, through the application of certain Korean officials, to hand over the charters on the ground that as the officials in question signed the documents upon the order of the Emperor, they desired them to show that their action was by order and not personal and it was necessary to show this in order to avoid punishement. Certified copies were given in each case, but these were pronounced of no value. I was privately assured at the time that it was a mere clumsy ruse to get possession of the documents in order to lose them.

I know that Ye Yong Ik tried to bribe a trusty Korean employee of Collbran and Bostwick to steal these charters from the Company's safe. I cannot make this public however, as it would lead to the persecution and probable death of the man and his family, were it known that he had been false to Ye and faithful to his employers.

Failing in everything else Ye has had these poor ignorant Koreans appointed as a committee of five, with the evident intention of shifting blame upon them as several of them are old time friends of mine and did not wish the appointment, though being entirely afraid to refuse.

I could not accept this arbitrary reopening of the case and so informed the Minister for Foreign Affairs in my despatch of April 7, copy enclosed. This official is entirely dominated by Ye Yong Ik, to whom all my communications have been at once referred. In this despatch I handed certain proposals of Mr. Collbran for a settlement of the controversy.

To this I received a reply dated April 9, asking me to meet the Committee and discuss the matter of price.

To this I agreed conditionally, as per my despatch of the same date, and I met the Committee on April 10' with Mr. Collbran.

The meeting seemed to be an somewhat satisfactory at the time, in that we secured what seemed to be an aparent offer of ¥700,000 for the repurchase of the property, which I took to be an abandonment of the question of a reopening of the case, as I wrote to the Minister for Foreign Affairs, as per my despatch of April 10. I learned afterwards however that Ye had no intention of paying any such sum but mentioned it as a ruse to secure a statement of the lowest amount upon which the matter might be settled, since he intended to present a most absurd counter claim of ¥ 800,000.

A new and disagreeable complication arose about this time in the action of Ye Yong Ik, who, instead of arranging for the purchase of the plant which now lights the palaces on a 35 year franchise, has given to an Englishman a contract for the purchase and installation of a separate plant for the palace. To this I have entered a remonstrance as per my despatch of April/4, on the ground that any such action will constitute a direct violation of the franchise now held by Collbran and Bostwick, and such violation will render the Korean Government liable to a heavy claim for damages.

In this connection I hand you a copy of my despatch to the Foreign Office dated January 23 last, in which I had to complain of an infringement of this franchise by the erection of telephone lines in Seoul by Japanese. The Koreans were delighted with this action as they had almost come to blows with the Japanese in their attempt to prevent the latter from erecting telephone poles in Seoul. When they found however that my complaint also included a telephone service being erected by the Korean Post and Telegraph Department, they were not so pleased and I received a deferred reply dated March 2.

Mr. Hayashi, the Japanese Minister, informed me on the 14'th April, that his people were very anxious to acquire this telephone franchise as well as most of the other rights of Collbran and Bostwick. I asked him why he had made to the Emperor that unfortunate promise that "he would not agree to the purchase of the property by a Japanese without the consent of the Korean Government". See my despatch No. 533 of November 21, page 6.

I told him that this promise had caused me most of the trouble of the past winter since the Koreans being assured that the property could not be sold, cared not to come to a settlement. Much to my surprise Mr. Hayashi said he had only stated that he would not agree to the purchase by a Japanese without first informing the Korean Government. He further told me that it was now his intention to write to the Household Department cancelling that agreement.

This, taken in connection with other information bearing on the same subject leads me to suppose that Mr. Hayashi has had more or less censure from his people and possibly from his Government, for having made this unnecessary agreement which was interpreted by the Koreans as I mentioned it in my No. 533, and which interpretation Mr. Hayashi allowed me to accept.

Bearing in mind recent reports of threatened violence toward the Company on the part of Ye Yong Ik, who was heard to caution Koreans against using the street cars on the penalty of being considered "traitors", I suggested to Mr. Hayashi on April 14 that if he now withdrew his promise, such action might possibly induce Ye Yong Ik, in his ignorant, stubborn rage, to attempt some violence, in which case it might be difficult for me to secure immediate protection, and as the trouble would be really of his own (Mr. Hayashi's) making, what might I expect if I should call upon him for temporary protection of the property. (The Japanese have a large police force in Seoul and a guard of 200 soldiers). He said he would let me know later. To this I have had no reply.

Mr. Hayashi called again on April 16 and told me that he had telegraphic advices to the effect that his people were very desirous of purchasing this property outright or of securing it upon a loan to the Koreans, a plan that we both favored as liable to cause less friction. He however said that his people did not wish to go above ¥800,000, an amount that was too low for Mr. Collbran to accept without loss, and since then as I stated at the beginning of this letter, the amount was raised, verbally, to ¥1,000,000. He said the matter would take some time to arrange but that he hoped to bring it to a satisfactory conclusion prior to the date of my expected departure on leave, June 1.

Although the matter is still open, Mr. Collbran has telegraphed me not to delay my departure on this account and I think that, with the assistance of Mr. Hayashi, Mr, Paddock will be well able to arrange either for the transfer of the property or for some agreement as to international arbitration. The latter however will simply defer the evil day and any award made would have to be collected by our Government.

On April 16'th. I received a despatch from the Korean Minister for Foreign Affairs, dated the 15'th. quoting a letter dictated by Ye Yong Ik, copy enclosed. This despatch was of such an insulting nature that I was obliged to return it with a note, dated April 17, giving my reasons for not accepting it.

On the 18'th I received another letter from the Minister for Foreign Affairs, again returning me the despatch of the 15'th.

On the same day this returned despatch appeared in a local newspaper well known to be under Government support. I therefore again returned the despatch, stating that I could not receive it as it was couched in undiplomatic language, and calling the Minister's attention to the discourtesy of publishing the letter, which publication might lead to disorders for which the Korean Government would have to be held responsible. At the same time, in order to facilitate an undestanding I again went into the matter of the mortgage; the acounts and claims; the question of the audit which had already been made by Imperial Order, and my attempts to have the whole matter referred to arbitration. See copy of this note enclosed.

I also enclose a copy of a note sent me on April 17 by Mr. Collbran, giving extracts from the mortgage and other documents showing the basis of his claim.

The insulting despatch was again sent me on April 27, for the third time, with a lengthy note in the way of an attempt to refute my arguements. Copy enclosed.

Wearying of this sort of action, I returned the despatch for the third time, with a despatch dated April 29 asking for an audience with the Emperor on the subject.

I again called upon the Foreign Minister however, in order to leave no attempt untried to bring him to a proper understanding of the situation. I found him most difficult to reason with being very dull of comprehension and quite under the control of Ye Yong Ik. I was able however to show him that if my conduct in the case was as described by him, threatening, and without precedent in the world in ancient or modern times, he should report the matter to my Government and have me recalled or suffer punishment himself for having unnecessarily insulted a foreign minister. He asked if I would accept the despatch if he should remove the objectionable passeges, to which I consented on the understanding that he should accompany the revised despatch with a note of apology.

When the revised despatch came to me there was not the promised apology, and I sent my Interpreter to the Minister with the despatch to state that I would not accept it unless he sent me an apology, without which I would not recall my request for an audience.

On May 6 therefore, I received the revised despatch with a suitable note, a copy of which I enclose.

I then withdrew my request for an audience and sent a reply to the accepted despatch, dated May 8, in which, in the kindest manner possible, I attempted to show just how the case stands and what the Koreans might expect. This despatch will merit your perusal.

While the Korean Government seem to hesitate at taking official action looking to the prevention of the operation of the electric plant, the publication in the newspapers of the Minister's unjust letter and the subsequent appearance of daily notices of a most unfair nature regarding Americans and this company particularly, has so incited the people that on the 15'th. instant, a man employed in the mint under Ye Yong Ik, posted notices on the streets to the effect that all Koreans who ride on the cars will be considered "traitors, while another low grade official made public speeches to the same effect. The latter was arrested at the request of the American manager of the electric company, and he is still in jail, though fear of Ye Yong Ik has so far prevented his being brought to trial, and the President of the Supreme Court has memorialized the Emperor on the subject.

This agitation has had some effect in reducing the daily revenues of the Company.

On the 16'th. instant I had a long interview with the Minister for Foreign Affairs on the subject. He disclaimed any government connection with this action and declared the man under arrest to be a mere "crazy" individual. I told him that I would anxiously await the action of the Korean Government in the matter since that would indicate to me whether the mans acts were sanctioned by the Government or otherwise.

Mr. Brown, Commissioner of Customs, who made an examination of the accounts of the Electric Company and a report - as unfriendly to Mr. Collbran as he could make it, has expressed to me his utmost disgust at the action of Ye Yong Ik in the matter. He told me recently that Ye had been to him repeatedly to obtain documents that he might use against the Company, but that he had refussed the request on the ground that he had made his report and sent in his suggestions but that no action had been taken upon either. Mr. Brown also told me that on several occasions he had tried to induce the Emperor to pay five or six hundred thousand yen on account, in accordance with the report of his audit, and that the balance be submitted to arbitration but he had obtained no satisfaciton whatever.

Of late the enemies of Ye Yong Ik have become somewhat stronger than since he was saved by the Russians, as mentioned in my No. 556, of December 18 last, since it is not supposed that any foreign power will again afford the man protection. He is now reported as being very ill at his home and not to be seen. This, taken with the announcement of my early departure has had a good effect upon the business under discussion. The Emperor has recently sent me messages to the effect that "bad people have come between us of late", adding that he "trusts only you (me) among the foreign representatives", at the same time adding that he wishes me to prevent his property from going to the Japanese.

My reply to this was that I had tried my best to prevent his going into this electrical development for which the country was not prepared, and I had done all I could to prevent the accumulation of this great debt, sending him a copy of my last despatch to the Foreign Office of May 8 (enclosure 16). I added that for eleven months past I had been worrying over this matter day and night in trying to effect an amicable settlement, but that the only way in which he could recover the property was by paying a million yen for the same, and that, as the Koreans cannot possibly operate the plant, this money if paid, would be a total loss within one year, while if the property were allowed to go to the Japanese, a million yen would be saved and the city would still have the benefit of the electric plant under capable management.

Japanese aggression is so feared here that it is doubtful if my suggestions will be readily acted upon. But if the Japanese do purchase the property they will do so with the full knowledge that they will have the encumbrance upon it of this Korean ill-will and they will have to protect the property. However, once the Japanese buy the property, the Koreans will soon acquiesce, as the Japanese have methods of persuasion not enjoyed by others.

There is no doubt however that the purchase of the property by the Japanese will cause much ill feeling toward Americans, for a time, on the part of the Koreans. That is on the part of some of them. This will be unjust since the thing complained of will have been of Korean causing entirely, but these people are very childlike in some respects, and like children, they soon recover from their fit of ill nature.

Horace N Allen

No. 239   Department of State
                                           Washington, July 3, 1903.

Gordon Paddock

Sir:

I have to acknowledge the receipt of Mr. Allen's No. 611 of May 25th last and accompaniments in connection with the continued active negotiations on the part of Japanese to purchase the mortgaged properties of the Seoul Electric Company held by Colbran and Bostwick, and in reply to inform you that the Department has carefully considered the contents of your despatch and of its enclosures.

The treatment of the questions involved is doubtless of a difficult character. It is the aim of the Department to cultivate friendly and cordial relations with all Governments and it is its constant policy to address them in a considerate and conciliatory manner even when the circumstances might seem to justify the assumption of a high and imperious tone, and the Department is confident that by conducting the negotiations in a firm, gentle, insistent and unyielding manner, you will be able to bring the Government of His Majesty to a complete understanding of the inflexible attitude of the United States Government in this case; that it desires and expects that no injustice will be done either to Colbran and Bostwick or to the Korean Government in the adjustment of their controversy, and that if they are unable to agree on a settlement which is just and mutually satisfactory, the whole controversy should be submitted to the determination of an international tribunal of arbitration.

Francis B. Loomis

No. 626   Legation of the United States
                                           Seoul, Korea, November 28, 1903.

Secretary of State

Sir:-

As a matter of record, I have the honor to bring briefly to date, the matter of the extensive claim of the American firm, Collbran and Bostwick, in connection with the building and operation of an electric plant in the city of Seoul.

In my despatch No. 611 of May 25 last, I brought this matter down to date, since which time, Mr. Paddock has addressed you in his No. 620 of June 30, in regard to the infringement of the original franchise, by the erection of a new lighting plant for the palace, by an English company, giving you a copy of his remonstrances to both the Korean Foreign Office and the British Minister. His remonstrances were without avail.

As I have fully explained in previous despatches on this subject, the whole trouble is caused by the man Ye Yong Ik, who holds so grrat influence with the Emperor as to be able to influence the latter, continually, against the best interests of the country, both in this and other matters.

His most recent attempt in connection with this claim was to confide certain papers to the dismissed American employee of the Korean Government, Raymond Krumm, prior to the latter's departure for America, together with an expense fund of Yen 2000, all of which Krumm was to use in inciting newspaper comment in America against this American claim; this Legation and myself, with the hope of compelling the Department to cause the claim to be dismissed. Mr. Krumm's advantage was to be; his expenses home; a new contract if he should succeed, and, what probably appealed to him most, a chance of injuring me.

A full account of this man and his conduct, will be found in my despatches Nos. 601. of April 23, 1903; 545, of December 2, 1902, and previous ones referred to therein.

Since writing my despatch No. 611 of May 25 last, the following despatches have been exchanged between this Legation and the Korean Foreign Office, upon the subject of this claim: -

On June 16 Mr. Paddock complained of the proposed erection of a competing electric plant in violation of the franchise, as per copy enclosed in his despatch No. 620 of June 30, and a copy of which I again enclose. On July 13 Mr. Paddock complained of intimmidation that was being used against the passengers on the electric road, in an attempt on the part of Ye Yong Ik to boycott the property.

To this the Foreign Office replied in an unsatisfactory manner, again requesting that the settlement of the matter be referred to Ye Yong Ik.s "Committee of Five". On July 20 Collbran and Bostwick asked assistance from the Legation in regard to this intimmidation, and desired that as inflammatory notices had been posted regarding the electric company, warning the people against using the railway, counter notices should be posted by the Government.

This request was forwarded to the Foreign Office by Mr. Paddock on July 21'st., but it only brought forth a refusal to do so and another reference to the "Committee of Five". To which Mr. Paddock replied on July 25'th. finally disposing of the "Committee of Five".

On July 23'rd. Collbran and Bostwick notified Mr. paddock of the stoning of their cars and again asked for relief.

In consequence of this riotous conduct Mr. Paddock presented a claim for damages and again asked for the posting of concilliatory notices in order to show that the Korean Government were not sanctioning this conduct. Enclosure date July 24.

This despatch brought forth simply an evasive letter dated July 25, again referring to the "Committee of Five", and this was followed by another despatch of July 27, in which the Foreign Office refused to entertain any claim for damages.

Owing to renewed and continued riotous conduct, well known as being inspired by Ye Yong Ik, since the people themselves appreciated and were using the electric railway, on July 31, Mr. Paddock again asked for the posting of concilliatory notices in pursuance of the statement of the Minister for Foreign Affairs that the trouble was being caused by irresponsible persons, this brought no response.

On August 10 Mr. Paddock again asked for the payment to the Company of damages to their property and receipts because of rioting and intimmidation for which the Korean Government had offered no adequate relief. The Minister for Foreign Affairs replied to this request on August 12, stating that no such claim would be allowed even though "one hundred letters and one thousand despatches" should be written on the subject.

On October 1"st. a Korean boy was accidently run over by running into an electric car while playing. The boy was unfortunately killed, and a mob at once arose, crying "death to the foreigner", and doing damage to the persons and property of the Amerians, some of whom had great difficulty in escaping with their lives. Mr. Paddock at once, on October 1, notified the Foreign Office and asked for protection. I enclose a list of the assaults committed by Koreans upon this property up to date of October 6

This rioting being continued, and the Korean Government failing to offer any adequate protection, even though informed that uniformed Korean soldiers and police were assisting the rioters, on October 4, Mr. Paddock wrote to the Foreign Office, threatening to telegraph you for assistance, but getting no prompt response, he very wisely asked Mr. Hayashi, the Japanese Minister, to afford him the protection of Japanese soldiers, which request was promptly complied with to the tremendous consternation of the Koreans, who had not counted on any such turn of events. This request of Mr. Paddock's was most fit and proper and I had previously notified my Japanese colleague that it might be made, and that I thought he should comply, since his own interference at the time of the fore-closure of the mortgage, was somewhat responsible for our present difficulties.

As though the rioting was not trouble enough, just at this time, on October 1, Mr/ Paddock received a request from the Foreign Office that the lights be removed from the palace. to this he complied, after consulting with Collbran and Bostwick, as per enclosure of October 2. Personally I regret this compliance, but Collbran and Bostwick thought best to comply under existing circumstances.

The presence of Japanese police as a protection to the electric power house, was most distasteful to the Koreans, and on October 9 the Foreign Office asked for their removal. As the employment of the Japanese induced the Korean Government to promptly afford necessary protection, Mr/ Paddock agreed on October 10, to remove the Japanese as soon as possible. They were soon removed. on November 14, the Foreign Office replied to Mr. Paddock's despatch of June 16 regarding the infringement of the electric franchise by the erection of a competing plant. This letter was naturally entirely unsatisfacotry as the Foreign Office took the ground that their was not infringement.

On November 16, Mr. Paddock again addressed the Foreign Office on the subject of damages due the Electric Co. for the failure of the Korean Government to protect them during the past summer.

To this the Acting Minister replied, refusing to entertain the subject and stating that he wished to hear no more on the subject. This despatch, as well as all other despatches on the subject were dictated by Ye Yong Ik, as I am confidentially informed by the Acting Minister for Foreign Affairs himself.

I have received repeated assurances from the Emperor that he regrets the occurrences of the past summer, and he has also assured me that he knew nothing of the Krumm incident, and that if the latter actually presents himself at the State Department in Washington, he, the Emperor will cause Ye Yong Ik to suffer therefor. I do not place any confidence in these statements for the Emperor is so entirely in the hands of ye Yong Ik, and is so grasping in the matter of collecting money by any and all means, that I am sure he has listened favorably to propositions looking to the setting aside of this claim, however chimerical such propositions might be. I do think however, that His Majesty would not have sanctioned any attempt to injure me. His friendship for me is a matter that has borne too many evidences of good faith.

As to this "Committee of Five", although I could not agree to recognize them, Mr/Collbran, in an attempt to do all that was possible to affect an amiable settlement of the matter under discussion, did agree to answer questions the committee might propound to him, providing his answers shpould be embodied in the report of the committee. I enclose a copy of these replies, which were not used as they would not suit Ye Yong Ik if embodied in this report.

As a further attempt to annoy the Electric Company, Ye Yong Ik has caused the Company to be requested to remove their primary wire from the palace. This cannot well be done without seeming to give up the franchise entirely, and moreover the wire feeds this Legation and some houses beyond. Mr. Collbran has therefore very properly refused to accede to this unnecessary request, and has warned the palace people that as the wire is heavily charged with electricity, any attempt to interfere with it will result in serious danger.

I enclose copies of the correspondence on this subject, with a letter from Messrs Collbran and Bostwick dated November 17.

Horace N Allen

No. 652   Legation of the United States
                                                     Seoul, Korea, January 24, 1904.

Secretary of State

Sir:-
I have the honor to hand you enclosed, confirmation of my telegram of today regarding a riot that occurred this morning as the result of the unavoidable killing of a Korean by one of the cars of the Seoul Electric Company, an American institution operating in Seoul.

I also hand you enclosed a copy of my letter to the Korean Minister for Foreign Affairs, explaining the whole circumstance and intimating that I shall make a claim for damages on behalf of the Electric Company when all the facts are known.

As I explained in my No. 626 of November 28 last, these instances of mob violence are not sufficiently noticed by the Korean Government, especially since Korean soldiers lead the mob of September 30 which came very near killing at least one American. Had I been here at the time I would have taken more severe methods on that occasion, but as it was a closed incident apparently, I did not wish to open it. In this case however I think it might be as well to bring home to the Korean Government the fact that such things must not be allowed, especially so in view of the Korean remonstrance to my getting up a guard, and continued publication of incendiary articles in the Korean newspapers, although in common with other of my colleagues I have called the attention of the Minister for Foreign Affairs to the danger of allowing these newspapers to continue such publications.

In this connection I hand you enclosed another copy of a translation of an article that appeared in the Chekuk Sinmun, in the issue of yesterday. You will note that in this article the editor calls attention to the "Boxer" uprising of 1900 in Peking, and praises the leaders of that movement.

Had it not been for the presence, and prompt appearance of our marine guard this morning, the riot of today might well have spread to the destruction of the electric power house as well as other property, and the destruction of life. It looks as though the affair of this morning was premeditated, as it occured near a newly placed pile of stones, and the Korean jinricksha man refused to listen to the warnings of the Korean motorman. I do not give the man credit for intending to sacrifice his life, but he would not leave the track and evidently may have intended to have his old and damaged jinricksha injured sufficiently to have given some shaddow of reason for the attack.

The ice on the track caused his plans, if such they were, to end in greater results to himself than he may have intended. I may add that the thermometer stood at -13 Farrenheit last night.

Horace N Allen

No. 254   Department of State
                                           Washington, February 27, 1904.

Horace N. Allen

Sir:
I have to acknowledge the receipt of your No. 652, of the 24th ultimo, confirming your telegram of the same date regarding the riot that occurred that morning as the result of the unavoidable killing of a Korean by one of the cars of the Seoul Electric Company, an American Corporation operating in Seoul.

With your despatch you enclose a copy of your note to the Korean Minister for Foreign Affairs, explaining the affairs and intimating that you will make a claim for damages on behalf of the Electric Company, when all the facts are known.

Taking everything into account, viz, the inherent prejudice of the Oriental against innovations like the electric car; the killing of the Korean by the car; the fact that the motorman was rescued from the mob; and the present unfortunate situation of Korea as a battleground between the Russians and the Japanese, you will not present any claim for damages.

John Hay

No. 670   Legation of the United States
                                           Seoul, Korea, February 16, 1904.

Secretary of State

Sir:-
I have the honor to confirm my telegram of today as follows:-
"Am informed that Head of the Government of Korea has ordered the Minister for Foreign affairs of Korea to open Wiju. I expect to receive official announcement in a few days in reply to my request of the fourteenth. Head of the Government of Korea also satisfactorily settled Electric Company matters".

Horace N Allen

No. 693   Confidential.   Legation of the United States
                                                               Seoul, Korea, March 8, 1904.

Secretary of State

Sir:-

In my despatch No. 682, of the 27'th ultimo, I advised you of the fact that the Korean Government was now showing marked courtesy in attending to matters presented by this Legation, in great contrast to the condition of affairs for the past two years, - during the supremacy of the man Ye Yong Ik, recently taken to Japan.

As a further evidence of this return to previous cordial relations, I now have the honor to inform you of the final settlement of the long disputed matters relating to the Seoul Electric Company, which was taken over by the American firm, Collbran and Boswick on default, to satisfy a mortgage.

I addressed you by telegraph on February 16 advising you of a settlement but owing to matters relating to a deferred payment I could not follow at once with a letter in detail.

As you will see from the enclosed copy of a letter to me of yesterday, from Mr. Collbran of Collbran and Boswick, the Emperor has decided to retain an interest in the Company, which is to remain in American hands, and thus prevent its sale to Japanese. He therefore - unexpectedly to the firm and to myself - proposed to purchase a half interest. This was arranged, without consulting me, by his paying Yen 750,000 ($325,000). Yen 400,000 ($200,000) being in cash and the balance in a promissory note bearing a provision that if it is not paid the Yen 400,000 will be forfeited.

Mr. Collbran has assured me, in justice to the Emperor, that in case of default, he will not take this large sum for nothing but will apply it to the payment of the indemnity claimed for non-fulfillment of a water works contract after great expense had been incurred, and then surrender the agreement entirely. As matters stand now however, he intends to complete the much needed water works and secure the capital for the same in the United States, thus relieving the Korean Government of the chief objection they seemed to have towards this enterprise.

In addition to all these matters the firm is given certain mining rights on a royalty to be paid the Korean Government of 25% net.

I hear privately that in addition to a mining concession privately granted the Russian subject, Baron Gunsburg in December, concessions have lately been granted to French; Belgians and English, while the Germans and Italians are requesting similar rights with some prospect of success.

I also understand that these other concessions are being granted on the basis of a cash payment ranging from yen 200,000 to 300,000. The royalty plan seems to me to be the more fair to the Koreans.

Mr. Collbran calls attention in his letter enclosed, to the fact that the cheque handed him was made out to him by Ye Yong Ik a year ago and withheld by the Emperor himself, thus giving Ye Yong Ik a pretext for stating that the Company had received and not accounted for this large sum. This makes more clear many things that have taken place during the past year and shows into what a deplorable state the Korean palace affairs had fallen.

It is pretty well known that the Emperor was actually in negotiation with the Russians for a guard of troops. I have no available proof of this, but intelligent Koreans believe it, and the Japanese are making it very uncomfortable for the Koreans who were supposed to be in charge of the negotiations, and it is supposed that it made the way more easy for the acceptance of the Protocol of February 23. Therefore, when the Emperor saw the humiliating spectacle of the retreat of all the Russians from Seoul after the destruction of their ships at Chemulpo, he was horrified and turned at once to his old friends the Americans.

I fully realize that this prompt and generous as well as voluntary settlement of the electric matters without consulting me, was made with the hope of wiping off all the feeling of resentment for the unkind treatment I have received and of gaining American sympathy. In fact His Majesty has said as much to me since. I have fully explained our neutral situation especially with reference to the recent alliance with Japan - though that was not sought by the Koreans. I have made no promises whatever, though I have assured His Majesty that if it becomes necessary to invoke the good offices of the United States in accordance with the provisions of our treaty with Korea, I am sure the request will receive prompt and kindly attention.

I am able to hand you enclosed a copy of the document given in settlement of the disputed Electric Company matters. In addition to this they have mining rights that have yet to be located.

Mr. Collbran leaves shortly for America to arrange the financial matters necessary to his undertakings. He asks me to keep these matters of his out of print until he is ready to have them made public. I have therefore marked this communication confidential.

These concessions cannot but tend very greatly to the development of American commercial interests in this land, since every such company constitutes a centre for the introduction of American capital and products. Under the new regimé into which Korea seems tending, it is to be hoped that these American companies will prosper without requiring so much attention as has this particular one in the past.

Horace N Allen

No. 746

Legation of the United States
Seoul, Korea, May 27, 1904.

Secretary of State

Sir:-

In my Number 500 of August 29, 1902, as enclosure 10, I handed you a copy of a water works agreement held by Messrs Collbran and Bostwick, an American firm, who were then trying to collect a large claim covering electric construction and failure to carry out water works agreements. This agreement called for the expenditure of Yen 200,000 ($100,000) per annum for some eight years, the money having been ordered by Imperial mandate, to be set aside by the Customs. The Commissioner of Customs, a British subject, Mr. Brown, was favorable to the project at first, apparently, but when he saw that the money was to come from his department his attitude changed and he is credited with having suspended all action on the matter, with the assistance of the British and Japanese Ministers.

One result of the settlement of the electric claim, which I detailed in my No 693 of March 8 last, was that the firm agreed to erect the water works as a company matter, furnishing the capital themselves and thus relieving the project of its one disadvantageous feature. This agreement has however to be kept secret for the time, as the firm were obliged so to promise the Emperor. Perhaps he does not wish to recall his order for the setting aside of Yen 200,000 per annum, which he may wish to use for other purposes. It is publicly known however that Mr. Collbran has gone to America to raise the necessary funds for this and other purposes, and while in Japan he met Japanese financiers connected with the Government, whom he expects also to interest in the project. This was known to the Japanese Minister here, as he gave Mr. Collbran letters of introduction to these parties.

The Japanese authorities here, as well as in Japan, have had full access to all the papers of this firm in connection with their long continued talk of purchasing the whole interest: - A thing they might easily have done had they not put it off too long, for after negotiating for over eighteen months and finally abandoning the project in December last, the full settlement detailed in my No 693 of March 8 last, compelled Collbran and Bostwick to decline offers made after the successful commencement of the present war.

The existence of this water works agreement was therefore well known to the Japanese, as was the unfriendly official report on the Collbran and Bostwick claims, made by Mr. Brown and forwarded as enclosure 4 in my Number 533 of November 21 1902, wherein Mr. Brown says that the Household Department "whenever the competent authority decides to introduce a system of water works into the city of Seoul, (is obliged) to give the contract to Messrs Collbran and Bostwick and to no other party".

In view of all this I was greatly astonished therefore to learn from a local newspaper of the 13th instant, that a system of water works was about to be installed without any reference whatever to the Americans. I therefore wrote an unofficial letter, as per copy enclosed, to the Minister of the Household, making inquiries as to the matter. He came to see me at once and made great assurances that the matter was a mere temporary one but he failed to see that the act was a direct violation of existing agreements. I urged him to see Mr. Bostwick and arrange some sort of compromise, but he failed to agree to do so. I also learned privately that the Emperor in sanctioning the project, had insisted that the Minister first see me and obtain my consent, and that the latter had announced that he had done so. I therefore wrote him again as per copy enclosed, protesting against the construction of the proposed water system except by Collbran and Bostwick. To this I received a reply dated May 19 as per copy enclosed. This being unsatisfactory I had a very serious interview with the Minister and I also sent copies to the Emperor of my letters to his Minister. It was evident the Latter was now quite worried, and in response to my third letter of May 20, he called upon Mr. Bostwick and after a long interview agreed to drop the project entirely. I enclose copy of a letter from Mr. Bostwick giving the chief points of this interview, and showing that the scheme had been successfully urged upon the Koreans by a Japanese subject, who signed an agreement to settle any interference that might arise from the Americans. I learned privately that of the Yen 25,000 paid as an initial payment, 15,000 was divided among the Koreans concerned, while 10,000 went to the Japanese contractor.

It is easily shown that the scheme was entirely non-feasible and would only have resulted in a complete waste of money.

On the 19th instant I visited Mr. Hayashi, the Japanese Minister, and laid the whole case before him. I felt that with the knowledge he possessed of the American documents in the case, he would assist me in preventing any such infringement by a Japanese subject, as he is well known to have great power over his people here. He seemed surprised to hear of the matter, though it had been in the newspapers, and said he would investigate it. I have not yet been favored with any intimation as to the results of his investigation. It may be the Japanese contractor on his return, will attempt to hold the Koreans to the terms of their contract.

Horace N. Allen.

No. 749   Legation of the United States
                                                     Seoul, Korea, June 1, 1904.

Secretary of State

Sir:-

I have the honor to hand you enclosed, the published Report for 1903 of the Oriental Consolidated Mining Company, being the American gold mining company operating a district in north-western Korea of some 500 square miles in extent, upon a concession obtained from the Korean Government.

The Directors of the Company are Messrs H. C. Perkins, President; Leigh Hunt, Vice President; Wm. L. Bull, a Second Vice President and Treasurer; J. B. Haggin; Ogden Mills; J. S. Fassett, and Wm. P. Palmer. The main office of the Company is at 38 Broad Street, New York City.

H. F. Meserve is the manager of the mines and lives on the concession, with an office and agent at Chemulpo Korea.

The Company operates eight mines besides having several others operated by Koreans as "tribute mines". Considerable prospecting work is also being prosecuted.

There are five mills in active operation on the concession, with a total of 200 stamps. The Company also operates three cyanide plants.

During the year 1903 the Company mined and milled 203,567 tons of ore, of a total value of $1,478,956,78 .

On December 31'st 1903 They had ore in sight, 1,058,746 tons, valued at $5,874,637,45.

The cost of mining per ton for 1903 was $1,005: For milling it was $0,5025 The total operating expenses per ton being $2,225. The yield per ton was $6,0655.

The total operating profit for 1903 was $762,315,84.

The Company employs from sixty to seventy white men and several thousands Asiatics, spending for labor alone in 1903 some $300,000.

They are now building a large dam to form a reservoir for a water power plant. Their mills will be run by electricity generated by this plant, which will cost when complete about $200,000.

They own one steam launch and six schooners, which run between the open port Chenampo, and the non-open port, Anju, from which the concession is reached by river or road, owing to the season.

The capital stock of the company is $5,000,000. $750,000 treasury stock is still held by the company. The company had a cash surplus on January 1'st, 1904 of $925,015,36.

Aside from the railways now being built under the auspices of the Japanese Government, this is the largest financial enterprise now being conducted in Korea. It is said to be the largest development undertaking of its kind in Asia.

Horace N Allen

No. 753   Legation of the United States
                                   Seoul, Korea, June 7, 1904.

Secretary of State

Sir:-

   In my No. 693 of March 8 last, handing you copies of documents relating to the settlement of the claims of Collbran and Bostwick and the Seoul Electric Company, which resulted in the purchase of a half interest in the concern by the Emperor of Korea, for Yen 750,000 ($375,000), Yen 400,000 of which was paid down and a promissory note for Yen 350,000 was given, with a clause allowing of the forfeiture of the first payment in case the deferred payment was not made in three months.

   I now have the honor to inform you that the whole balance of Yen 350,000 was paid over last night, thus relieving me of much anxiety lest I might be compelled to do something in favor of this forfeiture clause whereby the Emperor would be obliged to lose what is to him a very large sum of money.

                                   Horace N. Allen.

No. 875   American Legation, Seoul, Korea
                                   February 16, 1905.

Secretary of State

Sir:-

   In my No. 749 of June 1, last, I sent you the report of the operations of the American mining company in Northern Korea, known as the Oriental
Consolidated Mining Company, for the year 1903.

   I now have the honor to hand you enclosed, a copy of the report of the same company for the first half of the year 1904, this company having changed their method of reporting so as to have the year end on June 30th hereafter.

   From this report it will be seen that this company, in spite of the difficulties incident to the present war, having mined 81,952 tons of ore valued at $478,848,34, or $5,84 per ton, excluding a small amount from "tribute mines". The cost of mining the company's ore being $1,26 per ton. Showing a profit for operating for the six months of $162,183,10.

   The company is also completing an extensive water power for the generating of electricity for operating their mills.

                                   Horace N Allen

No. 891   American Legation, Seoul, Korea.
                                   March 30, 1905.

Secretary of State

Sir:-

   In my despatch No. 874 of the 14th ultimo, confirming my telegram of that date, I advised you of the formation of an American, British and Japanese syndicate to operate mines and other industries in Korea. I stated that in addition to participating in a mining concession owned by the American firm of Collbran and Bostwick, this syndicate would have equal interests in a mine long since applied for by the British Minister with no success, but which the Japanese Minister and myself would now second with success.

   I have the honor to inform you that this concession, which is for the very valuable Soo-an mine, has now been granted in principle and simply awaits the arrangement of details. Engineers have already arrived for the prosecution of the work.

   I hand you enlclosed the application of the British Minister for this mine, which application was seconded by the Japanese Minister and myself. I also enclose the reply to the same.

In this connection I also hand you enclosed a certified copy of the mining concession granted to the American firm Collbran and Bostwick on February 15th 1904, as well as a copy of the agreement granted to the Italian Minister for a mining concession, dated the 15th instant, mentioned in my 886 of the 17th.

Horace N Allen

E. U.S. Legation Business

No. 273   Legation of the United States
                                             Seoul Korea, June,10, 1897.

Secretary of State

Sir:-
    Referring to your letter of Feb. 27, no number, asking for an estimate of the cost of a suitable U.S. Legation building for this city, I beg leave to say that I judged that Icould best meet your wishes by giving you the cost of the buildings which other nations have thought sufficient for similar use.
    The English, the Japanese, the French and the Russians have erected Legations here. I have been greatly delayed in getting infomation as to the amount invested in the English plant, their accounts of building expenses are kept at Peking and while Mr. Jordan, the British Representative showed great willingness to give me the desired information, he could obtain it only by correspondence with their Representative in China. After all my waiting I am able only to get approximate figures in this case.
    It was completed in 1892 and consists of two buildings, one a residence and office for the Legation proper and one a Consular office. They are built of brick, each two stories in height and are of ample dimensions for their purposes. the cost was about $37,000 silver, equal at the time to about $33,300 gold. I send a photograph of the Legation building.
    The Russian Legation is one lofty story in height. It was built of brick covered with stucco and was begun in 1890. It is perhaps the most stately in appearance of any here and is large enough for present and all probable future wants. It was cheapened in construction at the expense of durability. The bricks are soft and the heavy rains and severe frosts make bad work with the stucco which has already begun to scale off, exposing crumbling bricks in many places.
    The cost was about $28,000 silver, at that time about $25,200 gold. But not only was the building poorly made, but Mr. Waeber, the Russian Chargé d'Affaires, being an architect, made all the plans and details and supervised the construction and made all purchases of materials without cost to his Government. He tells me that it would require at least $40,000 to replace the building now, correcting faults in construction and materials and paying usual prices for architects plans and supervision. I send a photograph of this structure.
    The present Japanese Legation is built of wood and is decidedly inferior in appearance. It has been enlarged until it meets present needs as to space. The whole cost to date has been $18,325 silver, which I cannot put into gold as it was spent at various times. The Japanese Government is about completing a very handsome brick and stone Consulate at a cost of about $80,000 silver ($40,000 gold) inclusive of grounds and numerous out-buildings for offices etc.
    The French are now erecting a fine building. Mr. V.C. de Plancy has furnished me with a photograph of the architects elevation, a copy of which I enclose, the estimated cost is $52,000 ($26,000 gold)
    The Germans are occupying rented houses as insignificant in appearance as our own.
    My judgment based on the best obtainable information is that from $25,000 to $30,000 gold, at present equal to about $50,000 to $60,000 silver, would be required to erect a Legation of proper size to meet our present and future needs. This amount of money judiciously expended would, I believe give us a structure which would not suffer by comparison with other legations in Seoul.
    I wish to say of the present buildings, that while we are somewhat straightened for room, we have found ourselves altogether comfortable in other respects and that repairs, improvements in drainage etc. which I have been allowed to make, have put the premises in good sanitary condition and that my successor need have no fears of danger to the health of himself or his family.
    For the outward appearance of the buildings nothing favorable can be said. I enclose a photograph.

                                             John M. B. Sill

Enclosures
    Four photographs
    <u>Note</u> I wish to add in explanation of this typewriting, that our present machine not being satisfactory, I have arranged to exchange it for a better one.

No. 1   Department of State
                                                 Washington, August 2, 1897

Horace N. Allen, Esquire
        Appointed Minister Resident and Consul General of the United States of America to Korea. (Now at Seoul, Korea.)

Sir
        The President by and with the advice and consent of the Senate, having appointed you to be Minister Resident and Consul General of the United States of America to Korea, and you having subscribed to the necessary oath of office, I herewith enclose to you the following documents:
        1. Your commission in that capacity.
        2. A letter of credence addressed to His Majesty the King of Tah Chosun, with an office copy of the same which you will communicate to the Minister for Foreign Affairs upon your asking through him, an audience of His Majesty for the purpose of presenting the orginal.
        3. A copy of the printed instructions to the Diplomatic Officers of the United States.
        4. A diplomatic and consular list of the United States.
        Your salary as fixed by law, will be at the rate of Seven Thousand five hundred ($7,500.) dollars per annum. You will also be allowed the sum of $2,300 yearly for rent and contingent expenses of your Legation and Consulate General, and Five hundred ($500.) dollars annually, for the services of an Interpreter. For your salary as it falls due, quarterly, for the contingent expenses and rent, and for the Interpreter's compensation, you will draw upon the Department of State.
        Your are referred to the printed Instructions to the Diplomatic Officers of the United States for detailed information and direction as to the mode of drawing your salary, and of rendering your accounts, as well as for the regulations relating to the expenditures of your Legation.
        Although extended instructions in regard to the conduct of your Mission may not be necessary it seems proper to refer as briefly as possible to the manner in which your despatches should be addressed, since you are accredited in a dual capacity.
        For the convenience of the Deaprtment, I may observe that your diplomatic and consular correspondence should be entirely independent of each other. The former should be addressed to the Secretary of State, and the latter to the Assistant Secretary of State. You will give to each, however, a distinct series of numbers commencing with No. 1, and continuing in regular sequence. At the top of the title page of your despatch, should be written, in accourdance with the subject, either "diplomatic" or Consular series", as the case may be.
        To become properly conversant with the business of the Legation, you will have recourse to the correspondence of your predecessors in the Mission recorded in its archives. Special instructions on important subjects between the two Governments will be sent from time to time as occasion may require.
        I enclose, also, the letter of recall of your predecessor Mr. John M. B. Sill, the office copy of which, you may send to the Minister for Foreign Affairs and present the original to His Majesty, at the time you deliver your letter of credence.
        The Department entertains the confidence that your intelligent and zealous attention to the interests of the United States, now confided to your care, will be eminently conducive to the harmony and friendly relations between the two countries which it is so much the desire of the President to maintain and strengthen.

                                                 Alvey A. Adee

No. 1   Legation of the United States
                                                 Seoul Korea, September 13, 1897.

Secretary of State

Sir;-
        I have the honor to acknowledge the receipt on the 11'th Instant, of the despatch No. 1, dated August 2, of Mr. Adee, Acting Secretary of State, advising me of my appointment by the President, by and with the consent of the Senate, to be Minister Resident and Consul General of the United States of America to Korea, and handing me my Commission; my letter of credence, with an office copy of the same; a copy

of the Instructions to the Diplomatic Officers of the United States, and a Diplomatic and Consular list of the United States, together with the Letter of Recall for Mr. Sill, with an office copy of the same.

I am deeply grateful to the President for the high honor he has conferred upon me, and I shall do all in my power to carefully carry out the spirt and letter of the instructions I have been favored with, and I shall endeavor by constant diligence and caution to give the fullest possible satisfaction to the Government in this new post of responsibility.

At once upon the receipt of the above named despatch and its enclosures, we communicated with the Minister for Foreign Affairs, giving him translations of the letters of the President, and an audience was appointed for today. At this audience Mr. Sill presented his letter of recall, and I delivered my letter of credence. We each made suitable remarks, to which His Majesty replied in gracious terms.

I herewith enclose a copy of my remarks and a synopsis of the reply of His Majesty.

With a further expression of my deep gratitude for the high honor you have conferred upon me,

Horace N. Allen.

Your Majesty:

In presenting my credentials as Minister Resident and Consul General of the United States of America, it gives me great pleasure to call Your Majesty's attention to the very cordial expressions of the President contained therein, of a desire for the maintainance and strengthening of the friendly relations that have so long existed between our two Governments and countries.

The Government and people of the United States entertain very kindly sentiments toward the Government and people of Tah Chosen, and in accepting the high post conferred upon me by these credentials, I wish to assure Your Majesty that it will be my pleasant duty to do all in my power, in conformity with my instructions, to further cement and strengthen these kindly feelings and friendly relations.

I have long been known to Your Majesty and I have had repeated kind expressions of confidence from your lips. By the exercise of caution and diligence, I hope in my new post to lose none of that confidence which I assure Your Majesty I appreciate most highly, but rather to enjoy to a still greater extent, the good opinion you have heretofore expressed yourself as entertaining of me; while at the same time, so fulfilling the instructions of my Government as to merit to as full an extent as possible, the confidence shown in me in appointing me to this post of importance and responsibility.

Reply of the King to the remarks of Mr. Allen.

The United States was the first of the Western Nations to make a treaty with Chosen. We feel that America is to us an Elder Brother (Korean Phrase).

We have long been sure of the good will of your government, and now we know by the appointment of yourself as Minister, that your Government considers our wishes, and that President M'cKinley, appreciates our country.

We have known you a long time, we know that you fully understand Korea and Korean politics, customs and manners. We feel sure that the appointment of yourself as your country's Minister here, will tend greatly to strengthen the friendly relations that have so long existed between our two countries.

We are glad to welcome you in your new capacity.

No. 4   Legation of the United States
                                                                    Seoul Korea, September 20, 1897.

Secretary of State

Sir;-

In conformity with my instructions I have the honor to report to you upon the condition of the Archives of this Legation upon assuming charge, and in so doing I will have to mention my own connection therewith to a certain extent.

When I entered upon my duties as Secretary of Legation here in 1890, I found the letters and other documents unbound, tied in bundles and stowed in out of the way, dusty corners. Many were missing. I secured duplicates of missing papers so far as was possible; called in a native binder and had everything neatly bound in suitable volumes, after which I carefully indexed them all and wrote up the books in proper order, so that after six months work everything was in good shape and of easy access.

Since that time I have readily kept the archives in proper order as prescribed by the regulations, and I think they will well bear a close inspection.

I would like to say a word in this connection about the office itself.

The office building is an old Korean house of very dilapidated external appearance. I have now arranged to have the most disreputable parts put in more decent shape by replacing the mud walls with walls of brick, fitted with glass windows instead of those of paper, at a small charge to the Contingent Fund. The office building has not so far had any of the small allowances for repairs.

Inside, the office presents a very business like appearance. The furniture is meagre but with a few additions from time to time it will be ample for the present building.

With the handsome legation buildings of other governments in close proximity to our place, and the fine palace buildings and customs offices going up next door, it is exceedingly humilliating to American residents and travellers to see their own Government so meanly housed. We own the Legation which occupies one of the best sites in Seoul and right in the centre of the foreign colony and the new palace buildings.

Horace N. Allen

Department of State
Washington, October 18, 1897

William F. Sands,
Appointed Secretary of the Legation of the United States of America at Seoul, Korea. Now in Washinton, D.C

Sir:
The President having appointed you Secretary of the Legation of the United States of America at Seoul, Korea, I enclose herewith your commission in that capacity.

The specified duties of the position to which you have been appointed must in a great degree be determined by circumstances or ascertained by the experience of the Legation. It will devolve upon you to transcribe the official communications of the Minister, and to record the same in suitable books, to be carefully preserved with the archives of the Legation. The classification and indexing of the originals of all despatches, notes, and official communications and the custody of the records, books, seal and cipher of the Legation will also be under your immediate control, - subject of course to the general supervision and direction of the Minister.

Section 1750 of the Revised Statutes authorizes a Secretary of Legation to administer oaths, take depositions, and generally to perform notarial acts. While this statute is not construed as mandatory, it is not thought you will fail to appreciate what can rightly be expected in this regard. You will be entitled to retain fees paid for such services. Should a seal be required, you will use that of the Legation.

Should the post of Minister become vacant during your connection with the Legation, it will be your duty to retain charge of the seal, cipher, records, books, and archives, and to take upon yourself the discharge of the ordinary functions of the mission as Chargé d'Affaires ad interim until the vacancy be otherwise supplied.

In the event of the Minister's absence from his post by permission, the duties of Chargé d'Affaires ad interim will in like manner, devolve upon you, and in such case you will be duly presented to the Minister for Foreign Affairs in that capacity.

It is to be distinctly understood that in either circumstance, this will not give you any claim to other compensation than that provided for the contingency by the Act of Congress of the 18th of August, 1856, namely, at the rate of fifty per centum of the regular salary attached to the Minister's office. This compensation is in lieu of your salary as Secretary of Legation, which ceases during the time you shall act as Chargé d'Affaires ad interim.

You will submit to the Department separate accounts therefor at the end of such term of temporary charge, and on receiving its authorization, you will draw on the Secretary of State for the amount due you as Chargé at the date of your draft.

Your compensation as Secretary of Legation will be at the rate of Fifteen hundred ($1,500) dollers per annum; and you will draw upon the Secretary of State for the amount of your salary as it becomes due, quarterly, commencing on the date of your oath of office. You will be entitled to salary for thirty days from that date prior to your departure for your post, while receiving instructions, and will draw for the same in like manner. In availing yourself of this authorization, you will be careful not to exceed, in the amount drawn for the sum to which you may be entitled in account with the United States at the date of your drafts.

John Sherman

No. 223

Legation of the United States
Seoul Korea, Jan. 19, 1900.

Secretary of State

Sir:-

I have the honor to inform you that the Korean Government, having made satisfactory arrangements, is now despatching foreign mails from Korea through its own post-offices, as I have already reported.

I have therefore, arranged for the transmission of sealed mail pouches between this Legation and the Department of State, and this letter goes forward by the first pouch.

As the pouches I am able to have made here, are not suitable for the purpose, I have the honor to request that I be supplied with such as are in use between the Department and other Legations. I presume such will be received in the ordinary course of the transmission of mails. In the meantime, I shall in all probability, use the open mails largely.

Horace N. Allen

No. 173

Department of State
Washington, June 27, 1901

Horace N. Allen

Sir:

The President desiring to show in every way his friendship and regard for the Emperor of Korea, has decided to raise the rank of your mission to correspond with that of the mission of Korea to this country.

I enclose herewith your commision as Envoy Extraordinary and Minister Plenipotentiary of the United States to Korea, and a blank oath of office, which, when sworn and subscribed to by you, should be returned to the Department for its files.

David J. Hill

No. 402

Legation of the United States
Seoul, Korea, September 20, 1901.

Secretary of State

Sir:-

I have the honor to acknowledge the receipt of five telegrams from you, on the overleaf, in regard to the lamented death of President McKinley, and to confirm my telegram of the 15'th. instant.

On yesterday, the date of the funeral, I held a memorial service at eleven o'clock, in the large brick, Methodist Church in front of this Legation. I enclose copies of the invitations to this service and of the programme of exercises.

His Majesty, the Emperor of Korea, sent as his official representatives to this service, Prince Ye Chai Soon; the Minister for Foreign Affairs, and the Minister of the Imperial Household. The members of the Cabinet also attended in court dress. The Foreign Representatives all attended in full uniform, and during the overture the Imperial Representatives and the Foreign Ministers filed in with me and occupied draped chairs in front of the pulpit. Almost the entire foreign community attended and the services were solemn and impressive.

I have received the most profound expressions of sorrow from native and foreign officials and the community generally, upon this our great bereavement.

I will strictly observe mourning until further instructed, and regret that I cannot furnish the Legation with mourning stationery.

It is very difficult to arrange for a suitable service such as that I held on yesterday, owing to the lack of facilities in this place. I wish therefore to record my gratitude to those who helped me to make the service a success, and chiefly to the Rev. Geo. Heber Jones, Superintendent of the Korean Mission of the American Methodist Church, for valuable suggestions and for conducting the service with the assistance of others; to Mrs. D. A. Bunker and Miss Katherine Wambold, for attending, with my wife, to the extensive draping of the church, and to Miss. Dr. Field, for furnishing the instrumental music, as well as to all to whom I applied for assistance.

I promptly conveyed to the Minister for Foreign Affairs for the Emperor, the message contained in your telegram received on the 17'th. instant.

Horace N Allen

No. 462   Legation of the United States
                                                  Seoul, Korea, May 20, 1902

Secretary of State

Sir:-

I am reluctantly compelled to bring to your attention a most aggravating case in which a young American, Raymond Krumm, of Columbus Ohio, now in the employ of the Korean Government, has threatened to kill David W. Deshler, a most estimable business man of Chemulpo Korea, and step-son of Governor Nash of Ohio. My reason for bringing the matter to your attention at this stage is that Mr. Krumm is preparing to make some sort of charges against me, presumably at the Department of State.

The facts are briefly as follows: - Through the kindness of Mr. Deshler, who is an intimate friend of W. H. Krumm, the brother of the Krumm in question, the latter was given employment in the construction of the Seoul-Chemulpo Railway, though he had not yet completed his course in engineering. W. H. Krumm was at the time employed in the same work and is now with the American Mining Company in North Korea.

Some time (about one year) after R. Krumm's arrival, he secured with my assistance, a lucrative position in the Korean service, on a five years contract as head of a survey bureau. I also showed him numerous and continued kindnesses, even to the extent of securing him at the Bank for Yen 5,000 ($2,500) for the purchase of some desirable property. After he had gotten into the property deal, very great difficulties were experienced in completing it as the Korean Government refused, on one pretext and another, to issue a deed. It transpired that the Emperor wanted the property for the mother of his youngest son, and I advised Mr. Krumm as he was in the Korean service, to come to some compromise on the question. To this he agreed. withdrew, agreed again and became most anxious to accept. After very great difficulty and some delay, I finally secured a most generous settlement. He was given Yen 10,000 for the property which had cost him but Yen 5,000 a few months before. Owing to delays in the final payments Mr. Krumm may have lost as much as $200 on exchange, all of which he was informed of beforehand and to which he fully assented. It is this loss from his 100% profits of which he seems to complain.

He seems to have conceived the idea that this loss was due to my action, and even insinuates that I was interested in getting the property, though I refused to join him in the matter and informed him that I made it a rule not to hold any interests in the country to which I am accredited. I kept him fully posted by word and letter of all that I was doing and he knew full well that I was doing all in my power for him and more than I was called upon to do. In fact he has ample evidence that I have never done him an unkindness and if I have erred at all, it has been on the side of favor to him. I never had the intention to do him an injury and I have never approached any such act.

He consulted his brother and Mr. Deshler in regard to a complaint he intended to bring against me, but they did their best to dissuade him from any such course. This angered him against them, particularly Mr. Deshler. They did not inform me of his intentions through mortification.

He finally became possessed of the idea that Mr. Deshler had taken from him a letter I had written him. He did not mention this to Mr. Deshler until months after the incident of the "stolen letter" which he graphically recounts. He made frequent and increasingly insulting demands for this "stolen letter" until on August 23, 1901, he wrote a most violent letter to Mr. Deshler, in which he threatened to shoot him on sight.

Mr. Deshler brought the matter to me on August 24, and for the first time I realized what the young man had on his mind. I was compelled to summon him to my office and have him make a written retraction of his threat, which he was induced to do only after very great difficulty. I offered him any explanation he might wish of my actions toward him <u>and also offered to let him have a copy of any letter I might have relating to his affairs.</u> He <u>declined</u> both offers.

His physician does not think him insane, yet he is a very dangerous man.

During my recent absence in the United States, the matter came up in an aggravated form. Krumm demanded a trial before Mr. Paddock, to recover the letter. Mr. Deshler was absent in Japan on account of sickness and did not return until about the time of my arrival.

After vain attempts to dissuade him from bringing the matter to trial, Mr. Paddock was obliged to set a date for and make all preparations for the suit. At this stage however, Mr. Krumm - evidently from reluctance to lose the costs of court - abandoned the case in a most insulting manner.

His conduct to Mr. Paddock has been insulting and exasperating in the extreme, but Mr. Paddock has held himself under control and has treated him with more courtesy than he deserves. In fact Mr. Paddock's handling of the whole case and the legal questions involved, deserves great credit.

As I presume Mr. Krumm will refer this whole matter to the Department of State, as he has announced he would do, with the intention of making me trouble of some kind, I have decided it to be my duty to lay the whole matter before you. I have therefore carefully collected all the documents I could obtain bearing upon the subject and now have the honor to hand them to you enclosed.

The file of papers is carefully jacketed in two parts The first closes with the retraction of the threat to shoot Mr. Deshler. The second relates to the incidents of the past winter, including the legal papers issued in connection with the abortive trial, and a copy of Mr. Krumms contract with the Korean Government.

It will not be necessary to peruse all these papers unless the matter is brought to the attention of the Department.

I may add that Mr. Edwin V. Morgan, Assistant to the Third Assistant Secretary of State, was Secretary of this Legation at the time of the incident herein described, relating to the property question.

Horace N Allen

No. 490   Legation of the United States
                                                                Seoul, Korea, August 18, 1902.

Secretary of State

Sir:-

I have the honor to acknowledge the receipt of your despatch, No. 200 of July 2, regarding the matter of a lawsuit brought by Mr. Raymond Krumm.

I note that the Department is constrained to point out that in his communication to Mr. Krumm of May 2d, Mr. Paddock was not justified in ordering Mr. Krumm to refrain from further communications of any kind with the Consulate or Legation, or in informing him that should it become necessary for him to transact any business with either, he would have to make his wants known through a third party, since Mr. Paddock has no power to curtail the rights of an American citizen to appeal to the agencies of his own nation in an extraterritorial country.

In reply I must relieve Mr. Paddock of all responsibility for the issuance of these instructions. He did so at my request and I alone am responsible.

The immediate cause for the issuance of these instructions was the last visit of Mr. Krumm to the Legation, when after conduct of the most insulting and exasperating character toward Mr. Paddock, he dared the latter to have him put out of the office, though there had been no mention of any such course. It was his evident desire in coming to the office, to so conduct himself as to force his ejection or arrest. He did not succeed.

The man is vicious and dangerous. He has threatened the life of his best friend. He has broken with his brother without cause, and he is known to carry firearms, from the fact that his native servant was reported in the papers recently, as having been injured by the accidental discharge of his masters revolver.

He has been treated with the greatest forbearance all during this absurd litigation he has tried to bring as a result of his threat to kill. He finally dropped the case himself, just the day before it was to be tried. I fail to see that he has any further occasion to communicate with the Legation or Consulate upon this subject. He has done so however, and his letters have in certain cases been so cleverly sent as to be received.

It seems to be asking a good deal of a judge that he must sit quietly and allow a dangerous man to threaten him in his own office. Mr. Paddock has heretofore controlled himself with great forbearance. I would regret very much to have it become necessary for Mr. Paddock to have the man ejected; to defend himself, or to order the arrest of Mr. Krumm. I think the latter would like to compel some such action. Hence the instructions to make his wants known through a third party.

However, in conformity with the views of the Department, communications from Mr. Krumm on subjects other than the law case which he dismissed himself, will be hereafter received.

Mr. Wm. H. Krumm, brother of the one in question, is now travelling in the wilds of Manchuria and I will not see him for some months in all probability. I will then, as instructed, show him the instruction to which this is a reply. No local medical court would find the man insane, in the general acceptance of the term.

Horace N Allen

No. 570   Legation of the United States
                                                    Seoul, Korea, February 2, 1903.

Secretary of State

Sir:-

In my despatch No. 519, of October 24, last, I had the honor to lay before you the necessity for making some early provision for an adequate interpreter service for Korea, and suggested the appointment of one or two student interpreters for that purpose.

I also mentioned the absence of adequate consular representation in this land and the fact that a salaried consul would, sooner or later, have to be appointed. Our Treaty with Korea forbids the appointment of merchants as consular officers.

At present I do all my own writing personally, which at times prevents my giving due attention to matters requiring investigation; the copying of the records is done by the constable (Jailer) and Interpreter, as the Secretary of Legation and Consul General is busy with details of office work and with his consular functions. A student interpreter would be of great assistance in the office without taking too much time from his language studies.

Several times of late the Secretary of Legaion and Consul General has had to be away for days attending to cases in the Korean court where Americans were the plaintiffs against Koreans. Also he has to make frequent trips to Chemulpo on consular business.

We should have a paid consular officer stationed at Chemulpo, with jurisdiction over the outputs, to which he would have to make annual visits, or oftener.

In the north of Korea we have a rich mining district 25 x 30 miles in extent, on a long term concession. These mines employ over 80 white men; under 100 Japanese; 300 Chinese, and about 3000 Koreans. They operate several very large mills and represent an investment of $5,000,000. This is a growing concern and is one of the most successful enterprises in Asia. H. C. Perkins of Washington, D.C. is the President; Leigh Hunt of Seattle is Manager, and Wm. Hearst; Lanman Bull; D.O. Mills, and J. Sloat Fassett, of New York are Directors. In a recent case of murder at these mines it was impossible for me to send a consular officer there to hold an investigation. I have just had two Koreans brought from the mines to Seoul for trial for an attempt to kill an American. Such cases would be much better tried on the spot where the evidence would all be available.

Americans built the first railroad in Korea and while it was sold to the Japanese, the electric railway and lighting plant with kindred enterprises, in Seoul, has become the property of the American contractors for the construction, through the failure of the Koreans to pay a debt of ¥ 1,500,000 ($750,000) - and the foreclosure of mortgage.

Last year over 250,000 cases of American kerosene were sold in Korea at about $375,000, and this business is steadily increasing. The Standard Oil Company have a main office at Chemulpo with a branch at Fusan, both being under American supervision. The Company now import kerosene direct into Fusan from America.

The largest rice mill business in Korea is conducted by an American at Chemulpo.

The total trade of Korea, export and import, is only about $13,000,000, and though it is difficult to ascertain the exact proportion of American business because American goods are mostly reimported from Japan, China and Manchuria, and are not diferentiated on the statistics, we are evidently getting our share.

Korea seems to be regarded by the Church people as the most successful missionary field today, and missionaries are coming by nearly every steamer. We now have some 200 of them at work in Korea. They require - and receive - constant attention, but I am greatly hampered by having no consular officer whom I can send to the locality in case of dispute or trouble.

Most of the import trade is in the hands of the Japanese and Chinese. The former maintain consulates at all the open ports, with imposing buildings in most cases. They have also a consulate in Seoul housed in a very imposing building and with a very large staff. The Legation in Seoul with a Minister Plenipotentiary, has two secretaries, two assistants and a number of clerks, besides a Japanese interpreter with a student assistant.

The Russians have a consulate at Masampo for the south of Korea and one at Chemulpo for this region and the north, while at their imposing Legation the Minister Plenipotentiary has three secretaries and an interpreter (Russian).

The British with simply an indirect trade in the hands of Chinese and Japanese mostly, and a small mining concession and an Englishman in charge of the customs service, have a consul at Chemulpo with a finely located, substantial house, while the Minister Resident and Consul General at Seoul, has two assistants, who with the Minister and Consul understand Asiatic languages. The Legation has also a British Constable and Korean interpreters.

The French with no commercial interests and simply the missionaries and politics to look after, have a most imposing legation building, with a Minister Plenipotentiary and two assistants, all three understand Asiatic languages, and one assistant has consular functions.

The Chinese have a Legation and Consulate (separate) at Seoul and consuls at the ports, with large staffs.

The Germans have a fine house for their consulate at Seoul, which has just been raised to a legation. They have few real interests, but at present they have a consul; vice consul and an assistant, all of whom understand Asiatic languages. The staff will probably be increased now that the consulate has been made a legation.

The Belgians, who have just established themselves in Korea and have neither subjects nor interests, have a consul general and vice consul at Seoul.

The Italians have also just established themselves in Korea and have no interests as yet. They have a consul at Seoul at present, with a consul general en route.

I should add that the Belgians have purchased a site in Seoul and are beginning the erection of a suitable house.

With the largest interests or rather the largest financial undertakings next to the Japanese, we have a fine site, on which we have a miserable old Korean house for a legation, and with a Minister Plenipotentiary, we have a secretary of legation who is also consul general, and a Jailer.

At present American interests are not neglected and without taking too much credit to myself, I may say that my intimate knowledge of Korean affairs; a smattering knowledge of the language, and some personal influence has enabled me to do more than a stranger would do, both during my own service as minister and for my chiefs when I was secretary. My successor will not be so well placed. It is therefore necessary to make some provisions for the future.

I would suggest that a consul be appointed for Chemulpo, with a salary of at least $2,500. If my request for the appointment of two student interpreters is favorably acted upon, one of these might be vice consul at Chemulpo, while the other could be deputy consul at Seoul, with the Secretary of Legation as vice consul as well.

I do not think it strictly necessary to have a consul general, though if that is considered necessary the Secretary of Legation could continue as Consul General, as at present. For years the German Representative has been merely a consul with diplomatic powers, as was the case with the French Representative, who is now Minister Plenipotentiary with the duties of a minister resident.

In accordance with precedent the United States could reserve a consular site at Chemulpo providing all such sites have not been reserved before action is taken. The price would not be great. At one time we owned a fine site at Chemulpo as a gift from the Korean Government, on which an American had erected a good house for the use of a consul. No such officer having been appointed, the site was given up and the same was acquired by the Korean Government as a residence for the Commissioner of Customs, who bought the house of the American. C. H. Cooper.

It would cost say $5000 to build a house, and the house and ground, with furnishings, wall, well etc, should be built for about $8,000. I think a building might be erected by an American on a contract for rental of from $600 to $800 per annum.

The Consul would need a Chinese writer at a cost of $300 per annum, and the allowance for contingent expenses would probably be the same as at other offices of a like nature, except that it would have to be sufficient to allow the consul to make several trips to the ports and the interior, annually.

Horace N Allen

No. 587   Legation of the United States
                                                          Seoul, Korea, March 14, 1903.

Secretary of State

Sir:-

I have the honor to make the following suggestions relative to our mail service with Korea.

In my No. 104 of May 5, 1898, I asked that arrangements be made with the Japanese Postal Authorities for a sealed diplomatic mail pouch service between the Department of State and this Legation. To this I received a favorable reply No. 81 of June 24, 1898. The Departments No. 107 of November 2, 1898, however, enclosed a letter from the Postmaster General to the effect that the Japanese Government had responded saying that it was not then able, owing to existing circumstances, to enter into such an arrangement.

In January 1900, the Korean Government began conveying foreign mails, under an agreement with the Japanese post-offices in Korea whereby the latter transports the pouches for the Korean post-offices. I was at once accorded the privilege of a closed pouch by the Korean office, having had much to do in helping in the establishment of the same.

I addressed you in regard to this matter in my despatches No's 223, January 19, 1900; 227, February 8, and 247, May 1. Your replies were favorable, No's 143; March 12; 145, March 21, and 150, June 22, 1900, - in which last named despatch you announced that the matter might be considered as satisfactorily settled.

The Korean postal service has not been altogether satisfactory. The French assistant M. Clemencet, has done most faithful work, but he has had assistants that were of little use. The mail usually leaves by the 7. A.M. train to catch the steamer of the same day, and our pouches have several times missed the steamer for the reason that the post-office employees were not up in time to attend to the departure of the mail. It has become necessary therefore, for the Constable to go personally and see that each pouch gets off, in one case he was obliged to take the pouch to Chemulpo; and has on several cases had to see it put on the train, for he found one pouch that had been left at the post office to be forwarded still there lying under a table, when he went some days later to send off another mail.

It has taken between fifty and sixty days for letters from this Legation to reach their destination in the United States, by our sealed pouches. It should not take much over thirty days.

I have also been obliged to make frequent complaints of the grossest irregularities in the handling of open mail arriving for Americans by the Korean postoffice. I fear these matters will not improve as the French Assistant is reported as intending soon to leave.

In talking over these matters with Mr. Hayashi, the Japanese Minister, in December, he asked permission to speak to his Government and ascertain why it was they could not grant us a closed pouch service. On his return from Tokio he informed me that the reason for that refusal was that at the time there was no railroad between Chemulpo and Seoul and the foot messengers could not well carry heavy pouches. Now that the railroad is in operation, he said his Government would gladly make the arrangement we asked for in 1898.

I think it would be well therefore to renew the request of 1898 and arrange for the transmission of closed pouches between the Department of State and this Legation, by the Japanese postal service.

It might be just as well not to give up the Korean arrangement, for the reason that the privilege was accorded the Korean Government of having a closed pouch service between their Foreign Office and their Legation in Washington; also it might be unfortunate to discourage them too much, and if in the future they should be able to afford a better service we might again use it. In the meantime unimportant matter might be occasionally forwarded by Korean mail just to keep the arrangement open.

Horace N. Allen.

No. 240

Department of State
Washington, July 27, 1903.

Gordon Paddock

Sir:

I have to acknowledge the receipt of your No. 614 of May 30 last, with enclosures, in regard to the advisability of establishing a United States consular office at Pengyang, or its port, Chenampo.

The policy of the Department for a number of years has been against the establishement of consular agencies in China and Korea. It is difficult in those countries to find suitable persons to accept the position of Consular Agent or unsalaried Consul for the reason that the fees of the office amount to little. The exercise of judicial functions by consular officers in Korea, make in important to appoint officers of a higher grade than Consular Agent, and wherever possible to have adequate salaries appropriated.

Furthermore, it appears from an examination of the statistics of Korean trade that of the cities of Korea, Chenampo ranks fourth in commercial importance, its foreign trade being only about 6 per cent of the total foreign trade of Korea as against 48 per cent at Chemulpo and 221/2 per cent at Fusan. China and Japan have consulates at Chenampo; at Chemulpo there are British and Russian Vice Consuls, a Chinese Consul General, and a Japanese Consul; at Fusan there is a Japanese Consul General, and a Chinese Consul. At Yuensan there is only a Japanese Consul.

The Department does not therefore think it advisable to appoint a consular agent at Chenampo or Peng-yang. It will, however, take into consideration the question whether Congress should be asked to appropriate a salary for a consulate at either Chemulpo, Yuen-san, or Chenampo, and to aid it in reaching a conclusion, it would be pleased to have you fully report to it touching the relative commercial importance of these places.

Francis B. Loomis

No. 632

Legation of the United States
Seoul, Korea, december 12, 1903.

Secretary of State

Sir:-

I have the honor to acknowledge the receipt of your despatch *(No 241)** to Mr/ Paddock of August 8 last, enclosing copies of correspondence from Honorable W. A. Day, Acting Attorney General, and from Mr. G. Van Vorst of Cleveland Ohio, regarding the alleged illegal confinement in the California State Penitentiary of a prisoner by the name of J. Flanagan, convicted in Korea. Mr. Paddock has handed me the letter to be answered.

Mr. Van Vorst states in his letter that Flanagan was in Korea as an expert miner, not a grubstake mining engineer. He further states that the man was convicted by a board of missionaries who had to convict someone of the crime in order to protect themselves, and that the man is confined in this country illegally as according to law unless a man commits a crime upon the Embassy grounds he is not legally responsible.

The facts in the case are, - as reported in my consular despatch No. 29 of December 21 1898, - that Flanagan was regularly convicted of murder in the consular court before myself, sitting with four associates chosen by lot, as required by the regulations for consular courts, from a previously published list of names

---

*Handwritten

of American residents suitable for such service. Three of these associates were missionaries. These gentlemen did not wish to serve as associates and one who was at first chosen secured his release together with another missionary defended the prisoner. The fourth member of the court chanced to be Clarence R. Greathouse, a distinguished lawyer of well known ability who had practiced for many years in San Fancisco and was afterwards United States Consul General to Japan. The court was regularly constituted and was distincly favorable to the prisoner, who, in the opinion of Mr. Greathouse, would have stood some chance of being acquitted had he not perjured himself so repeatedly, as though endeavoring to protect an accomplice.

As to the missioinaries being opposed to the prisoner or being under any necessity of protecting themselves, the latter I do not understand as they were in no way connected with the crime or the prisoner or his victim and such a statement would not be given any credence here at the time, or now, neither would the one regarding any opposition to the prisoner on the part of the missionaries. The presence of Mr. Greathouse as an associate was a safe guarantee that all legal requirements would be complied with.

Personally, it was a most greivous thing to me to have to sentence a man to life imprisonment and I did all I could to protect the prisoner and afterwards asked that the matter be laid before the President with the view of lightening the man's punishment. In Mr. Cridler's despatch, consular No. 15 of March 10 1899, an appeal was refused, and in a dispatch from the same of October 15 1900, No. 33, handing me enclosed an opinion from Attorney General Griggs, the latter states that "in this case Flanagan appears to have been guilty of wilful and deliberate murder, which, in this country, would have subjected him to the death penalty. He was, however, sentenced to imprisonment for life.

"I can find no ground whatever for advising the President to grant any pardon of any nature".

As to the occupation of the prisoner previous to the crime of which he was convicted, I must explain that the facts differ somewhat from the statements of Mr. Van Vorst. Flanagan was brought to Korea by the American mining Company. He went with the Manager of that company, Mr. Leigh Hunt, part way to the mines, but Mr. Hunt found him to be such an undesirable character that he dismissed him before reaching the mines in north Korea. Flanagan then came to Chemulpo where he remained with George Lake, who kept a small shop for the sale of liquors and other commodities, and just prior to the opening of a soloon by Lake in another part of the town, which saloon was to be largely under the care of Flanagan, Lake was found most brutally murdered in his bed. The evidence showed that Flanagan had made away with much of the contents of the new saloon to which it would have been very unpleasant to him to have Lake come, as he would have found the contents missing.

I enclose two copies of the printed Judgement, which gives a resume of the facts in the case.

I have had letters from Flanagan, one of which I have answered, stating that if he is able to throw any light upon the murder I would gladly do anything in my power to obtain justice for him, in case it can be shown that any injustice has been done him.

Horace N. Allen.

No. 687   Legation of the United States
                                                     Seoul, Korea, March 2, 1904.

Secretary of State

Sir:-

I have the honor to confirm my telegram of today as follows:-
"Naval officers have decided upon alterations necessary to barracks amounting to three hundred fifty dollars in gold. Will you sanction?"

In explanation I may add that the "barracks" is a frail building used as a shelter for the legation chairs and jinricksha, and most necessary for that purpose. I had proper doors hung and bunks erected, as well as glass lights inserted. The building is only 16 by 40 feet however and in this space the men have to eat sleep and pass the time, it is very small for thirty six men. It is proposed to extend the whole of the front side giving more floor and air space and making it more habitable as warm weather approaches.

The rest of the guard, sixty four men, are quartered at the office building of the Seoul Electric Company, where they are also very crowded. As conditions are today, some of these men might go to the ship to return if necessary, but the ship that brought them, the "Zaphiro" has returned to the Philippines;

the "Vicksburg" is very small and so crowded already that she cannot take any, and the "Cincinnati" has no arrangement for marines and is here but for a short call at any rate.

Horace N Allen

No. 715   Legation of the United States
                                                 Seoul, Korea, April 5, 1904.

Secretary of State

Sir:-
    I have the honor to bring to your attention the necessity of establishing a consulate in the north of Korea.
    In my No. 614 of May 30 last, I handed you a suggestion on the subject from one of our missionaries residing at the northern capital Pengyang.
    In your reply No. 240 of July 27 last, you asked for more information on the subject, and on November 25, in my No. 624 I stated that I would await the result of pending negotiations in order that I might reply intelligently.
    Now two new ports have been opened, or the intention of opening them has been officially announced. I refer to Wiju and Yongampo. Also, the Japanese Government is rapidly pushing the work of constructing a railway to connect Seoul and Wiju, so that this will in a short time become quite an important port. See my No. 713 of yesterday.
    Wonsan, Gensan or Yuensan, on the east coast, is a port of no immediate importance to us as we have no people there in business, and but little indirect trade.
    Fusan at the south is a large Japanese settlement where we have one American in business - the agent of the Standard Oil Company. A consulate does not seem to be necessary there though American ships, or ships chartered by Americans do come there with kerosene. We have no merchants residing at Masampo; Mokpo or Kunsan, and but little trade.
    Chemulpo is by far the most important port in Korea, but as it is but twenty five miles from Seoul and connected with this city by a railway, the consulate General at Seoul is quite able to attend to consular matters there for the time.
    At Pengyang we have some twenty missionary families permanently residing and continually in need of consular assistance. Chenampo is the port of Pengyang and a consular officer residing at Chenampo could well attend to Pengyang matters, especially as it is understood that the Japanese may connect the two places by rail, in the near future. The two towns are separated by about forty miles, and in the open season light draft vessels approach to within a few miles of Pengyang.
    About sixty miles north west of Pengyang is the important walled city of Anju, where the Japanese are now establishing a branch of the First Bank. About thirty six miles north east of Anju is the nearest point of the American gold mining conession, which has a company house at Anju as well as at Chenampo.
    This mining concession, which covers a district twenty five by thirty miles and operates a number of very extensive mills in that region, is one of the largest foreign enterprises being successfully operated in Asia. The company employs from sixty to one hundred white men, mostly Americans, who reside within the limits of the concession, many of them with their families. Some hundreds of Chinese and Japanese are employed in time of peace as well as about five thousand Koreans.
    The imports and exports for this company are declared at the port of Chenampo and it is a great inconvenience that there is no consulate nearer than Seoul. Men have frequently been obliged to come to Seoul to attend to consular matters, involving an absence from the mines of at least three weeks.
    The company's imports for last year, chiefly from America amounted in round numbers to $500,000 gold. The exported bullion to the amount of $1,200,000, and this will increase notably with the advent of peace.
    The completed returns of the Korean Customs for the whole year 1903 are not yet to hand, and I cannot well make up the complete statistics for the year from the monthly returns.
    For the year 1902 however, the aggregate returns for the chief ports were as follows: -

Chemulpo   Net value of the whole trade   Yen   12,243,373
Fusan   5,849,087
Gensan   4,023,152

Chinampo	3,093,436
Mokpo	2,071 569
Kunsan	1,294,890

The other ports had less than yen 1,000,000 *each*.

It is impossible to ascertain from these reports the just proportion of American goods handled, as, owing to the absence of consulates the goods usually come from Japan or China and go to the credit of those countries.

Of vessels entering and clearing, there were in 1902 at

Chemulpo, total steam vessels	1062
Of which there were American steamers	2
Of sailing vessels there were altogether	1971
Of which there were of American flag	10
At Chenampo during 1902 there were	
Steam vessels to a total of	566
Of which there were under the American flag	62
Sailing vessels total at Chinampo	1706
Under the American flag	104

These vessels flying the American flag were chiefly those belonging to the American gold mining company.

While therefore, Chinampo only ranks fourth among the ports of Korea in general trade, it ranks next to Chemulpo in strictly American commerce, and ahead of it in the matter of shipping.

I send you enclosed a sketch map showing the location of these ports; the proposed and present railways, and the approximate location of the American gold mines.

The only place in Korea where we really need a consulate at present, aside from Seoul and Chemulpo, now supplied by the Secretary of Legation and Consulate General, is at the port of Chinampo, where our interests are very large and growing.

A consulate at Chinampo could attend to all matters of a consular nature for Pengyang; the mines; Wiju and Yongampo.

At present Anju is not an open port though it may be made so later, except that it is not a harbor for vessels drawing over six feet. All customs matters for Anju and the north are attended to at Chinampo, and the supplies for the mines are cleared at Chinampo and then shipped on American vessels of light draft to the Anju river.

I recommend therefore that a regularly paid consular officer be stationed at Chinampo with jurisdiction over American consular matters in the region included by that port; Pengyang; Wiju and Yongampo.

As to the cost of such an establishment, I may explain that the missionaries in that region receive about $2,000,00 per annum in salary and allowances. I think therefore that a consul should be allowed at least $2,500,00 and a house for office and residence, with a sufficient contingent allowance to allow of his making necessary trips to the other places over which he would have jurisdiction.

As there are no houses at Chinampo for rent, one would have to be built. If the Government does not care to invest in such property however, a suitable house may be erected to order by someone on a promised rental of say $75 per mo.

$500 would be a necessary allowance for the employment of an interpreter, and in time a constable would be required, to serve as constable, jailer and clerk.

The entire outlay should come within $5,000 per annum.

Horace N Allen

No. 758   Legation of the United States
                                             Seoul, Korea, June 13, 1904.

Secretary of State

Sir:-

I have the honor to acknowledge the receipt of Mr. Loomis's despatch No. 262 of May 10, handing me copy of a letter from Mr. Raymond Krumm, charging me with malfeasance in office in connection with the contracts between the Korean Government and Messrs Collbran and Bostwick, and stating that the Department would be pleased to receive from me such explanations of the charges as I can furnish.

In reply I have the honor to refer you to my Despatches No. 462 of May 20, 1902; 490 of August 18, 1902 and 545 of December 2, 1902. No. 462 being a complete history of the case.

I have further to say that I am not and never have been interested in electric or other contracts, franchises or interests in Korea. I am not and never have been interested partly wholly or indirectly in any real estate in Korea aside from a summer place I have long owned, outside of Chemulpo. I am not directly or indirectly interested in any financial enterprises in Korea nor in the stocks, bonds or securities of such concerns nor have I any promises of any such future interest.

I have not undertaken the promotion, protection or furtherance of my financial enterprise here for the purpose of personal gain, and I refer to an affidavit made by me concerning the particular interest mentioned, - The Seoul Electric Company - being enclosure No. 7 in my despatch No. 462 of May 20, 1902.

As I did more in a purely personal way for Mr. Krumm, than I have done for anyone else in Korea, he should know whether I was in the habit of profiting or not. He had ample reason in his own experience, to know that such was not the case, for in the real estate transaction which he cites as having produced a rupture of his friendhsip with me, I went his security at the bank for Yen 5000 with which to make the purchase. He asked me then to join him in the matter, and I replied that it was my fixed principle not to make my investments in Korea since I might be obliged to decide matters relating thereto, and I politely declined his offer. In this particular case, the deed for the property could not be secured from the Korean Government as it was claimed the purchase was irregular as the place had been reserved for use by the Palace. I did however get a settlement whereby Mr. Krumm obtained, within a few months, Yen 10,000 for his investment of Yen 5000 of money obtained on my name as security. There was the usual delay of a few months in payment, and Mr. Krumm thereby lost a small amount in exchange, which loss he knew beforehand would probably occur and to which he had fully assented. See copies of correspondence regarding this matter, being enclosures No. 8 & 9 in my No. 462 of May 20. I may further add that Mr. Krumm owed his lucrative post in the Korean Government entirely to me.

As to the Seoul Electric Railway matter, wherein he accuses me of asking for an interest for a third pary to whom I was under obligations. I admit this fully and with pride. Mr. Collbran kindly offered me an interest in this venture which I declined as I considered it would not be proper. I did however suggest that he take into the undertaking two other Americans on the ground that they could be useful to him; they had long been here attempting to get such business and Mr. Collbran was comparatively a newcomer. I had no idea of profiting by this suggestion and I did not profit to the extent of one penny by the same. Mr. Krumm however, failed to connect himself with that company in their undertakings here, though he attempted to do so. Further, one of the men whom I recommended to Mr. Collbran, was the sponsor and friend of Mr. Krumm, and the man whom Krumm later threatened to shoot. It was this threat to kill that caused the Krumm matter to be brought to my attention as well as to the attention of the Consul General. His own brother Wm. H. Krumm, who was then in Korea, appeared against him as will be seen from the letter of Wm. H. Krumm, enclosure No. 6 in my No. 462 of May 20, 1902.

For this threat and attempts at violence upon the person of myself and the Consul General, Krumm should have been arrested, but realizing that that was the object he most desired, in order that he might have something on which to base a complaint, any such action was carefully avoided.

I may add that by speaking the word, I could easily have had Mr. Krumm dismissed from his employment with the Korean Government. I purposely refrained from doing so, though his conduct towards the Koreans was such that they would willingly have dismissed him and did promptly give him notice that his services would be dispensed with on the expiration of his contract in August 1903.

It is generally believed here by people who know him that Krumm is not in a sane mental condition.

Should this statement and my previous letters and documents not prove sufficient, and should the Department have any suspicion whatever that there is truth in the charges made by Mr. Krumm, I must demand an investigation. I have lived here twenty years and this is the only charge I have ever known to be brought against me. Further I am willing that the judgement of any and all Americans residing here may be taken if necessary, on the subject, without reference to me.

Horace N Allen

No. 811   Legation of the United States
                                           Seoul, Korea, October 19, 1904.

Secretary of State

Sir:-
        Referring to my No. 715 of April 5 suggesting the establishment of a consulate at Chenampo for that port and the other northern ports of Korea, and my No. 735 of May 7 relative to Japanese objections to the presence of an American consulate there because Chenampo is one of their bases, or was, I now wish to call your attention to the fact that auction sales of land at Chenampo are of quite frequent occurrence, being sold by the Korean local authority at the request of Japanese applicants. Such sales have moreover, occurred at a time when Chenampo was closed so that the usual announcement by the Korean local offical of the intended sale, was a mere farce, since no American could go to attend the auction.
        I am not aware that any American has been desirous of purchasing land at Chenampo during the period I mention, though Americans do own land there, but as it now stands the available ground seems to be largely bought up by the Japanese at a time when the Japanese Government was making it difficult or impossible for persons of other nationality to participate in the auction sales.
        I am also informed that in addition to the land thus acquired, the Japanese have taken not only the official ground belonging to the Russian Government but the property of Russian private citizens as well, which increases their holdings.
        The proximity of the American gold mines to Chenampo and the large colony of Americans at the near by city - Pengyang, makes it advisable that a consular officer should reside in that region. Having but one consular officer in Korea, namely the Secretary of the Legation, it is practically impossible for him to go to the various ports to look after American interests as is sometimes very desireable.
        The objections of the Japanese Government, cited in the above mentioned despatch No. 735, can hardly be of a permanent nature, and doubtless by the time arrangements could be made for the establishment of a consulate at Chenampo, these objections would be waived.

                                           Horace N Allen

No. 889*   American Legation, Seoul, Korea.
                                           March 21, 1905.

Secretary of State,

Sir:-
        Having learned by private advices that my successor has been appointed, I have the honor to request that I be allowed to time my departure so as to avoid the hottest weather, in case my successor does not arrive as soon as might be expected.
        I make this request owing to the ill health of my wife and the consequent necessity of avoiding Japan in July.
        In such event I would transfer everything to the Secretary of Legation and instal him as Chargé D'Affaires ad interim.

                                           Horace N Allen

----

*In a note not meant to be a part of the official diplomatic correspondence that followed this despatch and which was addressed to Mr. Adee, the Acting Secretary of State of April 24, a J. Y. J. stated "I think we might consent to this. I know that Mr. Morgan is in hope that Mr. Allen will leave before his arrival."

No. 287   Department of State
                                                            Washington, March 30, 1905.

Horace N. Allen

Sir:
        The President having accepted your resignation as Envoy Extraordinary and Minister
Plenipotentiary to Korea, and having appointed as your successor Mr. Edwin V. Morgan, of New York, I
enclose herewith your letter of recall, with office copy.
        In doing so I desire to express to you the Department's high appreciation of the intelligent zealous
and faithful conduct of the affairs of the mission during your incumbancy.

                                                            Alvey A. Adee

No. 26   American Legation, Seoul, Korea.
                                                            November 4, 1905.

Secretary of State

Sir:-
        In confirming my telegram of the 31st ultimo, reading as follows: -
                        Legation guard sailed today,
I have the honor to report that the marine guard of this Legation after a residence of twenty two months left
Seoul on the 30th of October and sailed next day for Cavite on the U.S. cruiser "Cincinnati" which arrived
on the 25th bringing orders from the Commander-in-Chief of the United States Asiatic Fleet to remove the
command.
        I desire to record the appreciation both of this Legation and the American community as well as of
the Korean and foreign residents of the good conduct of the marines who under somewhat difficult
circumstances maintained a standard of deportment and efficiency which reflected credit both upon
themselves and the service to which they belong.

                                                            Edwin V. Morgan

TELEGRAM. CIPHER.   Department of State,
                                                            Washington, November 24, 1905.

Morgan,
Amlegation, Seoul.

        In view of the recent convention between Japan and Korea by which Japan becomes the medium
for conducting the foreign relations of Korea, the representation of the United States in diplomatic matters
affecting American rights of treaty, persons and property in Korea is transferred to the American Legation at
Tokyo, such questions to be dealt with through channel of the Japanese Foreign Office. You are
accordingly instructed to withdraw from Korea and return to the United States, leaving the premises,
legation property and archives in custody of the Consul General, whose function as Secretary of Legation
ceases.

                                                            Root

No. 41   American Legation, Seoul, Korea.
                                          December 6, 1905.

Secretary of State

Sir:-

        With the confirmation below of my cipher telegram of the 28th of November in reference to my departure from Seoul, I have the honor to enclose copies of the notes addressed by me on that day to the Korean Minister for Foreign Affairs, to our Consul General for Korea and to the Chargé d'Affaires of the American Legation at Tokyo informing them that in conformity with your instructions I had intrusted the archives and property of the Legation to the care of the American Consul General at Seoul and was about to withdraw from Korea.

Text of telegram sent.
Secstate, Washington.
        Twentyeighth. I have informed Korean Minister for Foreign Affairs that in compliance with your instructions I have today placed the property and archives of this Legation in the hands of the United States Consul General at Seoul and am about to withdraw from Korea.
                                                    Morgan.

                                          Edwin V. Morgan

OTHER FOREIGN INTERESTS

A. England

No. 49

Legation of the United States
Seoul Korea, December 21, 1897.

Secretary of State

Sir:-

I have the honor to hand you enclosed, confirmation of my telegram of yesterday, regarding proposed seizure by England, of a Chinese or Korean port.

As I mentioned in that telegram, this information was given me confidentially, by Mr. de Speyer, who called upon me soon after I had mailed my No. 48, of yesterday's date. In the course of a long and intimate conversation, he told me in confidence, with permission to inform you, that certain intentions the Russian Admiral had entertained, had to be given up because of his urgent necessity for concentrating all his ships and forces to watch the English. I asked him if he feared they would retake Port Hamilton, and he replied that the constant flitting of English ships in and out of that harbor, was a mere blind; that the Admiral had ample assurance that they intended to take either Chusan (the important group of islands at the mouth of the Yang Tze River) or Port Arther. I intimated that it could not possibly be the latter, since, as it was now practically in Russian hands, such an attempt would surely cause trouble. He said that the Admiral was of the opinion that Port Arthur was the objective point, and that he was prepared to fight in defense of the place. I believe that the Russians would object just as strongly to English occupation of Talien Wan as of Port Arthur, because of their railroad interests in the peninsula, hence all this vigorous preparation for war.

While to me it seemed improbable that England would be courting any such difficulty, I considered that if the information received by the Russian Admiral was of such a character as to cause him to make all these warlike preparations, the Department had better be at once informed. Hence my telegram, to which I added as qualifying the whole, that the"British Consul thinks the object "is Port Hamilton". My No. 48, of yesterday explains this. Mr. Jordan could not answer my question, and left me to infer that he was of the opinion that Port Hamilton was to be occupied.

Mr. de Speyer said that he had called primarily to thank me most cordially for arranging the transfer of the American property at Chenampo, mentioned in my No. 48, of yesterday. He also told me that the matter of the Commissioner for the Korean Customs had been settled the day before. He said that by the agreement made in favor of Mr. Alexeieff, the latter was to have the selection of a subordinate to act as Chief of Customs; that overtures had been made to a Frenchman in the employ of the Chinese Customs Service, but that this gentleman had declined; that they had therefore on the 19'th. Inst. come to a definite understanding with Mr. Brown, the Englishman now in charge of Korean Customs, whose removal from the post of Adviser to the Finance Dept. to make room for the Russian - Alexeieff, was the subject of much of my late correspondence with the Department. He informed me that Mr. Brown had given him a written agreement on the 19'th, accepting the post of Chief Commissioner of Korean Customs, under Mr. Alexeieff, or his successor, as his superior officer; agreeing to sever his connection with the Chinese Customs Service, and to draw his pay only from Korea, and to make no attempt to show especial favors to English men or interests.

He further explained that in all this controversy, he had been acting without instructions, fully aware that if he failed his Government would dishonor him, while if he won he would be highly honored. The high honor has come in his promotion to the post of Minister to China. He said that Mr. Alexeieff had come here purely in the capacity of Agent of the Russian Treasury, and that it was his own (Speyer's) idea to place him in charge of Korean Finances. He blamed Mr. Jordan much for his lack of tact, which he claims was the cause of most of the trouble. I may add that Mr. Jordan makes the same accusation against Mr. de Speyer.

I took occasion to ask about the rumors of a loan to be made to Korea by the Russian Government. He frankly told me that no definite loan would be made, but a Russian semi-official agent was now here for the purpose of starting a "Russo-Korean Bank", and this institution would from time to time, loan Korea such sums as Mr. Alexeieff should deem to be necessary and wise. this Bank, he said, would finance the business of Korea, and would have a capital of not more than two or three million yen.

263

Mr. Speyer had much to say in praise of the strictly neutral attitude maintained by this Legation during the exciting controversy of the past two months. He dwelt very much also upon the friendly spirit existing between our two countries, and in frofuse personal commendation, seemed evidently desirous of pleasing, and of atoning for some unnecessarily harsh statements he had made soon after his arrival in Korea, and which I fully reported in former despatches.

Horace N. Allen

No. 234

Legation of the United States
Seoul Korea, March 17, 1900.

Secretary of State

Sir:-

I have the honor to inform you of the conclusion of negotiations covering the grant of a mining concession and location, in Korea, to an English firm known as the Pritchard-Morgan Syndicate.

This concession was signed at Seoul September 27, 1898, and was modeled after the similar concession granted to Americans; was for a period of twenty five years on a royalty of 25% net; it covered a district 13 by 20 miles in extent to be selected within two year from the date of the concession.

In the autumn of 1899, a district in the north of Korea near to the American mines, known as the Eunsan of Inzan Magistracy, was selected by the English firm, but it seems that this had previously been secretly promised to another Englishmen named Chance, who had no concession but was to work the mine for the Household Department. This is the man whom I mentioned in my No. 214 Nov. 18, as endeavoring to interfere with negotiations then in progress between an American Syndicate and the Korean Government, for a loan secured by the mines of the Household Department of Korea. The Pritchard-Morgan concession, antedating these negotiations, has never been opposed by Americans. This concession covered any district in Korean not included in the list of seven exceptions. The mine in question was not in that list, therefore it was held to be available under the concession.

The Koreans flatly refused to grant this district, and Mr. Morgan, who is a member of the British Parliament, telegraphed to Lord Salisbury, as he informed me, and the latter sustained his claim and instructed him to insist upon receiving the district in question. This removed the obstacle of the man Chance but the Koreans still stubbornly refused to grant the district.

Mr. Morgan then sent his mining people to these mines to take possession and he sent a large force of armed Japanese with them for protection, which force he had gathered in Seoul with the assistance of the Japanese Consul. This force was increased from time to time till I was informed by Mr. Morgan that he had 150 of the Japanese there. This was most objectionable to the Koreans and some conflicts took place, the Englishmen having to establish a "laager".

Mr. Jordan the British Charge dAffaires here, secured an audience with the Emperor to discuss this business, and he was reported as having used such violent and threatening language for a space of two hours, that the Emperor was made quite ill by the experience. This was in December last and from that time on the Koreans were most persistent in their refusal to grant the mine.

Finally in the present month, Mr. Morgan informed me that explicit telegraphic instructions had been sent by Lord Salisbury to Mr. Jordan, to secure an audience and inform the Emperor personally of the surprise of Her Majesty's Government at the refusal of the Korean Government to carry out its agreement and grant this mine.

An audience was refused on the grounds that Mr. Jordan had abused the last opportunity and had been rude. I was told moreover, on good authority, that a telegram had been prepared to be sent direct to Lord Salisbury by the Korean Foreign Office, complaining of Mr. Jordans conduct and explaining the refusal of an audience. I hear that this was not sent, though it caused much comment here and was noted in the papers in Japan, See Enclosures. Although this audience was not granted, the mining matter was placed in the hands of Mr. Sands, American Adviser to the Household Department, for adjustment and he informed me that he had arranged for a settlement on a cash payment, when the matter was suddenly taken out of his hands and quietly given to Mr. Morgan without compensation and without condition, as the latter informed me. He said he had agreed to remove the Japanese constabulary on satisfactory evidence of protection from the Korean Authorities.

I had been compelled to forbid the American Mining Company from loaning dynamite to the English Company, which loan they had urgently requested. Dynamite import is forbidden by treaty and the large amounts used by the American mines is imported on special permission at my request, in each instance, in accordance with our concession. I informed Mr. Morgan that my refusal was from no desire to hamper him but from necessity, and that I could only allow such loan upon written permission of the Korean Government. He expressed his satisfaction and thanked me for my attitude of friendly neutrality throughout the matter.

There has been no ill will between Americans and Englishmen in this Morgan matter, though the Russian Charge d'Affaires told me he was opposed to the grant and would so advise the Koreans.

I did have to inform Mr. Jordan in a friendly conversation, that I would be compelled to oppose the man Chance, in his attempts to get concessions for matters that were then under negotiation between my own people and the Korean Government. Chance has since left Korea without having obtained anything, and after vainly trying to get a concession for water works in Seoul, which an American Company already held a written official promise for.

Horace N. Allen.

No. 341

Legation of the United States
Seoul, Korea, May 3, 1901

Secretary of State

Sir:-

Referring to my despatch No. 339 of April 29, and previous despatches relating to the Brown Incident, I now have the honor to hand you confirmation, on the overleaf, of my telegram of today announcing the probable occupation by Great Britain of the Southern Korean islands known as Port Hamilton. These islands were occupied by England on April 15, 1885, and evacuated on Feb. 27, 1887, on a guarantee by China that they should not be allowed to go to any other power. Recent activity of the Russian Navy in and around the nearby port, Masampo, might well induce England, with the present provocation of the Brown Incident and the French loan, as well as the studied discourtesy of the Korean Government, to make a demonstration at that point.

It has been reported in the local papers here that the United States was about to occupy these islands, which report I took to be a ruse for announcing that the subject of the occupation of the port was under discussion and that the Japanese telegraph office, where they seem able to decipher all codes, might be responsible for the information. Telegrams from Japan now announce that Japanese telegrams from here openly state that England will occupy these islands.

I happen to know that the British ship "Bonnaventure" left Chemulpo by direction of Admiral Bruce, on April 28, for that region. I gave Mr. Gubbins, the British Charge d'Affaires, the opportunity of telling me anything he wished to in regard to the mission of the ship and his instructions. He seemed very anxious to inform me of something, and did tell me that he had very strong instructions; that his "hand" was "very strong". But he could not tell me what his instructions were. I have waited to learn something definite but as it is difficult to learn more at present, I have decided to telegraph you as per enclosed reading. I am reasonably sure that the Japanese know something definite in regard to the matter, and that their reports are not mere guesses.

For a description of these islands, and an account of a British demonstration made there in Dec. 1897, I refer you to my despatch No. 48 of Dec. 20, 1897. Russia has violated her reported agreement, therein mentioned, with England, in securing a special reservation at the port of Masampo. It would be most natural for England to occupy Port Hamilton in return, especially as she needs something with which to teach the Koreans a lesson, for being apparently led away by the suspected Franco-Russian combination.

Horace N Allen

Reading of telegram, May 3, 1901.
"British will probably occupy the island of Port Hamilton or (the) other Korean island."

No. 342   Legation of the United States
                                                 Seoul, Korea, May 4, 1901.

Secretary of State

Sir:-

I have the honor to confirm my telegram of today, as follows: - "British Admiral denies reports contained in my last telegram."

In explanation of which I have to say that Mr. Gubbins the British Charge d'Affaires, has been very mysterious in regard to this and kindred matters. He has informed me of very strong instructions he has received and led me to imagine his Government were contemplating some great move. When asked in regard to the published rumors of the proposed British occupation of Port Hamilton, he gave such an evasive answer as to lead one to suppose he could not reply without letting out information.

My German colleague, finding it impossible to learn anything from Mr. Gubbins, visited the British Admiral at Chemulpo, and a favorable opportunity having offered itself, he asked the Admiral as to the Port Hamilton reports, and was told that they were utter nonsense.

I am inclined to regard this as reliable and regret having sent the first telegram.

                                                 Horace N Allen

No. 538   Legation of the United States
                                                 Seoul, Korea, November 25, 1902.

Secretary of State

Sir:-

I have the honor to acquaint you with the settlement of a recent case wherein the Korean local authorities endeavored to collect likin taxes upon British goods transported to the interior of Korea by a Chinese merchant for sale, the same having paid full duty at the maritime customs house.

Mr. J. N. Jordan, the British Minister, took this matter up on the grounds that it was an infringement of the treaty under which foreign goods, upon payment of the tariff duty, are exempt from any additional tax, excise, or transit duty in any part of the country.

On October 20'th. last, Mr. Jordan brought this matter to the attention of the Korean Minister for Foreign Affairs and requested him to issue orders for the instant release of these goods and for the prevention of further molesting in any way of persons purchasing or selling such articles.

To this the Foreign Minister replied in an evasive manner, on October 30'th. claiming that the treaty between Korea and China, Article VIII, distinctly provides that Chinese merchants are forbidden to reside or open commercial establishments in the interior of Korea, and that the seizure of these goods was in the nature of a fine for illegal procedure, rather than a tax upon the goods themselves.

I understand Mr. Jordan, together with Mr. Hayashi, the Japanese Minister, had one or more joint interviews with the Minister for Foreign Affairs upon this subject, and on November 3'rd. Mr. Jordan again wrote offically on the subject, declining to agree with the Foreign Minister's contention as to a fine, and insisting upon his demands being complied with.

On November 12'th. the Foreign Minister informed Mr. Jordan that the goods had been restored to their owner and as a result of further correspondence, orders were finally issued to the provincial officers instructing them to abstain from any such attempts in the future.

By favor of Mr. Jordan, I am able to hand you for your confidential use, a copy of this correspondence, which will be kept on file here for future reference, as it establishes a precedent that will doubtless be useful to refer to.

                                                 Horace N Allen

No. 27   American Legation, Seoul, Korea.
                                                      November 6, 1905.

Secretary of State

Sir:-

With his despatch No. 891 of March 30, 1905, my predecessor Mr. Allen enclosed a copy of two notes exchanged between the British Minister at Seoul, Sir John Jordan, and the Korean Minister for Foreign Affairs, Mr. Yi Ha Yung, in which Sir John informed Mr. Yi that the British syndicate represented by
Mr. A. L. Pearse which applied in April, 1903, for permission to mine in the district of Su-An, in the Province of Huang-Hai-Do, Korea, had made arrangements under which the Mitsui Company of Tokyo, a Japanese firm, and Messrs Collbran and Bostwick, American capitalists, were to participate in the working of the Su-An property, each of the parties to subscribe a share of the necessary capital and hold an equal interest in the undertaking. The Foreign Minister in replying consented to lease the Su-An mine to the Compnay represented by the joint English, Japanese and American interests with the understanding that his consent should be regarded as an agreement in principle and should be confirmed by the conclusion of a contract lease embodying such stipulations as might be considered necessary to safeguard the rights and interests of all concerned.

I have the honor to inform you that this contract lease, on which the seal of the Foreign Office was affixed by the Foreign Minister as proof that he recognized the validity of the document, was signed before the British Minister by Mr. E. A. Elliott, as attorney for Mr. Pearse, on the 4th day of November, after several months of negotiation between the British and Japanese Legations and the Korean Ministry for Foreign Affairs during which important modifications were effected in the terms of the conditions of operation made necessary by the withdrawal from the syndicate of the Mitsui Company after their mining experts had examined and reported unfavorably on the Su-An district.

I enclose a copy of the ordinance for the Su-An concession and a history of the events leading to its signature.

                                                      Edwin V. Morgan.

B. France

No. 294   Legation of the United States
                                                      Seoul, Korea, November 6, 1900.

Secretary of State

Sir:-

Referring to my despatch No. 276 of August 31 last, regarding concessions said to have been granted by the Korean Government, I have now the honor to inform you that the concession to the Japanese for the Chik-San gold mines in Southern Korea, mentioned in that despatch, was actually granted at the time stated and is now being worked.

The renewal of the concession to a mysterious French syndicate for a railroad to connect Seoul and Weiju, mentioned in that despatch, seems also to be a fact, though I have heard many denials of the same. French railway engineers have now actually arrived in Seoul and have begun to make a survey of the part of the line between Seoul and the former captital - Song-do, which is on the route of the line to Weiju.

There seems to be a great deal of mystery about this railway project and I can learn nothing more definite than the information I gave you in the above cited despatch. The Japanese newspapers persistently report that the money for this project is to come from the Russo-Chinese Bank. I can obtain no confirmation of this rumor.

Meantime the French Chargé d'Affaires here is pressing the Koreans very strongly to obtain a gold mining concession, which he is said to desire for himself as he is reported as intending to leave the French service in order to engage in mining, being a qualified engineer.

The building of the part of the Weiju Railway to Song-do does not conflict with the steam tramway from Song-do to a point on the Han River near to Chemulpo, the contract for the construction of which was given to the American firm of Collbran and Bostwick. There is considerable doubt, moreover, as to the ability of the Korean Government to raise the money with which to construct this steam tramway.

Horace N Allen

No. 354   Legation of the United States
                                          Seoul, Korea, May 29, 1901.

Secretary of State

Sir:-

I have the honor to inform you that a local rebellion is in progres on the large Korean island of Quelpart, off the Southern coast of Korea. I cannot as yet learn many particulars in regard to it. The island is used as a place for sending political exiles and the inhabitants have the reputation of being a very unruly set. Conflicts are of rather frequent occurrence on the island, but this one is given importance by the fact that two French priests are in danger. A delayed telegram sent by one of the priests, by means of a junk to the telegraph stations at Mokpo, states that they are being beseiged. Rumor however, states that one of them has actually been murdered.

The paddle-wheel gunboat, "l'Alouette" of the French Navy, has been despatched to Quelpart, and another is to be summoned from Nagasaki, I understand.

Horace N Allen

No. 355   Legation of the United States
                                          Seoul, Korea, May 30, 1901.

Secretary of State

Sir:-

I have the honor to inform you that the rank of the French Representative at this place has been raised from Chargé d'Affaires, to Minister Resident, and on the 25'th. instant, Mr. V. Collin de Plancy presented his credentials, in audience with the Emperor, as Minister.

On his recent return from a leave of absence during which he had visited France, Mr. de Plancy, signed himself, Charge d'Affaires with the rank of Plenipotentiary, which he explained to mean that he had been promoted in his own service, but had prefered to accept this post of Charge d'Affaires, rather than take a position as Minister to one of the South American states.

French interests seem to be advancing in Korea, with the fostering care of Russia. The large body of French misionaries exert quite an influence in Korea, and some sixteen Frenchmen are now engaged by the Korean Government as advisers, farmers, military experts in connection with the arsenal, in charge of mines for the Korean Government, builders of railways, employees of the customs, and in other capacities.

The French Legation is one of the finest and most imposing buildings in Seoul. The furniture is excellent; the French Government having purchased an old chateau in order to secure this furniture for this Legation.

Horace N Allen

No. 360   Legation of the United States
                                          Seoul, Korea, June 7, 1901.

Secretary of State

Sir:-

Referring to my despatch No. 354, of May 29, regarding a rebellion said to be in progress on the island of Quelpart, off the south coast of Korea, I now have the honor to inform you that Captain Mornay (?) of the French gunboat "Surprise", who returned from the island on the 3'rd. instant, informed me that the two French priests whom he went, with his consort, the "Alouette" to succor, were found besieged in the chief town of the island. They were in dire straits when relieved. The Captain told me that 600 people had been killed in the various conflicts. This is thought to be an over-estimate, though my informant said he had himself seen one hundred corpses.

The Korean Government sent 200 soldiers to the island, who arrived there on the first. The difficulty was found to be so serious that reinforcements were desired and a further detachment is being despatched today.

The local newspaper of the 5'th. instant, - the "Han Sun Sin Po" places the blame of the insurrection upon Ye Yong Ik because of his having sent one of his men to the island as an official for the collection of increased taxes.

I am informed by Mr. de Plancy, the French Minister, that it is true that a number of Catholic christians were employed by the officials in collecting these taxes which seem to have been entirely out of proportion to the ability of the natives to pay.

This employment of the native christians brought about a general persecution of their brethren. It is reported that 150 native christians were killed.

If the islanders persist in their revolt, it will be difficult, if not impossible, for the Korean Government to put it down without foreign assistance. Two French gun-boats and one Japanese war-vessel, at once repaired to the island and it is not improbable that the incident may lead to foreign intervention.

The island, though quite large and occupying a most commanding position, possesses no harbors or places of safe anchorage. Had this not been the case it would hardly have remained so long a possession of Korea.

In his No. 158 of Dec. 31, 1888, Mr. Long, Secretary of this Legation and Charge d'Affaires ad interim, handed you an account of a trip he made to Quelpart, but a copy was not retained in the archives of this legation. He also sent the Department an illustrated article concerning the same trip, in his No. 164 of January 26, 1889, for publication by Harpers Brothers. In his No. 104 of March 27, Mr. Blaine states that this article was to be sent to Mr. Longs representative in New York. I have not seen the article but presume it may be of value in case Qyelpart disturbance demands the collection of information regarding the island.

Horace N Allen

No. 372   Legation of the United States
                                         Seoul, Korea, July 3, 1901.

Secretary of State

Sir:-

Referring to the matter of the rebellion on the Korean Island, Quelpart, mentioned in my No. 360 Of June 7, I now have the honor to inform you that the Korean troops aided by the presence of two French gun boats, seem to have succeeded in restoring order, while the hardships of the people have been lightened somewhat, it is said.

It seems that the actual number of killed amounted to about three hundred and that these were mostly christians or persons believed to be christian. It is impossible to secure accurate information suitable for a proper report. I have talked with Mr. Sands, the American Adviser, who went to the island on the ship carrying the first detachment of troops. I have also talked with the Captain of one of the French ships and with the French Bishop and the French Representative.

The substance of the information I have so received is: That the French priests have been at work on the island for something over one year: That almost, if not all the exiles on the islands are are Catholics: That the ex-interpreter of the French Legation, Mr. Ye Yin Yon - who is the mainstay of the Catholics in their controversies with the Korean Government and is the Korean agent of the French Legation - has mostly to do with the affairs of Quelpart, from which he derives a revenue and to which he nominates officials: That Mr. Ye Yong Ik attempted, with the aid and assistance of Ye Yin Yon, to collect increased taxes on most everything in the island; fishnets; trees; stone walls; pig sties, and everything upon which a tax could in any way be levied: That the islanders, who are very poor, refused to pay these unwarranted taxes and as no tax collectors were available among the inhabitants themselves, it was arranged that the christians, presumably exiles, would collect the taxes: That a conflict occurred and before quiet was restored all the known christians had been killed: That individual Japanese were found to be concerned in the uprising, since letters in Japanese were found upon the persons of the captured leaders, in which Japanese aid and assistance was promised them. I was further told that when the French gun-boat "Alouette" arrived, the insurgents dispersed at once, but on the appearance of a Japanese warship they promptly returned as though assured that they would receive assistance from the latter.

A conflict having occurred between the people and the tax collectors, it seems that the inhabitants collected at the town on the south of the island, under leadership of an ex-magistrate, and marched in two divisions around the island to the town of Chei Chu on the north, driving all the christians before them. Under the heading of christian seems to have been included all who were not native to the island. The fugitives were driven into Chei Chu, where many were killed. The two French priests are said to have been saved by the insurgent leader, until relieved by the arrival of the French gunboat "Alouette" which was soon followed by the Korean merchant ship "Han Sung" bearing one hundred Korean troops.

I enclose an extract from the "Korea Review" a magazine published in Seoul by an American school teacher in the employ of the Korean Government - H. B. Hulbert. This gives a translation of a report on the trouble by a Korean Magistrate.

The incident seems to have stirred up quite an anti-christian feeling and there are rumors of a spread of the trouble to neighboring regions, though I can get no confirmation of these rumors.

It seems to be regretted by the French as well as by the other western foreigners that the priests should have been drawn into this affair on Quelpart.

The Japanese newspaper published in Seoul, the "Hun Sung Sin Mun", has been particularly bitter in its attacks upon christians, especially those adhearing to the Roman Church. I fancied that this was due to the personal animosity of a reporter, for I was told by Mr. Sands that he had prevented a reporter of this paper from securing passage on the Korean ship returning from the island, and as the captured letters above referred to might seem to implicate persons of Japanese nationality, I thought the reporter might desire to make the case as strong as possible against the foreigners in order to vent his personal animosity and draw attention away from the matter contained in the letters. I find that others maintain a more serious view.

The repeated publication of such articles can only serve to inflame the people generally against all christians and may lead to serious results. As the control the Japanese officials here have been known to exercise over their newspaper people in Korea is so arbitrary and far reaching, the immunity these people seem to enjoy in this instance has given the matter an anti-French aspect, that, taken with the recent attempt to secure French concessions for loans and mines, and the attack upon Mr. Brown, with which Koreans more or less intimately attached to the French Legation, were chiefly concerned, has induced some people to see in these newspaper attacks upon the priests an anti-French and Russian movement. I have been asked by at least one of my colleagues if I did not think that the Japanese officials here would be glad to see a movement among the natives against the institutions fostered by the French and Russians. Considering the fact that no such movement could be controlled and would work harm to all, I cannot conceive that any Japanese official would willingly favor anything of the kind. At the same time, I must confess that if it is distasteful to the Japanese Legation to have such attacks published in the Japanese papers in Seoul, previous experience has shown that they can be promptly stopped.

I refer you to the above extract from the Korea Review, enclosure 1, for a translation of one of these attacks contained in the Japanese newspaper, while I enclose two further translations of other articles that have appeared up to June 28, Enclosures 2 and 3.

Horace N Allen

No. 397   Confidential.   Legation of the United States
                                                           Seoul, Korea, September 10, 1901.

Secretary of State

Sir:-

I have the honor to hand you enclosed an extract from the Japan Daily Mail of September 3, 1901, purporting to give an account of some of the schemes of France in Korea; alleging that these schemes are in the interest of Russia, and indicating steps that should be taken by Japan to counteract this influence.

I cannot say if the reported schemes are actually fostered by the French Minister, though the plan to raise Lady Om (the mother of the Emperor's youngest son) to the rank of Empress, is being actively urged by Koreans who have usually worked with the French.

I send you the extract as showing that the opinion seems to prevail in Japan, as in Korea, that the recent unprecedented activity of France in Korean politics, is really a Russian move since in that way Japanese (and other influences) may be minimized without a violation on the part of Russia, of the Lobanoff-Yamagata agreement.

Horace N Allen

No. 458   Legation of the United States
                                                                Seoul, Korea, May 9, 1902.

Secretary of State

Sir:-

I have the honor to inform you of the visit to Seoul of Admiral Bayle, Commander in Chief of the French Naval Forces in the Extreme Orient, and of the coincident inaugural ceremonies connected with the beginning of work on the Northwestern Railway. The Admiral arrived at Chemulpo on the 6'th. instant, with his Flagship "d'Entrecasteaux". He had an audience with the Emperor on the 7'th., and left the next day, after attending the railway inaugural ceremonies.

This railway is being built with Korean capital, by French engineers, using French materials. It is intended to connect Seoul with the northwestern border town Weichu, by way of the former capitals, Songdo and Pengyang. The contract for its construction took the place of a concession for the road given to a French Company in 1896 and surrendered by them in 1899. In my despatch No. 388, of August 15, 1901, I informed you that Mr. G. Lefevre, Secretary of the French Legation at Seoul, had obtained a three years leave of absence from his service and had accepted the Position of Superintendent of this railway.

The amount of money annually appropriated for this railway work is said to be but Yen 100,000 ($50,000) but as the President, Ye Yong Ik, controls Korean finances, it is thought that more money may be forthcoming. It was supposed that at least a part of the "French Loan" would be used for this purpose, but the Korean Government have so far refused to accept this loan, though it is still the subject of some discussion between the French Legation and the Korean Foreign Office.

The matter of this French loan was fully explained in my correspondence of last spring, in connection with the attempted removal of J. McLeavy Brown from the post of Commissioner of Customs.

At the railway caremonies on yesterday, speeches were made by the Korean President Ye Yong Ik; by other Korean officials; by the French Minister, and by the Doyen of the Diplomatic Corps, Mr. G. Hayashi, Minister from Japan. I enclose a copy of Mr. Hayashi's remarks.

Horace N Allen

No. 475   Legation of the United States
                                                                Seoul, Korea, June 18, 1902.

Secretary of State,

Sir:-

I have the honor to hand you enclosed an extract from the Kobe Chronicle of Jun 9'th. being a copy of a telegram relative to reported intentions on the part of France to engage ina quarrel with Korea. This surprising report naturally elicits much interest here.

France has more than twenty citizens inKorean employ as advisers; military experts; teachers in language and industrial shcools; in the building of railways, and in the postal department. The last named being the only really effective position so far as actual work is concerned.

I know of two, somewhat serious subjects of contention between France and Korea at present. The Koreans having failed to adjust matters with the French Legation in both cases.

One relates to the uprising on the island of Quelpart last summer, when a large number of native christians of the French catholic church, were killed and two Frech priests came near losing their lives, being saved by the timely arrival of a French and a Japanese war vessel. See my despatch No. 372 of July 3, 1901. Compensation for damages was demanded last winter by the French Minister, but so far the Korean Government has not complied with any such demands.

The other subject of contention is that of a preposed French loan to be secured upon the Korean Customs which resulted in the attempted dismissal of Mr. Brown, the Englishman in charge of the Customs, last year. See my despatch No. 365 of June 12, 1901 and the preceeding despatches of the same series therin referred to.

This subject was again up for discussion last December, when an agent of the syndicate proposing to make the loan, was present in Seoul. This syndicate, which was originally of partial English composition, is now said to be entirely French.

Mr. J. N. Jordan, the British Minister, informs me that at the December discussion of this loan project, he took a much firmer stand in opposition to it that did his predecessor, Mr. Gubbins, last year. He says also that he was able sustained by his Japanese colleague, Mr. G. Hayashi, who also was much stronger in opposition than when the matter first came up.

I took an active part in the matter in the spring of 1901, in protection American interests as represented by an agreement for the construction of water-works, which work was to be paid for from Customs revenues. I informed my French co9lleague at the time, of my steps and he was frank enough to tell me that he would have to take a similar course were he in my position.

My action did more than that of my British and Japanese colleagues to prevent the completion of the loan at the time, and incidentally to prevent the dismissal of Mr. Brown from his position in charge of the customs. It also resulted ingetting an Imperial order to Mr. Brown to set aside Yen 200,000 per annum for eiht years for the purpose of the construction of water-works and though we are now awaiting the fianl order of the Emperor to begin the work on the project. I consider that my efforts at that time were satisfactory and that the order obtained will precede any given for another purpose at a later date.

The reason for my action being more effective than that of my colleagues who wre, politically, more interested, was that I had an actual grievance to urge.

This Legation took no part in the discussion of the loan last winter, during my absence in the United States, except that Mr. Paddock, Chargé d'Affaires ad interim, in an audience obtained for another purpose, informed the Emperor that my objections to say such loan still held good.

In the recent discussions of this loan project, the Korean Foreign Office has persistently refused, on one pretext and another, to carry out its agreement to accept the loan or to offer any redress for its failure to do so.

The agent of the syndicate has recently left Korea as though he had given up the matter.

In the meantime the work on the Seoul - Weiju railway, which was supposed - though that was not stated - to be built by money received from this loan, has been stopped for lack of funds.

This incident of itself has never been regarded here as one of sufficient importance to form the basis of an international quarrel, if the contrary proves to be true, however, the file of despatches above referred to will furnish full details as to what took place in the matter of the loan last year.

Horace N Allen

No. 502   Legation of the United States
                                           Seoul, Korea, September 3, 1902.

Secretary of State

Sir:-

In my No. 498, of the 29'th. ultimo, reporting an Imperial audience given in honor of the Emperor's birthday, I mentioned that some consternation was caused by the fact that Mr. de Plancey, the French Minister, left the palace at once after the audience, without waiting for the luncheon that was to be served.

I am now informed by Mr. de Plancey why he took this action.

In my No. 372, of July 3, 1901, I mentioned the uprising on the Korean island - Quelpart, which had resulted in the death of some 300 native christians of the Catholic faith, and had well nigh resulted in the death of two priests, who were saved by the timely arrival of two French war vessels. The leaders of this uprising were tried in court here in Seoul, - the French legal adviser taking a part in the proceedings. The leader, a man named Chai, was found to be so guilty that he was mentioned for the death sentence, but this was commuted to life imprisonment. Four others were also sentenced to penal servitude for fifteen years each.

On the 18'th. August last, the official gazette announced that these men had all been pardoned and that Chai, the leader, was not guilty and that what had been told against him in court was a mass of falsehood.

Mr. de Plancey, in relating this to me, said that he had not been consulted or even informed; that the man Chai had so many friends near to the Emperor that he was able to bring enough influence to bear to secure this reversal, regardless of what the French Government might think; that though he had written a formal despatch to the Minister for Foreign Affairs, protesting against the action, he had been favored with no reply, therefore he had taken the manner above described to show his marked displeasure.

Mr. de Plancey told me that the French Bishop had recently returned from Quelpart, where he went with the French Admiral on August 8. The Bishop reported all quiet at Quelpart at present.

Horace N Allen

No. 597 Legation of the United States
Seoul, Korea, April 7, 1903.

Secretary of State

Sir:-

I have the honor to hand you a report concerning disturbances in the Korean Province, Whanghai, north west from Seoul, caused by the usurpation of magisterial powers by a French missionary and the consequent persecution of many non-catholic natives as well as of those belonging to the protestant faith. This has aroused great indignation among some of the Americans and some very violent utterances have been made in American publications in Seoul. I have done my best to quiet our people, and I think the matter is now pretty well in hand.

In September last, this matter was first brought to my attention by Rev. Dr. S. A. Moffett, of the Presbyterian Mission, 156, Fifth Avenue New York, with Rev. Mr. Hunt of the same mission. I asked them to see the priest concerned, Father Wilhelm, who has been held in high estimation here for years and who I thought could not countenance the acts of persecution complained of.

This course was not adopted apparently, and on October 22, last, the matter was sent to me in writing, by Dr. Moffett, asking that I take the matter up with the French Authorities and the Korean Government. As I will explain later, this correspondence got into print and will be found in enclosure 1. This correspondence did not show that the French priests were actually to blame for the trouble, as that came out later on, and from reading these reports I decided that the matter was purely a Korean one and I declined to burden the Legation with such controversies between native christians. I so wrote to Dr. Moffett, as per enclosure 2, again suggesting that he arrange for a private and amicable settlement of the matter, which seemed to me to be but one of the continual Korean disturbances incident to this badly ruled country.

Later on Rev. Dr. Underwood, (American - naturalized) Dr. Avison and Rev. J. S. Gale (both Canadian) of the same mission visited me and after discussing the situation and showing me more fully that the French priests were apparently doing wrong, it was agreed upon my suggestion that they should go to the French Bishop and lay the matter before him. This they did, meeting with a cordial reception. This action and a direct complaint by a Korean, brought the matter to the French Minister, Mr. de Plancy, who saw me about the matter and agreed to officially ask the Foreign Office to hold a public trial of the case at the provincial captial, Haichu. I was very much pleased with Mr. de Plancy's prompt action and his suggestion that I send some one to be present at the trial. I did not however, address the Minister for Foreign Affairs officially on the subject, but spoke to him personally. I have had no official correspondence on the subject with the Korean Government or the French Legation.

A very just Korean official from the Foreign Office was sent to Haichu as Inspector, with power to try the cases and to inflict punishment in all but capital cases. Mr. de Plancy sent his second secretary to attend the trial. Having no one I could spare for the purpose, I asked Dr's. Underwood and Moffett to represent me unofficially and simply gave them my card of introduction, with a document they were to show in case the card was not sufficient to obtain for them the courtesies necessary. I enclose a copy of this document, enclosure 3.

Messrs Underwood and Moffett comported themselves with apparent dignity and reserve, winning for themselves the praise of the Korean authorities and sending me excellent and full reports, without in any way dragging the Legation into the quarrel. I have copies of all these reports on file but will not send the whole mass along unless I am asked to do so. I will enclose copies of the principal court records which show the facts in the case very plainly and briefly.

These reports are as follows: - Report to the Foreign Office by the Governor of Whanghai, December 23, 1902, complaining of the action of the French priests and their followers and showing his inability to cope with the difficulty: Report of the Inspector, Ye Unk Yik, to the Foreign Office, complaining of the violent conduct of the French priest Wilhelm: Proclamation of Father Wilhelm, instructing all the people to refuse to pay taxes and offering to protect everyone who so refused: Testimony of Yang Hui Ok Accusing Father Wilhelm of having arrested, imprisoned and tortured him: Letter from the Governor of Whanghai to the Foreign Office asking for the recall of the French priests on the grounds of their having protected criminals from arrest and of having beaten his soldiers and police sent to make such arrests: Complaint of Tai Ho Pang, of robbery by native catholics: Complaint of Cho Soong Kil that catholics stole his wife: Complaint of Kim Pil Sin - a native protestant - of excessive torture for protecting some protestant Korean old women: Complaint of magistrate Kim Yun Oh, of extortion; torture and imprisionment at the order of Father Wilhelm: Complaint of Kwak Hui Hoo, that the leader of a catholic church robbed and otherwise ill-treated him: Case of Koak Ki Ho who complained that his uncle Whang, was tortured to death by the catholics, one of whom, Chang, was duly indicated for murder.

At the request of Mr. de Plancy I handed him copies in Chinese with translations, of the above court records to 14 inclusive. I also enclose a later document dated March 15, being a proclamation by the Inspector intended to quiet the people, who seemed in danger of bringing about an uprising.

Mr. de Plancy has telegraphed several times to the priest Wilhelm, to return to Seoul, and he instructed his Secretary to bring him back with him. Wilhelm has so far declined to come, even upon the further telegraphic order of his Bishop. Mr. de Plancy now tells me he contemplates sending again and bringing the priest even against the latters will.

The presence of the French secretary at the investigation did not seem to result in any especial good and he was complained of by the Koreans as preventing the arrest of accused Korean catholics, thereupon Mr. de Plancy recalled him and I then recalled the two American missionaries, so that the further investigation of the matter is now purely in Korean hands. The investigation has seemed to have a good effect in showing the natives that their government desires to protect them. It has further resulted in giving the Koreans a great appreciation of the methods of the American missionaries, who carefully abstain from any interference with the native officials and teach their followers to abide by the laws, however onerous the latter may be.

Mr. de Plancy has done all he could in the matter apparently, and has been most cordial in his relations with me throughout the whole discussion. He seems deeply to deplore the action of Father Wilhelm, who he says, seems to have "lost his head".

I must now explain a very disagreeable incident that occured in connection with this matter.

Rev. Homer B. Hulbert, a former missionary of the Methodist Church, though a congregational minister, is now employed by the Korean Government as a school teacher. He also publishes a monthly magazine called the "Korea Review". His publications are so inaccurate and at times so misleading, that complaints have been made at this Legation by several of the Foreign Representatives, of such misleading publications. I myself have frequently suffered in the same manner, through Mr. Hulbert's not taking the trouble to ask me in regard to the truth of matter he intended to publish about matters in the hands of this Legation.

After I had joined Mr. de Plancy, (unofficially) in promoting the investigation at Haichu, and had sent Messrs Underwood and Moffett to attend the trial then in progress, Mr. Hulbert published in his "Review" the long personal correspondence sent me on October 22 by Dr. Moffett, with a very bitter and one sided editorial note; all of which was republished in foreign newspapers in Japan, with most unfavorable comments upon the spirit of protestant missionaries in Korea.

Mr. Hulbert obtained these letters from Rev. J. S. Gale to whom I had handed them upon a telegraphic request from Dr. Moffett. Mr. Hulbert mentioned the letters in such a manner as to lead the reader to suppose he had received them from me.

I at once wrote to Mr. Hulbert commenting severely upon his action in publishing such matter with such violent comments, at a time when the whole case was in court, and of giving the impression that I had sanctioned the publication. I asked him to make an explanation, which he did in his next number, promising as usual to be more careful in the future.

In the "Review" for March, however, Mr. Hulbert again published full reports of the trial, with a long and most violent editorial, making out the case to be one between the United States and France.

Mr. de Plancy called upon me at once in regard to this publication. I was able to show him that it was most distasteful to me, and that I had done all I could to prevent anything of the kind. I asked him to suggest anything which he might wish me to do in the matter but he saw it would be useless for me to make any further attempt unless his secretary might perhaps bring an action against Mr. Hulbert for libel. This was not considered advisable by either of us. He then said he would complain to the Korean Foreign Office of the conduct of this American employee, and I could not but assent. I have heard nothing more in regard to the matter.

Horace N. Allen.

C. China

No. 216

Legation of the United States
Seoul Korea, Dec. 22, 1899.

Secretary of State

Sir:-

I have the honor to inform you that after an interruption of five years, diplomatic relations have again been established between Korea and China.

The treaty, a copy of which I sent you in my No. 215, Dec. 12, between Korea and China, has been finally exchanged and Mr. Hsu Sou Pung, who negotiated the treaty on the part of China, has taken charge of Chinese interests here as Envoy Extraordinary and Minister Plenipotentiary. China has also appointed consuls to reside at the Korean ports, Chenampo; Chemulpo; Fusan, and at Seoul. Korea has appointed Mr. Sim Sang Hun to be Minister Plenipotentiary and Envoy Extraordinary at Pekin.

Mr. Hsu, the new Chinese Minister, was Secretary of Legation in Washington in 1888, when the first Korean Legation was established there.

A public dinner is being given at the Korean Foreign Office tonight, in honor of this resumption of diplomatic relations, the mere negotiations for which have lasted nearly one year.

Horace N Allen

No. 261

Legation of the United States
Seoul, Korea, June 26, 1900.

Secretary of State

Sir:-

I have the honor to inform you that I was asked to an audience yesterday together with my colleagues to discuss with His Majesty the situation in China and its relations to Korea.

His Majesty expressed his deep regret at the disorders in China which were causing suffering, loss, and death to foreigners residing there, and asked if there was anything we could suggest that he should do in the matter. We urged him to see that order was preserved and that a similar uprising in Korea was promptly suppressed. He asked us to advise him from time to time in case we heard of any such uprising.

We suggested, moreover, that as the telegraph lines are reported broken and the regular steamships are generally removed from the routes connecting China and Korea, for use as transports, it would be well to employ a couple of the Korean Government steamers for a daily service between Chemulpo and Chefoo, for the purpose of bringing news of Chinese affairs and for carrying passengers and freight. He seemed pleased with the idea and said he would put the plan into effect.

In this connection I enclose a translation of a memorial presented by certain Koreans to the Educational Department, which is notorious as a conservative and Confusianary institution, calling foreigners savages and barbarians, frankly stating that they are making regulations with friends who share the same opinions as themselves -- which is favorable to the Confusian system -- and bitterly opposed to the Christian religion.

It is generally recognized that this refers to a union with the "Boxers" of Shantung. The thousands of Chinese residing in Korea have much influence over the Koreans and as they seem generally to sympathize with the "Boxers" it is not remarkable that they should find support from the Korean people.

Horace N Allen

No. 265   Legation of the United States
                                                               Seoul, Korea, July 17, 1900.

Secretary of State

Sir:-

I have the honor to hand you enclosed a confirmation of my cablegram to you of the 14th instant, concerning the news received from Danish missionaries in Manchuria of the spread of the "Boxer" movement to a point near the northern border of Korea and of the excitement this was causing among the Koreans in the North, where Americans are conducting at Pyengyang what has been called "the most successful mission station in the World". As some of my colleagues were sending this information by wire to their Governments, I thought it best to inform you also at once. I may add that since cabling I have received a telegram from Pyengyang to the effect that practically the excitement there has subsided.

I alluded also in my cable to the fact that the Foreign Representatives in Seoul were not informed of the intention of His Majesty to send a telegraphic message to the rulers of the Treaty Powers expressing his regret that their Ministers were besieged in Peking. His action has given more or less offense particularly to my German colleague Dr. Weipert, who was not consulted before a special telegram of condolence was sent to the Emperor of Germany upon the murder of his Minister at Peking. Dr. Weipert thinks he should first have been asked if the rumor were true and that then the wording of the message should have been submitted to him. He fears the telegram as phrased may be considered impertinent.

I sent a despatch to the Foreign Minister, as did most of my colleagues, asking to be informed upon the matter. See enclosure No. 2. It is supposed that no discourtesy was intended toward the Foreign Representatives but that an indiscreet foreign adviser pursuaded His Majesty to telegraph, not appreciating the proper usage in such a case. I have received a reply to my despatch with a copy of the telegram to President McKinley, a copy of which despatch, together with one of the telegram I now enclose.

Horace N. Allen.

No. 266   Legation of the United States
                                                               Seoul, Korea, July 18, 1900.

Secretary of State

Sir:-

I have the honor to hand you enclose a confirmation of my cablegram of the 16th instant, informing you of the destruction of a native Catholic mission in the neighborhood of Andung Shien, three miles from the frontier of Korea in Manchuria. I am somewhat anxious as to the safety of the American gold mines which are near this border and actually north of the frontier town Euichu and some fifty miles to the west. We have about sixty American citizens there and several millions of dollars have been invested in the workings of the mines. If the "Boxer" movement spreads into Korea I may have to ask for a vessel to go to the mouth of the Anju river, one day's journey from the mines.

I consulted Mr. Hayashi, the Japanese Minister, as to the truth of a published rumor to the effect that Japan was about to send 10,000 troups to Korea, 5,000 of which were destined for Euichu. Mr. Hayashi said the report was not true and that he did not think his Government would take any such action at present on account of the nervous condition of the Koreans and the fear of the misunderstanding of such a course by the Russian Government. He intimated that if conditions on the border should become more serious and if he were asked by the Korean Government and by most or all of his colleagues to take measures for the protection of Korea, he should advise his Government to act.

Mr. Pavlow, the Russian Chargé d'Affaires, appears decidedly concerned as to the safety of the northern Korean border and states that he as advised the Korean Government not to send troops to the North as it has announced its intention of doing. He fears that if the Chinese cross they will possess themselves of the arms and ammunition of the Korean soldiers and thus become more formitable than they are at present when they appear to be but ineffectively armed. He evidently greatly desires that I request a gunboat for the patrol of the mouths of the Yalu and Anju rivers and said that he thought he should add to a telegram he was sending to his Government the information that I was anxious for the safety of American subjects in the North.

It seems to me that both Russia and Japan are eager to take upon themselves the protection of Korea. Especially does this appear true of Russia in relation to the northern frontier.

Horace N Allen

No. 373

Legation of the United States
Seoul, Korea, July 5, 1901.

Secretary of State

Sir:-

I have the honor to confirm my telegram of today as follows:-
"Three thousand Chinese Banditti menace Korea frontier near the American mines. Three detachments Russian troops have been sent to intercept, also a war vessel. Japan consents and may make the same action. I think the measures taken will be sufficient".

On the 30'th ultimo, the Korean Government received alarming news by telegraph, from Weiju, to the effect that large bodies of armed Chinese were at Andong on the Manchurian side of the Yalu. The Japanese Legation had a police officer sent from Chenampo to report, and he has confirmed the Korean report. I learn from Mr. Pavlow, the Russian Charge d'Affaires, that upon his and other representations, his Government is sending a detachment of troops from Port Arthur; from Newchwang and from a war-vessel at Taku shan (west of the mouth of the Yalu) to try to intercept the Chinese and prevent their getting across the Yalu River into Korea. There is a considerable body of Korean troops on the Yalu and it is feared, especially by the Russians, that the Chinese may get the large store of ammunition possessed by these Korean troops. The Chinese have arms but are reported to be out of ammunition. Mr. Pavlow also tells me that he has asked that a gunboat be sent to the mouth of the Yalu to cooperate with the land forces and to send armed steam launches up the river. He told me that the Russian Commanders had instructions not to cross over into Korea unless further instructed. He told me that he had communicated fully with the Russian Minister in Japan.

I saw Mr. Hayashi and learned from him that the reports were true and that he feared there might be serious trouble on the border unless the Chinese were headed off and their leaders captured. He said that Mr. Pavlow had consulted with him frankly and gave me to understand, with some apparent elation, that in this instance Russia had first secured the approval of Japan before sending a gunboat to patrol the mouth of the Yalu. This of course was told me in confidence.

Mr. Hayashi also said that he thought his Government might send a war vessel to the mouth of the Yalu, at least a Destroyer, and that they would send a body of troops up the Manchurian bank of the Yalu in case it became necessary.

As the American gold mines, with their extensive and costly plant, are within thirty to fifty miles of the Yalu, I am naturally taking a deep interest in the movement, and will ask that a vessel be sent to those waters if I deem it necessary. At present I think the measures already taken, or contemplated, will be sufficient to prevent any serious danger to the mines.

I have instructed the manager of the mines, by wire, to send scouts to keep a close lookout on the border and to report to me.

The Mines have some eighty men now I believe, at their works (I refer to white men of course), with a full supply of rifles and ammunition and three machine guns, so that I think they would be able to do a great deal toward protecting themselves.

Horace N Allen

No. 376

Legation of the United States
Seoul, Korea, July 16, 1901.

Secretary of State

Sir:-

Referring to my despatch No. 373 of July 7, in regard to the movement of a large body of armed Chinese toward the norther frontier of Korea, and the measures taken to prevent them from crossing the Yalu river; I now have the honor to inform you that they were prevented from crossing into Korea by the prompt movement of the Russian troops to intercept them. They seem to have become alarmed and turned back into Manchuria. I understand the Russian troops are in pursuit of them.

I have telegrams from the American mines, situated near the Yalu river, to the effect that all is now quiet and that the only Chinese who crossed into Korea were Chinese refugees fleeing from the robbers.

The Japanese Minister informs me that as he considers the trouble as ended for the time, his Government will not send a force to that region at present.

The prompt action of Russia in policing the Manchurian frontier has, in this case, evidently prevented an invasion that might have had serious results for the extensive American mines in northern Korea.

A considerable body of Korean troops are still kept on the frontier to prevent incursions of Chinese.

Horace N Allen

APPENDIXES

APPENDIX A.

U.S. DIPLOMATIC PERSONNEL, 1895-1905

	Representative In Korea	Secretary Of State	President
1895	John M. B. Sill* (Apr. 30, 1894- July 17, 1897)	Richard Olney (June 10, 1895- Mar. 5, 1897)	Grover Cleveland (Mar. 4, 1893- Mar. 4, 1897)
1896			
1897	Horace N. Allen** (July 17, 1897- June 8, 1905)	John Sherman (Mar. 6, 1897 April 27, 1898)	William McKinley (Mar. 4, 1897- Sept. 14, 1901)
1898		William R. Day (April 28, 1898- Sept. 16, 1898)	
1899		John Hay (Sept. 30, 1898 July 1, 1905)	
1900			
1901			Theodore Roosevelt (Sept. 14, 1901- March 4, 1909)
1902			
1903			
1904			
1905	Edwin V. Morgan*** (June 26, 1905- Nov. 24, 1905)	Elihu Root (July 7, 1905- Jan. 27, 1909)	

*During this period Sill was absent from his post from Sept. 18, 1896 until Nov. 18, 1896. Secretary of the Legation Horace N. Allen served as Chargé d'Affairs ad interum.

**Minister Allen took two leaves of absence while Minister of the U.S. Legation; the first from Oct. 15, 1901 - April 2, 1902, and the second from June 3, 1903 - Nov. 20, 1903. Secretary of the Legation and Vice Consul General Gordon Paddock served as Chargé 'd'Affairs ad interum.

***The U.S. Legation was withdrawn from Korea on November 24, 1905. Edwin V. Morgan was reassigned to a Ministerial position in Cuba.

APPENDIX B.

KOREAN DIPLOMATIC PERSONNEL, 1895-1905*

	Minister Plenipotentiary To The U.S.	Minister for Foreign Affairs**	King/Emperor
1895	Yi Sông-su 李承壽 Dec. 30, 1893	Kim Yun-sik 金允植 Aug. 23, 1895	Kojong*** 高宗
1896	So Kwang-bôm 徐光範 Feb. 19, 1896	Yi Wan-yong 李完用 Feb. 12, 1896	
	Yi Pôm-jin 李範晉 Sept. 12, 1896	Ko Yông-hui 高永喜 Sept. 25, 1896	
		Yi Wan-yong 李完用 Oct. 12, 1896	
1897		Min Chong-muk 閔種默 July 2, 1897	
		Cho Pyông-jik 趙秉稷 Nov. 18, 1897	

---

*This information was gathered from several sources, the most important of which include the diplomatic correspondence, <u>Hanguk Imyong Taesajôn</u>, Shingu Munhwasa; Seoul, Korea, 1967, and Andrew C.Nahm's <u>Japanese Penetration of Korea, 1894-1910</u>, Hoover Institution Bibliographical Series, no. 5. Stanford: Hoover Institution, Stanford University, 1959.
**The title of "President of the Foreign Office" was changed to that of "Minister for Foreign Affairs" in August of 1895.
***King Kojong became Emperor on October 12, 1897.

Minister Plenipotentiary To The U.S.	Minister for Foreign Affairs	King/Emperor
	Min Chong-muk 閔種默 July 2, 1897	Kojong 高宗
1898	Cho Pyông-jik 趙秉稷 Mar. 29, 1898	
	Yu Ki-hwan 俞箕煥 May 30, 1898	
	Yi To-jae 李道宰 Aug. 8, 1898	
	Pak Che-sun 朴齊純 Aug. 25, 1898	
	Cho Pyông-jik 趙秉稷 Sept. 24, 1898	
	Pak Che-sun 朴齊純 Oct. 10, 1898	
	Min Sang-ho 閔商鎬 Nov. 28, 1898	

Minister Plenipotentiary To The U.S.	Minister for Foreign Affairs	King/Emperor
	Pak Che-sun 朴齊純 Dec. 7, 1898	Kojong 高宗
1899	Yi To-jae 李道宰 Mar. 24, 1899	
	Pak Che-sun 朴齊純 Apr. 10, 1899	
1900 Yi Chong-gi(Chargé) 李鍾基 March 16, 1900	Min Chong-muk 閔種默 Jan. 1900	
	Pak Che-sun 朴齊純 Apr. 10, 1900	
1901 Cho Min-hui 趙民熙 May 31, 1901		
1902	Cho Pyông-jik 趙秉稷 Jan. 30, 1902	
	Yi To-jae 李道宰 Dec. 17, 1902	

	Minister Plenipotentiary To The U.S.	Minister for Foreign Affairs	King/Emperor
1903		Yi Chi-yong 李址鎔 Aug. 18, 1903	Kojong 高宗
1904	Sin Tae-mu (Chargé) 申太武 Feb. 15, 1904	Yi Ha-yông 李夏榮 Apr. 2, 1904	
1905	Kim Chung Yông(Chargé) 金重永 June 29, 1905†	Pak Che-sun 朴齊純 Sept. 18, 1905†	

---

†On November 17, Japan assumed full control of all of Korea's relations with foreign countries.

APPENDIX C.

A BRIEF CHRONOLOGY
OF
THE FINAL PERIOD OF KOREAN-AMERICAN DIPLOMATIC RELATIONS, 1896-1905

<u>1895</u>
Apr.	17	Treaty of Simonoseki signed by Li Hung-chang ending the Sino-Japanese war
	23	Tripartate Alliance (Russia-Germany-France) force Japan to return some concessions following the Sino-Japanese War
Oct.	8	Queen Min murdered by pro-Japanese and Japanese elements

<u>1896</u>
Jan.		Dr. Philip Jaisohn (Sô Chae-p'il) returns to Korea
Feb.	10	King and Crown Prince flee to Russian Legation
	12	New Cabinet announced
Mar.	5	Ito Hirobumi arrives in Seoul
	29	American James R. Morse given concession for the Seoul-Chemulp'o Railway
Apr.	3	Torture officially abolished in Seoul Courts
	7	First issue of the *Independent* (Tong'nip Sinmun), published in Seoul by Dr. Philip Jaisohn
May	13	Waeber-Komura Agreement (Russia-Japan) signed in Seoul
June	3	Li-Lobanoff Treaty (China-Russia)
	9	Lobanoff-Yamagata Agreement (Russia-Japan)
July	16	Japanese Minister Hara Satoshi assumes duties
Sept.	18	Minister Sill leaves Korea for vacation and Dr. Allen assumes duties as Chargé d'Affaires ad interim
	28	The Council of State organized and Cabinet abolished
Nov.	4	Prince Ui Hwa sent to school in the U.S.
	18	Minister Sill resumes duties at U.S. Legation
	21	Construction of Independence Arch (T'ong'nip mun) by members of the Independence Club

<u>1897</u>
Feb.	20	King Kojong leaves the Russian Legation for Tôksu Palace
	24	Japanese Chargé d'Affaires Kato Masuo appointed as Minister
May		Russian Chargé de Speyer initiates the "Deer Island Episode" by demading Kojei Island as a Russian Coaling Station
Sept.	7	A. de Speyer replaces Waeber as Russian Minister
	13	Horace N. Allen replaces Sill as U.S. Minister Resident and Consul General
Oct.	5	Kiril A. Alexeev (Russian) arrives to take the place of McLeavy Brown (British) in the Korean Customs Department
	12	Coronation of Kojong as Emperor
	16	Choson becomes Tae Han Empire
	21	Son is born to Emperor Kojong and Lady Om
	25	Department for Foreign Affairs appoints Alexeev as Commissioner of Finances and Customs
	28	Agreements signed opening Mokp'o and Chinnamp'o
Nov.	3	Min Chong-muk dismissed as Foreign Minister for his refusal to sign documents of appointment for Kiril Alexeev
	22	Funeral ceremony for Queen Min who was posthumously given the title of Empress

<u>1898</u>

Jan.		Anti-Russian agitation of the Independence Club
	8	Death of the mother of Emperor Kojong, the wife of the Taewon'gun
	11	William F. Sands assumes duties as Secretary of the U.S. Legation
Feb.	1	Seoul Electric Company formed for the construction of lighting facilities and electric railways in Seoul
	1	Contracts awarded to American Company Collbran and Bostwick for electric railway and lighting plant
	15	U.S.S. Maine sunk in Havana harbor
	22	Attempt on the life of the Russian Legation Interpreter Kim Hong-yuk
	22	British Consulate General raised in diplomatic status to a Legation
	23	Taewon'gun dies
Mar.	1	Russo-Korean Bank opens
	23	Withdrawal of Russian advisors and military officers
	27	Concession given to U. S. citizen James R. Morse for the Seoul-Chemulp'o Railway
Apr.		Russo-Korean Bank closes
	12	Russian Minister de Speyer resigns and is temporarily replaced by N. Mativinia
	21	State of War declared between the U. S. and Spain
	25	Rosen-Nishi Agreement (Russia-Jap.) signed in Tokyo recognizing Japan's superior commercial interests in Korea and forbiding intervention by either party
	27	Dr. Jaisohn is paid for the remainder of his contract and asked to leave Korea
	27	U. S. forces engage Spanish fleet in the Philippines
July	7	Hawaiian Islands are annexed by the U.S.
	23	Cho Pyŏng-sik dismissed as Acting Prime Minister
Aug.		P'yongyang opened as a treaty port
	27	Kim Hong-yuk, former Russian Legation Interpreter, arrested and banished
	30	American George W. Lake murdered in Chemulp'o
Sept.	8	The Japanese obtain concessions for a railway from Seoul to Pusan
	14	Kim Hong-yuk attempts to assassinate the King and the Crown Prince with poison
Oct.	11	Mass meetings in support of greater civil liberties include groups of women
	12	Change of Cabinet
	27-28	Continued mass meetings of Independence Club
Nov.	11	John G. Flanagan convicted of the August murder of George Lake
	26	Independence Club dissolved by the Emperor
Dec.	10	Treaty of Paris signed between Spain and the U. S. ceding the Philippine Islands to the U.S. for $20,000,000

<u>1899</u>

Jan.	12	The new Russian Minister Pavlow arrives
	18	Pavlow replaces N. Matunine as Chargé d'Affaires
Mar.	29	Concession for whaling privileges given to Russia
May		Kunsan opened as a treaty port
		Masan opened as a treaty port
May	26	"Street-Car Incident" sparks riots against the Seoul Electric Company
June		Songjin opened as a treaty port
July	25	G. Hayashi named as Japanese E.E. and M. P.
Sept.	1	Charles W. Legendre, American advisor to the Korean Government, dies at his post
	11	Korean-Chinese Commercial Treaty signed
	18	Seoul-Chemulp'o railroad opened for passengers

Oct.	8	U.S. Minister Allen returns from vacation
	21	Clarence R. Greathouse, American legal advisor to the Korean Government, dies at his post
Nov.		Former U.S. Legation Secretary, William Sands, appointed as advisor to the Korean Household Department
	9	The partition of Samoa by the U.S. and Germany
Dec.		Foreign styled Library for King completed near U.S. Legation

1900

Jan.	2	The first foreign mail leaves Korea via the new Korean Postal Service
	13	An Kyûng-su returns to Seoul for trial with the Japanese Minister
Mar.	30	E. V. Morgan assumes duties as Secretary of the U.S. Legation
	30	Russo-Korean Kojei Island Agreement
May	16	Kwon Hyong-jin returns to Seoul for trial
July		Russia occupies Manchuria throughout the summer
		Korean King sends cargo of provisions and tobacco to the Allied troops involved in the Boxer rebellion at Tientsin
		Severe drought affects Seoul water supply and destroys crops in the countryside throughout the summer
	14	The Boxer disturbance reported to have spread to the northern borders of Korea
	9	Collbran and Bostwick receive contract from the Emperor to provide nickel blanks for minting Korean coins
	9	Uprising in the northern towns of Songjin and Kilju
Aug.	10	Collbran and Bostwick given a contract for bank and office building near Ch'ongno in Seoul
	14	Englishman T.D. Bland is murdered at the American Candlestick mines. Murder trial begins Jan. 2, 1901
	20	Cho Pyông-sik leaves for special mission to Japan
Oct.	3	Additional Fisheries Convention between Korea and Japan
	11	Two Americans attacked and robbed near Taegu
	20	Circular posted ordering uprising against foreigners
	27	V. Collin de Plancey appointed Minister Plenipotentiary for France
	10	Rumored anti-Western uprising does not occur
Dec.	17	Emperor Kojong appointed Honorary Knight Grand Commander of the most Eminent Order of the Indian Empire by Queen Victoria

1901

Mar.	29	Edwin V. Morgan transferred from St. Peterburg to serve as second secretary of the U.S. Legation
Apr.	6	Former U.S. Minister John M. B. Sill dies at his home in Detroit
	17	Postal Agreement signed between Korea and France
	18	Cho Pyông-sik is forced to resign as Prime Minister for his opposition to the French Loan
June	1	Korean gunboat arrives at Cheju Island to quell popular uprising against the French Priests and native Catholics
	27	Horace N. Allen's diplomatic rank raised to Envoy Extraordinary and Minister Plenipotentiary of the U.S. Legation
Aug.	5	Gordon Paddock assumes duties as Secretary of the U.S. Legation and Vice Deputy Consul General
Sept.	7	Fiftieth birthday of Emperor Kojong
	14	U. S. President William McKinley dies of gunshot wound
	19	Funeral ceremonies for President McKinley held in Methodist Church in Seoul
Oct.	15	Horace N. Allen leaves Korea for vacation in the U.S. and Gordon Paddock assumes responsibilities as Chargé d'Affaires
	17	Belgian-Korean Treaty ratified in Seoul

	Nov.		YMCA begins operations in Korea
		14	Italian Legation opens in Seoul
		15	Imperial Library adjoining U.S. Legation destroyed by fire

1902

Jan.	5	The buildings housing the Seoul Electric Company destroyed by fire but completely rebuilt by July
	30	The first Anglo-Japanese Alliance signed
Mar.	19	The Franco-Russian response to the Anglo-Japanese Agreement announced indicating that their "Dual Alliance" of 1895 extended to Asia
Apr.	2	Allen returns from the United States
May		The Korean Government objects to the issuance of "Shibusawa Money" by the Dai Ichi Ginko
July	15	The Danish-Korean Treaty signed
Sept.		Cholera epidemic causes problems in Seoul and throughout Korea
	22	Foreign community's celebration of Emperor Kojong's assession to the throne postponed from Oct. 18, 1902 to April 30, 1903
Nov.	27	Severance Memorial Hospital, donated by Louis H. Severance of Cleveland, Ohio, dedicated by Minister Allen
	28	Korean Prime Minister and Minister for Foreign Affairs petition for the punishment of Yi Yong-ik
	30	Yi Yong-ik takes refuge in the Russian Legation to avoid punishment
Dec.	1	Yi Yong-ik banished to his country home but pardoned on the 16th and completely restored to most of his former offices by the 17th
	2	Beginning of ten days of native celebration of the anniversary of the ascension of Kojong to the throne
	22	One hundred Korean emigrants start for Hawaii

1903

Feb.	5	American Clare W. Hess arrested for shooting a Korean at a native "stone fight" and released after paying medical bills and promising to leave the country
	10	Celebration of Emperor Kojong's ascension postponed a second time until autumn
Apr.		Russians begin to cut timber along the Yalu
	21	Russian troops occupy Yong'amp'o
May	26	Local friction reported between Japan and Russia over timber operations on the Yalu
June	3	Minister Allen departs for the U.S. leaving Gordon Paddock as Chargé
Sept.	30	Minister Allen meets with President Roosevelt to discuss the Korean situation
Oct.	1	Riots occur on the streets of Seoul as result of the accidental killing of a child by an electric car owned by an American firm
Nov.	20	Minister Allen returns from leave
Dec.	8	Minister Allen requests protection for American lives and property in the event of war between Japan and Russia
	14	Japanese forces land in Mokp'o to "protect Japanese nationals from rioters"

1904

Jan.	5	U.S. marine guard lands for the protection of U.S. interests in the expected conflict between Japan and Russia
	8	British land marine guard
	9	Additional Russian marines enter Seoul
	9	Italian marines arrive in Seoul by railroad
	23	Korea declares neutrality in the conflict between Russia and Japan
	24	Accidental killing of a Korean laborer by an electric car results in riots

Feb.	5	Diplomatic relations between Russia and Japan officially severed
	7	1500 Japanese soldiers arrive in Chemulp'o
	8	Japan attacks Russian positions at Port Arthur
	9	Russian ships *Varig* and *Koreetz* destroyed in Chemulp'o harbor
	10	Japan and Russia declare war on each other
	12	Russian Minister Pavlow, Russian subjects, and Legation guard leave Seoul under Japanese escort
	23	Japanese-Korean Protocol signed in which Korea agrees to "place full confidence in Japan"
	25	Wiju declaired an open port
Mar.	17	Ito Hirobumi arrives in Seoul and stays until the 26th
Apr.		Japanese push for concession of all Korean vacant lands "forests, hills, and streams."
	14	Imperial Palace adjoining the U.S. Legation partially destroyed by fire
May	18	Korea abrogates all treaties and agreements previously made with Russia
Aug.	20	Japanese-Korean Convention concluded giving Japan the power to appoint advisors
	22	Japanese-Korean Treaty (First Treaty of Protection)
Nov.	29	M. Megata arrives in Seoul to serve as Japanese financial adviser to the Korean Government
Dec.	21	U.S. citizen D. W. Stevens arrives to serve as Japanese adviser to the Korean Department for Foreign Affairs

1905

Jan.	2	Russians surrender Port Arthur to Japanese after seige
	5	Japanese announce that they will undertake the policing of Seoul because of the "inability of the Korean police" to keep order
	29	Japan's Daiichi Ginko becomes the Central Bank of Korea
Mar.	30	Japanese Government takes over Korean Bureau of Communications
May	25	Seoul-Pusan Railway completed
	28	Admiral Togo destroys Russia's Baltic fleet in the Tsushima straits
June	8	Minister Allen hands over charge of the Legation to Gordon Paddock pending the arrival of the new Minister
	25	Edwin V. Morgan arrives in Seoul to assume the duties as Envoy Extraordinary and Minister Plenipotentiary of the United States in Korea and presents his credentials to Emperor Kojong the following day
July	27	Taft-Katsura Agreement acknowledgs Japan's interests in Korea and U.S. interests in the Philippines
Aug.	25	The second Anglo-Japanese Alliance concluded
Sept.	5	Treaty of Portsmouth signed giving Japan the Russian leases on southern Liaotung Peninsula, Russian railroad interests in Manchuria, the southern Sakhalin Islands, and Russian recognition of Japanese paramouncy in Korea
	20	President Roosevelt's daughter, Alice, pays a 10 day visit to Korea
Oct.	5	Japan assumes full control of Korean Customs
	31	U.S. Legation guard leaves Korea
Nov.	9	Ito Hirobumi arrives
	17	Second Treaty of Protection signed giving Japan control of Korea's foreign relations and establishing a protectorate over Korea
	23	Japanese ambassador in Washington advises Secretary of State Root that Tokyo will control all of the foreign relations of Korea
	24	Withdrawal of U. S. Legation
	29	Former Korean Government leaders commit suicide to protest the Japanese protectorate
Dec.	4	Withdrawal of the German Legation
	21	Ito Hirobumi appointed as Resident General of Korea

1906

Jan.	6	Withdrawal of the French Legation
Feb.	12	Withdrawal of the British Legation
	14	Withdrawal of the Chinese Legation

APPENDIX D.

NATIONAL ARCHIVES MICROFILM

Despatches from U. S. Ministers to Korea, 1883 - 1905 (M134)

No. 1	Mar. 13, 1883 - Sept. 24, 1884
No. 2	Oct. 4, 1884 - Oct. 15, 1885
No. 3	Oct. 19, 1885 - Dec. 31, 1886
No. 4	Jan. 1, 1887 - Dec. 31, 1887
No. 5	Jan. 20, 1888 - Aug. 26, 1889
No. 6	Sept. 14, 1889 - Sept. 27, 1890
No. 7	Oct. 1, 1890 - May 28, 1891
No. 8	June 1, 1891 - Apr. 28, 1892
No. 9	May 1, 1892 - Apr. 24, 1893
No. 10	May 1, 1893 - May 31, 1894
No. 11	June 1, 1894 - June 30, 1895
No. 12	July 9, 1885 - Apr. 30, 1896
No. 13	May 1, 1896 - Nov. 27, 1897
No. 14	Dec. 1, 1897 - Aug. 27, 1898
No. 15	Sept. 8, 1898 - Jan. 30, 1900
No. 16	Feb. 3, 1900 - Mar. 26, 1901
No. 17	Apr. 1, 1901 - Apr. 26, 1902
No. 18	May 1, 1902 - Oct. 31, 1902
No. 19	Nov. 4, 1902 - Apr. 25, 1903
No. 20	May 8, 1903 - Apr. 30, 1904
No. 21	May 2, 1904 - Dec. 30, 1904
No. 22	Jan. 3, 1905 - Dec. 6, 1905

Notes From the Korean Legation in the United States to the Department of State (M166)

         No. 1   Sept. 18, 1883 - April 24, 1906

Notes to Foreign Legations in the U.S. from the Department of State, 1835-1906 (M99)

         No. 68   Jan. 10, 1888 - Aug. 11, 1906

Diplomatic Instructions of the Department of State to Korea 1801-1906 (M77)

         No. 109   March 1883 - Dec. 4, 1905

Despatches From United States Consuls in Seoul, Korea, 1886-1906 (M167)

         No. 1   Register, 1886-1906, and Despatches
                                 July 3, 1886 - Dec. 21, 1898
         No. 2   Jan. 19, 1899 - July 5, 1906

INDEX TO DOCUMENTS

INDEX TO DOCUMENTS

1. PERIOD OF RUSSIAN PREDOMINANCE

2. PERIOD OF EQUILIBRIUM AND DE FACTO KOREAN INDEPENDENCE

3. PERIOD OF MUTUAL ANTAGONISM AND AGGRESSION

A. Increasing Japanese Interests

B. Attempts to Secure an International Guarantee of Independence

C. Treatment of Korean Refugees

D. Continued Russian Presence

E. The Masanp'o Issue

F. The "Brown Incident," the French Loan, and Yi Yong-Ik

4. THE RUSSO-JAPANESE WAR

A. Northern Timber Concessions and Increasing Tensions

B. Open Hostilities

C. U.S. Position vis-à-vis the Combatants

5. THE ESTABLISHMENT OF A JAPANESE PROTECTORATE

6. THE UNITED STATES IN KOREA

A. Korean - American Relations

B. American Missionaries

C. American Advisors

D. American Business Interests

E. U.S. Legation Business

7. OTHER FOREIGN INTERESTS

A. England

B. France

C. China

ABOUT THE AUTHOR

Scott Burnett has worked in the field of Korean Studies for the past ten years as teacher, researcher, writer, consultant, and translator. He has training and experience in the Korean language as well as Chinese and Japanese. He is finishing his doctoral work in Korean History at the University of Washington and is currently teaching in the Korean Studies program at Brigham Young University in Provo, Utah.